QOHELETH

BHB
Baylor Handbook
on the Hebrew Bible

General Editor

W. Dennis Tucker Jr.

QOHELETH
A Handbook on the Hebrew Text

Robert D. Holmstedt, John A. Cook,
and Phillip S. Marshall

BAYLOR UNIVERSITY PRESS

© 2017 by Baylor University Press
Waco, Texas 76798

All Rights Reserved. No part of this publication may be reproduced, stored in a retrieval system, or transmitted, in any form or by any means, electronic, mechanical, photocopying, recording, or otherwise, without the prior permission in writing of Baylor University Press.

Cover Design by Pamela Poll
Cover photograph by Bruce and Kenneth Zuckerman, West Semitic Research, in collaboration with the Ancient Biblical Manuscript Center. Courtesy Russian National Library (Saltykov-Shchedrin).

This title has been cataloged at the Library of Congress
with the ISBN 978-1-60258-732-8.

Printed in the United States of America on acid-free paper with a minimum of 30 percent postconsumer waste recycled content.

TABLE OF CONTENTS

Contents

ACKNOWLEDGMENTS

If there is any true insight into Ecclesiastes among my writings, it is due to the truly excellent mentorship of Michael V. Fox. Michael didn't just teach me how to read wisdom texts, he taught me the wisdom and rewards of close reading. I am also grateful to the various groups of graduate students at the University of Toronto who studied Ecclesiastes with me and provided feedback on my ideas. I owe a great deal to a rich collaboration with John Cook, this volume being only one of many projects. And finally, I continue to be amazed at and deeply thankful for the longsuffering of Rachel, my beloved, for enduring the hours I spend reading or typing or listening to me talk my way through a difficult passage.

Robert D. Holmstedt, Toronto, July 25, 2017

I am indebted to Michael V. Fox for first guiding me through the Hebrew text of Qoheleth, and I am grateful to the students over the years at Asbury Theological Seminary and Asia Graduate School of Theology (Manila), with whom I in turn have had the pleasure of reading through Qoheleth and discussing its many grammatical and interpretive conundrums. And I am ever thankful for the support and encouragement of my family—for Kathy (אשתי אשר אהבתי), our four boys, Jared, Colin, Tage, and Evan, and our daughters-in-law, Becca and Amantha.

John A. Cook, Wilmore, Ky., July 25, 2017

I wish to acknowledge and thank my Doktorvater, Peter J. Gentry, for igniting in me simultaneously a love for linguistics (applied to biblical languages) and a love for Ecclesiastes. Both of these coincided in this project. As well, several students in the MABL program at Houston Baptist University bravely endured my reading classes in the Hebrew text of

Qoheleth and helped me wrestle with many thorny syntactic issues; I owe them a debt of gratitude. My wife, Cheryl, and our three children, John-Phillip, Kathryn, and Andrew, have patiently waited while I spent many hours of vacation and free time working on this project—thank you! Finally, I wish to thank Robert Holmstedt and John Cook for the invitation to collaborate on this volume. Although we come from varying ecclesiastical backgrounds and hold varying views on how best to analyze parts of Ecclesiastes, we are united in our desire to help others read Hebrew Bible texts informed by the best tools from modern linguistics.

Phillip S. Marshall, Houston, Tex., July 25, 2017

ABBREVIATIONS

For abbreviations not listed below, please consult The SBL Handbook of Style.

*	used in three ways: (1) to signal an unattested but reconstructed form (e.g., מֹדַעַת* in 1:1); (2) to signal a *Ketiv/ Qere* in the Hebrew text of the commentary; and (3) in the translation to signal the adoption of an emendation.
ANE	ancient Near Eastern
BDB	Brown, Francis, S. R. Driver, and C. A. Briggs. 1979. *The New Brown-Driver-Briggs Hebrew-English Lexicon.* Peabody, Mass.: Hendrickson.
BH	Biblical Hebrew
BL	Bauer, H., and P. Leander. 1922. *Historische Grammatik der hebräischen Sprache des Alten Testamentes.* Halle: Max Niemeyer.
c	common
Constr	construct
CP	complementizer phrase
DCH	Clines, David J. A., ed. 1993–2011. *The Dictionary of Classical Hebrew.* 8 vols. Sheffield: Sheffield Academic.
DP	determiner phrase
EBH	early Biblical Hebrew
ECM	exceptional case marking
f	feminine
GKC	Kautzsch, Emil. 1910. *Gesenius' Hebrew Grammar.* Trans. A. E. Cowley. 2nd Eng. ed. Oxford: Clarendon.
HALOT	Koehler, Ludwig, Walter Baumgartner, and Johann Jakob Stamm, eds. 1994–2000. *The Hebrew and Aramaic Lexicon*

of the Old Testament. Translated and edited under the supervision of M. E. J. Richardson. Leiden: Brill.

Hiph	Hiphil
Hith	Hithpael
HNPS	heavy noun phrase shift
Impv	imperative
Inf	infinitive
JM	Joüon, Paul, and Takamitsu Muraoka. 2006. *A Grammar of Biblical Hebrew*. Rev. ed. SubBi 27. Rome: Pontifical Biblical Institute.
Kt	*Ketiv*: the contextual form in the Masoretic Text of B19a (Leningrad Codex)
LBH	late Biblical Hebrew
m	masculine
MNK	van der Merwe, Christo H. J., Jacobus A. Naudé, and Jan H. Kroeze. 1999. *A Biblical Hebrew Reference Grammar*. Biblical Languages: Hebrew 3. Sheffield: Sheffield Academic.
MSS	manuscripts
MT	Masoretic Text
N	noun
Niph	Niphal
NP	noun phrase
p	plural
pro	pronoun
PP	prepositional phrase
Qr	*Qere*: the marginal form in the Masoretic Text of B19a (Leningrad Codex)
s	singular
SBH	Standard Biblical Hebrew
WO	Waltke, Bruce K., and Michael O'Connor. 1990. *An Introduction to Biblical Hebrew Syntax*. Winona Lake, Ind.: Eisenbrauns.
V	verb
VP	verb phrase

INTRODUCTION

The language of the book of Ecclesiastes has long puzzled scholars. After more than three centuries of critical study, terms like "aberrant" (Seow 1997: 11) and "idiosyncratic" (Schoors, 1) continue to be used to characterize the book's language. The linguistic profile of the book is indeed unique and appears to be a mix of styles, stages, registers, and dialects. For instance, the orthography has been linked with Phoenician, two words (פַּרְדֵּס and פִּתְגָם) have often been identified as lexical borrowings from Persian, multiple other lexemes or grammatical features have been labeled Phoenicianisms, Aramaisms, and Grecisms, and some items (e.g., the use of the relative element אֲשֶׁר in addition to the more common שֶׁ) have been associated with "late, vernacular" Hebrew (see Seow 1996 for a concise overview of the linguistic features commonly used in dating the book). With that said, the linguistic profile of every book in the Hebrew Bible is unique, and perpetuating the view that the grammar reflected in Ecclesiastes somehow deviates fundamentally from other examples of ancient Hebrew may well keep us from grammatical insight into the book.

In this volume of the *Baylor Handbook on the Hebrew Bible*, we build on our previous work in ancient (biblical and nonbiblical) Hebrew linguistics and on the book of Ecclesiastes both to present a substantive discussion of the notable grammatical issues one faces in Ecclesiastes and to apply our linguistic model in a verse-by-verse commentary. In the following sections, we offer a brief discussion of structure (§1) and then present the background and terminology necessary for understanding our grammatical analyses (§2), in-depth studies of the pronouns (§3), relative words (§4), and verbal system in the book (§5), and a final section on dating the language of the book (§6).

1

1. Literary Structure

Identifying Ecclesiastes' opaque structure remains a challenge. In the voluminous scholarship on the book, consensus has emerged only concerning the existence of the frame (1:1-2; 12:8-14) that distinguishes the author from the main character—the "I" voice of the book, Qoheleth.[1] Though the positions on the structure within the frame are myriad,[2] we find it useful to think of them in three basic categories: (1) there is no clear structure; the book is compilation of sayings or groups of saying similar to Proverbs (e.g., Lauha); (2) the structure reflects a progression of concepts and themes (e.g., Seow 1997; Longman); the structure is tied to the book's key phrases, such as the mentions of הֶבֶל "vanity," or the exhortation to enjoy life in 2:24-26; 3:12-13; 3:22; 5:17-19; 8:15; 9:7-10 (e.g., Wright; Rousseau); and (3) Qoheleth's ramblings reflect his disturbed psychological state; the progression and lapses reflect a psychological spiral (Bartholomew).

None of the articulations of the book's structure has gained broad acceptance; moreover, we have not found any particular structural analysis to be thoroughly convincing. Even the notion that there is a structural shift at 6:10, which demarcates the two halves of the book (Seow 1997: 45–46) seems arbitrary (note that the midpoint the Masoretes indicate in the margin of the Leningrad Codex concerns the number of words for copying purposes, not literary design). The only clear structural shift, in our opinion, is marked by the intrusion of the narrator at 7:27. The book is thus structured in two parts, marked at the beginning (1:2) and end (12:8) by the Qoheleth's motto and in the middle by the narrator's intrusion (7:27) (Christianson; Beldman). Although there does not appear to be a rigid pattern between the two halves, the first half of the book seems more oriented to Qoheleth's report of his experiment while the second half seems to wrap up the more general conclusions he draws from this.

Within the two halves of the book, the structure (or lack thereof) suggests to us that the psychological approach may be essentially correct, though the repetition and circling back to previously covered topics may also have explanation within the general wisdom *modus operandi*—to cover an issue from as many perspectives as possible. In this vein, we

---

[1] Note that throughout this work we refer to the book as Ecclesiastes and the main character as Qoheleth.

[2] See the useful surveys in Wright; Salyer; and Beldman.

could compare the principle behind the multiple dialogue cycles in Job with the apparent redundancy and regression within Ecclesiastes. Just as the author of Job used the cycles to impress the audience with the sense that Job's guilt or innocence had been thoroughly investigated, so Ecclesiastes has Qoheleth return again and again to the problem of toil, gain, death, and utility of wisdom to demonstrate the intractable tensions between what he expects of life in an ordered creation and what he experiences and observes.

For the usability of this volume, we have included smaller section headings in the commentary. The reader should note, though, that these headings are intended to be a *convenience for using the volume* and do not reflect any formal position on a structure within the book.

2. Linguistic Background

In our grammatical analysis we follow the approach taken in two previous volumes in the BHHB series: the Ruth volume (Holmstedt 2010) and the Esther volume (Screnock and Holmstedt) as well as numerous subsequent studies by the current authors (see the bibliography), including the syntactic database developed for Accordance Bible Software (see here: http://www.accordancebible.com/store/details/?pid=HMT -W4.syntax). In this section, we briefly describe the concepts by which we analyze the grammar of Ecclesiastes (we also suggest the reader consult the linguistic glossary and index at the end of the volume).

A. Syntactic Components: Constituency

Constituency refers to the analysis and determination of the units that combine to create larger structures. Thus, in politics, a constituent is a member of a geographic area served by a particular politician. In linguistics, constituents typically refer to the syntactic units that combine to form a clause. The relationship between these units is not just linear, but also hierarchical (see Jacobson; Carnie 2010). Consider the following clause:

(1)   A friend who read the Bible concluded that Ecclesiastes hates life.

Working backwards from the largest constituent, the entire clause, we can distinguish successively small syntactic units. Thus, *A friend who read the Bible* is the subject noun phrase (NP) of the clause and *concluded that Ecclesiastes hates life* is the verb phrase (VP). Those two constituents can be further reduced; for example, the NP *Ecclesiastes* is the subject of the VP *hates life* within the complement clause (a constituent) of the verb *concluded*. Further, the NP *life* is the object of the verb *hates*. And the complex subject NP of the main clause, *A friend who read the Bible*, can be similarly reduced into a number of constituents, so that in English, there is almost a one-to-one correspondence between a word and the lowest level of constituency.

Because the hierarchy of some phrases or clauses is not always easy to tease out before the structure is adequately understood—including which groups of words constitute constituents—linguists often use a variety of "constituent tests" to determine constituency (see Carnie 2006: 86–89). Such tests both confirm that this invisible and inaudible concept exists within grammar and give us evidence for discerning precisely what kind of structure we are dealing with in most instances. That is, they drive home the linguistic fact that constituents are a linguistic reality, even though we cannot "see" or "hear" them. In many cases, more than one test may be needed to conclude with some confidence that a particular group of words represents a constituent. Commonly used tests are coordination, replacement (by "do so" for VPs or "one" for NPs), clefting, and pseudo-clefting, though few of these transparently work for Biblical Hebrew (BH). Below we give one example of a constituent test that may have some applicability to Hebrew.

Pronoun replacement is one constituency test that works reasonably well for Hebrew—if a word or group of words can be replaced in a given phrase or clause by a pronoun, that word or group qualifies as a constituent (see Carnie 2006: 86–87). For example, in (1′) the group of words *A friend who read the Bible* can be replaced by the pronoun *he*, as we have done in (2).

(1′)   [A friend who read the Bible] concluded that Ecclesiastes hates life.

(2)   [He] concluded that Ecclesiastes hates life.

The grammatical acceptability of the pronoun replacement in (2) suggests that the group *A friend who read the Bible* functions in the clause as a single constituent.

Constituents, starting at the simplest level of words, combine with other constituents to create increasingly larger units, or phrases. When phrasal constituents are formed, the relationship between the smaller constituents within the phrase is hierarchical. That is, one item in a phrasal constituent shares its syntactic identity with (or "projects" its identity to) the entire phrase; this item is considered to be the phrasal

head. For instance, in the phrase *A friend who read the Bible* above in (1), the noun *friend* is the phrasal head and so the phrasal constituent is identified as a **noun phrase (NP)**.

Just as a noun phrase has a noun as its head, so all phrasal types have one constituent that is hierarchically dominant. Verbs project **verb phrases (VP)**, adjectives project **adjective phrases (AP)**, and so on with other lexical categories: adverbs (>**AdvP**), prepositions (>**PP**), determiners (>**DP**).

Constituents continue to combine until they form the highest phrasal level—the clause. The constituent relationships within a phrase or clause are often visually represented by bracketing or tree diagramming. If we bracket (1), the result is given in (3). Note that multiple brackets indicate further levels down in the hierarchy.

(3) [$_{CLAUSE}$ [$_{DP}$ A [$_{NP}$ friend [$_{CP}$ who [$_{VP}$ read [$_{DP}$ the [$_{NP}$ Bible]]]]]] [$_{VP}$ concluded [$_{CP}$ that [$_{DP}$ Ecclesiastes] [$_{VP}$ hates [$_{NP}$ life]]]]].

The tree diagram equivalent of (3), slightly simplified (i.e., eliminating the relative clause modifying the subject for reasons of space), is given in (4).

(4)

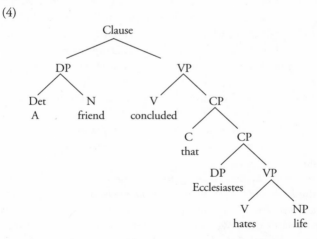

Both the bracketing and tree diagramming illustrate the hierarchical syntactic relationships among the words in phrases, though the tree diagramming is more visually explicit. (Note that the "tree" is upside down, since the highest node is the clause, which is the root in the tree metaphor, with the phrases and the nodes the "branches" and "leaves.")

What both methods of representation make clear is that phrases and clauses strongly tend to be *binary* in nature, that is, consisting of two lower constituents. For example, a DP consists of a determiner and an NP, a VP consists of a verb and its object DP/NP, and a clause consists of a subject and a VP. In fact, within generative syntax, binarity is taken to be a fundamental principle of phrase structure, so that even when a noun has multiple modifiers (e.g., an adjective and a relative clause), the phrase is structured so that there are only ever two branches (see Holmstedt forthcoming for further discussion).

B. Verbal Valency

Consistent with the hierarchical analysis of constituent structure, we employ the vocabulary and conceptual ideas of valency to analyze the nonverbal constituents within the VP. In terms of vocabulary, throughout this work we classify the nonverbal constituents within the VP as either **complements** or **adjuncts** of the verbal head. Traditionally, complements have been thought of as "required" (grammatically or semantically) by the verbal head, whereas adjuncts are "optional" (see, e.g., WO §10.2a). For example, in the sentence *He hit the ball into left field*, the transitive verb "requires" the NP *the ball*, but the PP *into left field* is optional; the sentence would remain grammatical and have the same basic semantics without the PP. Thus, the former constituent, *the ball*, is regarded as a complement and the latter constituent *into left field* as an adjunct. The traditional approach, however, cannot adequately account for expressions such as *He's hitting well* (such as in answer to the question about a baseball player, *How's he playing today?*). In this example, the head verb, *hit*, which is generally regarded as transitive and therefore requires a NP complement, is modified by the adverb *well*, which is arguably an adjunct—i.e., "optional."

Instead of the traditional concepts of "required" or "optional," we prefer to think in terms of hierarchy and constituent structure: constituents that are complements are more closely tied to their verbal head than are adjunct constituents. We can demonstrate the difference of "closeness" between the verbal head and complements versus adjuncts by the *do-so* test, which is analogous to the pronoun replacement test mentioned above. If we replace the verbal head with *do-so*, the head requires that its complement also be replaced; by contrast, adjunct constituents do not have to be replaced by the stand-in *do-so* expression. For example, in the expression *Bill hit the ball into left field, and John did so into right field*, the *did so* replaces the verbal head and its complement *hit the ball*, while the adjunct *into left field* is unrepresented by *did so*, thus an alternative one can be used, *into right field*. By contrast, we cannot replace only the verbal head without its complement by *do so*, demonstrated by the ungrammaticalness of the following expression: **Bill hit the ball into left field, and John did so the bat into the dugout.*

Even though it can be difficult at times to distinguish complements and adjuncts, especially in an ancient language, approaching the distinction in terms of hierarchy and constituent structure demonstrates that there is a real and measurable distinction between these two types of nonverbal VP constituents. In addition, it explains how the examples *He hit the ball against the wall* and *He's hitting well* can both be grammatical: in the second example, in answer to the question *How's he playing today?* about a baseball game, we interpret *He's hitting well* with an implicit complement *the ball*. This is evident from the fact that a follow up question *What's he hitting well?* would be strange in such a context. Many verbs elicit such implicit complements, even apart from contextual indicators. For example, the English *bake* implies baking bread or pastry; *read* implies looking at something legible; and *eat* implies ingesting something edible. If these actions apply to something other than these default complements, an overt expression is required: *Let's bake potatoes; I can read your mind; Eat my dust!* It is helpful, therefore, to think of implicit complements as of two types: either they are implied by the verb itself (as in the above examples) or they are implied from the context, either generally (as in *the ball* in the exchange about the baseball game), or elliptically, in which we can point to a specific word from the context that is the implicit complement (e.g., *She picked up her book and read (it)*; see אכל "eat" in Gen 3:6).

While recognizing variations in valency patterns for individual verbs, we find it expedient to refer to the verbs at times in the commentary by their typical structures, either as monovalent (one argument: the subject), bivalent (two arguments: the subject and a VP complement), or trivalent (three arguments: the subject and two VP complements). The following examples from Ecclesiastes illustrate these patterns in BH.

(5) Monovalent (no VP complement)

וְלָמָּה חָכַמְתִּי

Why have I [$_{\text{VP}}$ become wise?] (2:15)

(6)   Bivalent (one VP complement: NP, PP, infinitive clause, or direct
       speech)

הַחַיִּים יוֹדְעִים שֶׁיָּמֻתוּ

The living [$_{VP}$ know [$_{COMP}$ that they will die.]] (9:5)

(7)   Trivalent (two VP complements: NP, PP, infinitive clause, or direct
       speech)

אֶת־כָּל־זֶה נָתַתִּי אֶל־לִבִּי

I [$_{VP}$ gave [$_{COMP1}$ all this] [$_{COMP2}$ to my heart]] (9:1)

The system of *binyanim*, especially when they apply to a single root,
create contrasting valency patterns. For example, compare the bivalent
Qal verb of עשׂה (*he did x*; e.g., 2:5-6) with the monovalent Niphal of
the same root, נעשׂה (*it was done*; e.g., 1:14-15); similarly, compare the
bivalent Qal ראה (*he saw x*; e.g., 1:14) with the trivalent Hiphil, הראה
(*he showed x y*; e.g., 2:24).

C. Subordinate Clauses

Most subordinate clauses are clausal adjuncts (some are complements)
to a verb (relatives modify a noun) in a higher clause within which the
subordinate clause resides (see Holmstedt 2013d). Hebrew subordination is signaled by two methods: the use of subordinators or the type of
verb. The subordinators used in Hebrew fall into two categories, subordinating conjunction (e.g., כי) and the combination of a preposition and
conjunction (כאשׁר), and appear at the front of the subordinate clause.
Those used in Ecclesiastes are listed below:

(8) Subordinators in Ecclesiastes

אִם "if" (3:12; 4:10, 11, 12; 5:7, 10, 11; 6:3; 8:15, 17; 10:4, 10, 11; 11:3,
    6, 8; 12:14)

לוּ "if" (6:6)

אֲשֶׁר "that" (1:10, 13, 16; 2:3 [2×], 10, 12; 3:9, 10, 11 [2×], 14, 15, 22;
    4:1, 2, 3 [3×]; 4:9, 13, 15, 16, 17; 5:3 [2×], 4, 14, 17 [3×], 18; 6:1,
    2 [2×], 10, 12; 7:2, 13, 18, 19, 20, 21 [2×], 22, 26, 28, 29; 8:3, 4, 7,
    9 [2×], 10, 11, 12 [3×], 13, 14 [3×], 15 [2×], 16 [2×], 17 [2×]; 9:1, 2
    [3×], 3, 4, 6, 9 [3×], 10 [2×]; 10:14, 15; 11:5 [2×]; 12:1 [2×], 2, 6, 7)

שֶׁ "that" (1:3, 7, 9 [4×], 10, 11 [2×], 14, 17; 2:7, 9, 11 [2×], 12, 13, 14,
    15, 16, 17, 18 [3×], 19 [2×], 20, 21 [2×], 22, 24, 26; 3:13, 14, 15,
    18, 22; 4:2, 10; 5:4, 14 [2×], 15 [2×], 17; 6:3, 10 [2×]; 7:10, 14, 24;
    8:7, 14 [2×], 17; 9:5, 12 [2×]; 10:3, 5, 14, 16, 17; 11:3, 8; 12:3, 7, 9)

הַ "that"[3] (1:11 [3×]; 2:14, 16 [3×], 26; 3:9, 17 [2×], 21 [2×]; 4:1 [2×], 2 [2×], 3, 9 [2×], 10 [2×], 12 [3×], 14, 15 [2×], 16; 5:11 [2×]; 6:8 [3×]; 7:10, 19; 8:1, 13, 14 [2×], 17; 9:1 [2×], 2 [8×], 3, 4, 5 [2×], 11 [4×], 12, 15, 16; 10:4, 5; 11:5; 12:3, 5)

כִּי "because, when, if, that" (1:18; 2:10, 12, 16, 17, 21, 22, 24, 25, 26; 3:12, 14, 17, 19, 22; 4:4, 10, 14 [2×], 17; 5:1, 2, 3, 5, 6 [2×], 7, 10, 17, 19 [2×]; 6:2, 4; 7:3, 6, 7, 9, 10, 12, 13, 18, 22; 8:3, 6 [2×], 7 [2×], 15, 17; 9:3, 4 [2×], 5 [2×], 7, 9, 10, 11 [2×], 12; 10:4, 20; 11:1, 2, 6, 8, 9, 10; 12:3, 5, 13, 14).

Subordination that is signaled by the type of verb used primarily concerns Hebrew infinitives. The "infinitive construct" is often the clitic host for (and complement of) a preposition that overtly marks the infinitival clause as an adjunct of the verb in the higher clause (see, e.g., לָלֶכֶת in 1:2). These infinitives provide a wide range of subordinate clauses, such as temporal, purpose, and complement. The "infinitive absolute" used as the verb in a VP takes its tense-aspect-mood value from its governing verb and is used to present its clause both as subordinate and as focus-marked (see, e.g., שָׁבָה in 4:2; see also 4:17; 8:9; 9:11; and the commentary discussions).

D. Word Order

Although the basic word order of Hebrew is traditionally understood to be **verb-subject** (see, e.g., WO §8.3b; JM §155k), the discussion has markedly lacked grounding in the analysis of word order in general linguistics (see Holmstedt 2011). We maintain that the general shift in Semitic languages from typologically verb-subject to typologically **subject-verb** order had occurred in Hebrew by the time most of the Hebrew Bible was written down (Holmstedt 2005, 2009a, 2013d; cf. Joüon 1923 §155). More specifically, while some early books (e.g., 1 Samuel) may still reflect a "weak" verb-subject typology, the progression to subject-verb typology occurs through the monarchic and post-monarchic periods of ancient Israel, resulting in a "strong" subject-verb typology by the early postbiblical Hebrew of the Mishnah.

But a language's typological word order profile is not the end of the story. Typologically speaking, basic word order is most often identified

---

[3] On הַ as a subordinator, see Holmstedt 2010: 27–31 and 2016: 69–77. Note that the list of examples in Ecclesiastes includes cases in which the article and a preceding preposition have been fused, e.g., לַ.

as the word order present in "stylistically neutral, independent, indicative clauses with full nouns phrase (NP) participants, where the subject is definite, agentive and human, the object is a definite semantic patient, and the verb represents an action, not a state or an event" (Siewierska, 8; see also Mallinson and Blake, 125). However, this kind of clause may not be identical to the statistically prevalent word order of a given language, due to vagaries of human communication or genre conventions (Siewierska, 11–12).

Recognizing a distinction between basic word order and other derived orders that may be used more frequently is the key to the Hebrew situation. Hebrew narrative especially has a conventional form that utilizes a specific verb type, the past narrative *wayyiqtol*, which forces verb-subject order. Departure from the use of a clause with *wayyiqtol* triggers narrative implicatures like background information or simultaneity. Thus, it is accurate to say that the predominant word order in Hebrew narrative is verb-subject, but it is inaccurate to take this as underived and thus basic order. Rather, the basic, underived order is subject-verb, while a variety of grammatical factors—the placement of a constituent or certain grammatical words at the beginning of the clause, the use of an irrealis verb, the use of the past narrative *wayyiqtol*—trigger constituent movement and thus derivational orders often reflecting verb-subject. The list below summarizes the most common triggers to verb-subject order:

1. subordination (most commonly with פֶּן, אִם, אֲשֶׁר, כִּי, לְמַעַן)
2. clausal negation
3. irrealis verbs (irrealis *yiqtol* or *qatal*, jussives, cohortatives, imperatives)
4. topic or focus-fronting of a nonsubject constituent

The likely explanation for the marked difference between the basic subject-verb order of main clauses and the dominant verb-subject order in subordinate and negated clauses is diachronic. Cross-linguistic studies have demonstrated that syntactic change occurs first in nonembedded (i.e., main clause) structures and only later spreads to embedded structures (Holmstedt 2013d: 21). One indication that Hebrew continued to change during the span in which the Hebrew Bible was written is the different word order profiles we can detect in the different books. For example, finding a greater frequency of subject-verb order infiltrating subordinate, negated, and/or irrealis contexts within a given book (e.g., the subject-negative-verb clause in Eccl 1:15; 4:8; 5:9; 6:3; 8:5; 9:15;

11:4; and Esth 9:28b) strongly suggests a diachronically later linguistic stage (Holmstedt 2013d: 21–23; see below, §6).

Null copula clauses (so-called verbless or nominal clauses) also have the basic order subject-verb (or better, subject–null copula–complement). However, these clauses do not typically invert to verb-subject order when a subordinator or pragmatically fronted constituent precedes the subject. Rather, any divergence from subject–null copula–complement word order is when the subject or copular complement is fronted for topic or focus. Note that we take the Hebrew participle to be the complement of a copula, most often null, though occasionally overt (see Cook 2008). The word order implication is that participles should also have a basic subject-copula-complement[participle] order. Happily, this is indeed the case.

Finally, as copular items, we might expect יֵשׁ (positive) and אֵין (negative) to exhibit subject-verb (or, subject-copula-complement) word order. While this order does occur (e.g., וחלק אֵין־לָהֶם in 9:6), it is rare and the overwhelming pattern is either to use a left-dislocation that is resumed by the clitic pronoun on אֵין (e.g., וְהִים אֵינֶנּוּ מָלֵא in 1:7) or to have the אֵין or יֵשׁ first, followed by the copular subject and then complement (e.g., יֵשׁ אֶחָד וְאֵין שֵׁנִי in 4:8). The syntax of יֵשׁ and אֵין copular phrase structure has not yet adequately been studied and so remains an important desideratum in Hebrew grammar.

In sum, when constituents are moved from their default position (e.g., subject-verb-complement-adjunct), the reasons are either syntax (i.e., triggered inversion due to subordinating particles), semantics (i.e., irrealis verbs, negation), or pragmatics. Pragmatically motivated constituent movement in BH is for two primary reasons—to signal that a constituent carries either topic or focus information. Though it is possible for a topic-marked or focus-marked constituent to reside in its default position (where it would be marked by an item like focus גַּם or prosody) or to be moved to the end of the clause (e.g,. extraposition and right-dislocation; see Holmstedt 2014), by far the dominant strategy to signal such discourse information is to raise the marked constituent to the front of the clause (see Holmstedt 2009a: 126–29; 2011: 21–24).

Topic-fronting is used to signal a shift of "aboutness" (i.e., what the following assertions are "about"; the topic being typically the syntactic subject) between known discourse entities or to set the scene's circumstantial information, such as temporal or spatial PPs. An example of a scene-setting topic is the temporal phrase כְּ-PP in Eccl 5:3,

כאשר תדר נדר לאלהים אל־תאחר לשלמו. An example of topic for "about-ness" is the subject הארץ in the clause והארץ לעולם עמדת in Eccl 1:4. The fronted position of the PP לעולם before the participle (and null copula) indicates that the DP הארץ is also fronted, likely for focus (see discussion in commentary on 1:4).

Focus-fronting serves to establish a set of related items either from the discourse context or from shared knowledge of the world and then to set the focus constituent over against the other members of the set. The result is often associated with a sense of contrast, illustrated in Eccl 1:2:

(9) הֲבֵל הֲבָלִים אָמַר קֹהֶלֶת הֲבֵל הֲבָלִים הַכֹּל הָבֶל

"'A total הבל!' said Qoheleth, 'A total הבל! Everything is a הבל.'"

Note how the fronted direct speech (part of it, anyway) triggers the raising of the verb אמר in front of the subject קהלת. The reason for the focus-fronting is to contrast the audience's expected assessment (e.g., "it's all good") with the actual assessment given by Qoheleth.

Both topic and focus constituents may be fronted in the same clause, with the topic always preceding the focus, as the tree diagram below illustrates. Additionally, it is possible for there to be more than one of each type, which is what the *-marking in the tree diagram below represents. Note that the tree also shows where subordinators fit in nonmain clauses, as well as whence "extreme" topic-fronted constituents raise (see Holmstedt 2014 for further discussion).

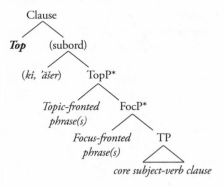

A final comment on word order in BH concerns the likely diachronic shift from a "weak" verb-subject typology to a subject-verb typology over the course of the centuries represented by the biblical texts. A contributor to this shift may have been the adoption and then abandonment of

the past narrative *wayyiqtol* form (later biblical and postbiblical Hebrew exhibit less frequent use of the *wayyiqtol* so that it is entirely absent in the grammar of rabbinic Hebrew—its only occurrences are in quotations of biblical material). At the core of the shift, though, is a reanalysis of subject fronting (for topic or focus) so that it was viewed as a pragmatically unmarked construction, resulting in a basic subject-verb order. Another participant in this shift is the modal system; for example, the loss of the irrealis *qatal* would strengthen the appearance of a general subject-verb pattern and likely encourage the acquisition of Hebrew as a subject-verb language. See Holmstedt 2013e for a fuller discussion of the shift to subject-verb in ancient Hebrew.

3. The Pronouns in Ecclesiastes[4]

This section addresses a noticeably idiosyncratic feature of Ecclesiastes' language—its use of the subject pronoun after a finite verb. Though superficially peculiar, this construction is actually well grounded in standard BH syntax and represents the use of the postverbal subject pronoun אֲנִי to formalize grammatically a literary method to describe Ecclesiastes' thought experiment: he did not do it alone, but with his לֵב as a dialogue partner.

A. The Problem of Postverbal Pronouns

Certain aspects of the first-person grammar of Ecclesiastes figure prominently in commentary upon the book: the use of the first-person narrative voice and the choice of the first-person pronoun אֲנִי over the longer form אָנֹכִי. The first-person narrative is not foreign to wisdom literature (see, e.g., Prov 1:10). The use of אֲנִי could either reflect its Hebrew origin as the "marked"[5] pronominal choice to signal higher status or importance (Revell 1995) or the later total displacement of אָנֹכִי by אֲנִי (see Mishnaic Hebrew); we suspect the latter is more likely (see §6 below on the dating of Ecclesiastes).

---

[4] This section has been adapted from Holmstedt 2009b; the reader should consult that study for the critical review of previous proposals concerning the 1cs pronoun in Ecclesiastes.

[5] Markedness theory developed out of the Prague School of linguistic analysis. The basic concept is, given two similar constructions, the one occurring more often and in a greater number of environments is unmarked while the one the occurs less often and in restricted environments is marked.

A third aspect of the first-person grammar that has not received due attention is the use of a first-person subject pronoun with a finite verb, an example of which is given in (10).

(10) דִּבַּ֤רְתִּי אֲנִי֙ עִם־לִבִּ֣י לֵאמֹ֔ר אֲנִ֗י הִנֵּ֨ה הִגְדַּ֧לְתִּי וְהוֹסַ֛פְתִּי חָכְמָ֖ה עַ֣ל כָּל־אֲשֶׁר־
הָיָ֥ה לְפָנַ֖י עַל־יְרוּשָׁלָ֑͏ִם וְלִבִּ֛י רָאָ֥ה הַרְבֵּ֖ה חָכְמָ֥ה וָדָֽעַת׃

"I spoke, I to[6] my לֵב: 'I—look—I made myself great and added wisdom (to myself) over any who was before me over Jerusalem.' And my לֵב has (also) seen much wisdom and knowledge" (1:16).

Set within the context of the Hebrew Bible, there are two features that distinguish Ecclesiastes' use of the subject pronoun: its presence and its syntactic placement. The first-person pronoun אֲנִי occurs 21 times in conjunction with a finite verb in the book. The book only has 81 first-person verbs within its 222 verses, so that more than one out of four verbs has a subject pronoun. A quick comparison with the rest of the Hebrew Bible, summarized in table 1, suggests that Ecclesiastes differs from the rest of the Hebrew Bible in its use of the 1cs pronoun as well as itself in the use of second and third-person subject pronouns.

The chart highlights a number of striking facts. First, the frequency of first-person pronoun with finite verbs is considerably higher in Ecclesiastes than in the rest of the Hebrew Bible. Second, Ecclesiastes' use of 1cs subject pronouns differs from its use of second and third-person subject pronouns. Third, the position of the 1cs pronouns is opposite the dominant pattern elsewhere: Ecclesiastes overwhelmingly places the 1cs pronoun *after* the verb whereas the subject pronoun in other biblical books typically *precedes* the verb. The much more common preverbal placement of the pronoun in the Hebrew Bible is illustrated in (11).

(11) כִּֽי־אֶֽהְיֶ֣ה עִמָּ֔ךְ וְזֶה־לְּךָ֣ הָא֔וֹת כִּ֥י אָנֹכִ֖י שְׁלַחְתִּ֑יךָ בְּהוֹצִֽיאֲךָ֤ אֶת־הָעָם֙ מִמִּצְרַ֔יִם
תַּֽעַבְדוּן֙ אֶת־הָ֣אֱלֹהִ֔ים עַ֖ל הָהָ֥ר הַזֶּֽה

"Because I will be with you and this will a sign for you that_I have sent you: when you take the people out of Egypt you shall honor God upon this mountain" (Exod 3:12).

---

[6] As HALOT (s.v. דבר) indicates, the verb דבר allows a number of prepositions to mark the person to or with whom the speaking is occurring: -לְ, אֵת, אֶל, and עִם are the most common, but -בְּ is also used; see, e.g., Num 12:6, 8; 1 Sam 25:39; Hos 1:2; Hab 2:1; Zech 1:9, 13-14; 2:2, 7; 4:1, 4-5; 5:5, 10; 6:4; Song 8:8. Since a one-sided conversation is what takes place in Ecclesiastes, we translate the preposition as "to" rather than "with." See also below, n. 16.

TABLE 1
Finite Verbs with Subject Pronouns in Ecclesiastes and the Hebrew Bible

	Ecclesiastes (222 vv. in B19a)	*Rest of Bible* (22,991 vv. in B19a)
1cs finite verbs	81	6,924
1cs pronouns w/finite verb	22 2 preverbal[7] 20 postverbal[8]	482 412 preverbal 70 postverbal
1cp finite verbs	0	1,032
1cp pronouns w/finite verb	0	31 26 preverbal 5 postverbal
2nd person finite verbs	39	6,861
2nd person pronouns w/finite verb	1 (preverbal)[9]	330 296 preverbal 34 postverbal
3rd person finite verbs	311	38,533
3rd person pronouns w/finite verb	5 4 preverbal[10] 1 postverbal[11]	561 468 preverbal 95 postverbal

[7] 1:12, 16 (2nd occurrence).

[8] 1:16 (1st occurrence); 2:1, 11, 12, 13, 14, 15 (2×), 18, 20, 24; 3:17, 18; 4:1, 4, 7; 5:17; 7:25; 8:15; 9:16.

[9] 7:22. Although 7:22 includes both an overt subject pronoun and mention of the לֵב, the second-person address makes it clear that Ecclesiastes is not speaking about himself or his לֵב, and thus this verse is not relevant for the "אֲנִי וְלִבִּי" argument. Even so, the function of the subject pronoun in 7:22 is worth examining: the overt, preverbal pronoun likely marks focus, communicating a contrast between the addressee and the servant mentioned in the preceding verse, e.g., כִּי גַּם־פְּעָמִים רַבּוֹת יָדַע לִבֶּךָ אֲשֶׁר גַּם־אַתָּה קִלַּלְתָּ אֲחֵרִים "your לֵב knows that also you [vs. your servant, from v. 21] have cursed others."

[10] 3:14, 7:29, 8:15, 10:10.

[11] 9:15.

In summary, while in general the use of the subject pronoun in the Hebrew Bible is a marked grammatical feature—relatively rare and used to signal a "topic"[12] or "focus,"[13] in Ecclesiastes it is strikingly frequent with the 1cs verbs. Moreover, the postverbal placement of the 1cs pronoun in Ecclesiastes contrasts both with the preverbal placement of second- and third-person subject pronouns in that same book and of all subject pronouns in the Hebrew Bible as a whole. All of this raises two closely related questions: Why is the 1cs pronoun used so much in Ecclesiastes and Why is it consistently placed postverbally? To answer these questions requires that we investigate features of the Hebrew pronominal system in general.

B. Hebrew as a "Pro-drop" Language

BH is a prototypical example of what is called a "*pro*-drop" or "null-subject" language (Naudé 1991, 1993; Holmstedt 2013b). The finite verbs are inflected with morphologically rich affixes (i.e., the verbal affixes are portmanteau morphs, carrying a bundle of person, number, and gender agreement features). In most languages with rich verbal morphology, overt subject noun phrases and pronouns are absent more often than not; i.e., they are "dropped." The subject noun phrases and overt subject pronouns are in complementary distribution with a covert/null pronoun (*pro*). The *pro*-drop status of BH explains why the Hebrew Bible—from early to late literature—exhibits numerous clauses lacking an overt subject, as in (12) and (13).

(12) כֵּן תַּכְעִסֶנָּה וַתִּבְכֶּה וְלֹא תֹאכַל

"Thus *pro* (= Peninah) would vex her and *pro* (= Hannah) would weep and *pro* (she = Hannah) would not eat" (1 Sam 1:7).

(13) וַיְבִיאֵם אֶרֶץ־שִׁנְעָר בֵּית אֱלֹהָיו

"And *pro* (= Nebuchadnezzar) brought them (to) the land of Shinar, (to) the house of his gods" (Dan 1:2).

---

[12] We take topic to isolate one among multiple known entities in the discourse or to set the scene (e.g., with temporal or locative phrases). See Holmstedt 2009a, 2014 for further discussion.

[13] We take focus to identify a constituent to be in a contrastive relationship with possible alternatives. A constituent is typically presented as carrying focus by syntactic position, intonation, or specific focus items (e.g., Heb רַק "only"). See Holmstedt 2009a, 2014 for further discussion.

While it is most common for an overt subject noun phrase or pronoun to be dropped when the agent/patient subject of the verb is the most recently used verbal subject, the examples in (12) and (13) illustrate that even a distant subject may be filled by *pro* if the referent is apparent from the context. In (12) the previous agentive subject to be mentioned (in v. 6) is Yhwh, but it is contextually clear that Peninah was the agent of vexation for Hannah. It is also clear that Hannah was the one who wept and not Peninah, even though Hannah has not been explicitly identified as an agent since v. 5. In both cases, the identity of the agent is sufficiently easy to reconstruct based on the context so that the use of overt subject noun phrases is unnecessary. Similarly, in (13) the last explicit agentive subject in the context is אֲדֹנָי "the Lord," but it is contextually clear that Nebuchadnezzar is the agent of the exile, making an overt noun phrase or pronoun to mark the shift between agents unnecessary.

The two examples in (12) and (13) demonstrate that an overt subject noun phrase or pronoun is often lacking in BH and yet the lack is syntactically licensed. Our explanation of (12) and (13) also illustrates how the identification of *pro* is related to the discourse: in Hebrew *pro* is used when its ability to access its antecedent within the discourse is high, the referring noun phrase subject is used when the accessibility is low, and an overt pronoun is used when the antecedent is marked for topic or focus.

Ecclesiastes exhibits the same *pro*-drop syntax as the rest of the Hebrew Bible, as (14) demonstrates.[14]

(14) וְנָתַ֤תִּי אֶת־לִבִּי֙ לִדְר֣וֹשׁ וְלָת֔וּר בַּֽחָכְמָ֔ה עַ֛ל כָּל־אֲשֶׁ֥ר נַעֲשָׂ֖ה תַּ֣חַת הַשָּׁמָ֑יִם

"And *pro* (= I) set my לֵב to seek and to investigate with wisdom concerning all that happens under the sun" (1:13).

When the overt subject 1cs pronoun is used with a finite verb in Ecclesiastes, we expect, then, that it is signaling that the 1cs referent (the speaker) is marked for topic or focus. But why does it use the unusual postverbal placement of the 1cs pronoun?

---

[14] For 1cs finite verbs without accompanying subject pronouns, see 1:13, 14, 17 (2×); 2:1, 2, 3, 4 (3×), 5 (2×), 6, 7, 8 (2×), 9 (2×), 10 (2×), 11, 15, 17, 18, 19 (2×), 20; 3:10, 12, 14, 16, 22; 4:1, 15; 5:12; 6:1, 3; 7:15, 23 (3×), 27, 28 (3×), 29; 8:9, 10, 14 16, 17; 9:1, 11, 13; 10:5, 7. The same hold true of second- and third-person pronouns: the overt pronouns occur with finite verbs many fewer times (1:13; 3:14; 7:22, 29; 8:15; 9:15; 10:10) than the verb with null *pro* (too many to list).

C. Subject Pronoun Syntax

By far the dominant order when pronouns are used with finite verbs is pronoun-verb (by at least four-to-one, with all pronouns), not verb-pronoun as we have in Ecclesiastes. Moreover, since an overt pronoun in a pro-drop language marks the subject with topic or focus status, the expected (and statistically dominant) position is initial, i.e., located somewhere in the clausal area preceding the final position of verb, as in (15), repeated from (11).

(15) כִּי־אֶהְיֶה עִמָּךְ וְזֶה־לְּךָ הָאוֹת כִּי אָנֹכִי שְׁלַחְתִּיךָ בְּהוֹצִיאֲךָ אֶת־הָעָם מִמִּצְרַיִם תַּעַבְדוּן אֶת־הָאֱלֹהִים עַל הָהָר הַזֶּה

"Because I will be with you and this will a sign for you that *I have sent you*: when you take the people out of Egypt you shall honor God upon this mountain" (Exod 3:12).

With that said, Hebrew clause structure does allow for postverbal focus constituents, as the constituents preceded by רַק and גַם in (16) and (17) demonstrate.

(16) וַיֹּאמֶר יְהוּדָה לְשִׁמְעוֹן אָחִיו עֲלֵה אִתִּי בְגוֹרָלִי וְנִלָּחֲמָה בַּכְּנַעֲנִי וְהָלַכְתִּי גַם־אֲנִי אִתְּךָ בְּגוֹרָלֶךָ

"And Judah said to Simon, his brother: Go up with me into my allotment and let us fight against the Canaanite, then *(I) shall go, I, too*, with you into your allotment" (Judg 1:3).

(17) וַתִּפֹּל שְׁבָא וַתִּקָּחֵם וְאֶת־הַנְּעָרִים הִכּוּ לְפִי־חָרֶב וָאִמָּלְטָה רַק־אֲנִי לְבַדִּי לְהַגִּיד לָךְ

"And Sheba fell (upon the livestock) and took them and they killed the servants by sword and *(I) escaped, only I alone*, to tell you" (Job 1:15).

Postverbal focus on the verbal subject, whether with pronouns or noun phrases, is much less frequent than preverbal focus. It is possible that this highly marked combination of the overt pronoun and the postverbal placement, which is unusual and thus syntactically marked (if not disruptive, similar to interjections and vocatives), is used for an even higher degree of focus-induced contrast than the more common preverbal focus. This is certainly suggested by the addition of the focus words גַם and רַק before the subject pronouns in (16) and (17).

An additional syntactic wrinkle in the use of subject pronouns is represented by examples like (18) and (19).

(18) וַיִּשְׁתּוּ הוּא וְהָאֲנָשִׁים אֲשֶׁר־עִמּוֹ

"And *pro* (they) drank, he and the men that were with him" (Gen 24:54).

(19) וַיַּכְבֵּד לִבּוֹ הוּא וַעֲבָדָיו

"And *pro* (he) hardened his לֵב, he and his servants" (Exod 9:34).

This type of construction is most often described as a way to highlight some feature of the subject, whether indicating a shift from a singular agent to a group, specified by the coordinate subject, as in (18), or emphasizing the primary agent-hood of the first constituent in the coordinate phrase, as in (19) (Revell 1993). This may be so, but it is not clear that the coordinate phrases are actually the syntactic subjects in these clauses since an overt subject of the verb may also appear (20).

(20) וַיֵּצֵא עוֹג מֶלֶךְ־הַבָּשָׁן לִקְרָאתֵנוּ הוּא וְכָל־עַמּוֹ לַמִּלְחָמָה אֶדְרֶעִי

"And Og, the king of Bashan, went out to meet us, he and all his people, for battle at Edrei" (Deut 3:1).

In (20) the coordinate phrase הוּא וְכָל־עַמּוֹ cannot be the syntactic subject since that position is already filled by the overt noun phrase עוֹג מֶלֶךְ־הַבָּשָׁן. Nor can the coordinate phrase be right-dislocated, since it is positioned before another prepositional phrase adjunct לַמִּלְחָמָה (see Holmstedt and Jones 2016). The phrase הוּא וְכָל־עַמּוֹ is instead an extraposed appositive to the syntactic subject, whether overt or null (see Naudé 1999; Holmstedt 2009c for an alternative hypothesis). When the syntactic subject is *pro*, the verb is often singular, even though the appositive is a compound NP that is plural. In accordance with the nature of apposition (Holmstedt and Jones 2016), the function of the appositive is to clarify the full extent of the semantic subject. When the subject is overt, the appositive not only clarifies the full extent of the semantic subject but also signals that that overt subject, which is resumed by the pronoun in the compound appositive, is the more salient (active) agent of the verb.

We thus have two grammatical explanations for the postverbal 1cs pronoun in Ecclesiastes: it may be to carry a postverbal focus on the subject or it may be within a compound appositive to the syntactic subject used to clarify the full set of verbal agents. Which grammatical construction (of perhaps both?) best explains the Ecclesiastes data is the remaining piece of the puzzle.

D. A Syntactic Solution and a Literary Explanation

In order to consider the grammatical options carefully, we must consider the full range of 1cs pronoun data in Ecclesiastes as a unified set, which is the purpose of table 2.

TABLE 2
The Use of the 1cs Subject Pronouns in Ecclesiastes

Col 1: Verb + Pro		Col 2: Verb + Pro-PP		Col 3: Other	
פָּנִיתִי אֲנִי	(2:11, 12)	דִּבַּרְתִּי אֲנִי עִם־לִבִּי	(1:16)	סַבּוֹתִי אֲנִי וְלִבִּי	(7:25)
רָאִיתִי אָנִי	(2:13, 24; 4:4; 5:17)	אָמַרְתִּי אֲנִי בְּלִבִּי	(2:1, 15; 3:17, 18)	סַבּוֹתִי אֲנִי לְיַאֵשׁ אֶת־לִבִּי	(2:20)
שַׂבְתִּי אֲנִי	(4:1, 7)				
יָדַעְתִּי גַם־אָנִי	(2:14)				
חָכַמְתִּי אֲנִי	(2:15)				
שָׂנֵאתִי אֲנִי	(2:18)				
שִׁבַּחְתִּי אֲנִי	(8:15)				
אָמַרְתִּי אָנִי	(9:16)				

In the first column are the occurrences of the 1cs subject pronoun without any coordinate phrase. In the second column the 1cs pronoun is immediately followed by a preposition and the noun לֵב "heart, mind." The third column presents what we consider to be the key to solving the problem: the first example has a singular verb followed by the 1cs pronoun coordinated with לֵב by the simple conjunction -וְ, the second example has לֵב as the verbal complement of an embedded infinitive following a finite verb and the 1cs pronoun.

At the center of the grammatical puzzle stands Qoheleth's לֵב. In Ecclesiastes[15] the לֵב is used differently than elsewhere in the Hebrew

---

[15] The noun לֵב occurs forty-one times in Ecclesiastes: 1:13, 16 (2×), 17; 2:1, 3 (2×), 10 (2×), 15 (2×), 20, 22, 23; 3:11, 17, 18; 5:1, 19; 7:2, 3, 4 (2×), 7, 21, 22, 25, 26; 8:5, 9, 11, 16; 9:1, 3, 7; 10:2 (2×), 3; 11:9 (2×), 10. It is used as a syntactic subject (1:16, 2:3, 10, 23; 5:1; 7:3, 4 [2×], 22; 8:5, 11; 9:3; 10:2 [2×], 3; 11:9), as an NP complement (1:13, 17; 2:10, 20; 7:7, 21; 8:9, 16), within a PP complement (3:11; 7:2; 9:1), within a noncomplement PP (1:16; 2:1, 3, 15 [2×]; 3:17, 18; 9:7; 11:10), as the NP clitic host of a bound noun (i.e., the "nomen rectum" of a "construct phrase") (2:22; 5:19; 7:26; 11:9), and as a conjunct in an adjunct phrase (7:25). There are clear cases in which לֵב is used in its more typical sense as one's inner self; notably these are all in reference to a לֵב that is not Qoheleth's specific one: 2:22, 23; 3:11; 5:1, 19; 7:2, 3, 4 (2×), 7, 21, 22, 26; 8:5, 11; 9:3, 7; 10:2 (2×), 3; 11:9 (2×), 10. There are

Bible. Rather than לֵב used with verbs of speaking to express the idiom for internal speech (i.e., someone thinking or speaking to himself), it is used as a full-fledged character in Ecclesiastes. To wit, the second-person imperative instead of the expected first-person jussive in 2:1 suggests strongly that Qoheleth treats his לֵב as an external conversation partner. There is no internal monologue in Ecclesiastes (contra Christianson, 19–97; Salyer, 175; and many others). Rather, Qoheleth uses his לֵב to observe himself investigating and testing the potential solutions to life's essential conundrum (contra Fox 1999: 78; Christianson, 195). The לֵב here is personified as an experiment partner distinct from himself (so also Fox 1999: 267).

It is in 1:16, given in (21), that Ecclesiastes first uses the postverbal phrase including the first-person pronoun אֲנִי to reinforce *grammatically* that the experiment was carried out in partnership by Qoheleth and his לֵב.

(21) דִּבַּ֣רְתִּי אֲנִ֤י עִם־לִבִּי֙ לֵאמֹ֔ר אֲנִ֗י הִנֵּ֨ה הִגְדַּ֤לְתִּי וְהוֹסַ֨פְתִּי֙ חָכְמָ֔ה עַ֥ל כָּל־אֲשֶׁר־
הָיָ֛ה לְפָנַ֖י עַל־יְרוּשָׁלִָ֑ם וְלִבִּ֛י רָאָ֥ה הַרְבֵּ֖ה חָכְמָ֥ה וָדָֽעַת

"*pro* (I) spoke, I with[16] my לֵב: 'I—look—I made myself great and added wisdom (to myself) over any who was before me over Jerusalem.' And my לֵב has (also) seen much wisdom and knowledge" (1:16).

Moreover, in v. 16 Qoheleth establishes that in addition to both parties engaging in the actual experiment, he and his לֵב dscussed their findings afterwards. Note how Qoheleth distinguishes what is true about just him, by using אֲנִי within the quote, and what is true of his לֵב apart from him: his לֵב had also seen much wisdom in the course of the experiment.

In 2:1 Qoheleth addresses his לֵב in the second person, which establishes the personification of Qoheleth's לֵב in the book. Qoheleth does not directly address his לֵב anywhere else in the book (the second-person

---

also verses in which Qoheleth references his לֵב but does not include the 1cs pronoun since he apparently intends no contrast or does not need to highlight the collaborative nature of the experiment: 1:13, 17; 2:3, 10, 15; 8:9, 16; 9:1.

[16] Elsewhere -בְּ prepositional phrases are spatial or temporal adjuncts when collocated with the verb אמר. Qoheleth, however, is manipulating the idiom אמר בְּלֵב, and so the nuance of the preposition must be taken from context. Here in 2:1 and also in 2:15; 3:17, 18, the preposition -בְּ marks the goal ("with X") or the indirect object ("to X") of the speech activity. Also see above, n. 6 for a discussion on the collocation of דבר and ב.

address in the remainder of the book is apparently aimed at Qoheleth's audience), but he does admit in 2:20 that he tried to influence the conclusions that his לֵב was drawing—his לֵב was not drawing the same negative conclusions about the value of his life's toil (2:10).

There certainly are cases of the 1cs verb when the 1cs pronoun is not overt—it is a grammatically optional strategy and thus Qoheleth is not compelled to use it to produce well-formed statements. What table 2 helps to show is that Qoheleth's pattern is to use the אֲנִי-plus-לֵב construction when he engages his לֵב in conversation (1:16, 2:1, 15; 3:17, 18) or when he and his לֵב take action together (7:25). He omits the pronoun more often than not, which is expected.[17] After the first instance of the אֲנִי-plus-לֵב construction in 1:16, Qoheleth repeats it to remind his audience that the experiment was carried out by the twosome. When he does not want to emphasize that the pair were engaged together, he omits the pronoun. And, finally, Qoheleth uses the 1cs pronoun but omits mention of his לֵב (the left column in table 2) when he wants to mark himself for focus. Once he has established that he and his לֵב carried out the experiment together, he is able to use the 1cs pronoun alone to identify the majority of experiences and conclusions as *his* rather than his לֵב's.

In its ancient Near Eastern (ANE) wisdom literature context, this literary device is similar to the personification of the *ba* in the Egyptian text *The Dispute Between a Man and His Ba*.[18] Seow notes this as well, but does not recognize it as an interpretive key to the book:

> [The personification of the "heart" (Eg. *ib*) or "soul" (Eg. *ba*)] is a literary device used in Egyptian pessimistic literature. So one reads in *The Complaints of Khakheperre-Sonb*: "He said to his heart: 'Come, my heart, that I may speak to you, and that you may answer me ... I speak to you, my heart, answer me! A heart that is approached must not be silent'" (see Gardiner, *Admonitions*, p. 105, line 1; p. 108, lines 5–6). A similar device is found in *The Dispute Between a Man and His Ba* (AEL I, pp. 163–69). Such texts typically present conflicting positions assumed, respectively, by the physical

---

[17] For a main clause finite verb without the postverbal pronoun אֲנִי and collocated with לֵב as a complement or adjunct, see 1:13, 17; 2:3, 10, 15; 8:9, 16; 9:1. For a main clause finite verb without the postverbal pronoun אֲנִי or לֵב as a complement or adjunct, see 1:12, 14, 16; 2:2, 4-9, 17; 3:10, 12, 14, 16, 22; 4:15; 6:3; 7:15, 23; 8:9-10, 14, 17; 9:11, 13; 10:5, 7.

[18] See Holmstedt 2009b for more on the comparison between Ecclesiastes' use of לֵב and the *ba* in *The Dispute Between a Man and His Ba*.

self and the heart or the soul. So, too, Qohelet speaks "with" ('*im*) his heart. Certainly the heart is personified in 2:1-3. (Seow 1997: 123; see also Shupak, 104, n. 13; 107, n. 9)

Based on the pronoun syntax and the use of the לֵב, it seems clear that Ecclesiastes has employed the basic literary presentation of the book on the ANE model much more closely than previously thought. The author has cast the book as the character Qoheleth's report of a probing dialogue between two investigators, the primary voice of the book, Qoheleth himself, and the silent voice of his לֵב. The two pursue different, even opposing, lines of inquiry and so strengthen the scientific nature of the experiment. Without testing more than one path in life, Qoheleth's experiment—and thus the book's argument—would be transparently facile.

In summary, the author of Ecclesiastes uses an ingenious grammatical device to signal that the fundamental shape of the book is a dialogue between the character Qoheleth and his personified לֵב. Qoheleth directs his לֵב "to know" wisdom and test the high moral ground for the experiment, while he sets himself to "knowing" foolishness, even if it means walking down some of the less seemly paths of life, all for the sake of determining אֵי־זֶה טוֹב לִבְנֵי הָאָדָם אֲשֶׁר יַעֲשׂוּ.

The I-and-my-לֵב strategy appears mostly in the first two chapters of the book and while the basic cooperative nature of the experiment is not jettisoned, the author invokes it infrequently in the rest of the book. As a literary convenience this differs little from the monarchic-Solomonic persona that is also dropped after chapter 2: once well established as a part of the audience's reception filter, the continued mention of such literary strategies is often uneconomical and even a distraction.

4. The Variation of שׁ and אשׁר in Ecclesiastes[19]

In no other biblical book is the distribution of שׁ and אשׁר like that in Ecclesiastes (68× vs. 89× respectively). To put this in perspective, while there are about 5,500 אשׁר clauses in the Hebrew Bible, there are only 139 occurrences of שׁ. Of these, 68 are in Ecclesiastes, 32 are in Song of Songs,[20] 21 are in various Psalms from Psalm 122 onward, and the

---

[19] This section has been adapted from Holmstedt 2013a; see also Holmstedt 2016.

[20] See Holmstedt 2016 for lists of all the relevant data mentioned from the biblical and nonbiblical sources.

remaining 18 are scattered in the Hebrew Bible, literally, from beginning to end. The distribution of אשר and שׁ in nonbiblical texts is somewhat similar. In epigraphic texts from the first millennium, there are 30 clear occurrences of אשר and none of שׁ. The Hebrew text of Ben Sira contains 29 cases of שׁ (and also 67 of אשר). In the Qumran nonbiblical texts, שׁ (including שׁל) occurs 145 times, but 124 of these are in just 2 texts: 57 in the Copper Scroll [3Q15] and 67 in 4QMMT[B,C] [4Q394–99]; the remaining 21 examples are so spread out that no one text uses שׁ more than twice. The Bar Kokhba period texts from Naḥal Hever and Wadi Murabbaʿat contain 118 occurrences of שׁ and none of אשר. Finally, שׁ dominates in the Mishnah, where אשר is used only 69 times, and all in biblical quotes or allusions (Segal, 42; Pérez Fernández, 50).

This distribution raises a host of questions, for the status of שׁ in general and its use in Ecclesiastes in particular. Scholars have suggested that the distribution in general and Ecclesiastes' use in particular reflects one or a combination of the following causes: dialect, style, register, and diachrony. The various proposals for the variation between שׁ and אשר in the Hebrew Bible were examined in Holmstedt 2013a and 2016. A brief summary of those findings follow.

The dominant proposal through the twentieth century was that שׁ reflected either a northern Hebrew origin or at least the influence of the northern dialect. This was ultimately connected to the almost certainly etymological origin of Hebrew שׁ from Akkadian *ša* (see Holmstedt 2007, 2016). The most reasonable pathway for this etymological connection from Akkadian to the biblical data is generally taken to include two intermediaries: northern Canaanite (e.g., Phoenician) and northern Hebrew. This seems plausible, that שׁ became the relative word of choice by change and diffusion within some Hebrew grammar in the north, from which it influenced some southern Hebrew grammar, particularly after 722 BCE, so that eventually it replaced אשר, the process and final result of which we see in Ecclesiastes and Song of Songs, respectively (see, among others, Gordon; Kutscher, 32, §45; Davila 1990; Rendsburg 2006). One problem with a simple northern-to-southern dialectal explanation is the complete absence of שׁ from any epigraphic text with a northern provenance. A second problem with this explanation, as Rendsburg notes, is that אשר is used in biblical texts often identified as northern in origin, e.g., Judges 5–8 and Hosea (1990: 114–16). For these two reasons, a *single* northern-to-southern explanation by itself is inadequate (more on this below).

Sensing the inadequacy in the dialectal explanation, some sought a sociolinguistic explanation, which takes two forms. The first is diglossia, a situation in which a language community uses a formal (high) variety for written media and a colloquial (low) variety for all normal discourse (Rendsburg 1990: 116–17; on diglossia in general, see Ferguson). The difficulty with a diglossic analysis of אשר and שׁ is that users in a diglossic situation do not mix the high and low varieties (Ferguson, 336; Kaye, 120). Thus, if the variation between שׁ and אשר reflects an intentionality, then the salient linguistic distinction is not diglossic variety but simply style (Young; Davila 1994).

Whereas dialectal differences in the textual evidence represent a linguistic accident—the differences reflect the separate origins of the contrasting linguistic forms—stylistic differences are not accidental. That is, characters are often distinguished by their speech in a range of genres, from plays to novels and other types of narrated literature (e.g., James Joyce's works). Speech may color the characters as old or young, educated or not, wealthy or poor, respectful or rude, local or foreign (for biblical examples, see Rendsburg 1996). This literary technique is not simply aesthetic, though: the differences are used to engage the reader and encourage the construction of a reader identity vis-à-vis the characters. While a stylistic explanation is compelling for a few of the שׁ and אשר variations (see Holmstedt and Kirk), it provides little guidance for Ecclesiastes or even Ben Sira, the two books that have a nearly equal use of both words (contra Davila 1994; Shlesinger). The nagging problem with the stylistic variation argument, at least for שׁ and אשר, is the lack of a clear pattern. For example, the variation between שׁ and אשר is not explained by the "lowbrow-highbrow" proposal: the variation occurs indiscriminately, sometimes in the same verse and in adjacent and parallel clauses: 1:10; 2:12; 3:14, 15, 22; 4:2; 5:4, 14, 17; 6:10; 8:7, 14; 10:14; 12:7.

The dialectal style and register analyses are inadequate, and the grammar of שׁ and אשר shows no noticeable divergences (both are used to nominalize clauses, mostly relative clauses but also some complement clauses, whether of verbs or prepositions). This leaves a diachronic explanation. Given that the great bulk of Hebrew texts in the Bible witness the use of אשר to the exclusion of שׁ, and also given that the Mishnah exhibits nearly the opposite case, the use of שׁ and the relegation of אשר to biblical quotations and allusions, it seems on the surface a logical proposal that the book of Ecclesiastes represents a middle point on this continuum of language change. Similarly, the many Aramaic-like features and Mishnaic-like features in the book have been adduced to support this relative placement of Ecclesiastes.

Without getting into the technical linguistic details (see Holmstedt 2012, 2013a, 2016), the likeliest diachronic story unfolds like so: by the end of the second millennium or early first millennium BCE, Hebrew used as its primary nominalizer the item אשר, which reflects the grammaticalization of a noun for "step, footstep." In roughly the same period (Middle Assyrian), the Phoenicians themselves may have adopted the etymologically distinct nominalizer שׁ from Assyrian, perhaps especially during Tiglath-Pileser I's (1114–1076 BCE) aggressive attention to northern Syro-Palestine. A dialect of Hebrew was similarly affected either at this time or three centuries later (due to intensity of contact with the Phoenicians during the Omride period), which may explain why שׁ appears in Judges 5.

The rare occurrences of שׁ in 2 Kings and Jonah, which are placed in the mouths of northerners or foreigners (Holmstedt 2006; Holmstedt and Kirk) suggest that שׁ was a marginal interpretable item for Hebrew speakers and used to signal "foreignness" in exilic (2 Kgs) and postexilic (Jonah) works. It is not until the Hellenistic period and the books of Ecclesiastes and Ben Sira that we see the change from אשר to שׁ truly take hold wth the latter's complete diffusion by the Mishnaic period (see Holmstedt 2016: 93–101 for a fuller discussion of the historical realities that are likely behind the replacement of אשר by שׁ).

5. The Verbal System in Ecclesiastes[21]

A. Introduction

The verbal system in ancient Hebrew, as in most languages, is a central component of the grammar, intersecting with numerous other grammatical features. As a result, the verbal system of Ecclesiastes has been of interest to scholars for as long as the language of the book has been an object of study. Not only is an understanding of the Hebrew verb forms in Ecclesiastes crucial for the philological/exegetical task, but the characteristics of the book's language have played an important role in constructing a history of the Hebrew language.

Dependent to some small degree on textual decisions, there are about 200 verbs that occur 700 times in total in the book of Ecclesiastes. The interpretation of these forms is addressed in the commentary. In

---

[21] This section has been adapted from Cook 2013.

this introduction we provide an overview of the verbal system in Ecclesiastes in the context of the verbal system in the broader BH corpus. This overview will facilitate the discussions of specific verbal forms in the body of the commentary. As the use of the verbal stems (*binyanim*) present no peculiarities in Ecclesiastes, this introduction focuses on the verbal conjugations—i.e., the *qatal* (which includes the so-called *weqatal* or *waw*-consecutive perfect), *yiqtol*, *wayyiqtol*, the participle, and the infinitives construct and absolute.

B. The Biblical Hebrew Verbal System

The following sketch of the BH verbal system is based on the extensive arguments presented in Cook 2012b. The semantic analysis of the BH verbal system in these works proceeds from the perspective of linguistic typology (i.e., the study of linguistic features across an array of human languages)—using observations about verbal systems in the world's languages to validate a model of the BH verbal system as a "realistic" grammar system.

As a starting point the following definitions are helpful. *Tense* is the grammatical marking of temporal location (past, present, or future) with respect to a deictic center, usually the "present" of the speaker; it is helpful to distinguish between *tense* as so defined and *temporal reference* in which temporal location is indicated by elements other than grammatical markings (e.g., discourse pragmatics). *Aspect* is limited in this discussion to *viewpoint aspect*, which refers to different "viewpoints" by which a speaker may portray the temporal unfolding of a situation, such as in progress (imperfective and progressive), as an undifferentiated whole (perfective), or as a resultant state of an action (perfect). *Mood* and *modality* are interrelated but distinct in their origins. *Mood* describes the basic binary distinction in language between "realis" statements that describe actual situations and "irrealis" statements about potential or nonactual situations, including conditional expressions, imperatives, optatives, and the like. Whether simple future expressions constitute realis or irrealis mood is debated among linguists. This category is most evident in the grammaticalization of the realis-irrealis distinction by indicative and subjunctive/optative mood in European languages (e.g., Greek). *Modality* derives from modal logic, which treats epistemic and deontic expressions of possibility and necessity. Apart from declarative modality, which is equivalent to realis or indicative mood, distinctions of modality can be thought of as forming a subset of irrealis mood insofar as these are frequently expressed by irrealis mood markings. In addition to epistemic and deontic, the main types of modalities expressed by irrealis mood are volitive/optative (will/desire), dynamic (ability), habitual, conditional, and final (purpose/result).

The following description is largely consonant with the typical, aspectual model of BH (e.g., WO chap. 29; MNK chap. 19). However, for this reason it is necessary to highlight the distinctive features of our analysis. To begin with, we want to be careful not to mislead by labeling the BH verbal system as "aspectual," as though aspect and tense or mood/modality are mutually exclusive semantic domains. Rather, verbal systems typically express a range of semantic categories that belong to the domains of tense, aspect, mood/modality. However, distinctions belonging to one or the other of these categories may be thought of as "in ascendancy." In BH the most frequently and widely employed verb conjugations, the *qatal* and *yiqtol*, form a central opposition of *perfective : imperfective* aspect, explaining the reference to BH as having an "aspectual" verbal system. This configuration, which according to one study is the most frequently found type among the world's verbal systems (Bybee and Dahl, 83), expresses different viewpoints on a situation: the perfective verbs express events as an undifferentiated whole, whereas the imperfective verbs express events as in progress. This opposition is well illustrated by the contrast of the English simple past *he walked to school* and past progressive *he was walking to school*. In the latter instance, the "in progress" viewpoint allows another action to interrupt temporally the imperfective situation, e.g., *He was walking to school, and his bike got a flat tire.*

This tidy opposition, which constitutes the heart of the verbal conjugation system, is complicated by the interrelatedness of tense, aspect, and mood/modality; the affect of discourse context on the interpretation of the verbal conjugations; and interaction with other conjugations in the system. For example, the relationship between tense and aspect leads to a default interpretation of perfective *qatal* as having past temporal reference and the imperfective *yiqtol* as nonpast temporal reference, as in other aspect-prominent languages (see Smith 2008). Within direct discourse or speech, which is temporally independent of the surrounding discourse (e.g., narrative), the *qatal* form expresses simple past time and the *yiqtol* simple future. However, outside of speech, in the predominant narrative discourse of the Hebrew Bible, the *qatal* conjugation more frequently expresses perfect aspect in all three times (i.e., past perfect, present perfect, and future perfect), while *yiqtol* appears in present imperfective, simple future, and an array of irrealis mood expressions. The most significant explanation for the statistical distribution of meanings for these two central conjugations is their "competition" with semantically related or similar conjugations. Linguists recognize that languages frequently develop semantically related forms that "compete" over time with each other and often lead to the eventual obsolescence of one (usually the older) of the constructions (see Hopper and Traugott, 9).

In ancient Hebrew we have two such examples of competing forms: the *wayyiqtol* and the *qatal* conjugations and the *yiqtol* and the predicatively employed participle. In each case the semantic overlap is significant but other factors help determine their distribution in the system. For example, *wayyiqtol* and *qatal* both express past perfective (i.e., past temporal reference and perfective aspect, as English simple past) events, but past tense *wayyiqtol* is specifically a narrative foregrounding verb whose appearance outside of narrative discourse is rare. As a result, *qatal* infrequently expresses past perfective events in narrative because of the dominance of *wayyiqtol* for that function in that context. This competition culminates in the dropping of *wayyiqtol* from the system altogether in post–BH, which raises the question of whether the mere three occurrences of the *wayyiqtol* conjugation in Ecclesiastes is due to the nonnarrative discourse type, or the relative lateness of the language, or both.

Similarly, the adjectival participle, when supported by a copula (i.e., used predicatively), expresses progressive aspect, which is semantically nearly identical with imperfective aspect expressed by *yiqtol*. This periphrastic construction with the participle is the statistically dominant means of expressing progressive/imperfective situations in BH, whereas the older *yiqtol* conjugation has developed an extensive range of irrealis mood meanings (commands, wishes, conditions, expressions of possibility, ability, etc.) as a result of this competition. In Mishnaic Hebrew the *yiqtol* is largely reduced to an irrealis mood and subordinate conjugation (see Pérez-Fernández, 108). This raises the question of whether the preference for the participle over *yiqtol* in proverbial sayings in Ecclesiastes versus the opposite tendency in Proverbs may be diachronically significant.

Mood has been introduced above as essentially binary: verbal constructions express events that are in some way "real" or "irreal" with respect to the discourse situation. The most familiar irrealis-mood constructions in BH are the morphologically distinct imperative-jussive (including cohortative) system. The complementary distribution among person and negation (i.e., imperative is limited to positive second-person commands, whereas second-person jussive is almost entirely limited to negative commands) indicates that conjugations together comprise a directive-volitive irrealis mood system to express speaker commands and wishes.

Importantly, when these directive-volitive forms appear with an overt subject (though rare) they almost always occur in verb-subject word order. This pattern suggests that the word order alternation notable with the two primary conjugations in the system, the *yiqtol* and *qatal*, correlates with a realis : irrealis mood distinction. Indeed, ample evidence has been produced over the past half-century that verb-subject *yiqtol* and verb-subject *qatal* (i.e., the so-called *weqatal* or *waw*-consecutive perfect) are irrealis mood expressions of these conjugations, respectively. The irrealis-mood construction of *qatal* and *yiqtol* appear in subordinate modal constructions (such as protasis-apodosis, purpose and result statements) and regularly express habitual situations.

The infinitive forms require little comment here except insofar as their labels as construct and absolute are opaque. The infinitive construct comes close to the traditional infinitive form in other languages, and in fact increasingly appears with the ל preposition "to" (almost exclusively in post–BH). The infinitive absolute functions predominately as an adverbial expression, often adding epistemic modality (certainty or doubt) to the finite verb it modifies.[22]

C. The Verbal System in Ecclesiastes

The verbal system in Ecclesiastes is largely consonant with the above description of the BH verbal system. The variations that the verbal system in the book exhibits are also in keeping with the sorts of historical changes that are clearly recognizable between BH and post–BH, lending support to the long-standing view that the grammar of Ecclesiastes represents some of the latest in the BH corpus. Here we summarize six distinctive features of the verbal system in Ecclesiastes that are significant for dating and interpreting the book.

The first and most noticeable feature of the verbal system in Ecclesiastes is its almost entire lack of the *wayyiqtol* form, which occurs only three times (1:17; 4:1, 7). Scholars have debated whether this lack of the narrative *wayyiqtol* is due to the lateness of the book (the form is obsolete in rabbinic Hebrew) or perhaps due to the "nonnarrative" and

---

[22] Hence, these are labeled the infinitive and adverbial infinitive, respectively, in Cook and Holmstedt.

"philosophical" character of the literature (e.g., Crenshaw, 60; Isaksson, 50). Although it is true that the book contains material quite distinct from the predominant prose narrative in the Hebrew Bible, there are several passages of successive narrative action in Ecclesiastes where the reader might reasonably expect *wayyiqtols* to appear but are absent (e.g., 1:12-13, 15; 9:14-15). At the same time, the three occurrences of *wayyiqtol* are atypical uses of the conjugation (see commentary). Together these facts suggest that the conjugation is rare in the book at least in part due to the historical factor of its declining use.

The absence of *wayyiqtol* in the "autobiographical narrative" of chapters 1–2 (as it is sometimes called, e.g., Isaksson) in preference of *qatal* forms—some sixty of them—may not simply be an accident of history.[23] The foregrounded events of Qoheleth's "experiment" are not typical prose narrative, in which past-perfective events are reported in the order in which they occur (i.e., temporal succession). The main actions Qoheleth undertakes are often distinct and so independently a part of the passage's foreground (versus background); i.e., there is no demand that they be interpreted as occurring in temporal succession. Thus, in many cases, there is a good argument that the use of the *qatal* in place of the *wayyiqtol* forms is motivated by literary concerns not language diachrony. Further, recognizing that Qoheleth's experiment is not in typical prose narrative raises the general exegetical question of whether these *qatals* express perfective-past ("I did this") or present-perfect ("I have done that") events. Answering this question hinges on the interpreter's decision as to whether Qoheleth's perspective is best understood to be his reflections on a recent past ("I have done this and done that") or a more distant past ("I did this and I did that"). These qualifications notwithstanding, some of the autobiographical *qatal* series remain syntactically comparable to passages elsewhere in the Hebrew Bible in which we find *wayyiqtol* series (cf. 2:2-6; 1 Kgs 6:1-5), suggesting that a literary explanation alone for the dearth of *wayyiqtol* forms in Ecclesiastes is insufficient (see §6 below).

Ecclesiastes presents two further general interpretive issues with regard to the *qatal* conjugation. The first has to do with the frequently occurring Niphal of עשׂה "be done" (1:9, 13-14; 2:17; 4:3; 8:9, 11, 14, 16-17; 9:3, 6), always in relative clause. Scholars typically translate these as present-generic, "(which) happens" (see Isaksson, 69–74; Fox 1999:

---

[23] Scholars differ on the precise number of *qatals* that make up this "narrative" thread because of differences of definition and analysis; see discussion in Cook 2013.

169, 265), as part of a broader tendency to render all generic or gnomic expressions such as these with a general present, because this is the
preferred English construction for such expressions. However, generic
expressions are not confined to a single TAM form in languages generally (e.g., boys will be boys; see discussion in Cook 2005), and thus
to be faithful to the literature of Ecclesiastes, we should interpret this
construction in conformity with our general expectations of the *qatal*
semantics and interpret it as a past-perfective "(which) happened" or a
present-perfect: "(which) has happened."

The other issue, closely related to the previous one, is the treatment
of the *qatal* Qal of היה, particularly in those passages where it functions
similarly to the Niphal of עשׂה (see 1:9; 3:15; 6:10; 7:24). Since היה is a
stative, some scholars (e.g., Isaksson) advocate rendering these instances
as present-stative, or even as synonymous with the Nifal עשׂה "(which)
happens" (so Fox 1999: 169, 265). The copula verb, however, frequently
presents a peculiar case in verbal systems, and the fact that BH has a
zero-copula strategy to express present-stative (i.e., verbless clause) suggests that the *qatal* of היה will frequently express a past-perfective (or at
most, a present-perfect) idea ("was" or "has been") in contrast with the
future-time expression of the *yiqtol* of היה ("will be"; see esp. 1:9; 3:25;
cf. comments on 3:15).

A second feature of the verbal system in Ecclesiastes is a decline
of the irrealis *qatal*, which we have reanalyzed the so-called *weqatal* or
waw-consecutive perfect. Schoors (88) argues that the form is altogether
absent in the book. This mistaken claim arises from the obscuring of the
word-order distinction of irrealis *qatal*: about a third of the *qatal* forms
in the autobiographical foreground, which are contextually realis qatals
in chapters 1–2 are *waw*-prefixed *qatal* constructions (e.g., 2:11-15,
18). However, close attention to the context of the *qatal* forms reveals a
small number of occurrences, sometimes without the prefixed *waw* (e.g.,
6:6; 10:10 with a preceding conditional word), other times with it (e.g.,
12:1-7 contains eight *waw*-prefixed irrealis *qatal* verbs that form the
lengthy temporal apodosis). Another notable example is the *waw*-pre-
fixed irrealis *qatal* verbs in the recurrent irrealis final expression preceded
by "there is nothing better than that …" (2:24 [2×] and 3:13 [2×]).

A third feature peculiar to Ecclesiastes is the ratio of *qatal* to participial encoding of stative predicates. In other parts of the Hebrew Bible
the *qatal* of statives regularly expresses *present* states (e.g., כִּי עַתָּה יָדַעְתִּי
"for now I know"; Gen 22:12; see Cook 2012b: 194–99). In Ecclesias-
tes, however, there is a notable increase in participial encoding of stative

predicates (e.g., גַּם־יוֹדֵעַ אֲנִי "Also, I know"; see 2:19, 22; 3:21; 4:2, 14, 17; 5:7, 9 [2×]; 6:10, 12; 8:1, 7, 12; 9:1, 5 [2×]; 11:5, 6), similar to the case with Qumran and rabbinic Hebrew. This seems to be diachronically significant as evidence of a change that cannot easily be explained as register or dialectal variation as *qatal* shifted toward becoming a past tense form, as it is in rabbinic Hebrew, new strategies for encoding present states emerged (see Cook 2012b).

A fourth feature also relates to the increased use of the participle. In contrast to the sentence literature of Proverbs, in which the *yiqtol* form is more frequent than the participle for generic expressions, Ecclesiastes exhibits a reversal of this trend: the sentence literature of Proverbs contains 272 generic *yiqtols* and 73 generic participles; by contrast, Ecclesiastes contains only about 51 generic *yiqtols* versus 110 generic participles (see Cook 2005: 124; 2013: 334 n. 91). As in the case of participial encoding of statives (above), this shift is best attributed to diachronic changes, namely, the encroachment of the progressive participle on the domain of imperfective *yiqtol*. Another feature attributable to this participle-*yiqtol* competition is the increased restriction of *yiqtol* to subordinate expressions in Ecclesiastes, anticipating its modal-subordinate function in rabbinic Hebrew.

Fifth, directive-volitive systems consisting of the imperative and jussive exhibit few distinctive patterns in Ecclesiastes except for a loosening of word order evident with the jussive. This may be related to the loosening generally of the realis : irrealis word order distinction that has obscured the irrealis *qatal* in the book (see above). In contrast to jussives in Genesis–2 Kings that almost always occur clause initially (see Shulman), in keeping with the subject-verb irrealis mood marking, the division is more balanced in Ecclesiastes: seventeen clause-initial jussives (2:1; 5:1 [2×], 5 [2×], 7; 7:9, 10, 16 [2×], 17 [2×], 23; 8:3 [3×]; 11:9) and 10 nonclause-initial jussives (5:1, 3; 7:18, 21; 9:8 [2×]; 10:4, 20 [2×]; 11:6) (see Joosten).

Sixth, and finally, the ubiquity of לְ preposition on infinitives construct (94 of 108 occurrences) in Ecclesiastes is distinctive and points toward the conventionalization of the construction in rabbinic Hebrew (see Pérez Fernández, 144).

6. Dating Ecclesiastes

The literature on the language of Ecclesiastes spans over three centuries and the views of the book's language have situated it within just about every historically permissible context, from Solomonic to late Hellenistic. Behind them all lies a clear consensus that the linguistic profile of Ecclesiastes differs markedly from any other book in the Hebrew Bible. Unfortunately, no such agreement on the reason for the differences has emerged. As Seow notes,

> Scholars have variously attempted to explain the aberrant character of Qohelet's Hebrew in terms of a foreign origin (i.e., the book was originally composed in Aramaic), heavy foreign influences (of Aramaic, Canaanite, Phoenician, Greek), a late date (with traces of "Mishnaisms"), dialectal origins (i.e., it was composed in northern Hebrew or a dialect like it), specialized vocabulary (i.e., the author used philosophical jargon), or vernacular elements (i.e., reflecting the Hebrew of everyday speech). (1997: 11)

The majority view through the twentieth-century and into the twenty-first-century has been that, whatever the precise explanation, the language of the book cannot reflect a Solomonic origin but a much later stage of Hebrew. The primary linguistic features used in the discussion fall into three categories: orthography (spelling), non-Hebrew words (loanwords from Persian, Aramaic, or Phoenician), and grammatical affinities with other biblical books considered to be late (LBH) as well as Mishnaic Hebrew. We will not take space to cover this well-trod ground here but refer the reader to the list of data (though not the conclusions) in Fredericks or the overview in Seow 1997 (11–21), and the discussion of the verbal system in the previous section.

Rather, we will pick up the discussion about Ecclesiastes' language in light of the vigorous debates about Hebrew diachrony and dating the language of texts that has occurred in the last decade, especially since the appearance of Young, Rezetko and Ehrensvärd 2008. The argument of Young, Rezetko, and those who have followed their lead boils down to the following points. First, the textual history of Hebrew texts is so complicated by transmission, including scribal updating, that the form of the texts cannot be relevant to dating the "original" compositions:

> If the text of any given biblical book was fluid then the language of that book was also fluid. (2008, 1:345)

> ... we cannot know to what degree our extant texts retain their original linguistic makeup. (2008, 1:359)

Second, what are commonly understood as diachronic stages of Hebrew in the biblical period are better taken as concurrent "styles" of Hebrew:

"Early" BH and "Late" BH, therefore, do not represent different chronological periods in the history of BH, but instead represent coexisting styles of literary Hebrew throughout the biblical period. These two general language types, EBH and LBH, are best taken as representing two tendencies among scribes of the biblical period: conservative and non-conservative. The authors and scribes who composed and transmitted works in EBH exhibit a tendency to "conservatism" in their linguistic choices, in the sense that they only rarely use forms outside a narrow core of what they considered literary forms. At the other extreme, the LBH authors and scribes exhibited a much less conservative attitude, freely adopting a variety of linguistic forms in addition to (not generally instead of) those favoured by the EBH scribes. (2008, 1:361)

Cutting through the obfuscation and special pleading (evident in subsequent works, such as Rezetko and Young; Rezetko and Naaijer 2016a, 2016b), the discerning reader will note that the two points are contradictory at their core—if textual transmission has so obscured the linguistic features of the compositions such that the extant texts make use of them for building a linguistic profile impossible, how is it that they continue to talk about languages from the "biblical" period at all? And how can they coherently propose that EBH and LBH existed as parallel "styles of literary Hebrew throughout the biblical period"? Contrary to the presentation of the volume, Young, Rezetko and Ehrensvärd 2008 should not be taken as an argument about the general viability of dating biblical texts linguistically; rather, as they clearly acknowledge later in Rezetko and Young, their 2008 volume is an exercise in using the dominant approach in Hebrew studies (not historical linguistics), associated closely with the work of Avi Hurvitz (see, e.g., Hurvitz 1990, 2006, 2007, 2012), to show its own inconsistencies (597–98).

The response to this challenge to linguistic dating of texts (and thus necessarily the linguistic features preserved in the texts) by Hebraists with training in general linguistics was clear: they may have demonstrated the weaknesses of a flawed approach to Hebrew diachrony, but their exaggerated rhetoric masks serious flaws in their own conclusions about the viability of using the data within the extant texts to date the biblical books (see Cook 2012a; Dresher 2012; Holmstedt 2012). In the sections below, we both follow a clear, linguistically based methodology for diachronic analysis and identify the linguistic features we conclude to be salient for situating the relative dating of the book of Ecclesiastes. Note that relative dating without any external dating information would not provide any way to locate the texts historically; thankfully there are enough (though more would be better) epigraphs on the early side and the evidence of Ben Sira, Qumran, and Mishnah on the later side to allow us to use the relative dating to provide reasonable historical approximations for the final form of the biblical books.

A. Historical Linguistics and Dating Ancient Texts

Any study of linguistic variation that proposes diachronic change as the explanation must address three core issues: *cause*, *mechanism*, and *effect*. Identifying the effect is typically the easiest task since it concerns the resulting sound, shape, sequence, or word that arises from the induced change. Cause and mechanism are more challenging to isolate, particularly since they are closely related. The cause of a given change falls into one of two categories that identify the source of the motivation: external and internal. The mechanisms by which changes occur fit into three broad categories: borrowing (externally motivated), reanalysis (internally motivated), and extension (internally motivated).

Once a change is identified, the subsequent history in the language becomes a focus of attention. One of the significant advances in Hebrew historical linguistics in the last ten years is a more robust understanding of the process by which change spreads through time within a speech community. Critically, while the process unfolds, both the old and the new forms coexist, often for hundreds of years (Wolfram and Schilling-Estes, 715–16). As a new linguistic entity (e.g., lexeme, syntactic pattern) enters usage, it is a minority form alongside the previously existing entity; over time, the usage of the new entity gains ground on the older entity, with increasing speed; as the new entity becomes dominant, the speed by which it pushes the older entity out of usage slows and the older entity never entirely disappears (Bailey, 77; Kroch 1989, 2001; Pintzuk).[24]

---

[24] Significantly, linguists have noted the frequency of the new form's appearance over time follows a Sigmoid, or "S"-shaped curve (Bailey; Kroch 1989; Pintzuk; Nevalainen and Raumolin-Brunberg, 53–82). This S-curve model effectively replaces Hurvitz' principles of opposition and distribution. Though few real language variations match the idealized S-curve in figure 1, this model provides us with a statistically grounded pattern to use as a baseline for comparison in discerning whether a given variant pair likely reflects a diachronic change or not. See Forbes 2014 for valuable criticism of the use of S-curves in language diachrony from a statistician's perspective

Table 3
The Diffusion of שׁ versus אשר in Ancient Hebrew

By Frequency[25]	אשר (Old)	שׁ (New)	% New-to-Old
Epigraphic texts	38	0	0
Exodus	309	0	0
Leviticus	309	0	0
Numbers	295	0	0
Deuteronomy	584	0	0
Joshua	265	0	0
Samuel	428	0	0
Isaiah	171	0	0
Jeremiah	460	0	0
Ezekiel	342	0	0
Hosea	12	0	0
Joel	12	0	0
Amos	18	0	0
Obadiah	4	0	0
Micah	16	0	0
Nahum	2	0	0
Habakkuk	3	0	0
Zephaniah	6	0	0
Haggai	7	0	0
Zechariah	44	0	0

and Forbes 2016 for a solution to the problem of applying the S-curve inversely (i.e., from the observed data to the relative ordering). Forbes 2016 is a convincing rebuttal of recent arguments against using the S-curve as a diagnostic tool (Rezetko and Young 2014; Rezetko and Naaijer 2016a,b). We thank Dean Forbes for giving us access to his papers in prepublication form.

[25] Five occurrences of שׁ in Judges 4–5 are likely due to an early incursion of שׁ, which was interrupted (see Holmstedt 2016: 93–101, 215–47). The single occurrence in Kings and the three in Jonah are placed in the mouths of foreigners and thus serve purely literary purposes (see Holmstedt and Kirk). These complications confirm that diachronic analysis must account for a full range of linguistic and historical factors, though they in no way delegitimize or make "facile" the use of the change and diffusion model and its corollary, the S-curve (contra Rezetko and Young, 237; see Forbes 2016 for a statistical defense of using the S-curve as a diagnostic tool, which is fundamentally an inverse problem, the regularization for which Forbes illustrates).

Table 3 *(cont.)*

By Frequency	אשר *(Old)*	שׁ *(New)*	% New-to-Old
Malachi	13	0	0
Proverbs	12	0	0
Ruth	42	0	0
Esther	99	0	0
Daniel	47	0	0
Kings	696	1	0.14
Genesis	411	1	0.24
Chronicles[26]	345	2	0.58
Ezra-Nehemiah	120	1	0.83
Job	40	1	2.4
Judges[27]	177	5	2.7
Qumran Sectarian[28]	1616	111	6.43
Psalms[29]	102	21	17.07
Jonah[30]	12	3	20
Ben Sira	70	22	23.9
Lamentations	9	4	30.8
Ecclesiastes	89	68	43.3
Song of Songs	1	32	97
Mishnah	69	11690	99.4
N. Ḥever and N. Ṣeʿelim	0	71	100
W. Murabbaʿat	0	47	100

[26] The frequency in the chart is for all of Chronicles. However, if only nonparallel passages are considered, there are only thirty-six אשר, resulting in a much higher (5.6 percent) relative frequency of שׁ.

[27] See n. 25.

[28] Andrew Jones has pointed out, "[I]n order for groups of texts to be useful in statistical analysis as a random sample, it is not permitted to organize the groups ahead of time to match the conclusions being sought by the research. Any groups of texts need to be formed for reasons independent of the distribution of the grammatical forms at hand, such as dating that is based on historical considerations" (5). Thus, we have not excluded 4QMMT or 3Q15, both known to reflect different linguistic profiles than the other Qumran texts.

[29] Though שׁ occurs only twenty-one times and all in Psalms 122–124, 129, 133, 135–137, 144, 146. However, following the same principle mentioned in n. 28, we take the book of Psalms as a whole in this analysis.

[30] See n. 25.

If we return to the distribution of אשר and שֹ that was discussed in §4, we find a clear example of the change and diffusion process. Consider the data presented above in table 3 (with modification from Holmstedt 2016: 243), taking אשר to be the "old" form and שֹ to be the "new" form, with the final column being the percentage of new-to-old (i.e., representing the diffusion of the new form).

A second illustrative example is the replacement of the *wayyiqtol* with *qatal* (see above, §5). We noted a marked avoidance of the *wayyiqtol* in Ecclesiastes—it occurs only three times. In fact, this accords with a noticeable increase in the frequency of *qatal* instead of *wayyiqtol* in later texts, in contexts in which *wayyiqtol* could have been used, such as following a fronted temporal clause (e.g., cf. Gen 22:4; Eccl 5:10). Though the decreasing use of the *wayyiqtol* in Hellenistic period texts has long been noted, it should be properly situated within a change-and-diffusion model of diachronic development. Below we provide the data from narrative texts (to which the first-person narrative of Ecclesiastes belongs).

Table 4
The Diffusion of Narrative *qatal* versus *wayyiqtol*

Book	All verbs	wayyiqtol (= old)	qatal (= new)	% new-to-old
Jonah	200	84 (42%)	38 (19%)	31.1%
Judges	2552	1139 (44.6%)	552 (21.6%)	32.7%
Genesis	5040	2105 (41.7%)	1105 (21.9%)	34.4%
Samuel	6239	2374 (38.1%)	1458 (23.4%)	38.0%
Ruth	414	138 (33.3%)	94 (22.7%)	40.5%
Kings	6054	2257 (37.3%)	1606 (26.5%)	41.6%
Chronicles	4286	1451 (33.9%)	1164 (27.2%)	44.5%
Nehemiah	973	264 (27.1%)	257 (26.4%)	49.3%
Esther	640	159 (24.8%)	165 (25.8%)	50.9%
Joshua	1930	592 (30.7%)	618 (32.0%)	51.1%
Ezra (Heb)	363	86 (23.7%)	95 (26.2%)	52.5%
Qumran	21375	708 (3.3%)	5712 (26.7%)	89.0%
Ecclesiastes	699	3 (.04%)	206 (29.5%)	98.6%
Mishnah	46202	32 (.007%)	14758 (32%)	99.8%

Overall there is a clear change in the use of the *wayyiqtol*, with Ecclesiastes near the end of the process. The obvious outlier in the chart is Joshua and the likely reason for this is the significant drop in the use of the *wayyiqtol* in Josh 13–23, which are only marginally narrative.

1. Externally Motivated Change: Borrowing

Languages borrow words from other languages for two primary reasons: *need* and *prestige* (Campbell 2004: 64–65). For Ecclesiastes the fact of borrowed words is not the question—all scholars admit the presence of both Persian and Aramaic loanwords in the book. Rather, the questions concern the likely reasons and their implications.

Prestige-borrowing, in particular, is often invoked to explain the increasing number of Aramaisms (e.g., זְמָן "time") as well as the few Persianisms (e.g., פַּרְדֵּס "garden," "royal enclosure") found in some biblical texts like Ecclesiastes. The prestige status for Aramaic came from its role as the administrative language of both the neo-Babylonian and Persian empires; for Persian the prestige status no doubt derived from the political dominance of the Persians from the sixth to fourth centuries BCE.

Whether words are borrowed due to need or prestige, it is important to recognize that the borrowed item is normally *adapted* and *accommodated* to the borrowing language's phonology and morphology (see Campbell 2004: 65–69). For instance, although the Hebrew אַשָּׁף "conjurer" entered either via Aramaic אָשַׁף or Akkadian *(w)āšipu*, the Hebrew word is the only one reflecting the gemination of the middle root consonant, which is likely because the word was imported as a *qattāl*-pattern noun, the nominal morphological category used for "nouns of profession" (JM, §88Ha and n. 49; also §87d).

The problem that adaptation and accommodation raise is one of identification: most cases of discernible borrowings in Hebrew come from other Semitic languages, which share a similar phoneme inventory and the triconsonantal root morphology. For all practical purposes, then, we should start by limiting ourselves to words whose shape falls outside the paradigmatic margins. As Campbell suggests, "Words which violate the typical phonological patterns (canonical forms, morpheme structure, syllable structure, phonotactics) of a language are likely to be loans" (2004: 70).

An example of a borrowed word that has been phonologically adapted is עֲבָדֵיהֶם (Eccl 9:1). There are two related features of the word's phonology that do not reflect paradigmatic Hebrew. First, the vowel under the second root letter (בְ) has not been reduced to *sheva* in an open syllable that is two syllables removed from the primary word stress. The expected Hebrew form is עֲבָדֵיהֶם (Zech 2:13). Second, if the vowel has not been reduced, then according to normal Hebrew morphophonology, it must be a long vowel, *ā*; if so, then this is a vowel that was not affected by the Canaanite shift (ca. 1400 BCE), in which *ā* > *ō*—a sound change that distinguishes Hebrew from Aramaic. If it had been affected, it would be vocalized like חֲמוֹר (< *ḥimār*). Since עֲבָדֵיהֶם, and its assumed singular form עֶבֶד (like the attested כְּתָב), does not fit the phonological and morphophonological patterns of Hebrew, it not only must have been borrowed but also must have been borrowed *after* the Canaanite shift. This, however, leaves a rather large temporal window for the borrowing, which leads to the corollary of identifying a loanword—identifying a historically reasonable context for the borrowing.

An author's use of foreign words, like Persian and Aramaic loanwords in the Hebrew Bible, necessarily assumes that his audience knows these words. Thus, it is not a matter of a linguistically cosmopolitan author throwing in a few foreign words for effect; rather, to utilize the intended nuance each carries requires that the words have become sufficiently diffused within the linguistic world of the audience so that the average reader will recognize the intent. Borrowing presumes a necessary level of *intensity of contact*. That is, if nonnative items are identified and they are not need-based lexical items (e.g., a name for a nonnative animal is imported with the animal), they must reflect intense contact between the language in question and the other language that is the source of the borrowed feature. Notably, among the factors that contribute to this contact intensity is "a high level of bilingualism" (Thomason, 689)—the use of prestige-based borrowing presumes that *both* the *author* and the *audience* understood such elements.

For Hebrew texts in the Bible, the implication is clear. The necessity of an intensity of contact and resulting bilingualism limits the earliest period for which an increase in Aramaic loanwords but no Greek influence is exhibited by texts to the Achaemenid period. From this point through the Hellenistic period and into the early Roman period, historical sources witness an increasing intensity of contact with first Aramaic and then, from the early Roman period onward, with Greek (see Heijmans; Janse on Greek loanwords in Hebrew). Not acknowledging the necessity of intensity of contact and bilingualism is the single most problematic weakness of studies discussing the *diachronic* implications of loanwords, such as Fredericks; and Young, Rezetko and Ehrensvärd 2008.

For words that pattern like Aramaic, such as זְמָן and *עֲבָד (attested only in the bound plural), it does not logically follow that their occasional occurrence in texts typically understood to be from the monarchic period requires one to conclude that either the word is not Aramaic or that Aramaic words in general are not an indicator of later texts. Such arguments naively overlook the distinction between prestige and need-based borrowing. It is only prestige-based borrowing that suggests intense language contact. With need-based borrowing, the loanwords often come with the introduction of the foreign entities. For example, the use of the Aramaic form עֲנָק "neck chain" in Judg 8:26 likely refers to a particular type of ornamental collar that only foreigners, in this case Midianites, used on their camels. The appearance of this word in Judges implies only that the item had been introduced into Israelite commerce via trade with Midianites. Thus, the presence of some Aramaic or even Persian words in texts otherwise considered pre-Persian period does not undermine the *informed* use of loanwords in the diachronic analysis of Hebrew (contra Young, Rezetko and Ehrensvärd 2008: 201–22; 280–311).

Now consider the two Persian words in Ecclesiastes: פַּרְדֵּס (2:5) and פִּתְגָם (8:11). First, it is worth noting that the latter does not accord to typical Hebrew phonology since the ג beginning a syllable after a preceding closed syllable does not have a *dagesh lene* (e.g., *פִּתְגָּם would be normal Hebrew phonology); moreover, both words have quadraconsonantal word skeletons, which stands in contrast to the normal triconsonantal skeletons of Hebrew morphology. Second, there is no clear need for either borrowed word. Admittedly, פַּרְדֵּס has a complicated story:

> The Hebrew term *pardes* is a loanword from the Old Persian **paridaida* (lit. "enclosure"), via the Median form *paridaiza*, which denoted a walled garden precinct, although of a very special type. It is attested in what are generally considered late books of the Bible, that is, those dating from the Persian period. The term *paridaiza* appears to have been specific to the Achaemenid Persian historico-cultural context (sixth–fourth centuries BCE). It came into Aramaic, and most likely from there into Hebrew, not from the domain of gardening or agriculture, as one might expect, but from the realm of government and administration, which represented the chief source of Persian lexical borrowings into imperial Aramaic, the official language of Achaemenid administration. In Late Babylonian inscriptions from the time of the Achaemenid ruler, Cyrus (ca. 530 BCE), the term occurs in the form *pardesu*. (Subtelny, 15–16)

Though the word is clearly not synonymous with Hebrew גַּן (contra DCH, s.v. פַּרְדֵּס), there is sufficient semantic overlap such that Hebrew גַּן could have carried a royal connotation with suitable modification, e.g., גַּן הַמֶּלֶךְ (2 Kgs 25:4; Neh 3:15). Thus, פַּרְדֵּס in Ecclesiastes can only be a prestige-borrowing intended to evoke an explicitly royal garden connected to a palace, used to bolster Qoheleth's royal self-presentation in the first part of the book.

Similarly, פִּתְגָם is a word that need not have been borrowed. The Hebrew words מִצְוָה or דָּבָר would have sufficed, depending on the intended nuance, "decision" or "announcement." The fact that פִּתְגָם is also used in Esth 1:20, in a royal setting, suggests that in Ecclesiastes the word is a prestige-borrowing intended to evoke a royal or court setting for the "decision." Importantly, the royal connotation associated with both words assumes a context in which the Hebrew speaking audience would be sufficiently familiar with Persian royal administration and the palace institution to process the author's intentions.

More than two Aramaic loanwords are typically identified for the book. Fredericks discusses forty-eight possible Aramaic words or calques on Aramaic phrases (217–41), which we list below for convenience:

אִלּוּ (6:6); אַרְיֵה (9:4); Niphal בהל (8:3); Piel (5:1; 7:9); בָּטֵל (12:3); בְּכֵן (8:10); בְּשֶׁל אֲשֶׁר (8:17); גּוּמָץ (10:8); דְּרְבֹנוֹת (12:11); הֶבֶל (1:2, 2; 12:8); הָוָא (11:3); הוֹלֵלוּת (10:13); זְמָן (3:1); חוּץ מִ- (2:25); חוֹר (10:17); חוּשׁ (2:25); חֵפֶץ (3:1, 17; 5:3, 7; 8:6; 12:1, 10); יְקָר (10:1); יִתְרוֹן (1:3); כִּשְׁרוֹן (11:6); כְּבָר (1:10); כָּל-עֻמַּת שֶׁ- (5:15); כָּשֵׁר (10:10; 11:6); כְּאֶחָד (11:6); מָכַךְ (3:19); מוֹתַר (10:20); מַדָּע (10:20); מְדִינָה (2:8; 5:7); מָכַךְ (2:21; 4:4; 5:10); מְדִינָה (2:8; 5:7); מַדָּע (10:20); מוֹתַר (3:19); מָכַךְ (10:18); מָלַךְ (4:14); מִסְכֵּן (4:13; 9:15, 16); נְכָסִים (5:18; 6:2); סוֹף (3:11; 7:2; 12:13); עָבַד (9:1); עַל דִּבְרַת שֶׁלֹּא (7:1); עָנָה (1:13; 3:10); סָכַן (10:9); עִנְיָן (1:13; 2:23, 26; 3:10; 4:8; 5:2, 13; 8:16); פֶּשֶׁר (8:1); קְרָב (5:19); עִנְיָן (1:13; 2:23, 26; 3:10; 4:8; 5:2, 13; 8:16); רְעוּת (2:17); רַעְיוֹן (1:17; 2:22; 4:16); שָׁכַח (4:2; 8:15); שֹׁהַם (9:18); שׁוּק (12:4, 5); שָׁלַט (2:19; 5:18; 6:2; 8:9); שִׁלְטוֹן (8:4, 8); שַׁלִּיט (3:18); תָּקַן (1:15; 7:13; 12:9); תְּקֶף (4:12; 6:10); תָּקַן (7:19; 8:8; 10:5).

We cannot discuss each of these examples (nor are we convinced that all of them are clear cases of borrowing). With that said, if the data are viewed through an informed historical linguistic lens, we do find the overall argument that the presence of two Persian and numerous Aramaic loanwords in Ecclesiastes contributes to its late Persian/early Hellenistic period linguistic profile. Finally, the borrowing of שׁ (likely from Late Babylonian in an exilic context; see Holmstedt 2016: 93–101) and its diffusion further situates the book of Ecclesiastes: the degree of diffusion suggests a relative position alongside the book of Ben Sira and closer to the end of the process (e.g., Mishnaic Hebrew).

2. Internally Motivated Change: Reanalysis and Extension

While borrowing has an external cause in language contact, internally motivated changes are responses to some perceived internal pressure on the language and are associated with the mechanisms of *reanalysis* and *extension*. Although it is not a hard and fast division, borrowing mostly concerns lexical items while reanalysis and extension affect grammatical structure or meaning. For the linguistic changes we have identified as operative in the language of Ecclesiastes, reanalysis is the primary mechanism.[31]

Reanalysis is the change of the underlying structure or meaning of a linguistic phenomenon without any structural change to the surface (phonological or morphological) manifestation (Harris and Campbell, 50). An example of reanalysis in Hebrew involves the conditional אִם in the oath formula. In the full formula, the אִם introduces a conditional clause, as it often does: "Thus shall God to you and thus shall he add, if (אִם) you do/do not …" (see 1 Sam 3:17). In many cases, though, the oath formula was abbreviated with the initial threat omitted, leaving only the אִם clause. In the abbreviated examples, the אִם takes on a negative connotation—i.e., "(you will be cursed) *if* you do it" > "don't do it!"—and אִם לֹא is interpreted positively—i.e., "(you will be cursed, *if* you do *not* do it" > "do it!" The negative אִם and positive אִם לֹא were then later used in non-oath contexts (e.g., Isa 22:14 and 1 Kgs 20:23, respectively; see JM 2006: §165).

A likely example of reanalysis in Ecclesiastes concerns the increase in subject-verb word order. As argued in Holmstedt 2013e, ancient Hebrew exhibits a shift from *verb-subject–to–subject-verb* word order profile (see Holmstedt 2013e). The cause and mechanism for word order changes are often difficult to untangle, and this is the case for the

---

[31] Extension is the opposite of reanalysis: it is a change to the surface pattern without any underlying modification (Harris and Campbell, 51). Paradigm leveling (or analogical change) is a classic example of extension. E.g., there is no good evidence that the second vowel of the Hiphil was a long /i/ before Hebrew, which suggests that Hebrew did not inherit the long /i/, but developed it. A likely source for this long vowel is the II-w/y verb class, in which the middle glide (w or y) assimilated to the adjacent vowel, producing a "long vowel" (e.g., *yaqwim → *yaqyim → *yaqiim = *yaqîm). This long vowel was then extended throughout the Hiphil paradigm, resulting in the pattern with which all Hebrew students are familiar יַשְׁמִיד and הִשְׁמִיד.

proposed verb-subject–to–subject-verb shift in BH. It is conceivable that the shift to subject-verb was due to language contact; however, since this shift occurred over hundreds of years, it is more likely that it reflects a long-term reanalysis. In particular, it is plausible and supported cross-linguistically that the topic- and focus-fronted subjects in the earlier basic verb-subject language were reanalyzed by successive generations of child learners as nontopic and nonfocus constituents, resulting in an acquired basic subject-verb pattern. As each generation reanalyzed the role of the subject in subject-verb clauses, Hebrew moved through a series of word order profiles: strong verb-subject → weak verb-subject → weak subject-verb → strong subject-verb.

There are a number of striking word order examples in Ecclesiastes that are otherwise difficult to explain. Consider the subject-negative-verb examples in וְנַפְשׁוֹ לֹא־תִשְׂבַּע מִן־הַטּוֹבָה (5:5), אֹהֵב כֶּסֶף לֹא־יִשְׂבַּע כֶּסֶף (6:3), וְאָדָם לֹא זָכַר אֶת־הָאִישׁ הַמִּסְכֵּן הַהוּא (8:5), and שׁוֹמֵר מִצְוָה לֹא יֵדַע דָּבָר רָע (9:15). The clear pattern in the majority of BH is for the negative לֹא to trigger verb-subject order (see §2D above); if the subject is subsequently placed in front of a negated verb, it reflects a subject that is marked (and thus fronted) for topic or focus (see Gen 16:1, where שָׂרַי has been fronted as a reactivated topic). The examples in Ecclesiastes, however, do not make clear discourse sense with topic- or focus-fronted subjects. If so, then the subject-negative-verb order reflects both the reanalysis of the topic/focus position in such clauses to be basic word order as well as the reanalysis of the negative such that it does not trigger verb-subject order.

We cannot present a full-fledged diachronic analysis of the language of Ecclesiastes. Such a study is much more involved than suggested by any of the surveys given in various commentaries, or even by the analysis in Fredericks. The studies in Cook 2012a, 2013, and Holmstedt 2012, 2013a illustrate the type of linguistic analysis that should be carried out on every salient feature in Ecclesiastes. In this overview we have only briefly introduced this approach and illustrated it with a few particularly useful examples.

In conclusion, there is no doubt that the linguistic profile of Ecclesiastes differs from most other biblical books. Historical linguistic study strongly suggests that the book's language occurs very late in the relative ordering of ancient Hebrew texts of the first millennium. With the external dating evidence provided by Hebrew epigraphs, Ben Sira, the Qumran texts, and the Mishnah, we can confidently situate the language of Ecclesiastes in the early to mid-Hellenistic period, close to that of Ben Sira and the Qumran texts.

A HANDBOOK ON THE HEBREW TEXT OF QOHELETH

1:1-11 Creation Is Ordered, but Humans Don't Benefit from It

The first chapter of the book frames the voice, themes, and method of the book. It is presented as the conclusions drawn about questions of meaning and behavior in life by a sage who has observed and intentionally experienced enough aspects of life to speak authoritatively.

In terms of voice, the title to the book attributes it to "the son of David, king in Jerusalem" which can only refer to Solomon (see comment on 1:1). However, if the writer had really wanted to identify Qoheleth as Solomon, he could have used Solomon's name. Instead, by suggestively associating Qoheleth with "son of David" the author creates a Solomonic persona based on the tradition of Solomon's wisdom for the rhetorical advantage of the book. The writer quickly drops the "king" persona after chapter 2. Note the mention of "all who were before me over Jerusalem" (1:16), which implies multiple kings before him, clearly excluding a Solomonic reference. Additionally, some of Qoheleth's comments later in the book about kings exhibit an outsider's perspective and lack any hint of familiarity with being a king himself (e.g., 4:13-16). Thus, the Solomonic persona is a literary device to cast the message as the highest wisdom from the famous king, known for both his wisdom and his luxury.

The themes addressed in the first section of the book, vv. 1-11, all relate to the organization of the world that humans experience (good and evil, righteousness and wickedness, life and death, eating and drinking, and so on). The question that guides Qoheleth's experiment and shapes his report of it is whether the order God embedded in the world can be discerned, at least enough to guide behavior. If so, then we may make wise choices and should expect to be rewarded correspondingly; if not, then how do we determine what is the best way to live? In this way the author uses the character of Qoheleth to interact with the basic underlying principle of the wisdom enterprise, that God allows humanity to see the order of his creation and so determine how to live successfully.

1:1   דִּבְרֵי֙ קֹהֶ֔לֶת בֶּן־דָּוִ֖ד מֶ֥לֶךְ בִּירוּשָׁלָֽם׃

These are the words of Qoheleth, the son of David, king in Jerusalem.

Verse 1 introduces both the book and the primary voice, that of Qoheleth. Between 1:2 and 12:8, the narrative framework is from the perspective of the first-person.

דִּבְרֵי֙ קֹהֶ֔לֶת בֶּן־דָּוִ֖ד מֶ֥לֶךְ בִּירוּשָׁלָֽם. The entire verse is either a syntactic fragment functioning as a title or a null copula clause with a covert subject: "(These are) the words of . . . ." Our translation reflects the latter option. See Prov 1:1 for a similar syntactic beginning, מִשְׁלֵ֣י שְׁלֹמֹ֑ה בֶּן־דָּוִ֖ד מֶ֣לֶךְ יִשְׂרָאֵֽל (see also Isa 1:1; Jer 1:1; Hos 1:1; Joel 1:1; Amos 1:1; Obad 1; Mic 1:1; Nah 1:1; Hab 1:1; Zeph 1:1; Mal 1:1; Prov 1:1; Song 1:1; Neh 1:1). Compare Exod 1:1 for a similar example, but with an overt subject, וְאֵ֗לֶּה שְׁמוֹת֙ בְּנֵ֣י יִשְׂרָאֵ֔ל (see also Deut 1:1). In this complex NP, דברי קהלת is the complement of the null copula, while the following phrases בן דוד and מלך בירושלם are appositives modifying קהלת. These appositives identify who this קהלת is in terms that assert his authority.

קֹהֶ֔לֶת. Participle ms Qal √קהל, derived from noun קָהָל "assembly" (see JM §88Fb). The root קהל occurs in BH as a verb only in the Niphal and Hiphil; however, in Aramaic the Peʿal occurs as a monovalent verb, "one who does something in the congregation." Even though it is feminine singular in form, the referent of קֹהֶ֔לֶת is clearly masculine singular, given Qoheleth's self-identity and the fact that the form קֹהֶ֔לֶת occurs with masculine agreement features on its verbal forms in 1:2; 12:8, 9, 10, and possibly 7:27 (depending on whether one emends; see discussion there). There are, however, other cases of this apparent gender mismatch in BH, e.g., פֹּכֶ֣רֶת הַצְּבָיִים "gazelle-catcher" (Ezra 2:57; Neh 7:59), סֹפֶ֫רֶת "scribe" (Ezra 2:55; 7:57), and *מֹדַ֫עַת "close relative" (Ruth 3:2) (it is also worth mentioning mismatch cases like אָב֥וֹת "fathers"). Muraoka suggests that singular feminine-for-masculine forms have "an intensive nuance" and compares Arabic forms like *rāwiyat* "a (great) narrator," to the simple form *rāwin* "narrator"; he also suggests that, in contrast with מוֹדַ֫ע "kinsman" (Ruth 2:1), the feminine form *מֹדַ֫עַת in (Ruth

3:2) "seems to mean close relative (probably masculine, speaking of a man)" (JM §89b; cf. GKC §122r; Whitley, 4–5). Finally, the lack of an article on the noun suggests either that it refers to a nonspecific entity, "an assembler" (often, rendered "a teacher" or "a preacher"), or that it is both specific and identifiable; that is, it has become a proper noun, "Assembler," much like the use of "smith" as the surname "Smith" in English or the end point of the development of the word שׂטן (10× as a common noun, "adversary," without the definite article [1 Sam 29:4; 2 Sam 19:23; 1 Kgs 5:18; 11:14, 23, 25; Ps 109:6; Num 22:22, 32]; 17× as a common noun with the definite article, indicating a specific [celestial] figure fulfilling the office of "the adversary, prosecutor" [Zech 3:1-2; Job 1:6-9,12; 2:1-4, 6-7]; and then once without the definite article as a proper name, "Satan" [1 Chr 21:1]). The proper name use of קהלת is the consensus understanding, especially for its occurrences in 1:2, 12; 12:9, 10 (and possibly 7:27), though the articular appearance of הקהלת in 12:8 is surprising.

בֶּן־דָּוִד. The lexeme בן is used both to refer to a kinship relationship "son" or "descendant" and to designate one of a group or type, such as species (e.g., בן אדם "human"; GKC §128v; WO §9.5.3a; JM §129j). Thus, here it could refer to the actual son or descendant of David, or someone who could be considered as belonging to the "Davidic" class, which presumably refers to royalty (i.e., "a member of the group known as 'David'"). As Seow notes, though, elsewhere in the Hebrew Bible, the collocation בן דוד strictly refers to Solomon or one of David's other historical sons not any of his more distant descendants (1997: 97). The use of the phrase here in v. 1 is perhaps building both on the allowable meaning for the term as well as the known biblical or traditional usage, thereby establishing the Solomonic *persona* for the voice of Qoheleth while also maintaining a "backdoor" meaning for the skeptical reader, who recognizes that the author was neither Solomon nor likely royalty (see Longman, 2–9 for a clear discussion of authorship).

מֶלֶךְ בִּירוּשָׁלַם. This is a collocation unique to Ecclesiastes: elsewhere מלך and ירושלם are in a bound relationship; i.e., "king of Jerusalem" (Josh 10:1, 3, 5, 23; 12:10). Making this collocation even rarer is the fact that NP-internal PPs as a whole are not common. That is, PPs overwhelmingly modify a verb or serve as complements in null copula clauses; they generally do not modify a noun. See 1 Kgs 10:26; 2 Chr 1:14; 9:25 for the same sequence, מלך בירושלם, in which the PP does not modify the noun but the verb in the clause. For other NP-internal PPs in Ecclesiastes, see 2:7, 13, 26; 3:1; 5:11; 7:6; 9:17; 12:6.

1:2   הֲבֵל הֲבָלִים֙ אָמַר קֹהֶ֔לֶת הֲבֵל הֲבָלִים הַכֹּל הָֽבֶל׃

"A total הבל*!" said Qoheleth, "A total* הבל*! Everything is a* הבל.

   Verse 2 presents Qoheleth's theme or motto and perhaps also the theme of the entire book (i.e., including the narrator's perspective in 1:1 and 12:9-14): הכל הבל. Together with 12:8, this verse also serves to create an inclusio demarcating Qoheleth's report concerning his investigation.

   הֲבֵל הֲבָלִים֙ אָמַר קֹהֶ֔לֶת הֲבֵל הֲבָלִים הַכֹּל הָֽבֶל. *Qatal* 3ms Qal √אמר. A complement-verb-subject clause, where the complement, which is the reported speech, is fronted for focus. The fronting subsequently triggered the raising of the verb higher than (i.e., in front of) the subject. The reason for the focus-fronting is to contrast the audience's expected assessment (e.g., "it's all good") with the actual assessment. The phrase הבל הבלים represents either a one-part null copula clause (but is it the subject or the complement of the null copula?) or a predication-less exclamation. We take it to be the latter, though it is possible (if not likely) that even exclamations like this should be formally analyzed as full clauses. The remainder of the reported speech, הֲבֵל הֲבָלִים הַכֹּל הָֽבֶל, presents a complex appositional phrase modifying the initial reported speech phrase followed by a separate summary clause; when the first NP הבל הבלים was raised to a focus position, it left the second, appositive הבל הבלים "stranded" in its original position. The clause הכל הבל is a null copula clause with subject-copula-complement order. The position of the quotative frame—circumscribed by the direct speech complement—is rare in the Hebrew Bible; besides here, 7:27, and 12:8, we have only found Isa 48:22; 57:18 (possibly), 21; 59:21; 65:7; 66:20; Jer 49:18; Mal 1:10, 14; 2:2; 3:10, 17.

   הָֽבֶל. The denotation of the noun הבל appears to be "breath, vapor." As used in Ecclesiastes, it must be a metaphor since it makes little sense for Qoheleth to assert that "everything" is literally "vapor." What the metaphor means, though, has long been and remains the subject of some debate. The following are those English glosses most commonly proposed: "ephemeral," "worthless, trivial," "empty, nothing," "incomprehensible," "deceit," and "senseless, nonsense" (see Meek for an exhaustive survey). Some suggest that the word is used in more

than one way in the book (see, e.g., Crenshaw, 57; Miller 2002 offers
a variation on this). Others disagree: Fox, for example, argues that the
term must have a single dominant meaning around which the book's
argument coheres (1999: 35); he proposes that Ecclesiastes' use of הבל
parallels Camus' idea of "absurd"—i.e., the "disjunction between two
phenomena that are thought to be linked by a bond of harmony or
causality, or that should be so linked. ... Absurdity arises from a contradiction of two undeniable realities" (1999: 31). We find Fox's absurd
idea attractive, though at the same time acknowledge that it seems a
bit anachronistic. Because we cannot find a single convincing English
gloss, and because this is a grammatical commentary, we have left הֶבֶל
untranslated throughout.

הֶבֶל הַבְלִים. This is a bound phrase in which the form of the first,
bound item does not reflect typical Hebrew morphology. Normally the
free and bound forms of a ms segolate noun are identical, e.g., מֶלֶךְ.
However, the form הֶבֶל is typical for an Aramaic bound word, including
segolate nouns; cf. the Aramaic forms צְלֵם in Dan 3:19 and עֲבֵד in 6:21
(GKC §133, BL §72x, 573x; JM §96Ae; Schoors, 75). The phrase הבל
הבלים as a whole, a singular noun bound to a plural form of the same
word, reflects a BH strategy for expressing the superlative (WO §14.5b,
d; 9.5.3j; GKC §133i; JM §141l).

הַכֹּל. The combination of the article and כל refers to "everything"—
i.e., the כל that is specific and identifiable (without being in a bound
relationship with an adjunct modifier, as in 1:7 כל־הנחלים "all of the
rivers"). The statement that "everything" is הבל is an exaggeration for
rhetorical effect; rather, הכל strictly refers to everything that was within
Qoheleth's purview during his investigation, although it might also be
taken as a logical extrapolation that Qoheleth makes based on what he
has observed.

1:3   מַה־יִּתְרוֹן לָאָדָם בְּכָל־עֲמָלוֹ שֶׁיַּעֲמֹל תַּחַת
הַשָּׁמֶשׁ:

*What profit belongs to a man in exchange for all his toil that he does
under the sun?*

Verse 3 moves from introduction and motto to Qoheleth's report of
his experiment. This verse appears to be a rhetorical question, especially
in the cynical context established by v. 2.

מַה־יִּתְרוֹן לָאָדָם. The syntax of this verse is more complicated than it may initially appear. The absence of an overt verb indicates that, whatever else is concluded, it is a null copula clause with the interrogative מה as the subject. From there, the challenge begins. The primary question concerns the copular complement: is it יתרון or לאדם? In the first option, if the complement is יתרון, the question is wide open: "What is profit for a man … ?" In the second option, the question is narrowed somewhat if יתרון is taken with מה (see JM §144d) and the complement is לאדם: "What profit (belongs) to a man … ?" The precise function of the PP לאדם changes depending on the overall syntactic choice: in the first option above, the ל preposition marks the person who would *benefit* from יתרון (if it exists); in the second option, the ל signals *possession*—whether or not a person owns (or, better in English, "receives, gets") profit is central to the question (on both uses of the ל, see WO §11.2.10d). Deciding between the two syntactic analyses of the entire clause requires a semantic judgment: Is the question about *what constitutes* יתרון for a person who toils or *what kind of* יתרון the toiling person receives? In seeking to resolve the semantic question, we find that the comparative data in Ecclesiastes are ambiguous. In 2:22 the interrogative מה is the subject of a copular clause, the possessive ל-PP is the copular complement, and thus Qoheleth seems to be asking, What (in terms of profit) belongs/will belong to the man who toils? (כי מה־הוה לאדם בכל־עמלו וברעיון לבו) (so also 6:8b). This notion is similar to the second reading we propose for 1:3. On the other hand, in 3:9 the interrogative מה is the subject of the null copula clause, "the profit of the worker" is the copular complement, and thus Qoheleth is asking, What is/constitutes the profit of the one who works? (מה־יתרון העושה באשר הוא עמל). This notion is similar to the first reading proposed. In the other three examples where Qoheleth employs the interrogative to question the value of one's labors (6:8a, 11, 12), the constructions bear the same syntactic ambiguity as 1:3. In the context of this verse, we find the second semantic option more felicitous—"what kind of profit belongs to a man in exchange for all his toil?"

יִתְרוֹן. The pattern *qitlōn* is used for abstract nouns and occurs only as a bound form; the free form could either be *qitlōn* (<*qitlān*) or *qətalōn* (<*qatalān*) (BL §500q; GKC §85u; JM §88Mb–c). Within the Hebrew Bible, these two -ōn afformative noun patterns occur with greatest frequency in the book of Ecclesiastes, with twenty-seven cases (for an average of 6/1000 words). Compare this, for example, to the highest occurrence elsewhere, which is in Numbers (32 examples of the noun pattern); since this book is far larger, however, the frequency is much lower: 1.28/1000 words. Moreover, whereas the lexical diversity of these nouns is minimal in Numbers (only two appear, עִשָּׂרוֹן and זִכָּרוֹן), Ecclesiastes uses nine different lexemes (חֶשְׁבּוֹן, זִכָּרוֹן, בִּטָּחוֹן, חֶסְרוֹן, שִׁלְטוֹן, רַעְיוֹן, כִּשְׁרוֹן, יִתְרוֹן, חֶשְׁבּוֹן). Given that the *-ān > Heb. -ōn affirmative reflects the nonapplication of the 14th-century BCE Canaanite shift (ā>ō), an isogloss distinguishing the Canaanite languages (including Hebrew) from Aramaic, and given that this sound change was not reapplied in the first millennium, the typical arguments that this pattern, which reflects normal Hebrew morphology, represents borrowing from Aramaic do not make good sense; see Introduction §6.

לָאָדָם. Lit. "to the man." The Masoretic vocalization indicates that the tradition takes this noun to be definite. Since the context suggests no specific real-world referent, it is best to understand this as the use of the article for generic nouns (i.e., nouns that refer to an arbitrary member of a species, genus, or kind). Generic nouns are often (but not always; see v. 4) accompanied by the article in Hebrew (as well as many other languages) since as a class the noun is identifiable to the hearer. English allows either a definite or indefinite article with generics (e.g., "the giraffe has a long neck" or "a giraffe has a long neck," both of which can be generic expressions), which explains our translation choice, "*a* man." See Baranowski and also Bekins for recent and linguistically insightful studies of the article in BH.

בְּכָל־עֲמָלוֹ. The בְ preposition here marks the entity given in exchange for the (hoped for) יתרון. This use of בְ is often called the בְ *pretii* ("the בְ of price") (JM §133c; WO §11.2.5d; MNK §39.6.3.2).

שֶׁיַּעֲמֹל. *Yiqtol* 3ms Qal √עמל. The relative clause modifies עָמָל. Since the root and meaning overlap between the head עָמָל and the verb within the relative יַעֲמֹל, the relative clause is most likely a nonrestrictive relative (see Holmstedt 2016: 205–14), serving to modify עָמָל with additional but obvious information for rhetorical impact. That is, a restrictive relative, which by nature defines or identifies the head, would be redundant in this case. The verb עמל is bivalent, typically occurring with an explicit complement (e.g., 2:21); however, in this relative construction (see 2:19-20; 5:17), the head is resumed as a null complement of the bivalent verb.

תַּחַת הַשָּׁמֶשׁ. This PP introduces an image that is used throughout the book. Those who exist "under the sun" are the living, as opposed to

those who no longer see, or have never seen, the sun (see 4:3; 6:5). The
English phrase "the light of day," as in "would he ever see the light of day
again?," is similar.

1:4   דּוֹר הֹלֵךְ וְדוֹר בָּא וְהָאָרֶץ לְעוֹלָם עֹמָדֶת׃

*A generation goes and a generation comes; that is, the world always
remains the same.*

Verses 4-7 are a short poem that provides the answer to the question posed in v. 3. Though v. 3 seems like a rhetorical question, Qoheleth goes ahead and answers it—cynically, of course. These verses give
Qoheleth the opportunity to showcase his real-world observations—i.e.,
the results of his experiment. In a nutshell he has concluded that while
there is a lot of activity in the world, nothing really new happens, and no
advantage is gained by those engaged in activity in the world.

It is tempting to take this proposition as a statement about the brevity of life: "humans come and go." However, the verbs are in the wrong
order to fit that idiom. The order "goes and comes" suggests that Qoheleth is asserting that human history is cyclical and so monotonous: one
replaces the other, and so humanity appears to undergo change, but the
"world" (humanity) never really changes.

דּוֹר הֹלֵךְ וְדוֹר בָּא. Participle ms Qal √הלך and √בוא. The form בָּא
is ambiguous (it could also be *qatal* 3ms Qal), but its parallelism with
the unambiguous participial forms הלך and עמדת support our analysis
here. Likewise in v. 5, the ambiguous form וּבָא is clarified by its parallelism with the unambiguous *qatal* perfective verb זָרַח. For participial
clauses, the order subject-verb is both basic and dominant (see Introduction §2D). The participle has long been understood as an "intermediate"
form between verbs and nouns, since sometimes it appears verbal (e.g.,
it takes NP complements), while other times it appears nominal (e.g., it
takes possessive clitic pronouns; GKC §116; see WO §37; JM §121).
Recent study, though, indicates that participles in BH are best understood as adjectives that encode an activity or event rather than a quality
(Cook 2008). Thus, when participles are used "verbally," they are actually
complements of a null copula. The core semantics of the Hebrew participle is progressive aspect, which is increasingly used also for habitual
and gnomic statements instead of the *yiqtol* (see Introduction §5). Here
the context suggests that the participle has a gnomic meaning—that "a

generation goes and a generation comes" is taken as an observable truth of human existence. Qoheleth uses this observable fact, against which one can hardly argue, to set up his corollary: so nothing ever changes.

דּוֹר. Note the lack of the article on the generic noun. As a generic, the noun דור refers to an arbitrary member of the class "generation." The hearer knows and thus can identify the class, even though a specific דור has not been established in the discourse. See also the comment on לאדם in v. 3.

וְהָאָרֶץ לְעוֹלָם עֹמֶדֶת. The position of the PP לעולם in front of the participle reflects focus-raising. Focus on the PP לעולם fits the context well, in that Qoheleth's point here is that the world *always* stays the same. If the PP לעולם has been raised for focus, it means that the NP הארץ must also be in higher-than-normal position in the clause. This also fits well, since as a topic, הארץ alerts the listener/reader to an agent/patient shift—from the cycle of individual generations to an assessment of the whole of humanity (all the generations, past, present, and future). An alternative, which we take to be less likely, is that both the subject הארץ and the PP לעולם are fronted for focus—הארץ because it is contrasted with both occurrences of דור in the first half of the verse, and לעולם because of the inherent contrast between it and something that happens sporadically or ceases at some point.

וְהָאָרֶץ. The use of the NP הארץ here is an example of synecdoche, the literary device by which the part is used to refer to the whole. In this case the author employs a specific type of synecdoche in which the container is used to refer to the contents (e.g., "White House" referring to the people filling roles in the executive branch of the U.S. government; "keg" referring to the beer that fills the keg). Thus, הארץ refers to humanity. (See also 10:16-17, where Qoheleth employs the literary device of personification to picture ארץ as a people, as opposed to a piece of land.) In keeping with the noncontrastive juxtaposition of the two halves of the verse, the ו conjunction is taken as the "epexegetical" use: "to clarify or specify the sense of the preceding clause" (WO §39.2.4). In the alternative interpretation mentioned in the last note, in which דור and הארץ are contrastive, הארץ would not refer to humanity, but rather to the world as opposed to the human generations of the first half. In this case, the two halves of the first do not work together (such that the second reinforces the first); they present opposites: humanity is cyclical, the world is static. Fox asserts that the nature of the physical world "has no relevance to the individual life" and so this interpretation is unlikely from a rhetorical perspective (Fox 1999: 166). Though it may be an exaggeration to state that the physical world is irrelevant, since the lessons Qoheleth gives here derive from observing the physical world, the central point stands—that Qoheleth is not comparing the static earth to the transience of human generations, but is presenting it in parallel with the phenomena in the natural world that follow. Thus we agree with Fox's basic point that the change (one generation goes and another comes) is an illusion: humanity does not really change. Similarly, the cycle of the sun and the wind and the rivers flowing to the sea give a deceptive appearance of "change"; nothing really changes in the end (and humanity cannot change any of it either).

עֹמָדֶת. Participle fs Qal √עמד. The verb עמד at its core means "to stand"; the context here suggests that the nuance is "to stand in place," so "endure, remain the same" (see BDB, s.v.; HALOT, s.v.; DCH, s.v.).

1:5   וְזָרַח הַשֶּׁמֶשׁ וּבָא הַשָּׁמֶשׁ וְאֶל־מְקוֹמוֹ שׁוֹאֵף זוֹרֵחַ
       הוּא שָׁם׃

The sun rises and the sun sets: for its place, it longs—it rises back there.

The sun's endless cycle is yet another example of the wearisomeness of the physical world. While the sages typically took such constancy as positive evidence of the creator's care, Qoheleth points to it as evidence of the wearisome fact that nothing actually changes in life.

וְזָרַח הַשֶּׁמֶשׁ וּבָא הַשָּׁמֶשׁ. *Qatal* 3ms Qal √זרח and √בוא (see note at v. 4 on the parsing of וּבָא). Both *qatal* perfective verbs are irrealis in these two clauses. The irrealis mood goes hand-in-hand with the habitual semantics of the statements (see Introduction §5). Notably, the verb-subject syntax also supports the irrealis interpretation of the verbal semantics, since subject-verb order is basic with realis verbs, whereas irrealis mood triggers inversion to verb-subject order (see Introduction §§2D, 5). The collocation בא השמש is used idiomatically for the sun setting (Seow 1997: 107; Krüger, 50, esp. n. 9). The article on השמש reflects the specificity and identifiability, and thus determination, of the referent for the listener/reader (see Baranowski for the use of the article in Ecclesiastes).

וְאֶל־מְקוֹמוֹ שׁוֹאֵף. Participle ms Qal √שׁאף. Since the referent is specific and identifiable, the nuance of the progressive semantics of the participle is habituality (rather than gnomic, for which the noun must also be generic, i.e., nonspecific). The word order reflects the focus-raising of the PP. As a focus-marked adjunct phrase, אל מקומו stresses that the sun returns to its place—no other route or destination ever occurs. Thus, the constancy and inevitable cyclicity of life is reinforced with evidence from the physical world. Although there is scant cognate evidence for the verb שׁאף (HALOT lists only Arabic *sahafa* "to gasp, thirst"), the lexica are in agreement on a basic meaning of "to gasp, pant" (and "trample," which clearly does not fit this context). In this verse what does it mean that the sun "pants" for its place? Commentators are of two opinions: the connotation is either (1) that the sun hurries (thus the panting) to arrive at its house every evening, or (2) that it longs for or desires to get home. In both cases, the concrete meaning "to pant" is understood simply as the symptom of either a physical activity (hurrying) or psychological state (longing). We find no strong indication which of the interpretations is accurate, though because שׁאף is found in a parallel stich with יאב "to long for" (Ps 119:131) we lean toward the psychological "longing" (contra Seow 1997: 107). Although this verb usually has an NP complement (e.g., Job 7:2), here (as in Amos 2:7) the complement is a PP, אל מקומו.

זוֹרֵחַ הוּא שָׁם. Participle ms Qal √זרח. The participle-pronoun (subject) syntax of the clause is quite unusual. Following the Masoretic interpretation, in which זורח and הוא are linked together prosodically by the *merkha-tifha* pair, results in a single, rather strange clause: "it rises there." Presumably the locative adverb שם refers to the sun's home. The problem with this is that the sun does not rise *there*; rather, it rises *from* there. Moreover, why is the participle in front of the subject pronoun? It could be to mark focus on the activity of rising, but this seems a stretch. If it were not for the Masoretic טעמים, we would see here two separate clauses, a one-item participial clause, "(it) rises," and a pronoun-adverb null copula clause, "it (is) there." Although abrupt, the sense of the three-stage sequence is clear: (1) the sun pants to get home, (2) has to rise again (and so depart from home), and (3) is there again (i.e., returns back home, panting). It is an excruciating image of weariness: "Its great, laborious trek across the sky merely brings it back to its point of departure" (Fox 2004: 5).

1:6   הוֹלֵךְ אֶל־דָּרוֹם וְסוֹבֵב אֶל־צָפוֹן סוֹבֵב | סֹבֵב
הוֹלֵךְ הָרוּחַ וְעַל־סְבִיבֹתָיו שָׁב הָרוּחַ:

Going to the south, turning around to the north—round, round goes the
wind, and upon its rounds the wind returns.

In this verse Qoheleth builds on the theme of the wearisomeness
of constancy in the physical world by considering the wind. The wind
is portrayed here as a single entity, similar to Qoheleth's unified view of
humanity despite the existence of multiple generations.

הוֹלֵךְ אֶל־דָּרוֹם וְסוֹבֵב אֶל־צָפוֹן סוֹבֵב | סֹבֵב הוֹלֵךְ הָרוּחַ. There
are three clauses here, but the subject of the first and second is delayed
until the end of the third. Syntactically, the delay of the subject הרוח
until the third clause in the verse is an exceptional case of a cataphoric
null-subject pronoun. Literarily, leaving the actor unspecified until the
last word creates a sense of mystery and so builds the reader's/listener's
interest.

הוֹלֵךְ אֶל־דָּרוֹם. Participle ms Qal √הלך. The אל-PP is the locative
complement of the motion verb. The noun דרום is used only in Ecclesiastes, Deut 33:23, Job 37:17, and the book of Ezekiel (21:2; 40:24, 27;
42:18). Elsewhere ימין, נגב, or תימן are used to refer to "south."

וְסוֹבֵב אֶל־צָפוֹן. Participle ms Qal √סבב. The verb סבב does not
take a complement; the אל-PP is thus an adjunct.

סוֹבֵב | סֹבֵב הוֹלֵךְ הָרוּחַ. The three participles here form a ver-
bal hendiadys, which means that the first two adverbially modify the
main activity expressed by הולך. The use of סבב in such proximity
to a preceding use (in the previous clause), its repetition here, and
its focus-fronted position drive home the never-ending cyclicity of
life—it is dizzyingly wearisome. The order participle-subject for הולך
הרוח is unusual, since the word order of participial clauses throughout
Hebrew is strongly subject-participle and is not affected by syntactic
triggers (e.g., כי, אשר), though the order may be affected by topic and
focus fronting (see Introduction §2D; Holmstedt 2009a, 2011). Here
the word order might reflect additional focus on the הולך, but we
prefer to see this as an example of poetic license—Qoheleth lines up
the three participles in a row and delays the subject for aesthetic effect.
The English equivalent, "round and round goes the wind," captures
the order and feel perfectly.

וְעַל־סְבִיבֹתָיו שָׁב הָרוּחַ. Participle ms Qal שוב√. As with the
preceding clause, the PP is focus-fronted to contrast the circular paths
of the wind with the logical alternatives (i.e., straight paths that actually go somewhere). The order participle-subject reflects Qoheleth's art-
istry and parallels the previous clause, creating symmetry. As with the
prior participles in this verse and in v. 5, the nuance of the progressive
semantics of the participles is habituality due to the actor's specificity and
identifiability.

1:7 כָּל־הַנְּחָלִים הֹלְכִים אֶל־הַיָּם וְהַיָּם אֵינֶנּוּ מָלֵא אֶל־
מְקוֹם שֶׁהַנְּחָלִים הֹלְכִים שָׁם הֵם שָׁבִים לָלָכֶת:

*All the rivers are going to the sea, yet the sea—it is not full! To the place
that the rivers go—there they go continually.*

This verse continues Qoheleth's consideration of the physical environment. Here he shifts from the sun (v. 5) and the wind (v. 6) to the
rivers and sea.

כָּל־הַנְּחָלִים הֹלְכִים אֶל־הַיָּם. Participle mp Qal הלך√. The participle presents a habitual activity. The אל-PP is the locative complement
of the motion verb.

וְהַיָּם אֵינֶנּוּ מָלֵא. This is a negative copula clause, with אין as the
negative and copula. Although it is possible to analyze the clitic pronoun
as the copular item (and then אין as a simple negative; see Holmstedt and
Jones 2014), in this case the pragmatics of left-dislocation fit the context
better (see also 5:11; 9:5, 16). As a left-dislocated constituent, הים is a
topic that is resumed by the 3ms clitic pronoun -נו, which itself bears
focus. The adjective מלא is the copular complement. The function of the
left-dislocation construction is to signal an agent switch (= topic) from
הנחלים to הים, which had been introduced in the previous clause in an
embedded position (as the complement of the preposition אל), and then
to focus the referent of הים by means of the resumptive pronoun attached
to אין: "Though the rivers flow to the sea, *the sea—it* is never full!"

אֶל־מְקוֹם שֶׁהַנְּחָלִים הֹלְכִים שָׁם הֵם שָׁבִים לָלָכֶת. Participles mp
Qal הלך√ and שוב√, and Inf Constr Qal הלך√. This clause presents a
rare example of a PP that is left-dislocated and then resumed within the
clause proper by the locative adverb שם (which is the focus-fronted locative complement of ללכת). The function of the dislocation is to signal a

switch in topic and to allow focus-marking within the clause proper—in this case, on שָׁם, the locative resumption of the dislocated constituent. Note that the noun מְקוֹם is pointed as the bound, clitic form, making the שׁ relative clause its clitic host. This is a strategy used to indicate that a relative clause is restrictive and thus identifies the referent of the relative head (see Holmstedt 2002, 2008a, 2016: 205–14). In this case, the מקום is the specific מקום to which rivers flow (i.e., the sea).

שָׁם הֵם שָׁבִים לָלָכֶת. The sequence of verbs is an interesting construction. Syntactically, the infinitive clause ללכת is the complement of the verb of motion שׁוב. But there are two options for understanding how this construction works semantically: (1) "they return to go there" or (2) "again they go there." In the first option, the semantic relationship mirrors the syntactic construction, with שׁוב the main verb "they return" and ללכת modifying the nature of the returning activity. In the second option, שׁוב is an auxiliary verb, providing the adverbial notion "again" (JM §102g; WO §39.3.1b). Qoheleth is not likely referring to the cycle of rain (that water evaporating from the sea rains over land and thus returns to the rivers), but about the endless and yet apparently futile flow of the rivers into the sea. In light of this, we take the adverbial function of שׁוב to be more fitting. Additionally, the progressive semantics of the participle שבים lends itself to an adverbial notion of "again and again," or, as we translate, "continually."

כָּל־הַדְּבָרִים יְגֵעִים לֹא־יוּכַל אִישׁ לְדַבֵּר לֹא־תִשְׂבַּע   1:8
עַיִן לִרְאוֹת וְלֹא־תִמָּלֵא אֹזֶן מִשְּׁמֹעַ:

All the words are wearying: man is not able to speak, the eye is not satisfied by seeing, and the ear is not filled from hearing.

In this verse Qoheleth's observations about life move to their climax: humanity. The cyclicity of vv. 3-7 observed in the poem about the physical environment is now extended to humanity. Qoheleth's rhetorical strategy is simple and effective. He has established his argument using observations with which the listener/reader can readily agree—all can see these cycles and note that despite the endless activity, they have no progress or fulfillment. Agreement on the four preceding "facts of life" allows him to apply his argument to humanity, making the debatable claim that humans never find real satisfaction, only limited fulfillment and frustration (cf. 6:7).

כָּל־הַדְּבָרִים יְגֵעִים. A null copula clause with the adjective יגעים as the complement. The *qatil* vocalization of יְגֵעִים is frequent with adjectives, especially those that are associated with stative verbs, which have no active *qotel* participle in the Qal. These *qatil* adjectives illustrate the fuzzy line between adjectives and participles (see Cook 2008). The semantics of stative יגע are expected to be monovalent, "to be(come) weary"; however, it may also be bivalent in much the same way that Qal מלא is (e.g., "be full" or "fill something"; see Seow 1997: 109). Fox (1999: 167) notes that כל־הדברים never refers to physical entities. Thus הדברים refers not to the cycles of the physical world themselves, but most directly to the aforementioned *descriptions* of them—note the definite article (though the following mention of "seeing" tempers the strictness of such a distinction). Human words fail to comprehend these cycles, and yet humanity does not cease trying, exhibiting the same wearying lack of progress as the natural cycles themselves.

לֹא־יוּכַל אִישׁ לְדַבֵּר. *Yiqtol* 3ms Qal (?) √יכל and Inf Constr Piel √דבר. The negative לא has triggered inversion to verb-subject order. The verb יכל "to be able" is almost always bivalent (it may be monovalent "to be capable" in 1 Sam 26:25; Jer 3:5; and Job 31:23) and takes an infinitival complement, here לדבר. The verb דבר is either monovalent, with an adjunct PP indicating the addressee, or bivalent, with a NP denoting a speech activity (like "this/these words" and "all the commands," often marked by את) or a clausal complement indicating the content of the speech (for an argument regarding the adjunct status of the addressee PP, see Holmstedt 2010: 182). No complement is present here, and the sense does not suggest that a covert one must be assumed. Rather, the meaning here is intentionally ambiguous, akin to the English statement "Words fail." In the context Qoheleth, as a wisdom sage, laments the insufficiency of words—to comprehend the wearisome cyclicity of the world, to discern anything new in life, and ultimately to discover anything profitable for humanity to do. The irony is, of course, that people do not stop speaking despite gaining no advantage by it (see 6:12; 10:14).

יוּכַל. The *binyan* of this verb is enigmatic. The semantics required by the context are "to be able," which best fit the Qal; but the morphology only fits the Hophal (<*yuwkal). Joüon and Muraoka argue for the Hophal analysis and suggests the following series of semantic shifts: "the original meaning of Hophal, *he will be made capable*, could easily, and may in fact, have weakened to *he will become capable, he will be capable,* becoming finally *he will be able to*, the causative meaning may then have gradually evaporated" (JM §75i).

לֹא־תִשְׂבַּע עַיִן לִרְאוֹת. *Yiqtol* 3fs Qal √שבע and Inf Constr Qal √ראה. The Qal of שבע occurs both as a monovalent form (e.g., Prov 27:20) and a bivalent form (e.g., 4:8; 5:9). No example occurs, however, of the bivalent pattern with an infinitive complement, which makes it most likely that the ל + infinitive clause לראות is a gerundive (or explan-atory/epexegetical) adjunct clause (i.e., "satisfied by seeing"; see WO §36.2.3e).

וְלֹא־תִמָּלֵא אֹזֶן מִשְּׁמֹעַ. *Yiqtol* 3fs Niph √מלא and Inf Constr Qal √שמע. Like שבע in the preceding clause, מלא (in the Qal or Niphal) can be either monovalent (e.g., 6:7) or bivalent (e.g., 11:3), including with infinitive complements (e.g., Hab 2:14). However, the monovalent pattern is rare (only 6:7; Exod 7:25; Job 15:32). In the other thirty-three occurrences of this verb the *content with or from which something* is *filled* is overtly expressed, usually as a bare NP (e.g., 11:3), but also with a מִן-PP (e.g., Ezek 32:6; cf. Ps 127:5 but with the Piel trivalent verb). Thus, the PP + infinitive clause משמע is the complement for תמלא, expressing the source of the content with which the ear is filled (see מלא DCH #3). The first of the three negative clauses in this verse is intentionally ambiguous (see above), and may be treated as looking backwards on the opening poem (so Fox 1999: 167) or forward to v. 9 (so the Targum; see Seow 1997: 110). These two latter, more specific, negative statements seem to point ahead less ambiguously to v. 9 and set up the frustration of human existence: though nothing new ever occurs, people nevertheless speak, look, and listen without ever finding satisfaction.

1:9   מַה־שֶּׁהָיָה הוּא שֶׁיִּהְיֶה וּמַה־שֶּׁנַּעֲשָׂה הוּא שֶׁיֵּעָשֶׂה
וְאֵין כָּל־חָדָשׁ תַּחַת הַשָּׁמֶשׁ:

Whatever has been—it is what will be. Whatever has happened—it is what will happen. There is nothing new under the sun.

Qoheleth's observations about the cyclicity of life leads him to this conclusion in v. 9: life is an oppressive stasis that admits no profit (v. 3) and no satisfaction (v. 8) for humanity regardless of how they might exert themselves to search for these.

מַה־שֶּׁהָיָה הוּא שֶׁיִּהְיֶה וּמַה־שֶּׁנַּעֲשָׂה הוּא שֶׁיֵּעָשֶׂה. *Qatal* and *yiqtol* 3ms Qal √היה, *qatal* and *yiqtol* 3ms Niph √עשׂה. Both clauses exhibit the same syntax: a left-dislocated indirect interrogative phrase resumed by the pronoun הוּא, which is the subject of a null copula clause with a null-head relative clause (e.g., "[the thing] that will be") as the copular complement.

מַה־שֶּׁ. This collocation only occurs in Ecclesiastes in BH (see also 3:15, 22; 6:10; 7:24; 8:7; 10:14), but is well attested in rabbinic Hebrew. It is often equated with, or taken as a calque of, Aramaic מה די (see Dan 2:28-29) or מה ז (Egyptian Aramaic; see Whitley, 10–11). Syntactically, it is a headed relative clause with an interrogative as the head. The combination of מה and שׁ produces a free choice relative, similar in function to English "whatever," "wherever," "who(m)ever," and "whenever" (cf. GKC §137c; WO §§18.2.c, e; 18.3e; JM §144fa–g; Schoors, 59–60). The implication of the free choice relative is that Qoheleth knows that *something* has occurred and that the same *something* will occur again, but he leaves the identity of that *something* unspecified, either out of indifference or lack of knowledge. In the context of the book and this verse, it is more likely that Qoheleth is letting the audience fill in the identity, as *anything* or *everything*, rather than admitting some sort of ignorance.

נַעֲשָׂה. We analyze this form as a *qatal* 3ms Niph, although the form is ambiguous and could also be the participle fs Niphal. In the context the tense contrast between the first pair, היה and יהיה (see Introduction §5), demands a *qatal-yiqtol* contrast here as well. Qoheleth contrasts the past with the present in both these pairs to underscore that in all time, including the present, nothing new exists or happens (cf. Fox 1999: 167). The most common meaning for the verb עשׂה in the Qal is "to do, make," and so the typical meaning in the Niphal is the passive "to be done." But throughout Ecclesiastes it is used as an agentless (semantically and syntactically) generic expression of what "has happened/occurred" (see Fox 1999: 175; Murphy, 11; see also Esth 2:11).

וְאֵין כָּל־חָדָשׁ תַּחַת הַשָּׁמֶשׁ. An אין copula clause, with כל חדש as the subject and the PP תחת השמש as the copular complement. The use of the negator here gives the statement universal temporal scope, summing up the previous past-future contrasts.

1:10 יֵשׁ דָּבָר שֶׁיֹּאמַר רְאֵה־זֶה חָדָשׁ הוּא כְּבָר הָיָה
לְעֹלָמִים אֲשֶׁר הָיָה מִלְּפָנֵנוּ:

A thing exists about which one might say, "See this—it is new!" It has already existed for the ages that were before us.

In vv. 10-11 Qoheleth builds upon his conclusion in v. 9 by pointing out its logical (v. 10) and psychological and emotional (v. 11) consequences. In v. 10 the idea that there is nothing new in life is simply the logical corollary of cyclicity.

יֵשׁ דָּבָר. In some cases יש functions as a noncopular, nonverbal "existential" predicator with the sense of "X exists" (see also 2:21, 4:8, and 6:1; similarly the use of היה with monovalent, existential semantics in 7:10). The subject of יש is the noun דבר, and it lacks any predicate complement, which is the prime indicator of its noncopular function.

שֶׁיֹּאמַר. *Yiqtol* 3ms Qal √אמר. We analyze the *yiqtol* here as irrealis mood expressing epistemic possibility: Qoheleth addresses the possibility that one *might* counter his conclusion (v. 9) by attempting to point out this or that as actually "new." Within the שׁ relative clause there is no resumption of the head דבר. Verbs of speech, like אמר, are often followed by an adjunct PP indicating the addressee (i.e., an אל-PP for "to speak *to someone*") or content (i.e., an על-PP for "to speak *about something/someone*"), although this PP may be covert (see Miller 1996: 333). Resumption of a relative head at an adjunct position when the relative verb is a verb of speech is optional and rare (see Holmstedt 2010: 182). Since English requires the preposition (although not the pronoun), it is necessary to insert one in translation, as we have done.

רְאֵה־זֶה חָדָשׁ הוּא. Impv ms Qal √ראה. There are two possible syntactic analyses of this sequence. The first is as two clauses, ראה זה and חדש הוא. The second is as a single complex clause, with הוא functioning as the copula of the embedded (unmarked) complement clause, "see (that) this is new." However, when the pronoun functions as a copula, it is positioned between the subject and copular complement, not after both (see Kummerow; Holmstedt and Jones). This fact, as well as the rarity of an unmarked complement clause (e.g., Judg 9:48: מָה רְאִיתֶם עָשִׂיתִי "what you have seen (that) I have done"; WO §38.8d; JM §175b), suggests that the two-clause analysis is more likely.

חָדָשׁ הוּא. A null copula clause, in which the fronting of the copular complement reflects focus-marking on חדשׁ (see Buth). The focus on חדשׁ fits the context, in which the opposing voice that Qoheleth sets up tries to find a counterexample to Qoheleth's claim that nothing is new (v. 9). The information structure does not lay focus on the identity of the item that the opponent points out but on its supposed newness. In other words, it is not the existence of the thing that is the issue but whether or not it is actually new.

כְּבָר הָיָה לְעֹלָמִים אֲשֶׁר הָיָה מִלְּפָנֵנוּ. *Qatal* 3ms Qal √היה. The subject is covert but clearly coreferential with both זה and הוא of the preceding two clauses. The PP (along with the embedded relative clause) is the complement of the copular verb היה. The adverb כבר is fronted for focus (to contrast the supposed "newness" of this thing with the fact that it has existed previously and is thus *not* new) and reinforces the past-tense semantics of היה. The adverb כְּבָר only occurs in Ecclesiastes (see also 2:12, 16; 3:15 [2×]; 4:2; 6:10; 9:6, 7) within the Hebrew Bible, but it is quite common in rabbinic Hebrew. Syntactically, it only appears before the verb (or copula); its preverbal position suggests that it is always fronted as a topic (scene-setting) or focus (contrastive) temporal adverb. The etymology of כבר is obscure. HALOT suggests that it is related to the biblical Aramaic conjunction בְּרַם "but, however, except, yet"; and phonologically it is Aramaic-like (i.e., reduction of the vowel in the pretonic open syllable in a nonbound form; see Schoors, 116–17).

עֹלָמִים אֲשֶׁר הָיָה מִלְּפָנֵנוּ. The plural of עולם is used only twelve times in the Bible: 1 Kgs 8:13; Isa 26:4; 45:17 (2×); 51:9; Pss 61:5; 77:6, 8; 145:13; Eccl 1:10; Dan 9:24; 2 Chr 6:2. GKC suggests that the plural of the word is a "plural of extension" and is used to "denote a lengthened period of time" (§124b). The gloss GKC provides is "eternity (everlasting ages)." More insightful and accurate is the description given in WO: "Plurals of extension indicate that the referent of the noun is inherently large or complex; the plural quality is the result not of a countable multiplicity, but of a multiplicity that is nonetheless perceived as real" (§7.4.1c). עולמים is not a count noun (even though the best English equivalent in this context, "ages," is a count noun), which explains the singular number features of the verb היה inside the relative clause אשר היה מלפננו. That is, the noncount semantics of עולמים override the plural morphology to the extent that verbal agreement features match the semantic not morphological number features of the noun. It is

similar to a mp verb used with morphologically feminine nouns such as
אָבוֹת "fathers" (see also Whitley, 11, Delsman, and Schoors, 157–59).

1:11 אֵין זִכְרוֹן לָרִאשֹׁנִים וְגַם לָאַחֲרֹנִים שֶׁיִּהְיוּ לֹא־יִהְיֶה
לָהֶם זִכָּרוֹן עִם שֶׁיִּהְיוּ לָאַחֲרֹנָה: פ

*No remembrance belongs to the former (generations); additionally, no
remembrance will belong to the latter (generations) that will exist, among
(those who) will be at the latter (time).*

In contrast to the logic of v. 10, Qoheleth here addresses the implications of his conclusion on the psychology of memory with its critical role in human interrelations and self-awareness, especially in orally
dominant cultures.

אֵין זִכְרוֹן לָרִאשֹׁנִים. An אין existential clause, with זכרון the subject, and לראשנים an adjunct, lit. "remembrance does not (exist/belong)
to/for the former generations." English prefers the structure using the
dummy pronoun "there" for existential sentences, which explains the
difference between the Hebrew syntax and our translation in all three
main clauses of this verse.

לָרִאשֹׁנִים ... לָאַחֲרֹנִים. The ל preposition in both phrases is used
to indicate the beneficiary of the action or event; i.e., the so-called ל of
(dis)advantage (WO §11.2.10d). The Masoretic vocalization indicates
that both adjectives, ראשנים and אחרנים, are preceded by the definite
article (the ה of which has syncopated following the clitic preposition;
JM §35e). But neither noun is specific; rather, both are generics—nonspecific, arbitrary, but nonetheless identifiable examples of the class represented by each (see Bekins on the generic use of the article in BH). In
addition, both adjectives are substantival with an assumed modified
noun such as *generations* or *people*. Seow (1997: 111) points out that in
the Hebrew Bible, the mp ראשנים refers to "former generations" (Lev
26:45; Deut 19:14; Ps 79:8), whereas the fp ראשנות refers to "former
things" (Isa 41:22; 42:9; 43:9, 18; 46:9). In Ecclesiastes mp אחרנים
occurs one other time (4:16), also with reference to latter generations
of people. In addition see 2:16, where the identical construction occurs
with *people* denoted as the prepositional complement in אין זכרון לחכם
"remembrance does not belong to the wise." Thus, Qoheleth asserts that
neither past nor future generations will be remembered, and so as generations pass on and new ones come (1:4) nothing ever changes.

זִכְרוֹן. The form of this noun is identical to the bound form of זִכְרוֹן, but the two must be allomorphs, or simple variants of the same noun, since both the context and Masoretic accents suggest that the noun here is not bound (Krüger, 49 n. 5; Schoors, 63). It is tempting to suggest also that the presence of an intervening preposition—the ל on לראשׁנים— prohibits זכרון from being a bound form, but prepositions can, in fact, intervene between a bound word and its clitic host (GKC §130a; WO §9.3d, 6b; JM §129a, c, m, n).

וְגַם לָאַחֲרֹנִים שֶׁיִּהְיוּ. There are two ways to analyze the syntax of the next clause. First, this expression could constitute a second clause with the subject, copula, and negative אין gapped from the first clause, "and also [remembrance does not exist] for the latter generations that will (yet) come." The function word גם may be used as an additive conjunction or a focus-marker (cf. MNK §41.4.5.2; van der Merwe). Here we take the גם as the additive "also" or "nor" (as the second option in a negative context). For גם in the book, see also 1:17; 2:1, 7, 8, 14, 15, 19, 21, 23, 24, 26; 3:11, 13; 4:4, 8, 11, 14, 16; 5:9, 15-16, 18; 6:3, 5, 7, 9; 7:6, 14, 18, 21, 22; 8:10, 12, 14, 16, 17; 9:1; 9:3, 6, 11, 12, 13; 10:3, 20; 11:2; 12:5. Alternatively, one might also analyze the expression וגם לאחרנים שיהיו as a left-dislocated constituent (signaling a topic-shift from "former generations" to "latter generations"), resumed by the 3mp clitic pronoun in the PP להם. In left-dislocation the grammatical function of the dislocated constituent in the core clause is sometimes retained by the constituent when moved to the front (e.g. 1:7 אֶל־מָקוֹם שֶׁהַנְּחָלִים; 1 Kgs 15:13 וְגַם | אֶת־מַעֲכָה אִמּוֹ וַיְסִרֶהָ הֹלְכִים שָׁם הֵם שָׁבִים לָלֶכֶת "and also Maacah his mother, he removed her"; and cross-linguistically, Greek examples like Rev 2:7, 17: Τῷ νικῶντι δώσω αὐτῷ "To the one who overcomes_DAT, I will give to him_DAT ....").

לֹא־יִהְיֶה לָהֶם זִכָּרוֹן עִם שֶׁיִּהְיוּ לָאַחֲרֹנָה. Yiqtol 3ms and 3mp Qal √היה. The verb-subject order of this clause is inverted from the basic subject-verb order due to the presence of the negative לא (see Introduction §2D). The PP להם is raised with the verb when, due to the presence of לא, it moves in front of the subject (זכרון); this is a consistent pattern with "light" PPs—they raise with the verb, whereas "heavy" PPs (i.e., those with a full NP complement) remain in their normal location below the subject unless they have been fronted for topic or focus. The PP עם is a verbal adjunct; the complement of עם is null and is modified by the ש (null-head) relative clause.

לָאַחֲרֹנָה. Unlike the previous two occurrences of the ל preposition, the preposition in this case is locating the event or action temporally (WO §11.2.10c). Syntactically, the PP is the complement to the copular verb יהיו. The feminine adjective אחרנה "last" has a contextually determined temporal nuance in this verse. The distribution of this adjective, which occurs fifty-one times in the Bible, establishes a clear pattern. The feminine singular occurs nine times (Num 2:31; Deut 13:10; 17:7; 1 Sam 29:2; 2 Sam 2:26; 1 Kgs 17:13; Eccl 1:11; Dan 8:3; 11:29), always as a prepositional complement, referring to "the last" time or place(ment). The masculine singular occurs twenty-two times (Exod 4:8; Deut 11:24; 24:3 [2×]; 29:21; 34:2; Isa 8:23; 30:8; 44:6; 48:12; Jer 50:17; Joel 2:20; Hag 2:9; Zech 14:8; Pss 48:14; 78:4, 6; 102:19; Job 19:25; Prov 31:25; Ruth 3:10; Neh 8:18), and the masculine plural occurs twenty times (Gen 33:2 [2×]; 2 Sam 19:12, 13; 23:1; Isa 41:4; Job 18:20; Eccl 1:11; 4:16; Ezra 8:13; 1 Chr 23:27; 29:29; 2 Chr 9:29; 12:15; 16:11; 20:34; 25:26; 26:22; 28:26; 35:27). Both masculine forms are straightforward adjectives, meaning "last, latter, second" (though translations often render the plural adverbially, e.g., Gen 33:2 וַיָּשֶׂם אֶת־הַשְּׁפָחוֹת וְאֶת־יַלְדֵיהֶן רִאשֹׁנָה וְאֶת־לֵאָה וִילָדֶיהָ אַחֲרֹנִים וְאֶת־רָחֵל וְאֶת־יוֹסֵף אַחֲרֹנִים "He put the maidservants and their children in front, Leah and her children next [lit. *the latter ones*], and Rachel and Joseph in the rear [lit. *the last ones*]" (NIV).

1:12-18 "I Am Qoheleth"

Verse 12 marks a shift in the first-person narrative flow of chapter 1. Though vv. 2-11 were introduced in v. 2 as the words of Qoheleth and so presumably from a first-person perspective, it is not until here in v. 12 that the first-person perspective is made overt by the pronoun אני and the verb הייתי. Note that no new observations are made in vv. 12-18; rather, Qoheleth introduces himself and his credentials, thereby establishing his authoritative voice, and provides a preview of his conclusions. Although we divide Qoheleth's autobiographical speech into smaller components for analysis, it should be noted that it encompasses 1:12–2:26.

1:12   אֲנִי קֹהֶלֶת הָיִיתִי מֶלֶךְ עַל־יִשְׂרָאֵל בִּירוּשָׁלָֽם׃

I am Qoheleth. I have been king over Israel in Jerusalem.

Significantly, besides 1:1, this is the only other verse in the book that explicitly identifies Qoheleth as a (former) monarch. It is perhaps the case that, after making the audience increasingly uncomfortable with his observations, the author (in the persona of Qoheleth) chooses this point to remind the audience of his credentials, thereby assuring them of his authority.

אֲנִי קֹהֶ֫לֶת הָיִ֫יתִי מֶ֫לֶךְ. *Qatal* 1cs Qal √היה. The primary grammatical question for this sequence is whether the whole is one clause or two. For the single clause analysis, the proper name קהלת is an appositive to the pronoun אני, which is the syntactic subject of the verb הייתי, with מלך as the complement and the על-PP as an adjunct: "I, Qoheleth, was king over ... ." The two-clause analysis separates off אני קהלת as a null copula clause, which serves to identify the speaker as the formerly named Qoheleth of v. 1; the second clause is a null-subject verbal clause: "I am Qoheleth; I was king ... ." Seow (1997: 119) notes that the former option appears in various West Semitic and Akkadian inscriptions (e.g., KAI 24.9; 26AI.16, 19–20, BI.9, 11, CII.5, 11; 215 I.19–20, 222 A3.2) but also that the latter mirrors the self-presentation formula in many West Semitic inscriptions (KAI 10.1; 13.1; 24.1; 26.I.1; 181.1; 202 A.2, 214.1; 216.1; 217.1). We follow Seow in preferring the second, two-clause analysis.

הָיִ֫יתִי. The verb היה is stative and the default rendering of stative + perfective *qatal* is a present-time state. However, the copular verb presents a special case insofar as it denotes primarily *tense* distinctions: with the perfective *qatal*, היה denotes past tense; with the imperfective *yiqtol*, היה denotes future tense (see v. 8 above); and a covert copula (or null copula) strategy signals present-time copular expressions (see Introduction §5). This view supports the past tense rendering "I was." However, though this fits the overall retrospective nature of Qoheleth's voice throughout the book, it complicates the Solomonic persona, since it implies that Solomon has died! The simplest solution is to interpret it as a present perfect "I have been" (so Seow 1997: 119; Fox 1999: 169; cf. Murphy, 11), implying that he is still on the throne but has been for a long enough time to give a retrospective on his experiment and life in general (hence the early Jewish interpretation that Solomon wrote the book as an old man in Midrash *Shir Hashirim Rabba* 1.1 [Gordis 1955: 39, esp. n. 2]). Another possible option is Krüger's (56) suggestion of an inchoative "I became king," which fits well with an irrealis interpretation of ונתתי in the following verse if that option is followed (see below). (See also Schoors, 172–73.)

עַל־יִשְׂרָאֵל בִּירוּשָׁלָ͏ֶם. These two PPs together narrow the possible intended referents to two: David and Solomon. The first PP was used of Saul, David, and Solomon, as well as northern kings, but the second PP limits it to David and Solomon.

1:13 וְנָתַ֨תִּי אֶת־לִבִּ֜י לִדְר֣וֹשׁ וְלָת֗וּר בַּֽחָכְמָ֔ה עַ֚ל כָּל־
       אֲשֶׁ֣ר נַעֲשָׂ֣ה תַּ֣חַת הַשָּׁמָ֑יִם | ה֣וּא | עִנְיַ֣ן רָ֗ע נָתַ֧ן
       אֱלֹהִ֛ים לִבְנֵ֥י הָאָדָ֖ם לַעֲנ֥וֹת בּֽוֹ:

I set my לב *to seek and to investigate with wisdom concerning all that has happened under the heavens. It is a severe task (that) God has given to men to be occupied with.*

In this verse Qoheleth introduces his experiment partner, indicating in the first half of the verse that he commissioned his לב. The second half of the verse is actually Qoheleth's preview of his לב's conclusion for the project. .

וְנָתַ֨תִּי אֶת־לִבִּ֜י. *Qatal* 1cs Qal √נתן, a trivalent verb (here with one NP complement and one compound infinitival complement). This phrase is often identified as the idiom נתן לב "set one's mind (to do something)." As the idiom, this collocation is often categorized as LBH, with the SBH expression either שים לב or שית לב (Seow 1997: 120). However, Ecclesiastes' usage does not engage the idiomatic phrase that many commentators mistakenly take it as (see note below on לבי). The verb נתתי is either a realis perfective used in the past time frame, "I set my mind," or an irrealis perfective describing a habitual action, "I would set my mind." If the former, it would most naturally refer to the "experiment" taken as a whole. If the latter, it would refer to a common activity. If the entire book is a thought experiment, the habitual fits with the created persona for Qoheleth as the wise monarch who had leisure ad infinitum to sit on his portico and search out the wisdom of the ages. If the book is a report of a "real" experiment, then the image of a young monarch testing various paths of life over time also suggests an activity that took place over many attempts. While either option is defensible, the realis perfective is preferable as it is more in keeping with the reported experiment that follows (see v. 16ff.) and because there is a decreased use of irrealis *qatal* in the book (see Introduction §5).

לִבִּי. The noun לב occurs forty-one times in the book of Ecclesiastes: 1:13, 16 (2×), 17; 2:1, 3 (2×), 10 (2×), 15 (2×), 20, 22, 23; 3:11, 17, 18; 5:1, 19; 7:2, 3, 4 (2×), 7, 21, 22, 25, 26; 8:5, 9, 11, 16; 9:1, 3, 7; 10:2 (2×), 3; 11:9 (2×), 10. It is used as a syntactic subject (1:16, 2:3, 10, 23; 5:1; 7:3, 4 [2×], 22; 8:5, 11; 9:3; 10:2 [2×], 3; 11:9), as an NP complement of the verb (1:13, 17; 2:10, 20; 7:7, 21; 8:9, 16), within a complement PP (3:11; 7:2; 9:1), within a noncomplement PP (1:16; 2:1, 3, 15 [2×]; 3:17, 18; 9:7; 11:10), as a genitive/nomen rectum of a bound phrase (2:22; 5:19; 7:26; 11:9), and as a conjunct in an adverbial adjunct phrase (7:25). There are clear cases in which לב is used in its more typical sense as one's inner self. Notably, the following are all in reference to a לב that is is not Qoheleth's specific לב: 2:22, 23; 3:11; 5:1, 19; 7:2, 3, 4 (2×), 7, 21, 22, 26; 8:5, 11; 9:3, 7; 10:2 (2×), 3; 11:9 (2×), 10. There are also verses in which Qoheleth references his partner-לב but does not include the 1cs pronoun, since he apparently intends no contrast or does not need to highlight the collaborative nature of the experiment: 1:13, 17; 2:3, 10, 15; 8:9, 16; 9:1. For more on Qoheleth's use of לב, see Holmstedt 2009b and Introduction §3.

לִדְרוֹשׁ וְלָתוּר. Inf Constr Qal √דרש and √תור. The two infinitival clauses together serve as the compound second complement for the trivalent verb נתתי. The Qal of תור means "to spy out, reconnoitre," but in the context of the book of Ecclesiastes, the meaning of "spy out" takes on the connotation of "investigate." Both דרש and תור are bivalent and usually take NP complements (18 out of 22 occurrences of תור; 105 out of 153 occurrences of דרש).

בַּחָכְמָה עַל כָּל־אֲשֶׁר נַעֲשָׂה תַּחַת הַשָּׁמָיִם. Qatal 3ms Niph √עשה. The close conjoining of the two bivalent infinitives strongly suggests one of the following PPs fulfills the valency requirement of both verbs; the other PP is then an adjunct. However, neither verb regularly takes a ב or על-PP as a complement: דרש occurs with a ב-PP complement in nine verses with the meaning "inquire of, consult with" (1 Sam 28:7; 2 Kgs 1:2–3, 6, 16 [2×]; 1 Chr 10:13-14; 34:26), and with על in just one case (2 Chr 31:9). Most versions and commentaries treat בחכמה as an adjunct of instrument or accompaniment "by/with wisdom" and the על-PP as the complement, some noting that חכמה is never the object or goal of inquiry in the book (Seow 1997: 120; also Krüger, 56; see also Schoors, 198–99); however, חכמה fulfills the complement role of the series of infinitives, לדעת ולתור ולבקש in 7:25. Nevertheless, the sense of

the adjunct בְּ-PP with תוּר in 2:3, where the complement is a following
לְ + infinitive, supports this analysis.

תַּחַת הַשָּׁמָיִם. This phrase is used here and in 2:3 and 3:1. Otherwise the more common phrase is תחת השמש: 29×—1:3, 9, 14; 2:11, 17,
18, 19, 20, 22; 3:16; 4:1, 3, 7, 15; 5:12, 17; 6:1, 12; 8:9, 15 (2×), 17;
9:3, 6, 9 (2×), 11, 13; 10:5. Seow distinguishes between these two: תחת
השמש refers to "the temporal universe of the living" or "this world" (as
opposed to the netherworld), while תחת השמים refers to "the universality of human experiences" or simply "the cosmos" (1997: 105).

הוּא | עִנְיַן רָע נָתַן אֱלֹהִים לִבְנֵי הָאָדָם לַעֲנוֹת בּוֹ. *Qatal* 3ms Qal
√נתן, Inf Constr Qal √ענה. The 3ms pronoun הוא is used in one of its
rare functions—to refer to a broad or vague entity, condition, or event
(what WO call the "neutrum" function; §16.3.5b). The reference for הוא
is either the activity of investigating or the object of investigation ("all
that happens under the heavens"); most commentators opt for the former, since, as Krüger notes, "in contrast to the following sections [as in
v. 14], the result of the examination [would be] stated before the reports
on its execution" (63 n. 12). Contra Seow (1997: 121), who claims that
"it" (הוא) refers narrowly to the investigative task Qoheleth has set for
himself, we see the referent as the investigative business that all humans
have been given by God (see also 3:10-12), since otherwise the reference
here to "men" (lit. "sons of man") would be nonsensical. Our translation reflects the unmarked relative clause that serves to modify ענין רע
(see 3:10, where Qoheleth does employ אשר to mark the relative clause
in the same expression). Resumption within a relative clause is dictated
by the valency requirements of the verb inside the relative. If the verb
requires a PP complement that is coreferential with the head of the relative, then overt resumption of the head must occur within a PP; if the
verb takes an NP complement, as here with נתן, the presence of resumption in BH seems to be determined by pragmatics and is not required
(see Holmstedt 2008b; 2016: 158–86). The verb נתן is trivalent, often
taking one NP complement and one PP complement. The phrase לבני
האדאם fulfills the PP requirement, and the NP complement requirement is fulfilled by null resumption of the head (though covert, it is easily recoverable from the context: "an unfortunate task, which God gave
[it] to the sons of man"). The infinitival adjunct, לענות בו, includes the
verb ענה with a PP complement בו (see 3:10). The 3ms clitic pronoun in
בו anaphorically refers back to the null resumption and thus to the head
of the unmarked relative ענין.

עִנְיָן. This noun, meaning "task, business, affair," is used only in Ecclesiastes (see also 2:23, 26; 3:10; 4:8; 5:2, 13; and 8:16). From the occurrences it seems to carry a negative connotation (i.e., disagreeable work, unhappy business).

1:14   רָאִיתִי אֶת־כָּל־הַמַּעֲשִׂים שֶׁנַּעֲשׂוּ תַּחַת הַשָּׁמֶשׁ
וְהִנֵּה הַכֹּל הֶבֶל וּרְעוּת רוּחַ:

*I have seen all the events that have happened under the sun, and look—
the whole thing is a* הבל *and chasing wind.*

In vv. 14-15 Qoheleth notes his own participation and expands on the conclusion he previewed in v. 13b. It is only in v. 16 that Qoheleth makes explicit the collaborative nature of his experiment, that he and his לב cooperate in this business (a collaboration that was only hinted at in v. 13).

רָאִיתִי אֶת־כָּל־הַמַּעֲשִׂים שֶׁנַּעֲשׂוּ תַּחַת הַשָּׁמֶשׁ. *Qatal* 1cs Qal √ראה, *qatal* 3cp Niph √עשה. On the meaning of Niphal עשה, see comment on v. 9. As with the verb נתתי in v. 13, the verb ראיתי can be analyzed as either a realis perfect ("I have seen"), given its relevance to his current (present-time) judgment, or an irrealis habitual, describing what Qoheleth frequently did during his experiment ("I would see"). Whatever mood choice one makes for נתתי in v. 13 must be followed for ראיתי here, and so we prefer the realis option for the reasons stated above (v. 13). The noun המעשים typically refers to "work, deed, accomplishment, achievement," but here it follows the semantics of the verbal usage of עשה and means "happenings, events" (so Fox 1999: 171).

וְהִנֵּה הַכֹּל הֶבֶל וּרְעוּת רוּחַ. A null copula clause with a compound copular complement, הבל ורעות רוח. The initial deictic exclamation, "hey!" or "look!" (traditionally, "behold!") directs the listener/ reader's attention to a following event or claim, which is often surprising or contrary to expectations (Andersen, 94–96). The article with כל refers to "everything" or "the whole" of something specific and identifiable (see 1:2), namely, "all the events that have happened under the sun"; "the whole thing" captures the sense well.

רְעוּת. This noun (which occurs 7× and only in Ecclesiastes—1:14; 2:11, 17, 26; 4:4, 6; 6:9) and רעיון (which occurs 3× and only in Ecclesiastes—1:17; 2:22; 4:16) appear to be derived from the same root, presumably רעה. However, what the etymology is and how we reach the common meaning "chasing, desire" or something similar is opaque. It is possible that the words were borrowed from Aramaic (HALOT, s.v.). Accepting the common meaning for רעות, the meaning of the whole phrase "chasing of wind" appears from the context to be something like "an ephemeral delight."

1:15 מְעֻוָּת לֹא־יוּכַל לִתְקֹן וְחֶסְרוֹן לֹא־יוּכַל לְהִמָּנוֹת׃

What is bent is not able to become straight, and what is lacking is not able to be counted.

Qoheleth reinforces his core conclusion that humanity has a "bad lot" by connecting his earlier conclusion (v. 9) that nothing changes with the human "task" (v. 13): there is no utility in doing anything, since nothing can be changed. (This verse foreshadows the slightly more ominous statement in 7:13.)

מְעֻוָּת לֹא־יוּכַל לִתְקֹן. Participle ms Pual √עות and *yiqtol* 3ms Qal √יכל (on this verb, see comment at 1:8). The participle מעות cannot itself stand as a syntactic subject; instead, the participle is within a null-head, unmarked relative clause, "the thing that is bent" (= "what is bent"). Although it is tempting to take מעות as a "substantival" participle (i.e., a participle used as a noun), we take this phenomenon to be more restricted in Hebrew grammar than many assume, limited to one of the few (mostly Qal) agentive forms (e.g., רֹפֵא, עוֹבֵד, יֹצֵר, בּוֹנֶה, שׁוֹפֵט, חוֹטֵא, and רֹעֶה, and less commonly from derived *binyanim* such as מְנַחֵם and מַצִּיל). However, when these forms are themselves modified by complements or adjuncts (such as adjectives and demonstrative pronouns), it is linguistically preferably to analyze the structure as a null-head relative clause (see Holmstedt 2016: 10–16). Note that the presence of the negative לא does not trigger inversion to verb-subject order. This may indicate that, after the inversion, the subject phrase was fronted for focus. However, subject-verb order is suspiciously common in Ecclesiastes and the book may reflect a shift further toward a strong subject-verb order, in which inversion to verb-subject is not consistent (see Introduction §2D).

לִתְקֹן. Inf Constr Qal √תקן. Commentators disagree on the valency of תקן in this verse. On the one hand, if it is bivalent, then this can only be an impersonal construction and the syntax of the clause quite different, with מעות as the complement (not subject): "what is crooked one is not able to straighten." On the other hand, if תקן in the Qal is monovalent, "to be(come) straight," מעות is the subject and תקן has no complement. In light of the factitive meaning of the Piel of תקן, "to make straight" (HALOT, s.v.), the monovalent Qal option is more likely.

וְחֶסְרוֹן לֹא־יוּכַל לְהִמָּנוֹת. On יוכל, see above. להמנות is an Inf Constr Niph √מנה. The precise nuance of חסרון is ambiguous. It is possible to understand "lacking" as less-than-whole. If this is the meaning for this verse, "to be counted" makes little sense and Fox is perhaps justified in proposing the emendation to המלות "to be filled" (1999: 172). However, if "lacking" can be a reference to whether something is fully present (locationally), then "to be counted" refers to the inability to count what is not (all) there (so Murphy, 12). On the subject-negative-verb order, see above on the first clause in this verse.

דִּבַּרְתִּי אֲנִי עִם־לִבִּי לֵאמֹר אֲנִי הִנֵּה הִגְדַּלְתִּי   1:16
וְהוֹסַפְתִּי חָכְמָה עַל כָּל־אֲשֶׁר־הָיָה לְפָנַי עַל־
יְרוּשָׁלָ͏ִם וְלִבִּי רָאָה הַרְבֵּה חָכְמָה וָדָעַת:

I spoke, I, with my לב, "I—look!—have made myself great and have added (to myself) wisdom over all who were before me over Jerusalem." And my לב (also) has seen much wisdom and knowledge.

In this verse Qoheleth elaborates on the commissioning of his לב in v. 13: he and his לב are conversation partners in the experiment. Recounting his greatness and wisdom—including the abundance of wisdom and knowledge shared by his לב (note how Qoheleth distinguishes what is true about just him from what is true of his לב apart from him by using אני within the quote)—establishes his and his לב's ability (resources) and authority (wisdom) to conduct the experiment and draw conclusions.

דִּבַּרְתִּי אֲנִי עִם־לִבִּי. *Qatal* 1cs Piel √דבר. Contrary to appearances, the pronoun אני is not the syntactic subject of the clause. If it were the subject, it would be placed before the verb. Instead, the postverbal position of the pronoun signals a specific pragmatic and literary strategy used in the book to highlight the collaborative nature of the experiment. This is what we call the "I-and-my-לב" analysis, syntactically similar to English "I spoke, me, myself, and I ..." (see Introduction §3; also Seow 1997: 123). Together the compound אני עם לבי forms a verbal adjunct with the complement of דברתי introduced by the speech complementizer לאמר.

דִּבַּ֫רְתִּי. As HALOT (s.v. דבר) indicates, the verb דבר allows a number of prepositions to mark the addressee adjunct; i.e., the person to or with whom the speaking is occurring: ־ל, אֶת, אֶל, and עִם are the most common, but ־בְּ is also used (see, e.g., Num 12:6, 8; 1 Sam 25:39; Hos 1:2; Hab 2:1; Zech 1:9, 13-14; 2:2, 7; 4:1, 4-5; 5:5, 10; 6:4; Song 8:8). Michael Fox has suggested (personal correspondence) that since the majority of occurrences of the דבר ב־ collocation occur in prophetic contexts, it may signal both intimacy and one-way communication rather than a genuine dialogue. A one-sided conversation is precisely what takes place in Ecclesiastes, and thus we translate the preposition as "to" rather than "with." The perfective דברתי might be analyzed as irrealis, continuing a description of what he "would do" followed by short (and exasperated) summaries. However, as with the *qatal* verbs in vv. 13-14, we prefer to understand the verb as a realis perfective used for past reference, with Qoheleth looking back and summarizing his experience.

אֲנִי הִנֵּה הִגְדַּ֫לְתִּי וְהוֹסַ֫פְתִּי חָכְמָה. *Qatal* 1cs Hiph √גדל and √יסף. Three syntactic features stand out in the clause. First, the overt subject pronoun אני is used even though the finite verb is fully inflected with person, gender, and number features. Hebrew is a type of language called "pro-drop" or "null-subject," which means that it allows an overt syntactic subject to be absent with inflected verbs (see Holmstedt 2013b). When the pronouns are present, they carry focus-marking. Here, then, Qoheleth is asserting that *he* (and no other) increased wisdom. The second notable feature is the position of the deictic exclamative הנה, between the subject pronoun and the verb. Intervening like this shows that the exclamative may also function as an interjection; i.e., a constituent that interrupts the phrasal syntax. The הנה, as a deictic exclamative, directs the listener/reader's attention to the subsequent assertion; its position strengthens the force of its use. Finally, the verb הגדלתי is often bivalent, "to enlarge something" or "make something great." If it is bivalent here, then חכמה is the only NP present to fulfill the valency. However, this would require taking the two verbs הגדלתי והוספתי as a compound (see Murphy, 12 n. 16a, "I greatly increased"). The alternative is to understand הגדלתי as an "internal" or "inwardly transitive" Hiphil, in which the agent is the same as the patient of the action (GKC §53d; JM §54d; WO §27.2f), thus "I made myself great." The NP חכמה is then the complement only for the verb הוספתי.

We have opted for this latter analysis. Semantically, both verbs are realis perfective with past-time reference. More specifically, a present-perfect rendering is preferred to a simple past inasmuch as these accomplishments result in a present position of greatness and wisdom that rhetorically supports the authority of Qoheleth in the eyes of the reader.

עַל כָּל־אֲשֶׁר־הָיָה לְפָנַי עַל־יְרוּשָׁלָם. *Qatal* 3ms Qal √היה. This PP is a verbal adjunct of הוספתי. Though it is not syntactically associated with the previous verb, הגדלתי, it can be assumed to apply to this verb in terms of the sense of Qoheleth's claim. The PP specifies that Qoheleth performed the activity of "increasing wisdom" (and, contextually, "making himself great") more than this specific set of other agents, "all who were before him over Jerusalem." (Given the report to follow, we should not think of Qoheleth's greatness as limited to his wisdom.) Notably, this assertion is logical only if there were multiple rulers in Jerusalem before Qoheleth. It is thus another hint that the speaker is taking on the "Solomon" persona (although he in fact is not), and that the author allows the façade to become transparent when doing so serves his rhetorical interest.

וְלִבִּי רָאָה הַרְבֵּה חָכְמָה וָדָעַת. *Qatal* 3ms Qal √ראה. Note that הרבה has the morphology of a Hiphil infinitive absolute. The infinitive absolute in general often functions simply as a reinforcing adverb, although other uses are possible (WO §35; JM §123). However, in the case of הרבה, the form seems to have been grammaticalized fully into an adverb meaning "many, much." As an adverb, הרבה regularly can modify either the verb or nominal constituents, and once even an adjectival form (7:16); at times it can even function in nominal roles, e.g. as the subject of the verb (2:7; also 2 Sam 1:4), as the complement of the verb (Hag 1:6; 2 Chr 25:9), or as a prepositional complement (Jer 42:2; Hag 1:9; 2 Chr 11:12; 16:8). In this case it modifies the conjoined phrase חכמה ודעת. The phrase חכמה ודעת serves as the complement of ראה and לבי is the subject. This clause has an important role in the rhetorical structure of the book, in that it clearly establishes the לב as an independent entity and so supports the "I-and-my-לב" analysis promoted in this commentary. The present-time judgment (from Qoheleth's perspective) rendered on the basis of the experiment makes a present-perfect interpretation of the realis perfective *qatal* preferable and is in keeping with the other *qatal* forms in the verse.

וָאֶתְּנָה לִבִּי לָדַעַת חָכְמָה וְדַעַת הוֹלֵלוֹת וְשִׂכְלוּת   1:17
יָדַעְתִּי שֶׁגַּם־זֶה הוּא רַעְיוֹן רוּחַ׃

I set my לב *to know wisdom; and knowing blindness and folly—I came to know that even this was chasing wind.*

Qoheleth describes the basic strategy for his experiment: there are two investigative paths, one for him and one for his לב. Qoheleth directs his לב "to know" wisdom, while for himself he chooses the other—and ultimately unsatisfying—path of "knowing" foolishness.

וָאֶתְּנָה לִבִּי לָדַעַת חָכְמָה וְדַעַת הוֹלֵלוֹת וְשִׂכְלוּת. *Wayyiqtol* past narrative 1cs Qal √נתן. Note the addition of the ה on the 1cs *wayyiqtol*, which illustrates an asymmetry in the *wayyiqtol* paradigm: whereas the shorter prefix forms are used (when possible) for the second- and third-person forms, e.g., וַיָּקֶם, וַיִּשְׁמַד, the first person often appears in the lengthened form, e.g., וָאֶשְׁלְחָה. The choice of the *wayyiqtol* here versus *qatal* form (cf. v. 13) is not easily explained; this is only one of three occurrences of this form in the book (4:1, 7; see Introduction §5). Scholars have suggested that the form is appropriate as a "narrative" past (e.g., "*So I applied*," Murphy, 11; Seow 1997: 124, with reference to Fox 1989: 174, who uses the term "narration" to describe vv. 16-18), but this only begs the question why the form is used here and not in other suitable narrative passages. Given the focus of v. 16 on establishing the authority of Qoheleth and his לב, we tentatively understand the *wayyiqtol* here to mark a transition back to the report of the experiment. The repeated use of נתן here as in v. 13 links these similar two passages (vv. 13-15 and 16-18): the first recounts the experiment and the conclusions drawn from it, while the second, in parallel fashion explains the basis of the experiment and its methods, along with reflections on the undertaking (similarly, Fox 1989: 174).

לָדַעַת חָכְמָה וְדַעַת הוֹלֵלוֹת וְשִׂכְלוּת. Inf Constr Qal √ידע, twice. This part of v. 17 is a well-known, interpretive crux in the book. As it stands, there are at least two syntactic analyses, and some commentators support emendation. The central question is whether the item וְדַעַת is a second occurrence of the infinitive "to know" or "knowing," as we take it, or the homophonous noun "knowledge" (so the ancient versions and some modern commentators, e.g., Longman, 77, 84). We see no grammatical justification for emending or revocalizing the conjunction in וְדַעַת so that it is understood as the second noun in a word pair—i.e.,

וְדַעַת as the second in a sequence of two noun pairs, "wisdom and knowledge, blindness and folly"—or for supposing that the second pair "looks like an addition based on 2:12a or 7:25" (Fox 1999: 173; cf. Seow 1997: 124–25). Accepting the text as it is and taking דַעַת as a second infinitive (since "knowing knowledge" is redundant), there are two primary syntactic interpretations. First, both infinitives can be taken together as the compound complement of the single preposition ל (this is not usual, but it does occur; WO §11.4.2a calls this "preposition override"). Thus understood, the clause means "I set my לב to know wisdom and (to) know blindness and folly." In this view Qoheleth has tasked his לב to experience these things while he, himself, observes it all and draws his conclusions. The second syntactic option is to take the second infinitive as a left-dislocated constituent in a second clause, resumed by זה, "knowing blindness and folly—I realized that also this was wind-chasing." Either option is grammatical; however, the second better fits the collaborative "I-and-my-לב" framework, although it admittedly reads against the Masoretic טעמים. (For other solutions, some involving emendation and some not, see, among others, Seow 1997: 124–26; Krüger 56–57.)

הוֹלֵלוֹת. This noun occurs here and in 2:12, 7:25, and 9:3. The similar form הוֹלֵלוּת occurs in 10:13. The latter form, with the וּת- ending, is clearly an abstract noun, "foolishness, blindness." Assuming that both forms are simply variants of the same word (an assumption that many share, as evidenced by translations), it is unclear why the וֹת- ending is used in four cases and the וּת- ending in one. Since an abstract meaning fits the context and matches the semantics and/or morphology of the surrounding nouns, it may be that the וֹת- form has been pointed incorrectly (so Goldman conjectures in *Biblia Hebraica Quinta* [2004]; see also Barton, 87 [for rebuttal of Goldman, see Meade and Gentry]) or that the morphologically fp ending has been used for the abstract (GKC §122p, q, s; WO §6.4.2b, 7.4.2; JM §88Mk).

יָדַעְתִּי שֶׁגַּם־זֶה הוּא רַעְיוֹן רוּחַ. *Qatal* 1cs Qal √ידע. The Qal of ידע is bivalent, with the nominalized clause שֶׁגַּם־זֶה הוּא רַעְיוֹן רוּחַ as the complement. In the context יָדַעְתִּי represents the intellectual result of Qoheleth's experiment: he realized the absurdity (according to him) of the pursuit of wisdom (דעת הוללות ושכלות). As such, we understand this instance of the *qatal* as an inchoative use of the perfective with the stative verb: "I came to know" (see WO §30.2.1b). Here גם is a focus marker, highlighting the fact that, among the set of options that Qoheleth and his לֵב are investigating, he has concluded that דעת הוללות ושׂכלות is ultimately useless (רעיון רוח). See comment on גם in 1:11.

זֶה הוּא רַעְיוֹן רוּחַ. There are two equally likely syntactic analyses for this clause. First, this could be a copular clause in which the pronoun הוא serves as the copula. Use of the pronominal copula was uncommon but not rare and existed throughout ancient Hebrew (see Holmstedt and Jones 2014). Second, זה could be left-dislocated and resumed by הוא, which is then the syntactic subject of the null copula clause. The pragmatic function of left-dislocation is to mark the dislocated constituent for topic (due to the position of זה) *and* focus (due to the presence of the resumptive הוא). The effect would be to direct the listener/reader's attention to זה (actually, the referent it points to—knowing foolishness) and contrasting it with alternatives (e.g., "knowing wisdom"): "I came to know that also *this—it* is wind-chasing." Both analyses make good sense: the dislocation option fits the context while the copular option fits the prosody suggested by the Masoretic טעמים (if they had read זה as dislocated, it would have had a disjunctive accent). The only feature weighing against the dislocation analysis of זה is the fact that it would be the second dislocation in the same clause since we take דעת to be a dislocated infinitive clause; such an analysis creates a highly complex structure, perhaps one too complex for processing. Based on the unlikelihood of such a complex structure, we opt for the simpler copular option. On רעיון, see comment on רעות in v. 14.

1:18   כִּי בְּרֹב חָכְמָה רָב־כָּעַס וְיוֹסִיף דַּעַת יוֹסִיף מַכְאוֹב:

Because in an abundance of wisdom exists an abundance of vexation, and he who will add knowledge will add pain.

Qoheleth makes this assertion, which is a generality (although one senses that it is grounded in his long-term observations), as support for the conclusion he draws at the end of v. 17.

כִּי בְּרֹב חָכְמָה רָב־כָּעַס. A null copula clause within a כי motive clause that is subordinate to the verb ידעתי of v. 17. The salient syntactic question concerns the identification of the subject and the copular complement—which constituent is which? At first glance, it may seem that a PP cannot be the subject of a copular clause, and indeed, it is rare (most examples are with ל + infinitive PPs; see WO §36.2.3b). This might suggest that רב כעס "abundance of vexation" is the subject and that the word order reflects the topic- or focus-fronting of the copular complement ברב חכמה. In fact, this analysis is contextually felicitous, since as a topic the PP complement would orient the listener/reader to what previously invoked item (in this case, חכמה within the PP) will now be discussed. Or, as a focus item, the vexing nature of חכמה is surprising; the audience no doubt expects the opposite, that *folly* leads to vexation. And yet, the identification of רב כעס as the subject remains suspect. The informational link to the previous verse is חכמה not כעס. One expects, then, that the informational link is also the entity about which something would be predicated (= subject). If it were the subject, ברב חכמה would likely also still be a topic, precisely due to its role as an informational linking item. In the end there is no clear way to determine which of the two analyses is more accurate. Until further research has been done on the acceptability of PPs in general serving as the syntactic subject, we default to the expected grammar and assign the status of subject to the NP רב כעס.

וְיוֹסִיף דַּעַת יוֹסִיף מַכְאוֹב. *Yiqtol* 3ms Hiph √יסף. This second clause falls within the scope of the initial כי and as such is a second supporting assertion. The first verb lies within a null-head, unmarked relative clause, "(the one) (who) adds knowledge," that serves as the syntactic subject. The second verb is the main verb of the clause with מכאוב as its complement. Typically the participle appears in such null-head relatives, and so we expect some semantic significance to the choice of *yiqtol*: by using the *yiqtol* forms, Qoheleth casts this proverb in the form of a prediction of what will happen if/when one pursues knowledge—essentially as a warning to the reader borne by his own experience (on the interpretation of the verbal conjugations in proverbial statements, see Cook 2005 and Introduction §5).

2:1-11 Qoheleth and His לב Investigate Pleasure and Toil

אָמַ֥רְתִּי אֲנִ֖י בְּלִבִּ֑י לְכָה־נָּ֛א אֲנַסְּכָ֥ה בְשִׂמְחָ֖ה וּרְאֵ֣ה   2:1
בְט֑וֹב וְהִנֵּ֥ה גַם־ה֖וּא הָֽבֶל׃

I said, I with my לב*: Come, I will make you experienced in joy; look upon (what is) good. See even this is a* הבל*!*

This verse is the only time that Qoheleth directly addresses his לֵב. Qoheleth does not do so anywhere else in the book (the second-person address in the remainder of the book is apparently aimed at Qoheleth's audience), but he does admit in 2:20 that he tried to influence the conclusions that his לֵב was drawing.

אָמַרְתִּי אֲנִי בְּלִבִּי. *Qatal* 1cs Qal √אמר. The syntactic subject is null, and the conjoined phrase אני בלבי is a verbal adjunct in the form of a null-verb small clause, lit. "I (saying) with my לֵב." On the "I-and-my-לֵב" framework, see Introduction §3 and comments on 1:16. Within the small clause, the PP בלבי is an adjunct to the elliptical form of אמר. Elsewhere בֿ-PPs are spatial or temporal adjuncts when collocated with the verb אמר. Qoheleth, however, is manipulating the idiom אמר בלב, and so the nuance of the preposition must be taken from context. Here in 2:1 and also in 2:15; 3:17, 18, the preposition בֿ marks the goal ("with X") or the indirect object ("to X") of the speech activity. The complement of the speech verb אמר is the quotation that follows, signaled by the change of verb (imperative) and addressee (second person).

לְכָה־נָּא. Impv ms Qal √הלך. Note the ה suffixed to the imperative: this is not a feature of the imperative paradigm, but a suffix added when the action of the verb is directed toward the speaker or when the action is simply for the speaker's benefit (Fassberg; similarly, Shulman). Note the second-person address directed at Qoheleth's לֵב as a call to action (see Introduction §3).

אֲנַסְּכָה בְשִׂמְחָה. *Jussive* 1cs Piel √נסה + 2ms clitic pronoun. The jussive (a term we apply to volitional prefixed forms for all persons) regularly expresses primarily commands and the speaker's will; here Qoheleth summons his לֵב and announces his intent toward his לֵב. The fully spelled clitic pronoun attached to the verb, which refers to his לֵב, is the complement of the verb, which is a bivalent Piel. In the collocation נסה ב, the verb usually means "test, examine" (e.g., 7:23), and the PP typically functions as an adjunct of means (e.g., God tests Israel by means of the Canaanites in Judg 2:22; 3:1, 4). However, this makes poor sense here (i.e., in what way is Qoheleth "testing" his mind?); rather, in keeping with a very few other instances (e.g., Exod 20:20; 1 Sam 17:39) the meaning here is "make someone undergo an experience" (a meaning that fits well within Piel's typical "factitive" sense). When the collocation נסה ב has this sense, the בֿ-PP is the second complement of the verb, expressing what the first complement experiences or is well experienced in ("I will have you experience/try out joy"). This sense is consistent with Qoheleth's concern to examine thoroughly various areas and make authoritative judgments on them.

וּרְאֵה בְטוֹב. Impv ms Qal √ראה. The ב-PP is the complement of the verb. The collocation ב + ראה here and elsewhere has the nuance "to take a look at, examine X" (BDB, HALOT, DCH, s.v.). The sequence of directive-volitive verbs expresses a complex of different nuances: the initial imperative serves as a call to action (almost like an interjection); the first-person jussive expresses Qoheleth's intent toward his לב, and the second imperative provides direction to the לב for fulfilling the intent expressed in the preceding first-person form.

וְהִנֵּה גַם־הוּא הָבֶל. A null copula clause, with an initial deictic exclamative, which focuses the reader's attention "with a sense of discovery" (Andersen, 94). The focus adverb גם is also used (see comment at 1:11); it contrasts the assertion that הוא (= "what is good") is a הבל, and not something else that the reader might expect to be absurd.

לִשְׂחוֹק אָמַרְתִּי מְהוֹלָל וּלְשִׂמְחָה מַה־זֶּה עֹשָׂה:　2:2

Regarding "laughing," I said, "Senseless!" Regarding happiness—what does it accomplish?

Qoheleth's description of his view during the experiment reflects the cynical and utilitarian attitude he had adopted. Laughter and happiness for him had no value since there was no observable benefit.

לִשְׂחוֹק אָמַרְתִּי מְהוֹלָל. *Qatal* 1cs Qal √אמר. The noun שׂחוק is classified as a noun by the lexica (BDB, HALOT, DCH); however, it is morphologically identical to a Qal infinitive. This example illustrates that the line between an action noun, such as "laughing," and the Hebrew infinitive, which is often gerund-like (WO §36.2.1c), is frequently so blurred as to be indiscernible. The ל-PP is an adjunct to the verb אמרתי, specifying what Qoheleth is talking about (on the ל of "specification," see WO §11.2.10d, g). The fronted position in the clause suggests that it has been raised as the topic, orienting the reader/listener to what is being discussed. The subject of אמרתי is null and the complement is the one-word direct speech מהלל.

מְהוֹלָל. Participle ms Polal √הלל (HALOT, s.v. הלל III). This single word direct speech functions as an exclamation, but syntactically it is a null-subject, null-copula clause: "(It) (is) senseless!"

וּלְשִׂמְחָה מַה־זֹּה עֹשָׂה. Participle fs Qal √עשׂה. As with the preceding clause, the initial ל-PP is a topic phrase that orients the reader/lis-
tener to the change from שׂחוק to שׂמחה. There are two ways to analyze
the syntax of this clause. First, one might consider this topic phrase to be
not simply fronted but left-dislocated and resumed within the clause by
זה. Or, given the parallel sentence-initial ל-PPs in the two clauses, one
might also consider this second clause to contain an elliptical (or gapped)
verb אמרתי with a topic-fronted adjunct PP ולשׂמחה, "and regarding
happiness (I said) What does this accomplish?" The interrogative clause
מה זה עשׂה is literally "What this does?" (or, in decent English, "This
does what?"). Note that the participle expresses progressive aspect: "This
(is) doing what?" However, this sort of generic statement is typically
expressed in English by the general present tense. The question is, of
course, rhetorical since Qoheleth's clear intent is to assert that it is worth
little to nothing.

תַּרְתִּי בְלִבִּי לִמְשׁוֹךְ בַּיַּיִן אֶת־בְּשָׂרִי וְלִבִּי נֹהֵג   2:3
בַּחָכְמָה וְלֶאֱחֹז בְּסִכְלוּת עַד אֲשֶׁר־אֶרְאֶה אֵי־זֶה
טוֹב לִבְנֵי הָאָדָם אֲשֶׁר יַעֲשׂוּ תַּחַת הַשָּׁמַיִם מִסְפַּר
יְמֵי חַיֵּיהֶם׃

I set out, along with my לב, *to drag my flesh along with wine (though my*
לב *was leading by wisdom), and to grasp foolishness, until I might see which
is good for humans, which they might do under the heavens (for) the number
of the days of their life.*

This verse begins the description of Qoheleth's investigation into
pleasure, the verdict of which he has given in advance in v. 2. The main
focus is on what Qoheleth subjects his body to, inasmuch as his focus is
on material pleasures (e.g., he employs wine).

תַּרְתִּי בְלִבִּי לִמְשׁוֹךְ בַּיַּיִן אֶת־בְּשָׂרִי. *Qatal* 1cs Qal √תור, Inf
Constr Qal √משׁך. The first part of the verse presents a grammatical
and interpretive crux. The problems are (1) what it means to תור בלב,
(2) what the root משׁך means in the context, and (3) how to relate both
the infinitive phrase למשׁוך ביין את־בשׂרי and the following conjoined
participial clause ולבי נהג בחכמה back to the main clause headed by the
verb תרתי.

תַּרְתִּי בְלִבִּי. The collocation of תור and בלב is often taken as
another way to express mental activity: "Qoheleth is not examining
material pleasures so much as his responses to them. Hence he goes
about, meditates, *within* his heart" (Fox 1999: 177, emphasis in original). Thus, the PP בלבי is often read as the mental space, "within my
mind" (e.g., Crenshaw, 69, 77; Longman, 87, 89), or the mental means,
"with my mind" (see, e.g., Seow 1997: 126–27). Fox argues that תור +
infinitive is equivalent to סבב + infinitive (2:20; 7:25), "showing the
beginning or the next stage of Qoheleth's investigation, as he 'turns' or
'goes about' from one thing to another" (1999: 177). The heart is the
area within which Qoheleth pursues his exploration not its object. Seow,
in contrast, argues that the meaning "explore, search" for תור makes no
sense in the verse (although he does not give a good reason for this judgment); he instead turns to the Arabic cognate's meaning "to flow, run,
go about" and then suggests that the collocation תור בלב means roughly
the same thing as תור אחרי בלבב "to follow the heart" (Num 15:39).
Against both views, if Qoheleth treats his לב as his experiment partner,
as we propose, then the ב preposition indicates accompaniment (WO
§11.2.5d) not location or means, and the meaning of תור in this context
is the same meaning found elsewhere (esp. 1:13), "to spy out, explore"
(DCH, s.v.; cf. HALOT, s.v.). On the absence of the personal pronoun
אני with this verb, see Introduction §3, where we argue that after the first
instance of the "I-and-my-לב" construction in 1:16, Qoheleth repeats it
to remind his audience that the experiment was carried out by the twosome. When he does not want to emphasize that the pair were engaged
together, he omits the pronoun.

תַּרְתִּי. This verb usually selects an NP complement, often marked
with אֶת, and only rarely occurs with prepositional phrases. However,
in Ecclesiastes it appears with a variety of complements: עַל-PP in 1:13,
ל-PP infinitive clause in this verse, and with an NP in 7:25. See comments in 1:13. As the introduction to his encounter with pleasure,
Qoheleth reports that he and his לב "set out" to investigate it.

לִמְשׁוֹךְ בַּיַּיִן אֶת־בְּשָׂרִי. The verb משך means "to drag, pull,"
although HALOT (s.v.) and many commentators suggest that it connotes here "to revive." However, "revive" is not the meaning in any other
biblical context or stage of Hebrew, and "pull the body along by means
of wine" is not an opaque image: the body is unwilling and must be
coerced with spirits to continue in the path that Qoheleth's experiment

has dictated. The meaning of לִמְשׁוֹךְ is best kept to its attested range, "pull, drag, draw," rather than the guesses that are motivated by the context of this verse (besides "revive," others have suggested "tempt" [NJPS]; "cheer" [NRSV; Longman, 89, Provan, 65]; "stimulate" [Barton, 77]; "bathe" [Lohfink, 51]). After all, the image of "dragging" oneself to do something is transparent (at least, in English), and in the context of Qoheleth's experiment it suggests that he induced himself to follow paths that he suspected might result in less than desirable experiences, all for the sake of determining אֵי־זֶה טוֹב לִבְנֵי הָאָדָם אֲשֶׁר יַעֲשׂוּ. Since תור is always bivalent, the syntactic role of the לִמְשׁוֹךְ infinitive clause is complement, providing the content of the experiment along with the conjoined infinitive clause וְלֶאֱחֹז.

וְלִבִּי נֹהֵג בַּחָכְמָה. Participle ms Qal √נהג. The verb נהג appears bivalent in eighteen of its nineteen occurrences, usually with an NP complement, but twice with a בְּ-PP complement (Isa 11:6; 1 Chr 13:7). Given word order and the nonsensical nature of taking וְלִבִּי as an NP complement, there are only two options for analyzing this clause: either נהג is monovalent and the PP בחכמה is the means, "and my לב led by wisdom" or נהג is bivalent and the PP בחכמה is the complement, "and my לב led wisdom." In the context the bivalent analysis makes little sense; rather, the sense is that Qoheleth's לב took the lead in the joint experiment (see 2 Kgs 9:20; cf. Ben Sira 3:26 in which the implied complement is reflexive: "lead oneself"). This clause provides further description of the main activity of "spying out," but shifts from Qoheleth's strategy to his לב's strategy. As such, it constitutes a *parenthesis* (see, among others, Barton, 77; Lauha, 48; Crenshaw, 78) and functions as what grammars typically call a circumstantial clause (WO §37.6b, e; JM §159). Parentheses are constituents (phrases, clauses, or even compound clauses, like Gen 1:2) that interrupt the flow of an "argument," whether the argument is at its core chronological (i.e., a narrative) or logical (i.e., an exposition, as in, e.g., many psalms). A test for identifying clausal parentheses in Hebrew is to ask the following questions (with answers for לבי נהג בחכמה from 2:3 indicated in brackets; in Ecclesiastes, see also 2:21; 4:8; 6:12; 7:6; 8:11, 16). First, does the clause in question add information about a specific constituent in the preceding clause and yet not appear to be a relative clause? [A: *Yes*—לב.] Second, does the clause in question overlap with the preceding clause in many of the constituents but add, say, one new constituent? [A: *Yes—לב is in the preceding clause and* חכמה *is a thematic word in the book.*] Third, does the structure of the clause in question differ from the structure of the clause on either side of it, especially the preceding clause? [A: *Yes—a change from qatal perfective to participle.*] If one or more answers are positive, then the clause is likely a parenthesis.

וְלֶאֱחֹז בְּסִכְלוּת. Inf Constr Qal √אחז. The verb אחז "to seize, grasp, hold on to" in the Qal is bivalent and takes either an NP complement (e.g., Judg 1:6 וַיֹּאחֲזוּ אֹתוֹ) or ב-PP complement (as here). Seow (following Biblia Hebraica Stuttgartensia) emends to וְלֹא אָחַז "and did not take hold," which he argues is a good parallel to נהג בחכמה and removes the awkwardness of taking ולבי נהג בחכמה as a parenthetical comment (1997: 127). The MT as it stands produces good sense (so also Fox 1999: 179)—the ו, as a phrase-edge marker, signals here that the main clause has been resumed (see, e.g., Deut 4:42; JM §176bc and n. 2; Holmstedt 2014). As the complement of the verb תרתי (conjoined with the earlier complementary infinitive למשך), the content of this clause is critical to understanding the nature of Qoheleth's experiment: Qoheleth took one path and set his לב on another—and Qoheleth's path included trying to understand folly. In accordance with the division of labor in 1:17, he indicates that his לב continued to be a source of wisdom even while he used wine to induce himself (lit. his "flesh") to explore the darker side of life.

עַד אֲשֶׁר־אֶרְאֶה אֵי־זֶה טוֹב לִבְנֵי הָאָדָם. *Yiqtol* 1cs Qal √ראה. Governed by the *qatal* תרתי of the main clause, this *yiqtol* is used in the past time frame with irrealis, epistemic semantics, "I might see." As a whole, this is a PP with the complement of the preposition עד being a clause introduced by אשר functioning as a complementizer (rather than a relativizer). In syntactic situations like this, one might be tempted to view the structure as that of a null-head relative clause where the null constituent is the complement of עד and is modified by the relative clause: "until (the time/eventuality) that I see … ." However, an important feature of relative clauses is that the head (even if null) must have an internal, relativized syntactic function within the relative clause in the form of overt or covert resumption (as well as an external function in the main clause). When there is no appropriate syntactic role *within* the relative clause for a putative null head, it is more likely that the אשר or שׁ does not introduce a relative clause but a complement clause (on this basic criterion, see Holmstedt 2001: 5; for further development, see Holmstedt 2013c: 293–94; 2016: 119–28; Marshall). Such an analysis is bolstered by the fact that in BH we also see other types of clausal complements of the preposition עַד, where analyzing the embedded clause as a null-head relative clause is not possible: an אִם-clause (Gen 24:19 "until they finish drinking"), a כִּי-clauses (Gen 26:13 "until he became very wealthy"; Gen 49:10 "until he/it comes"), and a nominalized infinitive clause (1 Kgs 18:29 "until the going-up of the offering"). The bivalent verb אראה takes as its complement the indirect speech/interrogative clause begun by אי (see WO §18.4a–b). The interrogative אי primarily presents a locative question: "Where?" But its use with the demonstrative זה in constructions like אֵי־מִזֶּה עִיר אָתָּה "where are you from, city-wise?" (1 Sam 15:2) may have led to the grammaticalization of אי with זה as "which," as in "which city?" We see this latter use only in this verse and 11:6, suggesting that it is a late development. In this case the אי זה modifies a null constituent, which we can contextually reconstruct as "path, way," while the complement of the null copula is the adjective טוב: "until I see which (path) is good for humans … ."

אֲשֶׁר יַעֲשׂוּ תַּחַת הַשָּׁמַיִם מִסְפַּר יְמֵי חַיֵּיהֶם. *Yiqtol* 3mp Qal √עשה. This relative clause modifies the contextually reconstructed item with אי זה, "path, way." The relative clarifies the force of Qoheleth's statement: he and his לב investigated two paths to figure out which was better for humans "to do under the heavens, all the days of their life." Semantically, the *yiqtol* is consonant with the irrealis, epistemic sense of the verb in the main clause. Grammatically, the relative clause could have as the relative head either בני האדם or the null constituent associated with אי זה. Contextually, we prefer the latter. This is supported by a feature of relativization: the verb יעשו within the relative is bivalent and so requires a complement. The valency would be filled by a null complement that refers back to the null head "path, way"; it would not be fulfilled by anything if the head were בני אדם. Also note that the NP מספר ימי חייהם is an adverbial (temporal) adjunct to the verb; the lack of the preposition on this phrase illustrates that Hebrew verbs do not require that adjuncts be explicitly marked, such as with a preposition or by having an overt adverbial form (see WO §10.2.2; JM §126a).

2:4   הִגְדַּלְתִּי מַעֲשָׂי בָּנִיתִי לִי בָּתִּים נָטַעְתִּי לִי כְּרָמִים:

I made my deeds great; I built houses for myself; I planted vineyards for myself.

In vv. 4-8 Qoheleth lists examples of how he carried out his experiment by amassing great things for himself. It is not entirely clear which "path" these things represent, but it is likely that they reflect סכלות, given Qoheleth's retrospective position while reporting. The "report" form Qoheleth uses is distinct from a "narrative," in which events are recounted in the order in which they occur. In contrast, the report makes no assumption of the order in which Qoheleth carried out his accomplishments, though some logically follow each other, such as making pools (v. 6) to water the gardens (v. 5). This report form explains the avoidance of the past narrative *wayyiqtol* form in preference for realis perfective *qatal* in this passage (see Introduction §5).

הִגְדַּלְתִּי מַעֲשָׂי. *Qatal* 1cs Hiph √גדל. The Hiphil of גדל is bivalent; the NP מעשׂי is the complement. This first clause does not describe anything in particular, but is a general preview statement. With גדלתי of the same root in v. 9, the verbs signals an inclusio for this part of Qoheleth's report.

בָּנִיתִי לִי בָּתִּים נָטַעְתִּי לִי כְּרָמִים. *Qatal* 1cs Qal √בנה and √נטע. Both verbs in the Qal are bivalent, and the NPs בתים and כרמים fulfill the valency of the respective verbs. The PP לי in both clauses is an adjunct indicating the beneficiary of the action (WO §11.2.10d).

עָשִׂיתִי לִי גַּנּוֹת וּפַרְדֵּסִים וְנָטַעְתִּי בָהֶם עֵץ כָּל־   2:5
פֶּרִי:

I made gardens, that is, royal gardens, for myself and I planted a tree of every fruit in them.

עָשִׂיתִי לִי גַּנּוֹת וּפַרְדֵּסִים. *Qatal* 1cs Qal √עשׂה. The PP לי indicates the beneficiary (WO §11.2.10d), and the NP גנות is the verbal complement of the bivalent עשׂיתי. The NP פרדסים, which is in apposition to גנות to clarify the precise type Qoheleth says he made, is one of two Persian words used in the book (פתגם is the other, in 8:11). While most translations render פרדס with some version of "park," or "orchard," the פרדס refers specifically to a cultivated enclosure within the royal grounds (see esp. Subtelny, 15–21). Interestingly, while gardens were intimately associated with kingship during the Assyrian empire, the Achaemenids, "for whom the notion of the garden as royal space was a central feature of their imperial ideology, linked the garden even more closely with the palace institution by integrating it architecturally in a single complex surrounded by a walled enclosure" (Subtelny, 18). Thus, the mention of making גנות ופרדסים is an explicitly royal claim. This fits the "royal resumé" style that Qoheleth is imitating in this section, vv. 4-11 (Seow 1997: 128).

וְנָטַעְתִּי בָהֶם עֵץ כָּל־פֶּרִי. *Qatal* 1cs Qal √נטע. The complex NP עץ כל פרי is the complement of the bivalent נטע and the PP בהם is a locative adjunct. That בהם is not a second complement (and thus that נטע is not trivalent) is suggested by the absence of a locative PP in the previous occurrence of the verb in v. 4. The claim that Qoheleth planted "a tree of every fruit" underscores the breadth of Qoheleth's accomplishment: in his gardens he experienced fruit of every sort. While this suggests a royal exaggeration, it may also point to a greater brag by intentionally hearkening back to Genesis 1 and 2, where another "planter" established a garden with fruit trees.

2:6   עָשִׂיתִי לִי בְּרֵכוֹת מָיִם לְהַשְׁקוֹת מֵהֶם יַעַר צוֹמֵחַ
       עֵצִים:

I made water pools for myself to water from them a growing tree forest.

עָשִׂיתִי לִי בְּרֵכוֹת מָיִם. *Qatal* 1cs Qal √עשה. This clause exhibits the same syntax as the use of עשיתי in v. 5. Note the placement of the complement ברכות—after the adjunct PP. All things being equal, the complement precedes any verbal adjuncts. What triggers the order in this example (and many like it) is the "light" nature of לי. It is a consistent pattern that light PPs (whether complement or adjunct) attach to the verb and raise with it in the course of the clause's development.

לְהַשְׁקוֹת מֵהֶם יַעַר צוֹמֵחַ עֵצִים. Inf Constr Hiph √שקה. The PP-infinitival clause is an adjunct to the verb עשיתי, indicating the purpose of the water pools. The PP מהם reflects the use of the preposition מן to indicate the means of an action (WO §11.2.11d). The position of the adjunct מהם mirrors the PP לי in the main clause (see above). Note the use of the mp suffix הֶם in the PP מֵהֶם for the fp antecedent ברכות. Such apparent lack of agreement occurs often with nouns that may be morphologically one gender but considered the other gender for agreement purposes (e.g,. אבות "fathers"). While the singular בְּרֵכָה is elsewhere feminine for adjectival agreement (see 2 Kgs 18:17; Isa 7:3; 22:9, 11; 36:2; Neh 3:16), the example here is one of only two plural occurrences in the Hebrew Bible (the other is in Song 7:5), and apparently ברכות was masculine in this author's grammar.

יַעַר צוֹמֵחַ עֵצִים. Participle ms Qal √צמח. The NP יער is the head of an unmarked participial relative clause, a very common construction. Within the relative clause, the subject is null and coreferential with the head יער and the verb צומח is monovalent (as it is always in the Qal), which means that it cannot take עצים as a complement (contra Gordis 1955: 207, who calls it as "accusative of specification"). Rather, the NP עצים is either an adjunct "tree-ish" or in apposition to יער; the latter option makes better sense: "a growing forest, (that is) trees." For other examples of an appositive separated from its anchor by other constituents, see Gen 48:15-16; Lev 2:9; 6:13; 14:24; Num 17:17; Deut 1:15; 2:10; Josh 22:10; 2 Kgs 22:16; Esth 9:30-31 (Holmstedt and Jones 2016).

2:7 קָנִיתִי עֲבָדִים וּשְׁפָחוֹת וּבְנֵי־בַיִת הָיָה לִי גַּם
מִקְנֶה בָקָר וָצֹאן הַרְבֵּה הָיָה לִי מִכֹּל שֶׁהָיוּ לְפָנַי
בִּירוּשָׁלָ͏ִם:

I acquired male and female servants, and home-born slaves belonged to me, also much livestock—cattle and sheep—belonged to me, more than all who were before me in Jerusalem.

קָנִיתִי עֲבָדִים וּשְׁפָחוֹת. *Qatal* 1cs Qal √קנה. The verb קנה "to acquire, create" is bivalent here with a null-subject and the compound NP complement עבדים ושפחות.

וּבְנֵי־בַיִת הָיָה לִי. *Qatal* 3ms Qal √היה. The copular verb היה is bivalent, taking a syntactic subject and a complement (here a PP לי). The ostensible subject, the mp head of the bound phrase בני, disagrees in number with the singular verb (if it were the subject, we would expect a plural verb form הָיוּ). Although there are cases of apparent lack of subject-verb agreement (GKC §145u; JM §150; see Holmstedt 2009c), it is extremely rare with subject-verb order. In this case it is likely that the syntactic subject is either formally (i.e., grammatically) or perceived to be (i.e., a "mistake" by the narrator) the clitic host NP בית, which is masculine singular. The Masoretic טעמים suggest by the placement of the אַתְנָחְתָּא that the היה clause ends with לי and גם initiates a new clause.

גַּם מִקְנֶה בָקָר וָצֹאן הַרְבֵּה הָיָה לִי מִכֹּל שֶׁהָיוּ לְפָנַי בִּירוּשָׁלָ͏ִם. *Qatal* 3ms and 3cp Qal √היה. The גם is here an additive conjunction, indicating that the following information (מקנה בקר וצאן) should be added to the previous statement (MNK §41.4.5.2). The compound NP בקר וצאן is an appositive to מקנה, indicating precisely what type of live-stock Qoheleth acquired. The adverb הרבה (see comment on הרבה in 1:16) is adjunct to the NP מקנה. The מן-PP following the verb היה and its complement לי is not a verbal adjunct but an adverb-internal adjunct to the adverb הרבה (see also 2 Sam 1:4; Jonah 4:11; 2 Chr 25:7), speci-fying that the quantity indicated by הרבה is grounded in a comparison with what other rulers in Jerusalem had acquired ("the things I had were much more than the things they had"). The distance between הרבה and its PP adjunct represents the extraposition of the adjunct (similar to HNPS; see also 2:17; 3:14, 22; 7:18, 20, 26; 9:11, 14, 15; 11:7): the מן-PP is a large constituent and such "heavy" constituents are often posi-tioned further down in a clause in order to avoid large (and thus hard-to-process) constituents in the subject position (as here). See Holmstedt 2014 on extraposition and related phenomena. In כל שהיו the plural verb suggests that the quantifier כל is resolved as a plural entity.

כָּנַסְתִּי לִי גַּם־כֶּסֶף וְזָהָב וּסְגֻלַּת מְלָכִים וְהַמְּדִינוֹת   2:8
עָשִׂיתִי לִי שָׁרִים וְשָׁרוֹת וְתַעֲנוּגֹת בְּנֵי הָאָדָם שִׁדָּה
וְשִׁדּוֹת:

I gathered for myself both silver and gold and royal and provincial property; I appointed for myself male and female singers and the delights of humans, many concubines.

כָּנַסְתִּי לִי גַּם־כֶּסֶף וְזָהָב וּסְגֻלַּת מְלָכִים וְהַמְּדִינוֹת. *Qatal* 1cs Qal √כנס. Like עשיתי in vv. 5-6, כנסתי is bivalent, with a null-subject and a compound NP complement; the PP לי indicates the beneficiary of the action (see WO §11.2.10d). The גם before the compound NP works with the ו (or sometimes with another גם) to indicate that the (usually two, here three) listed entities are all equally important (MNK §41.4.5.2ii); it is similar to the correlative conjunction pair "both ... and" in English. In the phrase וסגלת מלכים והמדינות, the first noun, סגלה refers to "private property" (HALOT, s.v.), and is bound to a compound clitic host מלכים והמדינות "kings and the provinces" (so Fox 1999:175; see WO §9.3b for compound clitic hosts). We understand the two nouns to modify the clitic head in an adjectival fashion, hence "royal and provincial" (WO §9.5.3). Seow notes that many commentators have problems with a compound in which one item, מלכים, lacks the article while the second, המדינות, has the article; in response, Seow takes המדינות as a concomitant phrase, "along with the provinces" (1997: 130). Both options are grammatically legitimate and there is no clear method for determining one to be more likely than the other.

Qatal. עָשִׂיתִי לִי שָׁרִים וְשָׁרוֹת וְתַעֲנוּגֹת בְּנֵי הָאָדָם שִׁדָּה וְשִׁדּוֹת 1cs Qal √עשׂה. See vv. 5-6 for the basic syntax of this clause. The connotation of תענוגת in this clause and the basic meaning of the lexical crux שדה ושדות continue to confound commentators. There are two central proposals. Some commentators take the תענוגת to have sexual connotations with the appositional שדה ושדות making the reference explicitly; thus, they assert that it is about concubines (derived from שדד "seize," as in "ones seized in war" > concubines—so Ibn Ezra and Ginsburg according to Seow [1997: 131]; or derived from שַׁד "breast" and by synecdoche [part for whole] > concubines—so Gordis [1968: 218–19]; see also Whitley, 21–22). Others, like Seow, dispute the concubine interpretation and take תענוגות to refer to "treasures" and שדה ושדות to refer to "chest, box," to hold the treasure, per rabbinic Hebrew (Jastrow, 1558). We can offer no definitive proof in favor of one or the other of the two proposals, although the concubine interpretation seems to fit well with the "human" acquisitions שרים ושרות and the larger context of trying to "seize foolishness" (2:3). The singular followed by a plural appositive of the same word is used elsewhere (דור דורים in Pss 72:5; 102:25) as an expression of multiplicity/plurality (Fox 1999: 180; Seow 1997: 131–32).

2:9   וְגָדַלְתִּי וְהוֹסַפְתִּי מִכֹּל שֶׁהָיָה לְפָנַי בִּירוּשָׁלָ͏ִם אַף חָכְמָתִי עָמְדָה לִּי:

I became greater and added more (things) than anyone who was before me in Jerusalem; even my wisdom stood by me.

Having listed some of his specific accomplishments (vv. 4-8), Qoheleth now engages in a more general reflection on what he has done (v. 9), leading to concluding statements from his לב and himself regarding the "experiment" (vv. 10-11).

גדל√ Qal 1cs *Qatal*. וְגָדַלְתִּי וְהוֹסַפְתִּי מִכֹּל שֶׁהָיָה לְפָנַי בִּירוּשָׁלָ͏ִם and Hiph √יסף, 3ms Qal √היה. Note the parallel with the same root collocation גדל and יסף in 1:16; here גדל is in the Qal whereas in 1:16, it was in the Hiphil (also in 2:4). Also, here the Hiphil of יסף lacks an overt complement; the null complement must be reconstructed from the context. The content and goal of vv. 4-8 suggest that Qoheleth is summarizing his acquisition of *things*; i.e., delights of this world, what Qoheleth judges to be "foolishness" (2:3). The head of the comparative מִן-PP (MNK §39.14.8; WO §11.2.11e.3) is not immediately clear: is it the verbal idea of "becoming greater and adding" (and so a verbal adjunct) or is it specifically the covert complement "things" (and so an NP-internal adjunct)? The context does not shed much light on the decision since it is equally believable that Qoheleth is contrasting his activity or the amount of his acquisitions. The only feature pointing in the direction of the verbal adjunct analysis is that the head of a comparative מִן-PP should be overt (note, in contrast, that the head of a partitive מִן-PP, "some of," is often covert). Therefore, we prefer to take the מִן-PP as a verbal adjunct modifying both verbs together (i.e., גדלתי והוספתי is a compound verb that together serve as the object of comparison). Alternatively, Fox takes הוספתי to be a finite verb used as an auxiliary, i.e., adverbially modifying גדלתי (1999: 180). Elsewhere the verb יסף in the Hiphil is used as an adverb "still, again, continually, increasingly" (WO §39.3.1b; JM §177b, c; DCH, s.v. Hiphil 2 "as auxiliary verb"), but the notion that "I increasingly grew more than …" or "I became increasingly greater than …" does not fit the context. Qoheleth's comparisons never seem to be "running" comparisons, as "to become increasingly greater" would be; rather, Qoheleth makes his comparative statements as if the objects or qualities being compared were complete and well in the past. In the relative clause שהיה לפני בירושלם, the null-subject is coreferential with the quantifier head כל; the complement of the copular verb is the closer PP לפני, and the PP בירושלם is a verbal adjunct of place.

אַף חָכְמָתִי עָמְדָה לִּי. *Qatal* 3fs Qal √עמד. Note the subject-verb order. The PP לִי is the complement of bivalent עמד; although the verb can be monovalent with the sense of "stand up, take a stand, stand still, endure" (2 Kgs 10:19; Isa 50:8; Josh 10:13; Exod 18:23), when it involves the notion of standing or remaining *in relation to places or people* (the vast majority of cases), a locative modifier is the complement (note that a locative complement appears to be optional, since in Exod 9:28 the locative complement is covert but readily recoverable from the context: "you will no longer stand [here] = you will no longer stay"). There are two questions in the interpretation of this phrase: (1) What does אף mean?; and

(2) What is the force of עמד ל? The adverb אף denotes that the clause or item that it modifies "adds" information related to the preceding. In some cases it is hardly discernible from ו (WO §39.3.4d), while in other cases it indicates that what is added confirms what has been stated in the preceding clause (i.e., "also") or is contrary to expectations given what the preceding clause asserted (i.e. "even") (MNK §41.4.3). Is Qoheleth, then, asserting something normal and expected—that his wisdom was with him during his acquisition phase? Or is he pointing out that, since his acquisition phase represented the epitome of סכלות, it is surprising that his wisdom stuck by him? Before any judgment can be made, it is necessary to consider עמדה לי. Typically the collocation used for the idiom "to stand by someone" is עמד על (see, e.g., Dan 1:4), whereas עמד ל means "to wait for someone/thing" (see, e.g., 1 Kgs 20:38) or "to attend to, serve someone." The issue here is whether Qoheleth used the collocation to say that his (personified?) חכמה (analogous to his לב, or something quite different?) waited for him while he pursued all these worldly delights (which would go with אף as "even"), or that his חכמה stood firm by him during it all (which would seem to fit אף as "also"). Seow takes the phrase to mean that his חכמה served him well during his experiences (1997: 132), and Fox takes it to mean that his חכמה did not desert him during the experience but served him well (1999: 180). We find no way to make a clear judgment on the meaning; the grammar is ambiguous. Since we understand Qoheleth to recognize that his past acquisitions represent folly and not wisdom, we tentatively suggest the contrary-to-expectation approach: even his wisdom waited patiently while he pursued such folly.

2:10   וְכֹל אֲשֶׁר שָׁאֲלוּ עֵינַי לֹא אָצַלְתִּי מֵהֶם לֹא־מָנַעְתִּי
אֶת־לִבִּי מִכָּל־שִׂמְחָה כִּי־לִבִּי שָׂמֵחַ מִכָּל־עֲמָלִי
וְזֶה־הָיָה חֶלְקִי מִכָּל־עֲמָלִי:

All (the things) that my eyes desired I did not withhold from them; I did not withhold my לב from any joy because my לב was happy from all my toil—and this was my share from all my toil.

וְכֹל אֲשֶׁר שָׁאֲלוּ עֵינַי לֹא אָצַלְתִּי מֵהֶם. *Qatal* 3cp Qal √שאל; *qatal* 1cs Qal √אצל. There are two analyses of the syntax of this clause that strike us as equally legitimate. On the one hand, כל אשר שאלו עיני may be taken as the fronted complement of the bivalent verb אצלתי, as we have translated: "all (the things) that my eyes desired I did not withhold from them." On the other hand, it is possible to take כל אשר שאלו עיני as a left-dislocated constituent, resumed by the 3mp clitic pronoun in the partitive PP מהם: "all (the things) that my eyes desired—I did not withhold (any of) them" (on the partitive מן, see WO §11.2.11e). Note the verb-subject order within the relative: the אשר has triggered inversion from subject-verb to verb-subject. The sense of the clause is that Qoheleth claims not to have set aside/reserved for later anything that his eyes desired. Rather, he indulged himself with everything that looked good.

לֹא־מָנַעְתִּי אֶת־לִבִּי מִכָּל־שִׂמְחָה. *Qatal* 1cs Qal √מנע. The verb מנע is trivalent, typically taking an NP complement indicating the patient (*what* or *who* is being withheld or restrained) and a מן-PP complement indicating the denied goal (e.g., Gen 30:2; Num 24:11; 1 Sam 25:26, 34; 2 Sam 13:13; Jer 2:25; 5:25; 31:16; 42:4; 48:10; Amos 4:7; Job 22:7; 31:16; Prov 1:15; 3:27; 23:13; 30:7; Neh 9:20). Here, as in the first clause, Qoheleth indicates that he did not withhold any joy from his לב. That is, he and his experiment partner enjoyed themselves fully.

כִּי־לִבִּי שָׂמֵחַ מִכָּל־עֲמָלִי. The כי anchors this clause to the previous clause and provides a motivation for the claim: this is at least one of the reasons why Qoheleth did not deny his לב any joy. We take the form שָׂמֵחַ to be an adjective functioning as the complement of a null copula clause with לבי as subject. Note, however, that the vowel pattern is also possible for the *qatal* 3ms of the stative verb שמח (which is how the Septuagint translator seems to have understood the word). The מן-PP is an adjunct of cause (WO §11.2.11d), providing the reason for the assertion that the heart was happy. The noun עמל, as Fox notes, can refer either "to the immediate source of pleasure, namely Qoheleth's wealth, or to the farther source, namely his toil" (1999: 180). We have translated as "toil" throughout for consistency, though often "acquisition(s)" might better communicate the intended nuance. This statement makes complete sense only within the "I-and-my-לב" framework: the two paths each partner takes result in different conclusions—the לב enjoys Qoheleth's עמל, even though Qoheleth hates it (2:18).

וְזֶה־הָיָה חֶלְקִי מִכָּל־עֲמָלִי. *Qatal* 3ms Qal √היה. The deictic anaphor זה, which is the subject of the clause, points back to something in the preceding clause (the main clause or perhaps just the subordinate כי clause) that Qoheleth identifies, by the copula היה, as his "share" (HALOT, s.v.). The NP-internal מן-PP is an adjunct indicating the source or origin of "my share" (WO §11.2.11d). Given what he says elsewhere about enjoyment of one's toil and one's share (i.e., 3:22; 5:18; 9:9; 11:2), Qoheleth passes judgment on what all his labor is worth, what he "gains" of any value from it: to wit, some joy in it.

וּפָנִיתִי אֲנִי בְּכָל־מַעֲשַׂי שֶׁעָשׂוּ יָדַי וּבֶעָמָל   2:11
שֶׁעָמַלְתִּי לַעֲשׂוֹת וְהִנֵּה הַכֹּל הֶבֶל וּרְעוּת רוּחַ וְאֵין
יִתְרוֹן תַּחַת הַשָּׁמֶשׁ׃

But (when) I faced, I, all my works that my hands had done and the toil that I had worked to do, See!—the whole (thing) was a הבל and chasing wind; there is no profit under the sun.

וּפָנִיתִי אֲנִי בְּכָל־מַעֲשַׂי ... וּבֶעָמָל. *Qatal* 1cs Qal √פנה. The presence of the pronoun אני and the apparent verb-subject (pronoun) order does not reflect typical Hebrew grammar; rather, it is connected to the "I-and-my-לב" strategy still in use at this point in the book. As we argued in Introduction §3, when Qoheleth uses just the 1cs pronoun, without any mention of his לב, he is explicitly signaling that the following action is what he did apart from whatever his לב was doing. Qoheleth is here contrasting his לב's evaluation of all his toil with his own. Syntactically, then, אני is not the subject, but a postverbal adjunct used as an interjection. The collocation of the verb פנה and the preposition ב is unusual; it happens only here and in Job 6:28. פנה is a bivalent verb, and everywhere it takes a ל or אל-PP complement to indicate the (mostly) locative goal of the "turning." Here and in Job 6:28, though, a meaning more closely connected to the associated noun פָּנֶה "face" is more felicitous: "to face." In both cases, the complement is a ב-PP; here there are two ב-PPs that combine as the single compound complement: בכל מעשי and בעמל (with their respective relative clauses).

בְּכָל־מַעֲשַׂי שֶׁעָשׂוּ יָדַי. *Qatal* 3cp Qal √עשׂה. The NP ידי is the overt subject of the verb עשׂו within the relative clause. The verb עשׂה is bivalent and here the required complement is the covert resumption of the relative head כל מעשׂי. (On the pattern of resumption within relative clauses, see Holmstedt 2016: 158–86.)

עָמָל שֶׁעָמַלְתִּי לַעֲשׂוֹת. *Qatal* 1cs Qal √עמל and Inf Constr Qal √עשׂה. As with the preceding relative clause, the relative head is resumed covertly (see 1:3). A slight grammatical twist is that the resumption does not occur with the bivalent main verb עמלתי in the relative clause but with the more deeply embedded verb לעשות. The infinitive clause satisfies the valency of עמלתי and the covert resumption satisfies the valency of לעשות.

וְהִגֵּה הַכֹּל הֶבֶל וּרְעוּת רוּחַ. The הנה is a deictic exclamative and draws attention to Qoheleth's repeated conclusion. The clause itself contains a null copula, with the subject הכל and the compound copular predicate הבל ורעות רוח. The past-tense interpretation derives from the past-time setting of Qoheleth's assessment on his work. By contrast, the following אין clause is best interpreted as a generic, universal statement; hence we use the general present to translate that clause. On the meaning of both הבל and רעות רוח, see comments at 1:2 and 1:14.

וְאֵין יִתְרוֹן תַּחַת הַשָּׁמֶשׁ. A null copula clause with אין as the negative, יתרון the subject, and תחת השמש the copular complement, lit. "profit does not (exist) under the sun." On אין clauses, see further 1:11. On יתרון, see comment on 1:3.

2:12-16 Qoheleth and His בל Investigate Wisdom and Folly

2:12   וּפָנִיתִי אֲנִי לִרְאוֹת חָכְמָה וְהוֹלֵלוֹת וְסִכְלוּת כִּי |
מֶה הָאָדָם שֶׁיָּבוֹא אַחֲרֵי הַמֶּלֶךְ אֵת אֲשֶׁר־כְּבָר
עָשׂוּהוּ:

I turned, I, to see wisdom and inanity and foolishness, that what the man who comes after the king (does)—(it) is (a thing) that they have already done!

In this transitional verse, Qoheleth characterizes his "experiment" as having been so thorough as to leave nothing "new" to be done—a thought that echoes the ideas from 1:9-11. In turn, this characterization lends authority to his statements that follow in the subsequent verses.

וּפָנִיתִי אֲנִי לִרְאוֹת חָכְמָה וְהוֹלֵלוֹת וְסִכְלוּת. *Qatal* 1cs Qal √פנה and Inf Constr Qal √ראה. On the postverbal אני, see the comment on v. 11. The complement of the bivalent פנה is the ל-PP infinitive clause לראות, which has the compound NP חכמה והוללות וסכלות as its complement. Gordis takes חכמה והוללות וסכלות as a complement clause with a null copula, with the ו ... ו structure as a *both-and*: "I saw that wisdom is both madness and folly" (1955: 210). While a complement clause may be unmarked (WO §38.8d; JM §157d), it is more often introduced by כִּי, אֲשֶׁר, or שֶׁ. Moreover, it is unclear why Qoheleth would equate חכמה with הוללות and סכלות. Instead, as we have argued with the "I-and-my-לֵב" framework, the goal of the experiment is to test all aspects of life.

.כִּי | מֶה הָאָדָם שֶׁיָּבוֹא אַחֲרֵי הַמֶּלֶךְ אֵת אֲשֶׁר־כְּבָר עָשׂוּהוּ

The second half of v. 12 has, as Gordis says, an ancient *crux interpretum* (1955: 210). Finding a contextually appropriate meaning in the text of the MT has generally defied interpreters, so that Fox concludes that v. 12b "makes no sense as it stands and is certainly corrupt" (1999: 182). For a concise survey of approaches to the text, including those that emend, see Longman, 96–97. We follow Gordis in keeping the text of the MT as it stands and similarly understand the sense to be that "Koheleth, in his assumed role of Solomon, wishes to assure the reader that he has experienced the ultimate in both wisdom and pleasure and that there is no need for any one else to repeat the experiment" (1955: 211). Below is our attempt at explaining the difficult Hebrew text as it stands.

כִּי | מֶה הָאָדָם. The כי introduces a second, appositive complement for the verb לראות; as such, it further specifies what Qoheleth means by observing wisdom and foolishness: a monarch should try to be productive in his reign, but the absurdity of life is that such activity has always been done and always will be done without observable progress (according to Qoheleth). The interrogative מה is the head of an unmarked relative clause, producing "what (that) the man ... does." It also appears to be left-dislocated and resumed by the null-subject of the next clause (see below). The problem with this analysis is that left-dislocation by definition requires overt resumption of the dislocated constituent. In a recent study Holmstedt (2014) proposes a separate category of "extreme fronting" for constructions like this (see also 3:13 and 4:11). Extreme fronting is similar to left-dislocation in that the initial constituent is marked as a topic; however, whereas in left-dislocation the resumption also provides for focus-marking within the clause proper, the extreme fronting does not.

הָאָדָם שֶׁיָּבוֹא אַחֲרֵי הַמֶּלֶךְ. *Yiqtol* 3ms Qal √בוא. The שׁ relative clause modifies האדם. Within the relative clause, the PP אחרי המלך is the complement for the verb יבוא, which is bivalent and takes a locative complement. Within the כי clause, there is no overt verb and a copula makes little contextual sense ("I turned to see wisdom, that what (is) the man who comes after the king?"; see Gordis 1955: 210–11). Thus, we understand this as a case where the verb must be reconstructed from the context as a copy of עשׂה. If the lack of an overt עשׂה is not the result of textual error, grammatically we could understand that this is a case of backwards gapping from the final verb in the clause: "what the man who comes after the king (does)."

אֵת אֲשֶׁר־כְּבָר עָשׂוּהוּ. *Qatal* 3cp Qal √עשׂה + 3ms clitic pronoun. If we maintain the MT's plural verb, it can be an impersonal construction, in which the reference is the kings who have preceded this one, or in which the identity of the agents are not in view but the agentive activity is (see WO §22.7; JM §152d). Many commentators note that numerous Hebrew MSS have the singular עָשָׂהוּ (reflected also in the Septuagint and Vulgate) and so suggest that the singular better fits the context, "he (= the king) has done it" (see, among others, Gordis 1955: 211). Fox advocates emending to the 1cs עָשִׂיתִי, but with weak justification (1999: 183). On כבר, see comment at 1:10. We suggest the following solution—it is a null copula clause with a null-subject and a null-head relative clause (marked as the complement by the presence of אֵת; see 4:3 and WO §10.3.2c).

2:13   וְרָאִיתִי אָנִי שֶׁיֵּשׁ יִתְרוֹן לַחָכְמָה מִן־הַסִּכְלוּת כִּיתְרוֹן הָאוֹר מִן־הַחֹשֶׁךְ:

I saw, I, that the profit of wisdom is more than (the profit of) foolishness, like the profit of light is more than (the profit of) darkness.

Qoheleth affirms that wisdom and folly are distinct, and that one is inherently better than the other. However, this affirmation simply sets up his case for absurdity, since, as he notes, the superior quality does not result in any substantive difference in life, such as a longer life.

וְרָאִיתִי אָנִי שֶׁיֵּשׁ. *Qatal* 1cs Qal √ראה. Once again, the postverbal pronoun אני is an adjunct used to indicate that the speaker, Qoheleth, not his לב, was the agent in this case. In other words this activity was not collaborative. See comment at 2:11. The complement of the bivalent ראיתי is the nominalized clause introduced by שׁ.

יֵשׁ יִתְרוֹן לַחָכְמָה מִן־הַסַּכְלוּת כִּיתְרוֹן הָאוֹר מִן־הַחֹשֶׁךְ. The יֵשׁ is the copula (see 1:10), with יתרון as the subject and the comparative מן-PP as the copular complement (MNK §39.14.8; WO §11.2.11e.3). The PP לחכמה is an NP-internal adjunct modifying יתרון. It indicates that this יתרון is the יתרון produced by חכמה (see WO §11.2.10d on this relevant use of the לְ). The preposition כ has as its complement an unmarked null copula complement clause, יתרון האור מן־החשׁך, which would normally be introduced as a nominalized element by אשׁר (so one might have expected כאשׁר; see, e.g., 4:17). The entire כ-PP serves as a comparative adjunct clause to the first copular predication; the כ compares the null copula clause it governs (with the subject יתרון האור and the copular complement מן־החשׁך) to the מן comparison of the main clause: "A is more than B like X is more than Y."

2:14   הֶחָכָם֙ עֵינָ֣יו בְּרֹאשֹׁ֔ו וְהַכְּסִ֖יל בַּחֹ֣שֶׁךְ הֹולֵ֑ךְ וְיָדַ֣עְתִּי
גַם־אָ֔נִי שֶׁמִּקְרֶ֥ה אֶחָ֖ד יִקְרֶ֥ה אֶת־כֻּלָּֽם׃

As for the wise man—his eyes are in his head. But the fool in darkness is walking. Yet I have come to know, even I, that one fate befalls them all.

הֶחָכָם֙ עֵינָ֣יו בְּרֹאשֹׁ֔ו. The initial NP is left-dislocated and resumed within the null copula clause by the 3ms clitic pronoun on עיניו. The left-dislocation signals that החכם is the topic and the resumptive pronoun carries focus: "The wise man—his eyes are in his head."

וְהַכְּסִ֖יל בַּחֹ֣שֶׁךְ הֹולֵ֑ךְ. Participle ms Qal √הלך. A null copula clause with הכסיל as subject, and the participle הולך as copular complement. The word כְּסִיל reflects the *qitīl*-pattern, which is used primarily for nouns, with only a few good candidates for adjectives (JM §88Eg). Yet, כסיל, along with the similar אֱוִיל "fool" and "foolish," appears to be a good candidate for both noun and adjective lexical entries. In this clause it seems most reasonable to take הכסיל as a noun, but in 4:13 כסיל modifies another noun and appears to be adjectival. The pragmatically unmarked word order for participial clauses is subject + immediately following participle. This particular participial clause exhibits double-fronting, where the ב-PP has been fronted to a marked position before the verb, and the NP הכסיל has also been moved to a marked position before the PP. In such cases of double-fronting, pragmatically the first constituent often signals a topic shift (here from the חכם of the previous clause to the כסיל), while the second constituent signals focus (here, the PP בחשׁך, which is the complement of הולך) (see Buth; Holmstedt 2014). The focus on בחשׁך serves to contrast the manner in which the fool lives with the manner in which the wise man lives (עיניו בראשׁו).

וְיָדַ֣עְתִּי גַם־אָ֔נִי שֶׁמִּקְרֶ֥ה אֶחָ֖ד יִקְרֶ֥ה אֶת־כֻּלָּֽם. *Qatal* 1cs Qal √ידע and *yiqtol* 3ms Qal √קרה. For the inchoative semantics of ידעתי, see the comment on 1:17. The גם אני serves to mark focus on Qoheleth (as opposed to his לב, which presumably drew different conclusions) and the שׁ clause serves as the complement for the verb ידעתי. Notice the subject-verb order within the complement clause; the order after function words like כי, אשׁר, and שׁ is consistently triggered to verb-subject. Thus, here the subject מקרה אחד must be focus-fronted, to contrast the one fate with what Qoheleth (and his audience) expect—that opposite fates belong to the wise and the foolish. Note that the verb יקרה is bivalent and takes an NP (here marked with את) as its complement.

2:15 וְאָמַרְתִּי אֲנִי בְּלִבִּי כְּמִקְרֵה הַכְּסִיל גַּם־אֲנִי יִקְרֵנִי וְלָמָּה חָכַמְתִּי אֲנִי אָז יוֹתֵר וְדִבַּרְתִּי בְלִבִּי שֶׁגַּם־זֶה הָבֶל׃

I said, I with my לב, "Like the fool's fate am even I; it will befall me! Why have I become wise, I, then, so much?" I spoke with my לב that this, too, was a הבל.

Fox's summary of v. 15 applies equally to vv. 13, 14, and 16 and is so on target that it is worth quoting in full: "In spite of wisdom's superiority, the foolish and the wise come to the same end. This leveling makes it pointless to grow very wise, but it does not, to Qoheleth's mind, eliminate wisdom's superiority" (1999: 184).

וְאָמַרְתִּי אֲנִי בְּלִבִּי. *Qatal* 1cs Qal √אמר. On the "I-with-my -לב," see comments on 1:16 and Introduction §3. The complement of אמרתי is the direct speech that begins with כמקרה.

כְּמִקְרֵה הַכְּסִיל גַּם־אֲנִי יִקְרֵנִי. *Yiqtol* 3ms Qal √קרה + 1cs clitic pronoun. The sequence of constituents initiates the direct speech complement of אמר. Unfortunately, the syntax is much more difficult than it might appear. Scholars typically take the initial PP to be a fronted adjunct of the verb יקרני and the גם־אני to reinforce the 1cs clitic pronoun in יקרני: "What happens to the fool will happen to me, too" (Fox 1999: 181; so also, among many others, Seow 1997: 118, 135; Longman, 95). Since a PP is not a likely syntactic subject for יקרה, this position assumes that the כ-PP has a null NP head, "(fate) like the fate of the fool." There are a few obstacles to this analysis that go unmentioned. First, the position of the גם־אני before its syntactic anchor (the 1cs clitic pronoun on יקרני) suggests that it has been focus-fronted; but why not simply use the

object marker in fronted position, i.e., ?בְּמִקְרֶה הַכְּסִיל אֹתִי יִקְרֶה Moreover, a fronted גַּם־אֲנִי implies in turn that the null NP head of the כ-PP
is also fronted, presumably as the topic. However, topic-marking on a
null NP is unlikely. But if the כ-PP does not represent a fronted constituent, then the גַּם־אֲנִי cannot be fronted—but if not fronted, then גַּם־אֲנִי
should follow its anchor (as in Gen 27:38). The solution to this challenge
is not entirely clear. We tentatively suggest reading against the accents
and take the comparative PP כמקרה הכסיל as the fronted complement
of a null copula clause with גַּם־אֲנִי the syntactic subject, also marked
with focus—the גם is necessary to indicate the focus since the only other
constituent is already fronted: "like the fate of the fool am even I! It will
befall me." In its fronted position, the כ-PP is a topic, orienting the audience to (in this case) a point of comparison. As in v. 14, the גַּם־אֲנִי serves
to mark focus on Qoheleth (as the rather surprising experiencer of the
same fate as the fool). The remaining constituent, יקרני, forms a distinct
clause by itself and clarifies Qoheleth's meaning appositionally, "that is,
it will befall me."

וְלָמָּה חָכַמְתִּי אֲנִי אָז יוֹתֵר. *Qatal* 1cs Qal √חכם. This is a syntactically unusual clause. The pronoun below the verb can be explained as
in 2:11, but the lower positions of the adjuncts אז "then" and יותר "too
much, so much" are very odd. The item יותר occurs only in this book
(2:15; 6:8, 11; 7:11, 16; 12:9, 12) and twice elsewhere: 1 Sam 15:15;
Esth 6:6. In 6:8, 11, 7:11, and 12:9, יותר functions as a substantive,
"advantage," though in all the other cases (including 1 Sam 15:15 and
Esth 6:6), it clearly functions adverbially, "excessively, too much" (see
HALOT, s.v.; DCH, s.v.).

2:16   כִּי אֵין זִכְרוֹן לֶחָכָם עִם־הַכְּסִיל לְעוֹלָם בְּשֶׁכְּבָר
הַיָּמִים הַבָּאִים הַכֹּל נִשְׁכָּח וְאֵיךְ יָמוּת הֶחָכָם עִם־
הַכְּסִיל:

Because remembrance is never for the wise alongside the fool; because
already (in) the coming days, all is forgotten. How the wise dies with the fool!

This verse details part of Qoheleth's motivation for the הבל conclusion about his experiment at the end of 2:15.

כִּי אֵין זִכְרוֹן לֶחָכָם עִם־הַכְּסִיל לְעוֹלָם. A copular clause with אין
as the negative copula (see also comment at 1:7). The PP לחכם is the

copular complement, and the ל preposition is used to indicate the beneficiary of the action or event, the ל of (dis)advantage (WO §11.2.10d).
The עם PP is an adjunct to the copula, indicating a comitative relationship, "along with, as well as, alongside," as it does at the end of this verse
(WO §11.2.14a–b; MNK §39.20.1ii). The adjunct PP לעולם combines
with the negative אין to mean "not ever," or "never."

בְּשֶׁכְּבָר הַיָּמִים הַבָּאִים הַכֹּל נִשְׁכָּח. Participle mp Qal √בוא and
qatal 3ms/participle ms Niph √שכח. The ב preposition that initiates this
clause is used causally (WO §11.2.5e) and the שׁ nominalizes the following clause so that it can serve as the nominal complement of the
preposition, lit. "because that already ..." (on the use of שׁ to nominalize
in Ecclesiastes, see Introduction §4). Within the nominalized clause, the
NP הימים הבאים is a temporal adjunct; often such adjuncts are introduced by prepositions, but this is not a requirement in Hebrew. As long
as the syntactic role of the constituent is apparent, explicit syntactic
marking is optional (this feature of Hebrew grammar is often described
under the rubric "adverbial accusative" [see WO §10.2.2], a case term
that is inappropriate for Hebrew). The participle באים is situated within
a ה-relative clause. The verb נשכח presents an example of homophony:
the same form is used for both the Niphal ms participle and the pausal
form of the *qatal* 3ms Niphal. The temporal NP הימים הבאים suggests
an expected future time frame, which in turn suggests that the participle
is the more felicitous verb. Note that the adverb כבר and the adjunct
NP הימים הבאים are both fronted as contextualizing topics (it is doubt-
ful that Qoheleth is contrasting "the coming days" with, e.g., "the past
days," making a focus interpretation of the fronting unlikely). Whether
the verb נשכח is taken as a participle or *qatal* determines whether the
subject הכל is in normal position (for a participle) or is also fronted
(for a *qatal*, since the topic-fronted בשכבר phrase would normally trigger inversion to verb-subject order). If fronted, then it is likely focus-
fronting, intended to make it explicit that no one and nothing escapes
ephemerality.

וְאֵיךְ יָמוּת הֶחָכָם עִם־הַכְּסִיל. *Yiqtol* 3ms Qal √מות. The first
word, איך, is an interrogative meaning "how, in what way?" (HALOT,
s.v.); it is also used in rhetorical exclamations, particularly in elegiac
contexts (e.g., Isa 14:12; Lam 1:1). Thus Seow asserts that "Qohelet is
lamenting the death of the wise and the fools alike" (1997: 136). The
presence of the interrogative at the front of the clause triggers inversion
to verb-subject order.

2:17-26 Qoheleth's Conclusion:
Hate Toil, Enjoy What You Can

2:17 וְשָׂנֵ֙אתִי֙ אֶת־הַֽחַיִּ֔ים כִּ֣י רַ֤ע עָלַי֙ הַֽמַּעֲשֶׂ֔ה שֶׁנַּעֲשָׂ֖ה
תַּ֣חַת הַשָּׁ֑מֶשׁ כִּֽי־הַכֹּ֥ל הֶ֖בֶל וּרְע֥וּת רֽוּחַ׃

I came to hate life, because the event that has happened under the sun was terrible to me, because everything is a הבל *and chasing wind.*

The frustration that has been building for Qoheleth now comes to a climax with this outburst. Fox argues that this is Qoheleth looking back—a retrospective describing part of his journey but not the end point: "As his account moves forward, he tempers his frustration with discoveries of good things, and his affirmation of life grows stronger" (1999: 184).

וְשָׂנֵ֙אתִי֙ אֶת־הַֽחַיִּ֔ים. *Qatal* 1cs Qal √שׂנא. An inchoative interpretation of the stative שׂנא here and in the following verse makes good sense if Seow's characterization is correct: Qoheleth's hatred of life is a result of his experiment and subsequent reflections on his work.

כִּ֣י רַ֤ע עָלַי֙ הַֽמַּעֲשֶׂ֔ה שֶׁנַּעֲשָׂ֖ה תַּ֣חַת הַשָּׁ֑מֶשׁ. *Qatal* 3ms Qal √רעע and 3ms Niph √עשׂה. The word רַע could be parsed as either a ms adjective or a *qatal* 3ms verb. The fronted position, due to the presence of the כי trigger, strongly suggests that it is a verb. If רע were an adjective, the clause would be copular, but without the normal subject-predicate order; thus רע would be in a focus-fronted position (although the reason that רע would be marked for focus in this clause is unclear, lending further support to the verbal analysis). It may be that the entire subject has been shifted rightward (i.e., toward the end of the clause)—a case of HNPS which is used to make processing the clause easier (see comments at 2:7; 3:14, 22; 7:18, 20, 26; 9:11, 14; 11:7)—and how it simplifies the processing of this clause is unclear. Thus, we prefer the verbal parsing and triggered inversion analysis. The position of the adjunct PP עלי reflects that common pattern whereby "light" PPs raise with the verb in the triggered inversion process. The כי clause provides one motive for Qoheleth's rather strong statement, that he hates life. Why? Because what happens in life is deeply disturbing (רע). As Fox points out, the noun מעשׂה does not refer to a singular event but to a "collectivity of events" (1999: 184).

כִּי־הַכֹּל הֶבֶל וּרְעוּת רוּחַ. This second כִּי clause may either present another motive for שָׂנֵאתִי or, if it overlaps enough with the content of the first כִּי clause, be an appositive that reformulates the first
motive clause. We take the latter analysis to make the most sense, that
Qoheleth's evaluation that "what happens in life is terrible" is simply
reformulated using his common refrain: הכל הבל. On הבל, see 1:2; on
רעות, see 1:14.

$$2:18 \quad \text{וְשָׂנֵאתִי אֲנִי אֶת־כָּל־עֲמָלִי שֶׁאֲנִי עָמֵל תַּחַת} $$
$$\text{הַשָּׁמֶשׁ שֶׁאַנִּיחֶנּוּ לָאָדָם שֶׁיִּהְיֶה אַחֲרָי:}$$

*I came to hate, I, all my toil, which I did under the sun, which I must
leave it to the man who comes after me.*

Qoheleth continues his emotional rant, moving from life in general
(v. 17) to his specific experience. In particular, he resents that what he
works for in this life does not endure for him beyond death.

שָׂנֵאתִי אֲנִי אֶת־כָּל־עֲמָלִי שֶׁאֲנִי עָמֵל תַּחַת הַשָּׁמֶשׁ. *Qatal* 1cs
Qal √שׂנא. The null copula relative clause has a free 1cs pronoun for
the subject and an adjectival copular complement (עָמֵל). Note that the
adjective עמל has some verbal characteristics—here and in 2:22, 3:9, and
9:9—in that it takes a covert complement by virtue of resumption within
the relative clause, "toil, which I did under the sun." On the postverbal
1cs pronoun, see comment on 1:16 and Introduction §3. That Qoheleth
hates his עמל is balanced within the book by the fact that his לב enjoys
it (v. 10). The relative clause שאני עמל תחת השמש appears redundant at
first glance: why characterize "toil" by saying that it was "what I toiled
for"? The reason for the relative clause is the addition of the information
תחת השמש—Qoheleth is sure to keep his audience focused on the problems of this life; i.e., what happens "under the sun." This is in keeping
with the nature of nonrestrictive relative clauses, which modify the head
by providing additional information that is unnecessary in order for the
reader/listener to identify the referent of the head. If the relative clause
were restrictive, it would serve to narrow (or restrict/define) the referent
of the head to the acquisitions toiled for under the sun (as opposed to
some other acquisitions not toiled for under the sun). Here, however,
Qoheleth is not interested in commenting about a subset of all his toil;
rather, he is reminding the reader that the entirety of his toil is, in fact,
done under the sun (and therefore its ultimate value and permanence is

suspect, see 1:3, 14; 2:11, 17). See Holmstedt 2016: 205–14 for a fuller discussion on restrictive and nonrestrictive relative clauses.

שֶׁאַנִּיחֶנּוּ לְאָדָם שֶׁיִּהְיֶה אַחֲרָי. *Yiqtol* 1cs Hiph √נוח + 3ms clitic pronoun and *yiqtol* 3ms Qal √היה. The *yiqtol* could be taken as expressing the simple future, but Qoheleth's complaint underscores the inescapable fate of death that he, like all humanity, must undergo; therefore, an irrealis epistemic sense of "must" fits the context better. The שׁ clause is taken as a causal by some (Seow 1997: 136; Fox 1999: 185), but there is no grammatical reason to take it as anything other than a relative. As a relative, this second שׁ clause also modifies עמלי; multiple relative clauses for the same head is called "stacking." This second relative clause is, like the first one, nonrestrictive. The clitic pronoun attached to the verb אניחנו resumes the head עמלי and serves as the first complement of the trivalent verb אניח; the PP לאדם is the second complement. Within the ל-PP a third relative clause modifies the head אדם, which is the resumptive null-subject, and the PP אחרי is the complement of the copula יהיה.

2:19 וּמִי יוֹדֵעַ הֶחָכָם יִהְיֶה אוֹ סָכָל וְיִשְׁלַט בְּכָל־עֲמָלִי
שֶׁעָמַלְתִּי וְשֶׁחָכַמְתִּי תַּחַת הַשָּׁמֶשׁ גַּם־זֶה הָבֶל׃

Who knows whether he will be a wise man or a fool and will rule over my toil that I did and concerning which I became wise under the sun. This too is a הבל!

וּמִי יוֹדֵעַ הֶחָכָם יִהְיֶה אוֹ סָכָל. Participle ms Qal √ידע and *yiqtol* 3ms Qal √היה. The first clause is simply a question: "Who knows?" The complement of bivalent ידע is a complex clause—an embedded interrogative that governs three further clauses. These clauses present the options implied in the open question, which picks up the concern expressed in v. 18: What kind of man will come after him and take over the product of all his toil? The subject of the first clause within the interrogative is null and by this zero anaphora reactivates האדם שיהיה אחרי from the preceding clause. The complement of the copular יהיה is the adjective חכם (functioning nominally, "a wise [man]"), which is fronted for focus. The second clause has both a null-subject (the same אדם as the first clause) and a gapped verb יהיה from the first clause; only the copular complement סכל is overt. The use of יהיה instead of the expected copular שׁ is motivated by the tense requirements: the copular שׁ would be interpreted "(whether) he *is* a wise man or a fool," whereas the יהיה

form keeps the relinquishment clearly in the future (cf. v. 21). The inter-rogative ה on החכם typically triggers inversion to verb-subject order, but this is both obscured by the use of a null-subject and overridden by the focus-fronting of חכם.

וְיִשְׁלַט בְּכָל־עֲמָלִי שֶׁעָמַלְתִּי וְשֶׁחָכַמְתִּי תַּחַת הַשָּׁמֶשׁ. *Yiqtol* 3ms Qal √שלט, *qatal* 1cs Qal √עמל and √חכם. The verb ישלט "to have power ב/over" occurs only in "late" texts (i.e., Neh 5:15; Esth 9:1; Ps 119:133; Dan 2:39; 3:27; 5:16; 6:25). Seow argues that, in the Persian period, שלט has the nuance of having the right of disposal for property, a trans-ferable right (1997: 136). Fox counters that there is no evidence to sug-gest that the verb ceased having the "right of disposal" nuance after the Achaemenid period, thus making it possible that the word is used with this meaning even in the Hellenistic period, where Fox situates the book (1999: 187). Fox also notes that שלט seems to be used in Ecclesiastes with the meanings of both "control, rule" and the "right of disposal," and that this accords with later rabbinic Hebrew and Aramaic usage. Thus, Fox concludes that שלט in Ecclesiastes "favors a post-Achaemenid dat-ing" (contra Seow). Regarding the semantics of the noun עמל, this clause provides a perfect example of why, although this noun denotes "toil," it also can connote the *product* of one's toil (see comment at 2:10). This man who comes will rule, not over Qoheleth's toil, but over those things which his toil produced for him (a metonymy of cause for the effect). The two *qatal* forms in the relative clauses are governed by the same head, כל־עמלי. With bivalent עמלתי as the verb within the relative, the relative head is resumed covertly as the complement: "the toil that I did (it)" (see the collocations עמל ב/ל in 2:11, 21; 5:15; 8:17; the comple-ment is lacking in 1:3; 2:19-20; 5:17). However, the stative חכמתי is monovalent, and so it must resume (again, covertly) the relative head as a specifying adjunct: "and in conjunction with which I became wise" (cf. על כל־העמל in v. 20). The inchoative meaning of the stative verb fits best here in the context of Qoheleth's acquiring wisdom (among other things).

2:20   וְסַבּוֹתִי אֲנִי לְיַאֵשׁ אֶת־לִבִּי עַל כָּל־הֶעָמָל
שֶׁעָמַלְתִּי תַּחַת הַשָּׁמֶשׁ:

I turned around, I, to put my לב *in a state of despair about all the toil that I did under the sun,*

וְסַבּוֹתִי אֲנִי לְיַאֵשׁ אֶת־לִבִּי. *Qatal* 1cs Qal √סבב and Inf Constr
Piel √יאשׁ. Again, on the postverbal 1cs pronoun אני, see comment at
1:16 and Introduction §3. The verb סבב is monovalent in the Qal; the
ל + infinitive clause is an adjunct indicating purpose. For יאשׁ, HALOT
and DCH provide "to despair" as the sense of monovalent *Niphal* and
"cause to despair" for bivalent Piel. In this verse Qoheleth describes how
he tried to convince his לב that his toil was not enjoyable, apparently in
response to the positive conclusion that the לב had already drawn: כִּי־לִבִּי
שָׂמֵחַ מִכָּל־עֲמָלִי in 2:10.

עַל כָּל־הֶעָמָל שֶׁעָמַלְתִּי תַּחַת הַשָּׁמֶשׁ. *Qatal* 1cs Qal √עמל. The
עַל-PP is an adjunct for the verb יאשׁ and indicates what Qoheleth's לב
was supposed to despair about: Qoheleth's toil in life (for this use of על as
specifying topic, see WO §11.2.13g; MNK §39.19.4i). On the relative
clause, see comment on v. 18.

כִּי־יֵשׁ אָדָם שֶׁעֲמָלוֹ בְּחָכְמָה וּבְדַעַת וּבְכִשְׁרוֹן　2:21
וּלְאָדָם שֶׁלֹּא עָמַל־בּוֹ יִתְּנֶנּוּ חֶלְקוֹ גַּם־זֶה הֶבֶל
וְרָעָה רַבָּה:

because there is a man whose gain is by wisdom and by knowledge and by
skill, but to a man who has not done it he must give it, his portion (this too
is a הבל and a great tragedy!)

Qoheleth now justifies his behavior toward his לב. Much like the
reasons he provided for his own early response to the experiment, that he
hated life (vv. 17-19), he points out the basic injustice of someone inher-
iting the fruits of toil who has not worked for it. Whether or not Qoheleth had in mind a specific אדם in this verse, it quickly becomes the basis
for addressing the plight of all humanity with the generic אדם in v. 22.

כִּי־יֵשׁ אָדָם שֶׁעֲמָלוֹ בְּחָכְמָה וּבְדַעַת וּבְכִשְׁרוֹן. Whether this
כי clause is an adjunct to the main verb of the last verse, סבותי, or
the infinitive יאשׁ depends on our semantic judgment—does Qoheleth
turn around "because there is a man ..." or does he depress his לב
"because there is a man"? The latter makes better semantic sense to us,
though both options are syntactically acceptable. Within the כי clause,
אדם is the subject of the ישׁ nonverbal predicator. The ישׁ clause here is
a rare example of an existential statement. That is, no quality, location,
or identity is the complement of the ישׁ; the proposition is simply that

this entity "exists." With such existential statements, English grammar prefers a different construction, with the dummy pronoun "there" and the syntactic subject positioned on the other side of the copula. Within the שׁ relative clause modifying אדם, the NP עמלו (note that its 3ms clitic pronoun resumes the head אדם) is the subject of a null copula clause, with a compound PP complement, בחכמה ובדעת ובכשרון. The predication is semantically underdetermined, since formally the statement "his עמל is in/by/with חכמה, etc." is not logical. Rather, one must reconstruct an appropriate semantic value for the copula, in this case "made, accomplished, achieved." The ב preposition on all three parts of the complement is used to signal the *means* by which the man introduced has achieved his עמל (WO §11.2.5d)—he toiled and, by wisdom, knowledge, and skill, he achieved a positive gain; alternatively, the ב may indicate the cause or origin, that this man's עמל resulted from his wisdom and skill (WO §11.2.5e). Grammatically, the two options are distinct; in terms of the proposition within the narrative, the difference is negligible.

וּלְאָדָ֞ם שֶׁלֹּ֣א עָמַל־בּוֹ֮ יִתְּנֶ֣נּוּ חֶלְקוֹ. *Qatal* 3ms Qal √עמל and *yiqtol* 3ms Qal √נתן + 3ms clitic pronoun. The *yiqtol* is best analyzed as expressing epistemic necessity, implied as brought on by death: the man who has acquired things by his wisdom, etc., cannot avoid death, when he *must* relinquish it all to someone else. Note that this clause is within the domain of the initial כי clause and constitutes a second part of the reason Qoheleth gives; both clauses together form the situation that explains why he put his לב into despair over his עמל. The syntactic structure of the clause (with its attending pragmatic effects) can be analyzed in three ways. First, חלקו at the end might be appositive to the anaphoric clitic pronoun attached to the verb יתננו, whose antecedent is עמלו in the previous clause. The man's עמל was his portion (recalling by analogy how the לב's happiness in Qoheleth's labor is Qoheleth's portion, 2:10), but that portion must be relinquished because of death. Hence, his portion is given to another (this connects to v. 22 and the concern for enduring gain for one's toil). The ambiguity of "his" on "his portion" may be intentional—it makes sense referring either to the man who relinquishes it or the one who receives it—to each it is equally their "portion." Second, with similar semantics but a different syntactic structure, this example could present one of right-dislocation (less common than left-dislocation, but attested nonetheless; see Holmstedt 2014). The PP לאדם would be the second (recipient) complement of the trivalent verb

נתן, and the clitic pronoun attached to the verb is the first complement (the patient, or what was given). The surprising grammatical issue (likely due to the relative rarity of right-dislocation in the Hebrew Bible) is that the referent of the clitic pronoun is not identified. Overwhelmingly, pronouns in Hebrew are anaphoric devices, coreferential with a previously invoked NP. On this analysis, here the pronoun must be cataphoric: its antecedent (so to speak) is not identified until the right-dislocated NP חלקו is given (see Seow 1997: 137–38). Cross-linguistically, the function of right-dislocation is (1) to reactivate an item that has not been used for some time in the discourse, or (2) to make an implicit item explicit, and sometimes (3) to mark the constituent for focus (Ziv; Ashby; for BH, see Holmstedt 2014). The NP חלק was first mentioned in 2:10, as Qoheleth's "portion," but it is not clear that this is the same item. Thus, rather than a reactivated NP, it is more likely that this clause illustrates the second use of right-dislocation: that the NP חלקו was left implicit in the clause proper and not specified until its dislocated position at the right edge of the clause. Additionally, if the motivation in using the dislocation structure is to heighten a tension by delaying an important piece of information, it would also make sense that חלקו bears focus. The effect of all this is to drive home the absurdity that what one toils for in life, and so the earned reward, must be passed on to another. A third analysis is to take the PP ולאדם שלא עמל־בו as a left-dislocated constituent, moved to the front of the clause as a topic. In this scenario Qoheleth introduces two new participants into the discourse. The first—the man who actually works for his gain—is presented with a יש construction and a restrictive relative clause that defines precisely the kind of אדם under consideration. Next, Qoheleth introduces a second participant— the man who does not work for his gain but gets what the first man toiled for. To aid in the processing of these participants, the second man is introduced using a left-dislocation, signaling a topic-shift, ולאדם שלא עמל־בו, which is resumed in the clause proper by the 3ms clitic pronoun on יתננו, thus (with subscripts to aid the interpretation): "*For there is a man$_i$ who his$_i$ toil$_k$ is by wisdom, knowledge, and skill. But to the man$_j$ who$_j$ did not do it$_k$—he$_i$ gives him$_j$ his$_j$ portion!*" Since left-dislocated constituents technically have no syntactic role in the clause proper, this ל-PP would not be a fronted (recipient) complement of the trivalent verb נתן; rather, the valency is filled first by the 3ms clitic pronoun in יתננו (marking the recipient, normally signaled with an ל-PP complement), and secondly by the NP complement חלקו. For the possibility that left-dislocated constituents may retain the syntactic marking from their role in the base clause after moving (in this case, the preposition לְ), see comment on 1:11.

גַּם־זֶה הֶבֶל וְרָעָה רַבָּה. This clause, with its slight difference from other instances, is both Qoheleth's refrain in the book and his specific judgment at this point about the injustice done to the one who toils.

2:22   כִּי מֶה־הֹוֶה לָאָדָם בְּכָל־עֲמָלוֹ וּבְרַעְיוֹן לִבּוֹ שְׁהוּא
         עָמֵל תַּחַת הַשָּׁמֶשׁ׃

because what endures for man in exchange for all his toil and striving of his heart, which he has done under the sun?

Here Qoheleth justifies his negative judgment at the end of v. 21—it is all a הבל because nothing endures for the working man in exchange for all his work. The energy one expends reaps nothing in the end. Futility characterizes the human existence.

כִּי מֶה־הֹוֶה לָאָדָם בְּכָל־עֲמָלוֹ וּבְרַעְיוֹן לִבּוֹ. Participle ms Qal √הוה. This כי clause provides the motive or explanation for the זה הבל ורעה רבה at the end of v. 21. The use of the participial form of the Aramaic-like copula (cf. BH היה) is rare (it occurs here, Exod 9:3, and Neh 6:6 in the Hebrew Bible) and seems to stress the enduring nature of the statement (Fox 1999: 188). The interrogative מה is the syntactic subject, the PP לאדם is the copular complement, and the two ב-PPs are adjuncts providing the price paid or exchanged (WO §11.2.5d). If, as the MT pointing indicates, there is an article in the form לאדם, then it functions either anaphorically (referring back to the first man in v. 21), or generically, referring to mankind (see Baranowski, 39). We think the latter more likely, given that Qoheleth seems to be characterizing human existence generally in this and the following verses on the basis of what he has observed. On רעיון, see 1:14.

שְׁהוּא עָמֵל תַּחַת הַשָּׁמֶשׁ. A null copula clause with 3ms pronoun הוא as the subject and the ms adjective עמל as the copular complement. Inside the relative, the head's resumption is null. Formally, the שׁ relative clause modifies the nearer antecedent, רעיון לבו, but contextually it fits both כל עמלו and its syntactic head רעיון לבו. Whatever the precise head, it is not overtly resumed within the relative.

כִּי כָל־יָמָיו מַכְאֹבִים וָכַעַס עִנְיָנוֹ גַּם־בַּלַּיְלָה לֹא־ 2:23
שָׁכַב לִבּוֹ גַּם־זֶה הֶבֶל הוּא:

Indeed, all his days are pains and grief is his business; even at night his mind has not "lain down to sleep." This, too—it is a הבל!

כִּי כָל־יָמָיו מַכְאֹבִים. A null copula clause with כל ימיו as the subject and מכאבים as the copular complement. Seow suggests that מכאבים is the subject and כל ימיו is the copular complement, translating "in all their days is pain" (1997: 138). While a preposition is certainly not obligatory to get the sense that Seow wants, the NP with the anaphoric link (the 3ms clitic pronoun on ימיו) is the best candidate for the subject; thus, there is little to commend Seow's analysis. The כי clause as a whole either introduces a motive for the question in v. 22 or is an exclamative, "indeed!," which signals Qoheleth's exasperation about the answer to the question asked in v. 22. We prefer this latter interpretation. The mp NP מכאבים might reflect the use of the plural for an abstract idea (WO §7.4.2), i.e., "suffering"; but the more concrete "pains, sufferings" (in the sense of "full of pains") seems to be equally fitting.

וָכַעַס עִנְיָנוֹ. The subject of this null copula clause is עינינו. The 3ms clitic pronoun on the noun grounds the statement to the previous discourse by referring back to the man of v. 22. The copular complement, which provides information newly added, is כעס. Note the vocalization of the ו conjunction: the *qameṣ* occurs especially on monosyllabic or disyllabic nouns with penultimate word stress (as here). Typically the word is also in pause, although sometimes (as here) it is prepausal (JM §104d). Although it is syntactically possible that מכאבים וכעס is a single compound complement (with כל ימיו as a temporal adjunct), the Masoretes clearly did not read the sequence as such due to their placement of a disjunctive טעם (the רביעי) between the two words. The word order (predicate-subject) reflects the raising of the complement due to focus: though Qoheleth has been lamenting the lack of an enduring return for one's toil, here he switches rhetorical gears and asserts that if one receives anything, it is *grief*.

גַּם־בַּלַּיְלָה לֹא־שָׁכַב לִבּוֹ. *Qatal* 3ms Qal √שכב. The focus-fronted (and focus-marked by גם) PP בלילה is a temporal adjunct of שכב. It carries focus because one's mind not resting at night is contrary to expectation. Sleep typically provides at least a semblance of rest. Here and in

v. 22 are two occurrences of לֵב that are not part of the "I-and-my-לֵב" framework; instead, the sense here is simply "mind." Both the fronted PP and the negative are triggers for inversion to verb-subject order, which occurs here with שָׁכַב לִבּוֹ. Though a generic statement, it is expressed as a pattern of behavior based on a past event: the pattern is that his heart has not lain down at night.

גַּם־זֶה הֶבֶל הוּא. A null copula clause. The use of the הוא here may look like the pronominal copula, but הוא used as the copula is rarely (if ever) in clause final position (Kummerow 2013: 88, n. 67; Holmstedt and Jones 2014). Additionally, a left-dislocation analysis fits the pragmatics, with the זה as both topic and focus (by virtue of the גם) and also the הבל focus-fronted, "Also this, it is a הבל!"

2:24 אֵין־טוֹב בָּאָדָם שֶׁיֹּאכַל וְשָׁתָה וְהֶרְאָה אֶת־נַפְשׁוֹ
טוֹב בַּעֲמָלוֹ גַּם־זֹה רָאִיתִי אָנִי כִּי מִיַּד הָאֱלֹהִים
הִיא:

A better thing does not exist for man (than) that he eat and drink and show himself good in his toil. Even this I saw, I, that it is from the hand of God.

After describing all his frustration over the absurdity of life—that one works and works but does not reap anything truly lasting—Qoheleth shares his conclusion: what else can you do but enjoy the here and now?

אֵין־טוֹב בָּאָדָם שֶׁיֹּאכַל וְשָׁתָה וְהֶרְאָה אֶת־נַפְשׁוֹ טוֹב בַּעֲמָלוֹ. *Yiqtol* 3ms Qal √אכל; *qatal* 3ms Qal √שתה and Hiph √ראה; null copula. The main clause is a null copula clause with אין as the negative copula, טוב as the subject, and the PP באדם as the copular complement. Many commentators (e.g., Barton, 96) suggest that באדם is a scribal error for לאדם, which is found in 6:12 and 8:15. But against this, see אֵין טוֹב בָּם (3:12), in which the preposition ב is apparently used to indicate the beneficiary of the "better than" comparison: "there is nothing better for them. ..." Alternatively, the ב may indicate the sphere in which the comparison is valid (WO §11.2.5b): "a better thing does not exist *among* man. ..." Notably, many commentators (Barton, 96; Fox 1999: 189) also emend to משיאכל in order to match the pattern of טוב מן

comparative statements used elsewhere in the book (see 3:22; 4:3, 6, 9, 13; 5:4; 6:3, 9; 7:1, 2, 3, 5, 8, 10; 9:4, 16, 18). It is possible that this minor emendation could be justified textually by proposing a scribal error such as haplography (the omission of one of two identical letters in a sequence), such that the scribe wrote the מ at the end of אדם and then in error assumed he had already written the מ to begin the comparison. Yet, the מן is not present on all the comparative statements in the book. In both 3:12 and 8:15, the basis for the comparison is introduced by כי אם "but," leaving the comparison itself implicit (i.e., מן "than," is absent). Recognizing that the מן is not an absolute necessity for the comparison enables us to suggest a simpler analysis than emending: שׁ in this verse nominalizes the finite verbal clauses so that syntactically they function as the point of comparison (just like the infinitives do in 3:12 and 8:15), and the comparison itself is unmarked (similarly, Seow 1997: 139). The verbs in the finite clauses headed by שׁ are irrealis, expressing a mild directive ("should") or wish ("might"). The first two verbs, אכל and שׁתה, are typically understood as requiring a complement of what is eaten or what is drunk. However, as with the English "eat" and "drink," the complement for these two verbs is often implicit, as here: i.e., "eat (something edible) and drink (something potable)." The Hiphil of ראה is trivalent; its valency is satisfied by the two complement NPs את־נפשׁי and טוב. The PP בעמלו is an adjunct to this last verb, indicating the sphere (WO §11.2.5b) in which humans must make themselves see good.

גַּם־זֹה רָאִיתִי אָנִי כִּי מִיַּד הָאֱלֹהִים הִיא. *Qatal* 1cs Qal √ראה and null copula. The cataphoric demonstrative in גם זה is the complement of bivalent ראיתי; its fronted position reflects raising for focus (which is reinforced by the focus particle גם). Although the audience does not yet know the content of זה (i.e., what Qoheleth saw), the grammar signals to them that it is unexpected and thus contrasts with what would be expected (hence the focus marking). The postverbal position of אני is addressed in the comment to 1:16 and the Introduction. The כי clause is in apposition to the deictic pronoun זה and provides the content of "this." Once again, Qoheleth makes a contrary-to-expectations claim and signals it by focus-fronting the unexpected information: the impermanent and terminal daily pleasures of eating and drinking are from the hand of God. The use of the feminine זה and היא reflect the common use of feminine pronouns and nouns for abstract ideas (WO §6.4.2; 6.6d).

2:25   כִּי מִי יֹאכַל וּמִי יָחוּשׁ חוּץ מִמֶּנִּי:

Because who can eat? Who can suffer apart from him/me?

This is a כי motive clause for the claim at the end of the last clause, that the limitations on human reward in life are of God's making.

כִּי מִי יֹאכַל. *Yiqtol* 3ms Qal √אכל. Typically a כי before a finite verb triggers inversion to verb-subject order. However, both this and the following verb are irrealis, expressing dynamic ("ability") modality—one cannot do anything apart from God's superintending work (below). Here the subject is the interrogative מי and the focus-fronting of interrogative phrases obscures the triggered inversion by changing the order back to subject-verb. The verb אכל is often bivalent, but in many cases no complement is specified. In such cases it is likely that the verb is formally monovalent and describes the generic activity of eating versus a specific eating event (in which the complement would be specified somewhere within the immediate discourse).

וּמִי יָחוּשׁ חוּץ מִמֶּנִּי. *Yiqtol* 3ms Qal √חושׁ. This clause continues the previous one and remains within the domain of the initial כי. The meaning of the clause presents multiple problems. First, the lexical semantics of the verb חושׁ are unclear. One root חושׁ means to "hurry, hasten"; a second, rarer root appears to mean "feel pain" or "be painful" in Job 20:2 (HALOT, s.v.; DCH, s.v.). Neither meaning makes good sense in this verse, which leaves commentators and translators (both ancient and modern) grasping for straws. The proposed etymologies and contextual meanings are plethora; for surveys, see Gordis 1955: 216–17; Fredericks, 225; Seow 1997: 139–40; Longman, 108–9; Fox 1999: 189. The proposed etymology that we find compelling is to connect חושׁ with Mishnaic חושׁ "to feel, suffer, be troubled" (Jastrow, 441), because if the two questions match the two types of people contrasted in v. 26 (see, among many others, Seow 1997: 140; Fox 1999: 189), whatever יחושׁ means, it must be contrastive in some way with יאכל. Thus, the logic of the statement is that if one does not eat, or if one is unsure if and when the next meal will be had, one is troubled or suffers. The phrase חוץ ממני is an adjunct to the verb.

חוּץ מִמֶּנִּי. This phrase presents the second and third difficulties in this verse. The second challenge is the unique (for the Bible) collocation חוץ מן, which means "except, without" in rabbinic Hebrew (Jastrow, 438). Rather than the later nuance "except," we suggest that the biblical meaning "outside" combines with the preposition מִן to produce "apart from." Assuming the questions are rhetorical (the obvious answer to both is "no one"), the sense is that no one eats or worries (i.e., doesn't eat) apart from the one who controls and oversees such things, God. And here is the third difficulty—the 1cs clitic pronoun on the preposition, producing "apart from me" or "without me," does not seem to fit the context, which is why most commentators follow the Septuagint and other ancient versions (and some Hebrew MSS), assuming that a scribe has erroneously misread and miscopied the final ו as a final י and that the intended meaning is "apart from him (i.e., God)" (for those who depart from MT and read a 3ms pronoun, see Seow 1997: 140–41; Fox 1999: 189; Longman, 108–9; Gordis 1955: 217; Barton, 97). However, in the attempt to resolve the difficulty of this verse, one should not too hastily dismiss the possibility that the 1cs pronoun is original (for commentators who retain 1cs, see Krüger, 58, 72; Lohfink, 56; Murphy, 24–26; Schoors, 50–52). On text-critical grounds, מִמֶּנִּי is the *lectio difficilior,* and one could account for how a 3ms pronoun arose in the tradition (by way of smoothing out the difficulty) more easily than one could account for how a more difficult reading (the 1cs pronoun) could arise from the easier one (the 3ms, if that is original). If the 1cs reading is retained, how does one explain the meaning of this clause in the context? Note that in 2:20, we see the independent 1cs pronoun following the 1cs verb (וְסַבּוֹתִי אֲנִי); Qoheleth is trying to dissuade his לֵב from the positive evaluation that it had made earlier in 2:10. Within a few verses in 2:24, a similar construction occurs, which may serve as a kind of envelope/inclusio: גַּם זֹה רָאִיתִי אָנִי. Between these two occurrences of postverbal אֲנִי in 2:20, 24 (which focus on Qoheleth to the exclusion of his לֵב), he provides three כִּי clauses which serve as motivations/reasons for why he would try to make his heart despair over the toils under the sun (recall how in 2:10 Qoheleth had said that his לֵב rejoiced מִכָּל עֲמָלִי). Thus, Qoheleth uses the entire unit, 2:20-24, to demonstrate that he knows better than his לֵב about these matters, and that his conclusion is correct. Verse 25 could then be taken to be a rhetorical question that functions as a concluding, parenthetical metacomment about his credentials to direct his לֵב (rather than as a continuing part of the argument about the emptiness of one's toil under the sun). The parenthetical nature of v. 25 is evident from the fact that, if it were extracted, the flow of the argument would appear to be uninterrupted. The כִּי clause of v. 26, then, would provide the reason for what is asserted in v. 24 rather than v. 25 (*pace* Gordis). If

v. 25 is parenthetical, then what is its purpose? Perhaps it is a concluding comment to bolster Qoheleth's credential to direct his לֵב away from its all-too-quick, and naïve assessment earlier. If the 1cs pronoun is retained, the sense of חוּץ מִן would be better understood as "except" (this is not an insurmountable problem, since the collocation is otherwise unattested in the Hebrew Bible, and the absence of the meaning "except" prior to rabbinic Hebrew is not an argument against the presence of such a meaning earlier), and the verse would read as follows: "For who can eat, and who can worry, except for ME?" That is, Qoheleth's assertion would contrast his own experience with that of his לֵב—"Who eats/worries, except for me (rather than my לֵב)?" In the end, although we have described a way to maintain the MT's 1cs pronoun in מִמֶּנִּי, we find it difficult to decide between the clearly simple emendation to 3ms, מִמֶּנּוּ, and the possible (though somewhat forced) explanation for the 1cs מִמֶּנִּי. We have left both options in the translation.

2:26   כִּי לְאָדָם שֶׁטּוֹב לְפָנָיו נָתַן חָכְמָה וְדַעַת וְשִׂמְחָה
וְלַחוֹטֶא נָתַן עִנְיָן לֶאֱסוֹף וְלִכְנוֹס לָתֵת לְטוֹב לִפְנֵי
הָאֱלֹהִים גַּם־זֶה הֶבֶל וּרְעוּת רוּחַ׃

Because to a man who is good before him, he has given wisdom, knowledge, and joy; but to the offender he has given the business of gathering and collecting in order to give (everything) to the one who is good before God. Even this is a הבל and chasing wind.

This verse presents a second כִּי clause justifying the claim at the end of v. 24, and it parallels the short contrastive set of questions in v. 25. The contrast in this verse is not between the saint and sinner but between the one who toils and the one who takes life easy. As Fox says at the end of a long exposition:

> The fortunate man's "wisdom" could be the good sense (*da'at, ḥokmah*), the savvy, to do what benefits him, which in the context means taking it easy and enjoying what falls to one's lot. This is what Qohelet recommends doing, and he naturally considers this behavior wise, even if he himself lacks this type of wisdom. The toiler has turned out to be foolish and "offensive," while the fortunate, easygoing man has seen wisdom or its fruits fall into his lap, and it was certainly wise of him not to exert himself. But for all that, there has been an asymmetry of effort and result, and this is absurd. It offends Qohelet's sense of fairness. (1999: 190–91)

כִּי לְאָדָם שֶׁטּוֹב לְפָנָיו נָתַן חָכְמָה וְדַעַת וְשִׂמְחָה. *Qatal* 3ms Qal
√נתן. The main verb נתן is trivalent and takes the compound NP as the
first complement ("what" is given) and the fronted PP לאדם as the second complement (the recipient). God's control of one's lot is underscored
by the use of the realis *qatal* verbs for these generic statements: God *has*
apportioned these lots. The subject is not explicit, but can be reconstructed from the context as האלהים. The PP לאדם is fronted for contrastive focus, as is its contrastive pair לחוטא in the next clause. Within the שֶׁ
relative clause modifying אדם, the subject is null (and coreferential with
the head אדם), and the null copula has the adjective טוב as its complement. The PP לפניו is an adjunct to the null copula. Note that the collocation טוב לפני occurs only in Ecclesiastes (here twice and in 7:26).

וְלַחוֹטֶא נָתַן עִנְיָן לֶאֱסוֹף וְלִכְנוֹס לָתֵת לְטוֹב לִפְנֵי הָאֱלֹהִים. Participle ms Qal √חטא, *qatal* 3ms Qal √נתן, Inf Constr Qal √אסף, √כנס, and
√נתן. The ms participle חוטא is used as an agentive noun, "an offender"
(see comment at 1:15). The ל-PP that contains חוטא is the second complement of נתן. The first complement, "what" is given, is a complex NP,
עינן followed by a long compound infinitival modifier, לאסוף ולכנוס לתת
לטוב לפני האלהים. Within this compound modifier, the bivalent verb
אסף has a null complement—what the offender gathers is not specified
but is presumably either something specific, such as grain, or more general, such as wealth. The second infinitival clause לכנוס is syntactically
parallel and a near synonym to לאסוף. As with the verb אסף, the complement of the bivalent כנס is null and must be reconstructed. Within the
book כנס is used twice elsewhere: in 2:8 for gathering כסף וזהב and in
3:5 for gathering אבנים. The context of this verse suggests כסף וזהב is
more likely intended than אבנים. Though the complement of לכנוס is
null, it has an overt adjunct, the purpose infinitival clause לתת לטוב לפני
האלהים. This final clause presents an observed truth that would reinforce
the more mainstream notion of just deserts but which is for Qoheleth yet
another example of the absurd asymmetry in life.

לָתֵת לְטוֹב לִפְנֵי הָאֱלֹהִים. Within this infinitival clause, the first
complement of the trivalent לתת is not made explicit; contextually it can
only be the product of the אסף and כנס activity. The second complement, though, is specified by the complex PP לטוב לפני האלהים. The
adjective טוב is used as a substantive, "a good man," and is further modified by the PP לפני האלהים. This PP is what is called an NP-internal
modifier, a type which is semantically restrictive: this is not any good
person, but one whose goodness is tied to his status "before God."

גַּם־זֶה הֶבֶל וּרְעוּת רוּחַ. See comments at 1:2 (for הבל), 11 (for גם), and 14 (for רעות).

3:1-15 Creation May Be Ordered,
but That Order Is not Clear

This section, 3:1-15, contains the famous "catalogue of times" (vv. 1-8), followed by Qoheleth's commentary (vv. 9-15). Here Qoheleth takes up a theme important in wisdom literature, "proper time" (von Rad, 138–43); as the proverb says, שִׂמְחָה לָאִישׁ בְּמַעֲנֵה־פִיו וְדָבָר בְּעִתּוֹ מַה־טּוֹב: "a man has joy in the answer of his mouth and a word in its time—how good!" (Prov 15:3). A significant component of the wisdom enterprise centers on determining not just what kind of behavior leads to success in life, but *when* that behavior is appropriate.

3:1   לַכֹּל זְמָן וְעֵת לְכָל־חֵפֶץ תַּחַת הַשָּׁמָיִם: ס

For everything exists a season and a time, for every delight/matter under the sun:

Verses 1-8 are structured as a rhythmic poem, using the עת + infinitive collocation as the structuring device. Verse 1 serves as the introduction, and v. 9 signals the end of the poem and the beginning of Qoheleth's commentary.

לַכֹּל זְמָן וְעֵת. A null copula clause with the copular complement fronted, presumably for focus: "a season and a time (exists) for *everything* (and I mean everything)." If לכל were not fronted, the relationship between לכל and the subject זמן ועת would be ambiguous: it could be an NP-internal (restrictive) modifier, "a time-for-everything exists," or a copular complement, "a time exists for everything." The fronting of לכל clarifies the syntax: since a restrictive modifier like an NP-internal PP or a restrictive relative cannot be fronted without its head, לכל can only be the copular complement. Assuming that this pattern applies to the other ל + infinitives in vv. 2-8 helps us to analyze the syntax of the entire poem. The ל preposition on the copular complements in vv. 1-8 indicates either the beneficiary (WO §11.2.10d), "a time exists *for the benefit* of everything," or the possessor (WO §11.2.10f), "a time *belongs to* everything." The preposition allows both meanings and perhaps both were intended, or at least the ambiguity was intentionally allowed. The use of the bound construction in vv. 4b, 5ab, and 8b (e.g., "a time *of* wailing exists") does not clarify the issue, since noun cliticization in Hebrew has a considerably flexible semantic range (see WO §9.5.3–4 for an overview of the "species of the genitive"). Although the compound זמן ועת is new information, it is also the syntactic subject. In fact, both the subject and the entire predicate present new information—nothing links the beginning of this chapter to the preceding discourse. The noun זְמָן "season" is of the same Aramaic-like pattern as עֲבָד (9:1) and קְרָב (9:18). The word itself occurs here and in Neh 2:6, Esth 9:27, 31, and Dan 2:16; 3:8; 4:33; 7:12. In nonbiblical texts, it occurs in Ben Sira (43:7) and the Mishnah, etc., as well as Imperial Aramaic (Hoftijzer and Jongeling, 332). It might be evidence of Aramaic borrowing, but it could also be a general Semitic word, since it also appears in Akkadian as *simānu* (see Schoors, 60–61; Mankowski, 54–55). While the vast majority of commentators and translations follow the Masoretic טעמים and break the verse, between זמן and ועת (i.e., into two clauses), we find Linafelt and Dobbs-Allsopp's argument compelling: the typical analysis defies lineation conventions in the Hebrew Bible and that the verse is best analyzed as a single clause, with the final PP an "extension" of the preceding PP.

לְכָל־חֵפֶץ תַּחַת הַשָּׁמָיִם. This PP is appositional to the fronted לכל at the beginning of the verse; as an appositive, it defines כל not as everything in general, but as every חפץ in human existence (תחת השמים) (similarly, see Krüger, 76). The root חפץ typically means "to take pleasure, desire, delight in" (HALOT, s.v.), and the noun חֵפֶץ, which occurs seven times in Ecclesiastes (3:1, 17; 5:3, 7; 8:6; 12:1, 10), typically means "joy, delight, wish" (HALOT, s.v.). However, most take the noun to have the nuance of "matter, business" here and in 3:17; 5:7; 8:6; this latter nuance is supported by the parallelism of כל חפץ with כל המעשה in 3:17 (similarly in Isa 58:13; cf. 1 QS 3.17; CD 14.12; Sir 10:26, and RH [Jastrow 492]). The PP תחת השמים modifies חפץ as an NP-internal modifier; i.e., the PP belongs within the NP and identifies or defines it as a restrictive modifier.

3:2   עֵת לָלֶדֶת וְעֵת לָמוּת עֵת לָטַעַת וְעֵת לַעֲקוֹר נָטוּעַ:

A time exists for birthing and a time exists for dying, a time exists for planting and time exists for uprooting something that is planted.

This verse initiates the sequence of gerundive infinitives that ends with the two nouns "war and peace" in v. 8.

עֵת לָלֶדֶת וְעֵת לָמוּת. Inf Constr Qal √ילד and √מות. Note that many translations and commentaries present ללדת as a monovalent, passive verb, "be born" (e.g., Delitzsch, 259; Longman, 111; Fox 1999: 207); however, there is no other example of a monovalent meaning for the Qal of ילד. Rather than force strict logic on the passage, the verb should be given its standard agentive meaning and the pair as a whole allowed an allusive reference to the beginnings and endings of life (so also Murphy, 29; Seow 1997: 160; Krüger, 75).

עֵת לָטַעַת וְעֵת לַעֲקוֹר נָטוּעַ. Inf Constr Qal √נטע and √עקר. The verb נטע is bivalent and so often has an overt NP complement (e.g., Gen 2:8; Josh 24:13). When a verb that usually has a complement occurs without one, the complement is typically either elliptical (i.e., a null complement with a meaning supplied by the context) or implicit. Implicit complements in BH are common in reflexive statements (where we often fill in "himself" or "themselves" in translation) and with certain verbs that suggest prototypical default complements based on cultural knowledge to allow underspecified, indefinite null complements, such as with "eat," "drink," and "bake." נטע appears to be a verb that allows underspecified, indefinite null complements, not only here, but also in Isa 65:22 and Jer 1:10. The verb עקר occurs in the Qal only here (it also occurs once in the Niphal [Zeph 2:4], once in the Hithpael [Dan 7:8], and 5× in the Piel [Gen 49:6; Josh 11:6, 9; 2 Sam 8:4; 1 Chr 18:4]). The single Qal occurrence here appears to be bivalent, with the complement (a null-head, unmarked relative with a ms Qal passive participle נטוע) created from the same root as the preceding verb, perhaps both to signal a sense of logical completion and for euphony.

3:3   עֵת לַהֲרוֹג וְעֵת לִרְפּוֹא עֵת לִפְרוֹץ וְעֵת לִבְנוֹת:

A time exists for killing and a time exists for healing, a time exists for breaking down and a time exists for building.

עֵת לַהֲרוֹג וְעֵת לִרְפּוֹא. Inf Constr Qal √הרג and √רפא. This pair of verbs is bivalent, most often with NP or clitic pronoun complements (e.g., Lev 20.16 and Gen 20.17, respectively—רפא also takes ל-PP complements). Here both verbs allow the underspecified, indefinite null complements (see comment on נטע in v. 2). As with the nonlogical opposition of לָלֶדֶת and לָמוּת in v. 2a, here, too, the contrast is not strictly logical (the antonym of killing would better be לְחַיּוֹת "to preserve life" and the antonym of healing לִפְצֹעַ "to injure"). Rather, הרג and רפא are opposites in a more general sense, speaking to intentional actions concerning a life; it is also possible that the pair is grounded in the context of battle (Longman, 115).

עֵת לִפְרוֹץ וְעֵת לִבְנוֹת. Inf Constr Qal √פרץ and √בנה. Again, these verbs are bivalent, though the complements here are underspecified, indefinite null constituents (see comment on נטע in v. 2). The order of the verbs is not what the reader might expect—first one builds and then one may tear down what is built. The converse order here may proceed from the warfare context of siege and rebuilding, but it also may be more general than warfare, since anytime a structure (e.g., grain storage facility, house) begins to fall apart, it is advisable to tear down and rebuild before the building falls on its own, possibly causing damage, injury, or even death.

3:4   עֵת לִבְכּוֹת וְעֵת לִשְׂחוֹק עֵת סְפוֹד וְעֵת רְקוֹד:

A time exists for crying and a time exists for laughing, a time of wailing exists and a time of gaiety exists.

עֵת לִבְכּוֹת וְעֵת לִשְׂחוֹק. Inf Constr Qal √בכה and √שחק. Both verbs are monovalent.

עֵת סְפוֹד וְעֵת רְקוֹד. Inf Constr Qal √ספד and √רקד. Unlike all other occurrences in vv. 2-8, the ל preposition is not used with these two infinitives (or כנוס in v. 5ab). There are two possible syntactic analyses: either (1) the absence of the ל is irrelevant and the construction is identical to those with the ל (JM §124b; see 1 Sam 15:22), or (2) the infinitive is part of the subject and is the clitic host for the noun עת (i.e., עת is bound to the infinitive; see WO §36.2.1c; Gen 29:7, 40:20). If the second option is taken, then there is no copular complement, making the statement a bare existential one: "a time of wailing exists." The deviation from the ל + infinitive pattern is a case of poetic license: the author uses a slightly different form, and possibly a different syntax, though the essential meaning remains the same. It could be that this deviation from the pattern is a structural signal that vv. 4b-5ab (i.e., כנוס) marks the halfway point of the poem, just as the deviation in v. 8b signals the end of the poem (Linafelt and Dobbs-Allsopp, 252). Even if this is correct, it unfortunately does not help us determine which syntactic structure is intended: whether the infinitive is the copular complement or the clitic host of עת within the subject. We have translated with the bound construction simply in order to communicate the literary signal in English. The same options apply for v. 5a-b (see also 12:12).

3:5   עֵת לְהַשְׁלִיךְ אֲבָנִים וְעֵת כְּנוֹס אֲבָנִים עֵת לַחֲבוֹק
וְעֵת לִרְחֹק מֵחַבֵּק:

A time exists for casting stones and a time exists for collecting stones, a time exists for embracing and a time exists for being distant from embracing.

עֵת לְהַשְׁלִיךְ אֲבָנִים וְעֵת כְּנוֹס אֲבָנִים. Inf Constr Hiph √שלך and Qal √כנס. The verbs in both halves are multivalent and each is followed by a complement, the NP אבנים. The verb השליך (always Hiphil) means "to throw" with nearly the same range of connotations as in English; thus, it is used for throwing objects, throwing something away, taking something off, removing something to another location, casting fish hooks, casting one's cares on God, etc. It is overwhelmingly trivalent, with an NP complement indicating the thing thrown and a locative PP complement indicating the goal of the throwing. Some occurrences lack a locative complement (e.g., Ezek 20:7), resulting in a general meaning "to throw (something) out/away." That is the notion here, where stones are thrown aside, as in a field or during building. Similarly, gathering stones occurs in the context of building structures such as walls and cisterns. The verb כנס is bivalent with אבנים its NP complement. Note the lack of the ל on the infinitive כנוס; see note on v. 4b. The verb כנס occurs only eleven times in the Hebrew Bible: in the Hithpael in Isa 28:20; in the Piel in Ezek 22:21; 39:28; Ps 147:2; and in the Qal in Pss 33:7; 147:2; Eccl 2:8, 26; 3:5; Esth 4:16; Neh 12:44; 1 Chr 22:2). It may be a lexeme characteristic of later BH, but the infrequent usage prevents any strong assertions.

עֵת לַחֲבוֹק וְעֵת לִרְחֹק מֵחַבֵּק. Inf Constr Qal √חבק and √רחק and Piel √חבק. The verb חבק, in both the Qal and Piel, is bivalent, and so an NP (Prov 5:20) or ל-PP (Gen 29:13) complement is expected. The absence of an overt complement forces a generalized implied interpretation—embracing generally, or embracing *something* (but *what* is left

unspecified). Rather than a lexical opposite, this pair uses the same verb
חבק but contrasts the positive with the negative by using the verb רחק.
Syntactically, the infinitive רחק, which is monovalent in the Qal, takes
the מן-PP + Piel infinitive חבק as a locative (source) adjunct.

3:6 עֵת לְבַקֵּשׁ וְעֵת לְאַבֵּד עֵת לִשְׁמוֹר וְעֵת לְהַשְׁלִיךְ:

*A time exists for seeking and a time exists for losing, a time exists for keep-
ing and time exists for throwing out.*

עֵת לְבַקֵּשׁ וְעֵת לְאַבֵּד. Inf Constr Piel √בקש and √אבד. As with
most of the other verses in this poem, the Piel verbs בקש and אבד are
bivalent, but here allow underspecified, indefinite null complements (see
comment on נטע in v. 2). When in parallel with בקש, the connotation
of אבד in the *Piel* is "to give up as lost" (HALOT, s.v.); in later Hebrew it
comes to mean simply "to lose (something)" (Jastrow, 2, "to waste, lose,
forfeit, destroy"). While this latter nuance is not quite accurate for the
biblical passage, it makes a much smoother English translation, which is
why it is used here.

עֵת לִשְׁמוֹר וְעֵת לְהַשְׁלִיךְ: Inf Constr Qal √שמר and Hiph √שלך.
Once again, the bivalent verbs שמר and השליך occur here with underspecified, indefinite null complements (see comment on נטע in v. 2). On
the meaning of השליך, see the comment on v. 5a.

3:7 עֵת לִקְרוֹעַ וְעֵת לִתְפּוֹר עֵת לַחֲשׁוֹת וְעֵת לְדַבֵּר:

*A time exists for rending and time exists for sewing together, a time exists
for being silent and a time exists for speaking.*

עֵת לִקְרוֹעַ וְעֵת לִתְפּוֹר. Inf Constr Qal √קרע and √תפר. Again,
both verbs are bivalent but occur here with the null complements signaling a prototypical constituent associated with the activity represented by
the verb, e.g., "rending (clothes)" and "sewing (clothes)."

עֵת לַחֲשׁוֹת וְעֵת לְדַבֵּר. Inf Constr Qal √חשה and Piel √דבר. The
verb חשה is monovalent and stative. Its counterpart, דבר, is bivalent
but here (like so many other verbs in the poem) allows the underspecified, indefinite null complement, for the general activity of "speaking
(words)."

3:8 עֵת לֶאֱהֹב֘ וְעֵת לִשְׂנֹא֒ עֵת מִלְחָמָה וְעֵת שָׁלֹ֑ום׃ ס

A time exists for loving and a time exists for hating, a time exists for war and a time exists for peace.

This verse brings the catalogue of times to a close, moving the audience to Qoheleth's explication of its significance.

עֵת לֶאֱהֹב֘ וְעֵת לִשְׂנֹא֒. Inf Constr Qal √אהב and √שנא. These two verbs (both bivalent with underspecified, indefinite null complements) are perhaps the only, and at least the best, set of antonyms in the poem.

עֵת מִלְחָמָה וְעֵת שָׁלֹ֑ום. Notice the use of nouns instead of the infinitive pattern. It certainly would have been possible to maintain the use of the infinitives, with לְשָׁלֹם* (an unattested form) and לְהִלָּחֵם. It is possible, then, that the nouns are a linguistic signal, in this case, that the list of times has come to an end. On the syntax of the departure from the lamed + infinitive pattern, see also the comment on v. 4b.

3:9 מַה־יִּתְרֹון֙ הָעֹושֶׂ֔ה בַּאֲשֶׁ֖ר ה֥וּא עָמֵֽל׃

What is the profit of the worker in exchange for (the labor) that he does?

As the audience should now recognize, Qoheleth's rhetorical questions demand a negative answer. In this case he begins his explication of the poem concerning fitting times by asserting that there is no profit for the one who works.

מַה־יִּתְרֹון֙ הָעֹושֶׂ֔ה. Participle ms Qal √עשה. A null copula clause with the interrogative מה fronted as the complement and the NP יתרון העושה as the subject. The participle עושה here is an agentive noun (see comment at 1:15), which is the clitic host for יתרון in the bound structure. See also the comment at 1:3 on slightly different מה יתרון structure there.

בַּאֲשֶׁ֖ר ה֥וּא עָמֵֽל. A null copula clause with a pronominal subject (הוא) and adjectival copular complement (עמל) (for similar relative clause syntax, see 2:18, 22). As with the similar statement in 1:3, the ב here is the ב *pretii* ("the ב of price") (JM §133c; WO §11.2.5d). The head of the relative clause is null, contextually inferable as עָמָל "toil, acquisition" (cf. 9:9) and resumed covertly within the relative. Note that the ב on באשר cannot go with the verbal adjective עָמֵל inside the relative clause since Hebrew does not allow pied-piping (i.e., raising of the prepositions with the relative words, as in English *in which, to whom,* etc.; see Holmstedt 2016: 155–58). Rather, the ב of באשר introduces a PP that is an adjunct to the null copula of the main clause מה יתרון.

3:10 רָאִיתִי אֶת־הָעִנְיָן אֲשֶׁר נָתַן אֱלֹהִים לִבְנֵי הָאָדָם
לַעֲנוֹת בּוֹ:

I have seen the occupation that God has given to men to be occupied with.

The second piece of his slowly building interpretation of the poem in vv. 1-8 is based on empirical data: he has observed what he is about to describe.

רָאִיתִי אֶת־הָעִנְיָן. *Qatal* 1cs Qal √ראה. On the meaning of עִנְיָן, see comment at 1:13.

אֲשֶׁר נָתַן אֱלֹהִים לִבְנֵי הָאָדָם לַעֲנוֹת בּוֹ. *Qatal* 3ms Qal √נתן and Inf Constr Qal √ענה. The relative clause modifies the noun הענין restrictively (i.e., it defines what kind of עִנְיָן is invoked). The trivalent verb נתן often takes an NP complement of the thing given and a PP complement for the recipient or goal. Here the NP complement is the null resumption of the relative head, הענין, and the PP complement is לבני האדם. The ל-PP infinitive clause is an adjunct (of purpose) to the verb נתן. The PP בו is the complement to the bivalent infinitival verb ענות; the 3ms clitic pronoun in the PP בו refers back to the relative head הענין via an anaphoric chain that goes through the null resumption within the main level of the relative (see also discussion of the almost identical construction in 1:13).

3:11 אֶת־הַכֹּל עָשָׂה יָפֶה בְעִתּוֹ גַּם אֶת־הָעֹלָם נָתַן
בְּלִבָּם מִבְּלִי אֲשֶׁר לֹא־יִמְצָא הָאָדָם אֶת־הַמַּעֲשֶׂה
אֲשֶׁר־עָשָׂה הָאֱלֹהִים מֵרֹאשׁ וְעַד־סוֹף:

He has made everything fitting in its time; yet he has put "eternity" in their mind without man's ability to find out the work that God has done from beginning to end.

This verse functions as the interpretive key to Qoheleth's use of the catalogue of times in vv. 1-8. The link with the poem is unambiguous: the word עת in the PP בְעִתּוֹ. The statement begins surprisingly positive: no one in ancient Israel would be likely to argue against the notion that God has created the world so that everything fits together. But for

Qoheleth, the disturbing truth is that God has not created humans with a corresponding ability to discern the pattern! The implications of this assertion are catastrophic for the wisdom enterprise in general. The assumption that drives the search for wisdom is that patterns in creation lead to principles that guide behavior resulting in reward or punishment. If, as Qoheleth here argues, such principles are fundamentally beyond human discernment, there is no way to know how to negotiate life. Qoheleth's use of the theme of "proper time" effectively pulled the rug out from under his fellow sages.

אֶת־הַכֹּל עָשָׂה יָפֶה בְעִתּוֹ. *Qatal* 3ms Qal √עשׂה. Note the complement-verb order; the adjective יָפֶה means "beautiful" and also "fitting," "right," which are more appropriate here. The Qal verb עשׂה is typically bivalent, but it also has a trivalent meaning "to make X (from/into) Y" (e.g., Gen 27:9; see DCH s.v. #2b; GKC §117ii). The NP אֶת־הכל is the first complement and יפה is the second. The ב-PP is a temporal adjunct to the verb.

גַּם אֶת־הָעֹלָם נָתַן בְּלִבָּם. *Qatal* 3ms Qal √נתן. Trivalent נתן typically takes an NP complement and a PP complement expressing recipient or, as here, location, thus accounting for the distinction in meaning between "give" (with recipient PP) and "place/put" (with locative PP). The function word גם is here best taken as an adversative, "yet, however" (HALOT); the noun עלם "eternity" is an interpretive crux. There are three common solutions. First, Seow represents those who take 'eternity' to make good sense: "The noun ... refers to a sense of that which is timeless and, as such, stands in contrast to *'ittô* 'its time.' Qohelet's point is ironic: God who has made everything right in its time has also put a sense of timelessness in human hearts" (1997: 163). However, the only way this could be ironic is if God made human understanding "timeless," i.e, without a sense of time. Since this does not fit with the meaning of עֹלָם, Seow's proposal does not make good sense. A less objectionable variation of this solution interprets עלם as "duration" (Murphy, 34–35; cf. NRSV "a sense of past and future"), a time including the various types of עת. This approach has support in the near description of God's work as lasting לעולם "forever" (3:14). Humanity is stymied by knowledge of the endless passing of "times" (see 1:3-8), because they also have no understanding of the principles by which things happen when they do. Crenshaw represents a second view, maintaining the consonants but deriving the noun from the root עלם "to be hidden" (Niphal). The derived noun supposedly denotes "what is hidden" and connotes "what is unknown"; thus, Crenshaw translates the phrase as "he has put the unknown in their mind" (note that Crenshaw conflates עלם "to be hidden" [Niphal] and עלם "to darken" [Hiphil], which HALOT lists as two distinct roots). Finally, Fox represents those who emend: he emends to the noun עָמָל, which is used throughout the book. The emendation to עמל gives the entire passage a greater negative cast: "the best evidence for this reading is 8:17, which echoes 3:11 in wording and ideas. There Qohelet uses the verb *'amal* to designate man's hopeless endeavor to grasp (*limso'*) that which God has brought to pass ..." (1999: 211). Our translation above retains the first, more traditional gloss, though it is not without difficulty. Finally, note the 3mp clitic pronoun in לבם; the plural pronoun must refer proleptically to האדם in the next clause (see also the discussion on בם and חייו in v. 12).

מִבְּלִי אֲשֶׁר לֹא־יִמְצָא הָאָדָם אֶת־הַמַּעֲשֶׂה. *Yiqtol* 3ms Qal √מצא. The verb expresses dynamic (ability) modality in this context. The initial sequence מבלי אשר לא is, as Seow (1997: 163) notes, without parallel in the Hebrew Bible. Both בְּלִי and מִבְּלִי mean "without" but also function simply as a negative for finite verbs (HALOT; cf. Jastrow, 172). But "without that man can (does/should) not grasp the deed that God has done" is nonsensical. Although this is a unique collocation (see Schoors, 147–48 for a brief discussion of past proposals), it is not inexplicable. The explanation requires recognizing two grammatical features. First, the אשר nominalizes the finite verbal clause so that it can function as the complement to מבלי. For the author of the book, the pattern in which מבלי negates a noun (and not a verb) must have become dominant, thereby necessitating the nominalization of the clause by אשר. Second, Hebrew allows double negation as a strategy to intensify the negative polarity of the statement. That is, in Hebrew, unlike English but quite like many of the world's languages, two negatives do not cancel each other out and thus reverse the polarity of the clause. מבלי includes negative semantics in that it comments on the "lack" of something, and the לא with the finite verb within the אשר clause reinforces the negative and makes it clear what the author intends. As a whole, the מבלי PP (with its אשר clause complement) is an adjunct to the verb נתן and describes an attendant circumstance of the event. Within the אשר clause, את־המעשה functions as the complement of bivalent ימצא.

אֲשֶׁר־עָשָׂה הָאֱלֹהִים מֵרֹאשׁ וְעַד־סוֹף. *Qatal* 3ms Qal √עשה. This restrictive relative clause modifies the head המעשה, which is resumed covertly as the complement of bivalent עשה. The correlative

PPs with מִן and עַד form a compound adjunct of time to the verb. The noun רֹאשׁ commonly has the sense "head," but in temporal contexts "beginning" is the appropriate gloss (cf. רֹאשׁ הַשָּׁנָה "the new year" in Ezek 40:1).

3:12   יָדַ֗עְתִּי כִּ֣י אֵ֥ין טֹ֖וב בָּ֑ם כִּ֣י אִם־לִשְׂמֹ֔וחַ וְלַעֲשֹׂ֥ות
טֹ֖וב בְּחַיָּֽיו׃

I have come to know that there is no good (thing) among them [human-ity] except to take joy and to do pleasure in one's life,

As with his other יֹדַעְתִּי statements, in vv. 12-13 Qoheleth moves from his observations about the unknowability of "proper times" to his conclusion for human behavior: since man cannot find what is truly good, he might as well enjoy what he can. In the face of such intellectual frustration, Qoheleth advocates a constrained hedonism (the limits of which become clearer in 7:2-4).

יָדַ֗עְתִּי כִּ֣י אֵ֥ין טֹ֖וב בָּ֑ם. *Qatal* 1cs Qal √ידע and אין negative cop-ula. The stative verb expresses an inchoative idea here (i.e., "coming to know" in the course of his reflections), as in 1:17 and 2:14. Rather than בם, two MSS read באדם, which is likely a scribal correction to make the phrase אין טוב בם accord with the similar phrases in 2:24 and 8:15. But the 3mp suffix on בם likely refers back to האדם (with generic use of the article for "humanity, mankind, human beings") in v. 11 anyway, so no emendation is necessary (so Seow 1998: 164; con-tra Fox 1999: 212; see also 3:11, where the 3mp clitic pronoun is used on בלבם in the same clause that uses ms האדם, both having "mankind" as their referent).

כִּ֣י אִם־לִשְׂמֹ֔וחַ וְלַעֲשֹׂ֥ות טֹ֖וב בְּחַיָּֽיו. Inf Constr Qal √שׂמח and √עשׂה. This clause is an exceptive clause subordinate to the negative copula אין clause. Contextually, the PP לעשׂות טוב בחייו is likely not the more frequent meaning "to do (moral, ethical) good," but rather "to do pleasure," i.e., "to enjoy oneself" (Seow 1997: 164; HALOT). Note the 3ms clitic pronoun on בחייו, which stands in contrast to the 3mp clitic pronoun in בם in the preceding clause. The referent of both pronouns is האדם (mankind) in v. 11. We suggest that the plural pronoun be under-stood to refer to the corporate plurality, similar to "people," whereas the switch to the singular pronoun in בחייו reflects a shift to individual refer-ence, "each person."

3:13   וְגַם כָּל־הָאָדָם שֶׁיֹּאכַל וְשָׁתָה וְרָאָה טוֹב בְּכָל־
עֲמָלוֹ מַתַּת אֱלֹהִים הִיא:

and also the whole (portion) of man is that he eats and drinks and experiences goodness in all his acquisition(s)—it is the gift of God.

וְגַם כָּל־הָאָדָם שֶׁיֹּאכַל וְשָׁתָה וְרָאָה טוֹב בְּכָל־עֲמָלוֹ. *Yiqtol* 3ms Qal √אכל and *qatal* 3ms Qal √שתה and √ראה. The גם is additive (see comment on 1:11). The syntax of this verse is challenging. The שׁ clause is not a relative modifying כל אדם but a nominalized clause. The question is how the שׁ clause relates to what comes before, כל האדם, and what comes after, מתת אלהים היא. Many versions and commentators understand כל האדם as a left-dislocated constituent resumed by the pronoun היא at the end of the verse, "every man who eats and drinks and experiences goodness in all his acquisition—it is the gift of God." But the 3fs היא is not an appropriate resumption for the 3ms כל האדם. Rather, כל האדם can be read as we do in 5:18 and 12:13; i.e., elliptically for something like כל חלק האדם, "the whole portion/lot of humankind." If so, then כל האדם is the subject of a null copula clause and the שׁ nominalized clause is the copular complement, "and also, the whole of man *is* (*consists of*) that he eat and drink and enjoy good in all his toil/acquisition." In all three passages that use the כל האדם phrase (3:13; 5:18; 12:13), our proposed elliptical rendering makes good contextual sense. In 3:13 the thing that makes Qoheleth's assertion informative is not that humans should eat, drink, and enjoy (he has already told us that in 2:24), but that these activities are "the whole (portion) of man" and a gift of God! Likewise in 5:18, after asserting (in v.17) that the good that he has seen is that eating/drinking/enjoying are appropriate, for that is חלקו ("his portion"), he proceeds to say, גם כל־האדם אשר נתן־לו האלהים עשר ונכסים והשליטו לאכל ממנו ולשאת את־חלקו ולשמח בעמלו זה מתת אלהים היא. Both 3:13 and 5:18 may represent premature conclusions of Qoheleth as he investigates life under the sun: what human life ultimately consists of is taking joy in the pleasures and benefits that God has given. But perhaps this is a foil for 12:13, where the final voice of the book comes to the conclusion of matters, and there he uses the collocation כל־האדם one final time to assert that something else constitutes the "whole of man": סוף דבר הכל נשמע את־האלהים ירא ואת־מצותיו שמור כי־זה כל־האדם.

מַתַּת אֱלֹהִים הִיא. A null copula clause in which the copular complement has been fronted for Focus. The 3fs pronoun היא refers back to the assertion made in the preceding clause; assertions and ideas, similar to abstract concepts, are grammatically feminine in BH. Given the high level of cynicism in Qoheleth's intellectual anthropology (i.e., the limits on human discernment), it is plausible that the reference to the "gift of God" is darkly ironic—for the sage, this gift is a pretty poor consolation prize.

3:14   יָדַ֗עְתִּי כִּ֤י כָּל־אֲשֶׁ֨ר יַעֲשֶׂ֤ה הָאֱלֹהִים֙ ה֣וּא יִהְיֶ֣ה
לְעוֹלָ֔ם עָלָיו֙ אֵ֣ין לְהוֹסִ֔יף וּמִמֶּ֖נּוּ אֵ֣ין לִגְרֹ֑עַ
וְהָאֱלֹהִ֣ים עָשָׂ֔ה שֶׁיִּֽרְא֖וּ מִלְּפָנָֽיו׃

I have come to know that all that God does, it will be forever. There is no adding upon it and there is no diminishing from it—God has done (it) that they should be afraid of him.

Verses 14-15 present a second conclusion that Qoheleth draws: God has made the world like this; since discerning how to behave by observation is impossible (and thus one may easily offend the creator), one can only live in fear of divine retribution.

יָדַ֗עְתִּי כִּ֤י כָּל־אֲשֶׁ֨ר יַעֲשֶׂ֤ה הָאֱלֹהִים֙ ה֣וּא יִהְיֶ֣ה לְעוֹלָ֔ם. *Qatal* 1cs Qal √ידע and *yiqtol* 3ms Qal √עשׂה and √היה. The כי nominalizes all four following clauses as a compound complement of the bivalent verb ידעתי. As in 1:17, 2:14, and 3:12, an inchoative sense for the stative is most fitting ("I have come to know"). The initial כל modifies a null head to the following relative, resumed covertly as the complement of the generic verb יעשׂה (the participle is more frequent in Ecclesiastes for generic expressions; see the Introduction). As a whole, the null-head restrictive relative is a left-dislocation resumed by the pronoun הוא in the following copular clause. The copular יהיה is generic, but casts the observation as a future prediction versus the present-tense interpretation of a null copula (see Cook 2005).

עָלָיו֙ אֵ֣ין לְהוֹסִ֔יף וּמִמֶּ֖נּוּ אֵ֣ין לִגְרֹ֑עַ. Inf Constr Hiph √יסף and Qal √גרע. The collocation of אין and a ל-PP/infinitive clause carries a modal nuance (WO §36.2.3f #40, 42), "cannot, must not, may not" and occurs almost exclusively in LBH (Esth 4:2; 8:8; Ezra 9:15; 1 Chr 23:26; 2 Chr 5:11; 14:10; 20:6; 22:9; 35:15; cf. Sir 10:23 (2×); 39:21; 40:26; cf. 1 Sam 9:7; Hag 1:6) and in Qumran texts (1QS 3.16; 1QH 7.28; see Qimron, 78–79). The "standard" BH method for negating an infinitive is to use לְבַלְתִּי, but this does not carry a negative irrealis (whether dynamic, directive, or epistemic) nuance. The subject of the אֵין copula is the לְ-PPs/infinitive clauses, לְהוֹסִיף and לִגְרֹעַ, out of which the PPs עָלָיו and מִמֶּנּוּ, respectively, have been focus-fronted.

וְהָאֱלֹהִים עָשָׂה שֶׁיִּרְאוּ מִלְּפָנָיו. *Qatal* 3ms Qal√עשׂה and *yiqtol* 3mp Qal √ירא. The verb עשׂה is bivalent; the complement is unexpressed here but may be inferred from the כֹּל phrase at the beginning of the verse. Note that within the שׁ clause, the verb יִּרְאוּ is defectively spelled for יִירְאוּ, resulting in a form that looks identical to BH "they saw" (from ראה; see GKC §16h for the role of *metheg* in disambiguating the forms). The role of שׁ is the interpretive challenge in this clause. Fox interprets the שׁ as a purpose particle: "God *intends* for people to fear him (thus *še-* introduces a purpose clause), but he does not impose that fear. By enforcing human ignorance and helplessness, God *occasions* fear but does not directly cause or 'make it'" (1999: 213; similarly, Delitzsch, 265–66; Whitley, 34; Schoors, 143; Seow 1997: 165; Longman, 113). There are three legitimate grammatical options. First, the relative clause may be extraposed—i.e., moved from its normal position following its head, הַאלהים in this case, to a lower position, after the verb עשׂה in this case. Relative clause *extraposition* is common when the relative clause is "heavier" than the remainder of the clause (i.e., the single word עשׂה here). As such, it is related to the well-known phenomenon "heavy noun phrase shift" (see 2:7, 17; 3:22; 7:18, 20, 26; 9:11, 14, 15; 11:7). If we were to move it back to its original place, we can more easily see how this option works: הַאלהים שׁיראו מלפניו עשׂה, "God, whom they fear, did (it)." The second option is to take the שׁ clause as a covertly headed relative clause that is an appositive to הַאלהים (similar to the above explanation, the appositive placed after the verb reflects HNPS). A literal gloss reflecting this syntactic analysis is "God did (it), (he) whom they fear." The first and second analyses, while syntactically distinct, do not differ much from each other in meaning; however, they provide a very different meaning for the clause in the verse compared to how we translated it above. In the relative analysis, one cannot infer that God intends that people fear him; rather, they simply do. That is, the relative clause is descriptive of the situation but says nothing about God's character or plans. However, the third grammatical option for the clause includes intentionality: the שׁ is a nominalizer for לְמַעַן, which has been omitted. The result is an understood purpose, "(for the purpose) that. ..." In this analysis the שׁ is technically still a nominalizer, but one can see how

שׁ might have been reanalyzed in cases of abbreviation like this so that by Mishnaic Hebrew it seems to introduce just about any subordinate clause. If this third option is correct, it must be the path by which שׁ, and also just a few cases of אֲשֶׁר, came to be associated (by ancient speakers as well as modern grammarians) with causal, purpose, result, or temporal meanings (see Holmstedt 2016: chap. 7).

3:15 מַה־שֶּׁהָיָה֙ כְּבָ֣ר ה֔וּא וַאֲשֶׁ֥ר לִהְי֖וֹת כְּבָ֣ר הָיָ֑ה
וְהָאֱלֹהִ֖ים יְבַקֵּ֥שׁ אֶת־נִרְדָּֽף׃

Whatever is—it was already, and what is to be already has been, and God will seek what is pursued.

The final statement of Qoheleth's exposition on proper times follows the dark view of God's work in v. 14 by reiterating his earlier point that life is cyclical and by making explicit that God is behind it.

מַה־שֶּׁהָיָה֙ כְּבָ֣ר ה֔וּא. *Qatal* 3ms Qal √היה and null copula clause. On מה שׁ, see comments on 1:9 and 3:22. On כבר, see comment at 1:10. The expected tense interpretation of the *qatal* copula and null copula make poor sense both within the immediate context and given the similar sentiment expressed in 1:9: "What has been already is" (cf. 1:9 "Whatever has been—it is what will be"). Rather, we would expect the null copula to come first followed by the perfect, to express "What (is) already has been" (see Fox 1999: 192). The difficulty is that there would then be no "landing site" for the enclitic שׁ, thus the *qatal* of the stative copula is used with the marginal meaning of a present state: "What is … ." This in turn prompts the avoidance of the overt *qatal* of the copula in the second clause, which might be misread as a tautological statement "What has been already has been." The immediate context added to comparison with 1:9 makes it clear that the comparison is between *past* and *present*, on the one hand, and *present* and *future*, on the other. Thus, it is possible to decipher here that the stative היה is present tense, referring to what is, and suggesting that the null copula must be contextually interpreted as past tense to make the expected contrast (see Cook 2017: 327).

וַאֲשֶׁ֥ר לִהְי֖וֹת כְּבָ֣ר הָיָ֑ה. Inf Constr and *qatal* 3ms Qal √היה. The null head of the אשר relative cause ("[the thing] that") is the subject of the copula היה, with כבר focus-fronted; this null head is also resumed within the relative clause as the null-subject of a null copula clause, which has the infinitive לִהְיוֹת as its copular complement ("[the thing] that [it] [is] to be").

וְהָאֱלֹהִים יְבַקֵּשׁ אֶת־נִרְדָּף. *Yiqtol* 3ms Piel √בקשׁ and Participle ms Niph √רדף. Fox notes that רדף is a near synonym of בקשׁ and thus translates this clause as "God seeks what has already been sought" (1999: 213). The obvious problem is the meaning of such a statement. Fox follows Crenshaw in explaining that this refers to the fact that "God ensures that events which have just transpired do not vanish into thin air. God brings them back once more, so that the past circles into the present" and thus there is nothing new under the sun (quoted from Fox 1999: 213–14). Differently, Seow notes that the Niphal of רדף is associated with the wind pushing something along and so summarizes the clause as "God will look after what people have pursued in vain" (1997: 165–66). This makes less sense than the Fox/Crenshaw proposal, although neither are truly satisfying. The last part of the verse remains enigmatic.

3:16-22 Neither Life nor Death Provide Justice

Qoheleth's view of death mirrors his view of life—he cannot see how any clear sense of justice reigns in either, leading him to conclude that the best one can do is to enjoy what one has now, since tomorrow, living or dead, is guaranteed to be neither better, nor even as good.

3:16 וְעוֹד רָאִיתִי תַּחַת הַשָּׁמֶשׁ מְקוֹם הַמִּשְׁפָּט שָׁמָּה
הָרֶשַׁע וּמְקוֹם הַצֶּדֶק שָׁמָּה הָרָשַׁע׃

And again I saw under the sun the place of justice—there was wickedness!—and the place of righteousness—there was wickedness!

With this verse Qoheleth shifts to another observation about the wicked and righteous, in this case, that wickedness is in precisely the places that it should not be (by all typical construals of the ordered cosmos, anyway).

וְעוֹד רָאִיתִי תַּחַת הַשָּׁמֶשׁ מְקוֹם הַמִּשְׁפָּט שָׁמָּה הָרֶשַׁע. *Qatal* 1cs Qal √ראה and a parenthesis with a null copula clause. The PP תחת השמשׁ is an adjunct to the verb and the NP מקום המשׁפט is the first half of the compound complement. The adjunct עוד functions as a constituent adverb (i.e., adverbs that modify the predicate by specifying the time, place, or manner, see WO §39.3.1d) with either a temporal quality, "still, yet" (WO §39.3.1h) or a scalar quality, "again, continually" (scalar referring to descriptions of something, like verbal action, along a continuum or grade—here, a grade of identity of the action or event; the two sides of the continuum would be a repeated situation ["again"] or an uninterrupted one ["continually"]; WO §39.3.1i). Here עוד is scalar not temporal.

וּמְקוֹם הַצֶּדֶק שָׁמָּה הָרֶשַׁע. The second מקום is the second half of the compound NP complement of the bivalent verb ראיתי. The parentheses that follow each מקום NP contain null copula clauses. Both parenthetical clauses also function as exclamatives, with a focus-fronted (locative) copular complement: "*there* was wickedness!" (twice). The focus-fronting serves to contrast the fact that Qoheleth has observed, with the natural expectation, that in both places one would more likely find righteousness *not* wickedness. Our gloss, "there (was) wickedness," is not to be understood as an existential statement in which English uses the dummy word *there* (as in, "There are crazy things happening!"); Hebrew does not use שם/שמה as a dummy word. Finally, the longer form of שם with penultimate stress, שָׁמָּה, has the postposition known as the locative/directional ה. However, it need not always indicate direction or motion; it can also be locative, see, e.g., Ruth 1:7: וַתֵּצֵא מִן־הַמָּקוֹם אֲשֶׁר הָיְתָה־שָׁמָּה "So she set out from the place where she was *there*" (WO §10.5b; JM §93f; GKC §90d).

3:17   אָמַרְתִּי אֲנִי בְּלִבִּי אֶת־הַצַּדִּיק וְאֶת־הָרָשָׁע יִשְׁפֹּט
הָאֱלֹהִים כִּי־עֵת לְכָל־חֵפֶץ וְעַל כָּל־הַמַּעֲשֶׂה שָׁם:

I said, I with my לב, "The righteous and the wicked God will judge," because there is a time for every matter and over every deed there.

Following his observation about wickedness in v. 16, here Qoheleth returns to the conversation with his לב. Neither the purpose of the conversation nor its content are entirely clear; it could be that Qoheleth builds on his observation that wickedness exists in places of righteousness by asserting that God judges both types of people equally (when one would expect only the wicked to receive judgment). If the choice of *yiqtol* for the generic statement is significant, the event is presented as a future inevitability (see Cook 2005: 128), in which case Qoheleth is perhaps making a concession to traditional wisdom: a time will come when the wickedness that appears where righteousness is expected (v. 16) will be dealt with. However, this is of little consolation, given the reference to

proper times here because no one can discern when that time of judgment will be.

אָמַ֤רְתִּֽי אֲנִי֙ בְּלִבִּ֔י. *Qatal* 1cs Qal √אמר. On אני and בלבי, see comment on 2:1.

אֶת־הַצַּדִּיק֙ וְאֶת־הָ֣רָשָׁ֔ע יִשְׁפֹּ֖ט הָאֱלֹהִ֑ים. *Yiqtol* 3ms Qal √שפט.
This clause is the speech complement of אמרתי. The fronting of the
compound complement את הצדיק ואת הרשע is for focus: the truth
(which Qoheleth asserts or uses to parrot traditional wisdom?) that God
judges *both* the righteous and the wicked stands in contrast to the conclusion one might draw from the exclamations in v. 16 that the wicked
may escape God's judgment. Confidently identifying the contrast of the
focus element, however, requires more clarity on the interpretation of the
statement as a whole.

כִּי־עֵ֣ת לְכָל־חֵ֔פֶץ וְעַ֥ל כָּל־הַֽמַּעֲשֶׂ֖ה שָֽׁם. A null copula clause with
עת as the subject and the compound PP ל ... על as the copular complement, just as with the poem in 3:1-8. The כי clause makes better sense if
it is understood to be subordinate to the verb of the matrix clause, providing a rationale for Qoheleth's act of saying, rather than subordinate
to the verb of the embedded speech complement, God's act of judging
(although it does not transparently motivate the act of speaking either).

3:18   אָמַ֤רְתִּֽי אֲנִי֙ בְּלִבִּ֔י עַל־דִּבְרַת֙ בְּנֵ֣י הָֽאָדָ֔ם לְבָרָ֖ם
הָאֱלֹהִ֑ים וְלִרְא֕וֹת שְׁהֶם־בְּהֵמָ֥ה הֵ֖מָּה לָהֶֽם:

*I said, I with my לב, concerning humans, "God should test them and
should see that they are cattle, they to themselves,"*

In another brief conversation with his לב, Qoheleth remains
opaque (Fox 1999: 214 thinks the text is corrupt beyond reconstruc-
tion). What precisely is the point of equating humans with cattle? It
is possible that Qoheleth returns to the theme of human limitation: if
they cannot discern God's order so as to behave wisely, how are they
any better than domestic beasts, who only live to eat, drink, work, and
rest? If this notion is behind this statement, then Qoheleth might be
suggesting that God ought to examine his own creation to see how
absurd the situation really is.

אָמַ֤רְתִּֽי אֲנִי֙ בְּלִבִּ֔י עַל־דִּבְרַת֙ בְּנֵ֣י הָֽאָדָ֔ם. *Qatal* 1cs Qal √אמר. On
אני and בלבי, see comment on 2:1. The PP על דברת בני האדם is a verbal

adjunct specifying the subject matter of the speech (for this use of עַל, see WO §11.2.13g; MNK §39.19.4i).

לְבָרָם הָאֱלֹהִים וְלִרְאוֹת שְׁהֶם־בְּהֵמָה הֵמָּה לָהֶם. Inf Constr Qal √ברר and √ראה. A null copula clause with האלהים as the subject and a compound ל-PP/infinitive as the copular complement. This use of the infinitive is related to the modal semantics with the ל-PP/infinitive in 3:14; thus, here "God is to test and to see" communicates a modal sense of obligation, "God should test and see" or "God ought to test and see." The שׁ clause is the complement of the infinitive ראות. Within the complement clause, the 3mp pronoun הם is the subject of a null copula clause and the NP בהמה is the complement. The two constituents at the end of the clause, המה להם, do not appear to serve any core syntactic role. The most plausible analysis is that המה להם is a right-dislocated phrase (the opposite of left-dislocation, or "casus pendens") that links back to הם within the clause, focusing the human self-awareness that will be gained (see Holmstedt 2014 on right-dislocation). Not only will God discover that humans are simply beastly, they appear as such even to themselves. Goldman (77*–78*) suggests that "the preposition of להם is to be understood as a ל *relationis* … introducing the meaning: 'even in their own estimation.'"

3:19   כִּי מִקְרֶה בְנֵי־הָאָדָם וּמִקְרֶה הַבְּהֵמָה וּמִקְרֶה
אֶחָד לָהֶם כְּמוֹת זֶה כֵּן מוֹת זֶה וְרוּחַ אֶחָד לַכֹּל
וּמוֹתַר הָאָדָם מִן־הַבְּהֵמָה אָיִן כִּי הַכֹּל הָבֶל:

because the fate of man and the fate of the cattle—one fate belongs to them!; like the death of the one—thus is the death of the other, and one spirit belongs to all, and the advantage of man over cattle is nothing. Indeed, everything is a הבל*!*

The whole verse (except for the last clause) is governed by the initial כי and consists of multiple reasons for Qoheleth's conversation with his לב in v. 18. The last clause is either an additional reason (functionally an exclamative in this context) or a concluding interjection (with an asseverative כי). The point of the verse is to belabor the injustice that humanity, the supposed culmination of creation (Qoheleth seems to assume a Genesis 1 or similar cosmology), fares no better than cattle, in life (v. 18) or death (v. 19).

A. כִּי מִקְרֶה בְנֵי־הָאָדָם וּמִקְרֶה הַבְּהֵמָה וּמִקְרֶה אֶחָד לָהֶם A null copula clause with an initial left-dislocation that is resumed by a partial copy of the dislocated NP מקרה. The subject of the null copula is the NP ומקרה אחד, and the copular complement is the possessive ל-PP. This verse expresses a similar sentiment with respect to humanity and humans as the wise and the fool in 2:14-15.

כְּמוֹת זֶה כֵּן מוֹת זֶה. A null copula clause, in which the initial PP כמות זה is left-dislocated and then resumed by the focus-fronted adverb כן within the clause proper. The fronted adverb כן is the copular complement of the clause, while the NP מות זה is the subject. The left-dislocation of the כ-PP allows it to function as the clausal topic and then also, by virtue of resumption with the fronted כן, also bear focus-marking. As the topic, the כ-PP orients the audience to the anchor of the comparison; with focus the כ-PP/כן chain isolates and restricts the nature of the death of humans to the particular option in view. The antecedent of the first זה is בהמה, with which humanity is compared, and the antecedent to the second זה is בני האדם. When contrasted pairs are mentioned (along the lines of the English expressions "the one … the other"; "this one … that one," or "some … others") BH employs the same demonstrative pronoun (זה) for both alternatives (WO §17.3c, §17.4.2d; see also Isa 6:3; Josh 8:22; 1 Kgs 22:20).

וְרוּחַ אֶחָד לַכֹּל. A null copula clause with "normal" subject-predicate order, with the possessive ל-PP as the complement, and a NP (with an intervening attributive adjective) as the subject. For ל indicating possession, see JM §133d; MNK §39.11.1.3; WO §11.2.10d.

וּמוֹתַר הָאָדָם מִן־הַבְּהֵמָה אָיִן. A null copula clause with אין (appearing here in the rare form of the nonbound substantive "nothing," instead of its more frequent negative copula role) serving as the copular complement. The subject is the complex NP ומותר האדם מן־הבהמה, in which the comparative מן-PP is NP-internal to the bound structure מותר האדם (for comparative מן, see MNK §39.14.8; WO §11.2.11e.3).

3:20   הַכֹּל הוֹלֵךְ אֶל־מָקוֹם אֶחָד הַכֹּל הָיָה מִן־הֶעָפָר
וְהַכֹּל שָׁב אֶל־הֶעָפָר:

Everything goes to one place; everything came from the dirt and everything returns to the dirt.

This verse is a restatement of the normative view of the afterlife in the majority of the Hebrew Bible, building on the view of human substance in Genesis 2 (see also 12:7): there is nothing meaningful after this life; the grave is the final stop. Such a view makes inequities in life all the more tragic since there is no afterlife during which justice could be achieved.

הַכֹּל הוֹלֵךְ אֶל־מָקוֹם אֶחָד. Participle ms Qal √הלך. The אֶל-PP provides the locative complement for the normally bivalent verb of motion הלך (which here, as participle, functions as the complement of a null copula clause having הכל as the subject). On כל with the article, see comment on 1:2.

הַכֹּל הָיָה מִן־הֶעָפָר. *Qatal* 3ms Qal √היה. The מִן-PP is the copular complement, in this case indicating a source or origin (WO §11.2.11b; MNK §39.14.1; JM §133e). The use of the copula verb with a directional expression like this (with the sense "arise, come, come about") is similar to the statement about the דבר יהוה in the prophetic books (Hos 1:1; Joel 1:1; Mic 1:1; Zeph 1:1).

וְהַכֹּל שָׁב אֶל־הֶעָפָר. Participle ms Qal √שוב. The predicate could be parsed as a *qatal* or participle. In the context, used as a generic expression like הולך, it is the participle. It contrasts with the overt past-tense היה that precedes it. As with הלך in the first clause, שוב in the Qal is a bivalent verb of motion and takes the אל-PP as its locative complement.

3:21   מִי יוֹדֵעַ רוּחַ בְּנֵי הָאָדָם הָעֹלָה הִיא לְמָעְלָה וְרוּחַ
        הַבְּהֵמָה הַיֹּרֶדֶת הִיא לְמַטָּה לָאָרֶץ:

Who knows (if) the spirit of mankind—it is what goes up above, while the spirit of the cattle—it is what goes down to the earth?

The concept of the human spirit going up while the animal spirit goes down is a departure not only from the typical view of the afterlife elsewhere in the Hebrew Bible but also from what Qoheleth just said in v. 20! Here in v. 21, Qoheleth appears to present a novel view of the afterlife, which he neither endorses or dismisses. Conceptually, this may reflect the Platonic view of the human versus animal soul; if so, then it is plausible that Qoheleth recognized that some of his intended audience may have adopted this Hellenistic belief. His mention of it is thus a rhetorical move to head off any response that justice may be meted out in the afterlife. For Qoheleth, it matters not which view of the afterlife his audience adopts—it is life "under the sun" that is the problem.

מִי יוֹדֵעַ. Participle ms Qal √ידע. The verb ידע is bivalent; the complement is compound, consisting of both clauses that follow, which are best understood in the irrealis context set up by מי יודע as an unmarked conditional, like 2:19 but without the interrogative ה (contra Goldman, who in the BHQ critical apparatus favors taking the ה on העלה as the interrogative ה, not the article). Unlike most of Qoheleth's questions, this one does not seem to be a rhetorical question, but an open-ended one.

רוּחַ בְּנֵי הָאָדָם הָעֹלָה הִיא לְמָעְלָה. Participle fs Qal √עלה and null copula clause. Here and in the next clause, the initial NP is left dislocated and resumed by the pronoun היא. In the clause proper, the copular complement העלה, which is a null-head ה-relative clause ("the one that goes up"), is focus-fronted in order to contrast the two assumed categories of spirits—those that go up and those that go down after death. The PP למעלה reinforces the directional idea of the verb and serves as a locative PP complement of the verb עלה within the ה relative. Qoheleth's question seems to assume that it was conventional wisdom that human spirits go up and animal spirits go down; in his frustration, what Qoheleth is questioning is whether this indeed is the case (based on his observations of the world about him).

וְרוּחַ הַבְּהֵמָה הַיֹּרֶדֶת הִיא לְמַטָּה לָאָרֶץ. Participle fs Qal √ירד and null copula clause. The syntax and pragmatics is identical to the previous clause.

3:22 וְרָאִיתִי כִּי אֵין טוֹב מֵאֲשֶׁר יִשְׂמַח הָאָדָם בְּמַעֲשָׂיו כִּי־הוּא חֶלְקוֹ כִּי מִי יְבִיאֶנּוּ לִרְאוֹת בְּמֶה שֶׁיִּהְיֶה אַחֲרָיו:

And I saw that a better thing does not exist than that man takes joy in his works, because it is his portion, because who can lead him to consider whatever will be after him?

This observation echoes a conclusion that Qoheleth gave in vv. 12-13. Here the sentiment is restated, not as a conclusion but as an empirical fact: the afterlife is even less knowable than life under the sun, and even though it, too, is fundamentally unknowable and there is no discernible "absolute good" (v. 12), at least one can take comfort in the smaller "goods."

וְרָאִ֔יתִי כִּ֣י אֵ֥ין טוֹב֙ מֵאֲשֶׁ֣ר יִשְׂמַ֣ח הָאָדָ֔ם בְּמַעֲשָׂ֑יו. *Qatal* 1cs Qal √ראה, negative existential אין, and *yiqtol* 3ms Qal √שמח. The כי clause is the complement of ראיתי, fulfilling the verb's bivalency requirements. Within the כי clause, the substantive adjective טוב "a good (thing)" is the subject of the existential negative אין. The comparative מִן-PP is a copular adjunct. Within the מִן-PP, the אשר nominalizes the following verbal clause so that it can function as the complement of the preposition מן. The verb שמח can be either monovalent (see 2:10; 3:12; 8:15) or bivalent with a בְּ-PP complement, as here (see also 4:16; 5:18; 11:8, 9). Note the typical verb-subject-complement order following אשר.

כִּי־ה֖וּא חֶלְקֽוֹ. A null copula clause. This כי clause, as well as the following כי clause, provides the rationale for the conclusion implicit within the main clause. The pronoun refers back to the activity of taking joy in his works.

כִּ֣י מִ֤י יְבִיאֶ֨נּוּ֙ לִרְא֔וֹת בְּמֶ֖ה שֶׁיִּהְיֶ֥ה אַחֲרָֽיו. *Yiqtol* 3ms Hiph √בוא + 3ms clitic pronoun, Inf Constr Qal √ראה, and *yiqtol* 3ms Qal √היה. In the higher clause, the interrogative pronoun מי is the subject and the 3ms clitic pronoun as well as the infinitive לראות are the two complements of the trivalent (in the Hiphil) verb יביא, which is perhaps to be analyzed as irrealis dynamic (ability) in the context. The infinitive ראות is bivalent: here the subject is null and identified from the higher clause (which is common in infinitival clauses); the earlier 3ms clitic pronoun is the subject and the complement a בְּ-PP. Within the בְּ-PP, the interrogative מה is combined with שׁ, resulting in a free-choice relative, like English "whatever." The implication of this construction is that the speaker cannot know the content of the man's future (i.e., "what" will come after) but simply that something (whatever it is) will come after (see 3:11). See also 1:9; 3:15; 6:10; 7:24; 8:7; 10:14.

4:1-3 Better Off Dead?

Verses 1-3 present the first of three new sets of observations (the second is in vv. 4-6, the third in vv. 7-12, and the fourth in vv. 13-16). This first of these new sets represents Qoheleth's conclusion after considering the oppression that occurs in life. He toys with a grim conclusion that shares much with Job's own in Job 3: for those who endure oppression, not to have lived is better than to have lived or lived and died.

וְשַׁבְתִּי אֲנִי וָאֶרְאֶה אֶת־כָּל־הָעֲשֻׁקִים אֲשֶׁר   4:1
נַעֲשִׂים תַּחַת הַשָּׁמֶשׁ וְהִנֵּה | דִּמְעַת הָעֲשֻׁקִים וְאֵין
לָהֶם מְנַחֵם וּמִיַּד עֹשְׁקֵיהֶם כֹּחַ וְאֵין לָהֶם מְנַחֵם:

Then I turned, I, and I saw all the oppressions that happen under the sun. And look, the tears of the oppressed—they have no comforter; from the hand of their oppressors (comes) power, and they have no comforter,

וְשַׁבְתִּי אֲנִי. *Qatal* 1cs Qal √שוב. The verb שׁוב can be either mon-ovalent, especially when it refers to the activity of "returning," or bivalent with a locative complement. Here the verb does not have any locative complement; this and its proximity to another finite verb, וָאֶרְאֶה, have led many commentators to suggest that שׁוב here is functioning in its adverbial capacity (BDB s.v, #8; HALOT:s.v, #5; WO §4.6.2; 39.3.1). That is, the verb שׁוב collocated with a second verb (finite or infinitive) can mean "to do X again" (see 1:7). This is the syntactic explanation given in, for example, Seow (1997: 177), Longman (133), and Fox (1999: 219). However, all three also note that it makes little sense that Qoheleth was "returning to see oppressions," since he has not previously mentioned seeing oppressions. We can thus dismiss such contradictory explanations. Here the verb שׁוב is functioning in its monovalent capac-ity and signals, like פנה (2:11, 12) and סבב(2:20; 7:25), that Qoheleth is "turning" to yet another observation.

וָאֶרְאֶה אֶת־כָּל־הָעֲשֻׁקִים. *Wayyiqtol* 1cs Qal √ראה. Note the "long" form of וָאראה; see comment on ואתנה in 1:17. This is one of only three *wayyiqtol* forms in the book; as with the other two (1:17 and 4:7), while semantically the function aligns with its use elsewhere in the Hebrew Bible, there is no compelling explanation for its use in just these three instances in Qoheleth. In 1:17 we noted that it may mark a transition by its inherent contrast with the dominant use of *qatal* forms. A similar explanation might be suggested here, but then why has the author begun with the *qatal* form? We tentatively suggest that the *wayyiqtol* serves to unite the initial two events in a narrative sequence (i.e., here the two verbs express a narrative sequence "I turned, I, and [then] I saw …"), which contrasts with many of the other of Qoheleth's actions as discrete, nontemporally successive (i.e., nonnarrative) events (see Introduction §5).

הָעֲשֻׁקִים אֲשֶׁר נַעֲשִׂים תַּחַת הַשָּׁמֶשׁ. Participle mp Niph √עשׂה. The complement of bivalent וָאראה is the noun עשקים, which shows the nominal pattern *qaṭūl*, which is used for adjectives, Qal passive participles, and some nouns, including both action nouns and abstract nouns. Typically the abstract uses appear in feminine form; with the abstract עֲשֻׁקִים "oppression(s)," there is no attested singular (so it could be either עָשׁוּק* or עֲשׁוּקָה*), with only an attested mp form. The אֲשֶׁר relative clause modifies the head "oppressions," which is resumed by a null-subject within the null copula relative clause. Within the relative clause, the participle נַעֲשִׂים is the copular complement, which is itself modified by the locative PP adjunct, תַּחַת הַשָּׁמֶשׁ (on this verb in Ecclesiastes, see 1:9, and on the phrase, see 1:3, 14).

וְהִנֵּה | דִּמְעַת הָעֲשֻׁקִים וְאֵין לָהֶם מְנַחֵם. Passive Participle mp Qal √עשק. An אֵין negative copula clause, with a left-dislocated NP דמעת העשקים that is resumed by the clitic pronoun inside the PP להם. To be precise, the clitic host, עֲשֻׁקִים, within the bound construction is the salient constituent that is resumed by the 3mp clitic pronoun in להם. The form עֲשֻׁקִים can be explained two ways in this case. Either this is a Qal passive participle within a null-head, unmarked relative clause, "(those who) are oppressed," which is simply homophonous with the abstract noun in the preceding clause, or both occurrences are the abstract noun and this second occurrence is a case of an abstract noun used for a concrete reference. With either explanation, the connotation is "oppressed ones."

וְאֵין לָהֶם מְנַחֵם. Participle ms Piel √נחם. In the negative copula clause, the subject is the ms participle מנחם. The Piel נחם is bivalent, but the lack of an overt complement with the participle form suggests that this is an agentive noun, "comforter" (see comment on 1:15). Though one could suggest that this is a null-head, unmarked participial relative, there are enough occurrences of מנחם in the Hebrew Bible without a complement to support the identification of an agentive noun based on the participial form (besides here, see 2 Sam 10:3; Nah 3:7; Pss 69:21; Job 16:2; Lam 1:2, 9, 16-17, 21; 1 Chr 19:3). The possessive PP להם (JM §133d; MNK §39.11.1.3; WO §11.2.10d) is the complement of the negative copula אֵין.

וּמִיַּד עֹשְׁקֵיהֶם כֹּחַ. Participle mp Qal √עשק + clitic 3mp pronoun. In this null copula clause, the subject is כח and the complement is the מִן-PP, which has been fronted for focus and communicates that, whatever power is possessed, it is only in the hand of those who are oppressive, and they wield it for themselves. In this copular clause, the מִן-PP complement suggests a motion interpretation of the copula, which is why we have translated it as "comes." This illustrates how the null copula in Hebrew interacts with both the subject and complement in its semantic interpretation. Within the מִן-PP functioning as the copular complement is the Qal participle, which is itself inside a null-head, unmarked relative; the 3mp clitic pronoun attached to the participle is the complement of the bivalent עשׁק, thus, "(those) (who) are oppressing them."

וְאֵין לָהֶם מְנַחֵם. Longman suggests that the repetition of this phrase is stylistic and" expresses Qoheleth's passion and despair about the subject" (134; similarly Seow 1997: 178).

4:2   וְשַׁבֵּחַ אֲנִי אֶת־הַמֵּתִים שֶׁכְּבָר מֵתוּ מִן־הַחַיִּים
אֲשֶׁר הֵמָּה חַיִּים עֲדֶנָה:

(while) I praise the dead, who have already died, more than the living, who are yet living.

וְשַׁבֵּחַ אֲנִי אֶת־הַמֵּתִים. Inf Abs Piel √שׁבח and Participle mp Qal √מות. Note that the bound and free infinitive forms are identical in the Piel. The Piel שׁבח is bivalent, with the 1cs pronoun אני the subject and the NP המתים the complement. The infinitive is functioning as the verbal predicate of this clause. The infinitive absolute used as a finite verb occurs in Hebrew narrative but is not common (WO §35.5.2; JM §123x). In Ecclesiastes it occurs here and twice more in the book, though those constructions differ slightly (see Cook 2013: 322, and comments on 8:9 and 9:11). Although further study of this phenomenon is needed, it appears that constructions like ושבח אני—i.e., the infinitive "bound with *waw* and functioning in place of a finite verb—closely approximates its use as an adverbial complement, for in both constructions the infinitive qualifies a leading verb" (WO §35.5.2d). If v. 2 is to be taken as subordinate to one of the main clauses in v. 1, the thrust is that חיים in v. 2 should be read as the עשקים in v. 1, and that Qoheleth is musing about how it is better to be dead than to be oppressed. We have attempted to signal the subordination of this infinitive clause in translation with the connector "while." A further intriguing feature of this occurrence in Ecclesiastes is the infinitive-pronoun order, which is a common narrative pattern in some Amarna Canaanite texts (14th c. BCE) and a few Phoenician texts (Kulamuwa [KAI 24; 9th c. BCE], Karatepe [KAI 26; 8th c. BCE]; and Yahawmilk [KAI 10; 6th c. BCE]) but a very rare pattern in

Hebrew (besides here, see only Esth 9:1). The temporal distance between the Amarna and Phoenician texts, on the one hand, and the Ecclesiastes and Esther occurrences, on the other, make any direct connection implausible (JM §123x n. 36; contra Dahood 1952a, b; see Introduction §6). See also Isaksson, 63–65; Schoors, 178–80.

שֶׁכְּבָר מֵתוּ. *Qatal* 3cp Qal √מות. Fox takes this שֶׁ clause and the אשר clause later in the verse as causal, thereby avoiding what he perceives as semantic redundancy. He suggests that both clauses "give the grounds for the declaration [that the deceased are more fortunate]" (1999: 218–19). We do not find the causal analysis of שֶׁ or אשר in Ecclesiastes compelling (see Introduction §4; Holmstedt 2016). The שֶׁ and אשר clauses in this verse are straightforward relatives, with null resumption of the head as the covert subject in the first and overt resumption as the 3mp subject pronoun in the second. The nuance that Fox (and Ginsberg) want to see is still available, even if their syntactic analysis is rejected. As nonrestrictive relative clauses, the שֶׁ and אשר clauses do not provide information that defines their respective heads (which would be their function if they were restrictive); rather, they provide a nondefinitional quality of the מתים and חיים that is salient in the comparison. It is the fact that they have *already* died (not some other conceivable quality) that makes those who are dead better off than the living, who are unfortunately (in Qoheleth's opinion) *not yet* dead. The relative clauses clarify the grounds for Qoheleth's declaration but in a syntactically different way than Fox understands.

מִן־הַחַיִּים אֲשֶׁר הֵמָּה חַיִּים עֲדֶנָה. This מִן-PP presents the anchor of the comparative construction (MNK §39.14.8; WO §11.2.11e.3) and is an adjunct to the verb שבח, even though it stands in comparative relationship with the NP המתים. Within the אשר clause, the null copula has the 3mp pronoun המה (resumptive for החיים) as its subject and the NP חיים as the copular complement. The adverb עדנה is a copular adjunct. The pronoun המה does not carry topic or focus—it is syntactically required in order to create a grammatical copular clause. That is, in contrast to verbal relative clauses, copular relative clauses overwhelmingly exhibit an overt subject, presumably to avoid syntactic ambiguity: in this case, if המה were missing, one could interpret חיים עדנה as the subject and copular complement, respectively, resulting in semantic nonsense ("living are still"). English does not require the overt pronoun in the same way, which is why we have omitted it in translation.

עֲדֶנָה. This form, as well as the similar one in 4:3, appears only in Ecclesiastes in the Hebrew Bible. HALOT suggests that עד in 4:3 is a combination of עַד and הֵן, and עדנה here in 4:2 a combination of עַד and הֵנָּה; the similar temporal expression "still, yet" appears in Jewish Babylonian Aramaic as עֲדַיִן and is common in Modern Hebrew.

4:3 וְטוֹב מִשְּׁנֵיהֶם אֵת אֲשֶׁר־עֲדֶן לֹא הָיָה אֲשֶׁר
לֹא־רָאָה אֶת־הַמַּעֲשֶׂה הָרָע אֲשֶׁר נַעֲשָׂה תַּחַת
הַשָּׁמֶשׁ:

And better than the both of them is (the person) who has not yet existed, who has not seen the evil event that has happened under the sun.

וְטוֹב מִשְּׁנֵיהֶם אֵת אֲשֶׁר־עֲדֶן לֹא הָיָה. A null copula clause with טוב as the complement and null-head relative אשר אדן לא היה as the subject. The complement טוב may be focus-fronted (presumably to strengthen the "good," versus bad, nature of comparison) or the subject NP may be extraposed as an example of heavy NP shift (see Holmstedt 2002: 303–5 for a brief discussion and sources; see also 2:7). It is unclear which analysis is correct. The מִן-PP is part of the comparative "better than" construction and is syntactically an adjunct within the structure of the טוב adjective phrase (for "better-than" sayings in Ecclesiastes, see 4:3, 6, 9, 13; 5:4; 6:9; 7:1-3, 5, 8; 9:4; note that only 9:4 does not have טוב as the first constituent). On את marking the subject of a null copula clause (here a null-head relative clause), see WO §10.3.2c and comment on 2:12.

עֲדֶן. On the form, see note on 4:2. The position of the adverb could be taken as focus—i.e., "the person who *still* doesn't exist"—but it may also be unmarked for any pragmatic feature. A thorough study of adverb syntax for BH has not been undertaken (and the data are admittedly sparse).

אֲשֶׁר לֹא־רָאָה אֶת־הַמַּעֲשֶׂה הָרָע אֲשֶׁר נַעֲשָׂה תַּחַת הַשָּׁמֶשׁ. *Qatal* 3ms Qal √ראה and Niph √עשה. For the meaning of Niphal עשה in Ecclesiastes, see 1:9. This relative clause appears to be a second, stacked relative modifying the head null head "(the person)." Whereas the first relative אשר עדן לא היה was restrictive, stacked relatives are appositive, adding information unnecessary for identifying the relative head but nonetheless considered important by the author. A syntactic-semantic twist with this relative is that nonrestrictive relatives cannot modify a null head, since the head must be identifiable without the relative. However, the relative clause before this one, by virtue of being restrictive, identified the null relative head; in doing so, it created an appropriately identified head (even if it remains null) to license this nonrestrictive relative. This is an excellent example of the role of linearity in semantic interpretation. By virtue of the second relative, Qoheleth is able to specify why he considers the not-yet-existent to have a better existence than both the living and the dead—the not-yet-existent do not and have not experienced the troubles of life.

4:4-6 Work Isn't Always Worth It

It is somewhat ironic that vv. 4-6 are not entirely clear. What seems to emerge out of Qoheleth's statements is his analysis of those whose response in life is to work harder for greater gain. His assessment?—such striving results in no real gain.

וְרָאִיתִי אֲנִי אֶת־כָּל־עָמָל וְאֵת כָּל־כִּשְׁרוֹן הַמַּעֲשֶׂה   4:4
כִּי הִיא קִנְאַת־אִישׁ מֵרֵעֵהוּ גַּם־זֶה הֶבֶל וּרְעוּת
רוּחַ:

I saw, I, all the acquisition(s) and all the success of work—that it is (out of) the jealousy of a man because of his neighbor. This, too, is a הבל *and chasing the wind.*

Verses 4-6 present a second set of observations signaled by רָאִיתִי אֲנִי. This set moves from the troubles one experiences at the hands of others to the troubles that proceed from one's own actions: jealousy, self-destruction, and anxious toil. Here Qoheleth employs traditional wisdom sayings (4:5-6), but he begins the set with his by now familiar refrain, thus reframing the traditional sayings to serve his own argument.

וְרָאִיתִי אֲנִי אֶת־כָּל־עָמָל וְאֵת כָּל־כִּשְׁרוֹן הַמַּעֲשֶׂה. *Qatal* 1cs Qal √ראה. The verb ראה is bivalent in the Qal. The subject is a null 1cs pronoun (signaled by the matching 1cs features on the verb) and the complement is the compound NP אֶת כל עמל ואת כל כשרון המעשה. On the (nonsubject) status of the postverbal 1cs pronoun אני, see 1:16 and 2:11.

כִּי הִיא קִנְאַת־אִישׁ מֵרֵעֵהוּ. A null copula clause. The syntactic explanation proposed for examples like this (see also וַיַּרְא אֱלֹהִים אֶת־הָאוֹר

כִּי־טֹוב; Gen 1:4, etc.), that the complement NP of the higher matrix clause "anticipates" the assessment of the lower כי clause (i.e., that the Hebrew reflects a reordering of "I saw that X is ..."; see JM §177i; Seow 1997: 179), is nonsense linguistically. Rather, the כי clause is a second complement of the verb ראיתי, appositional to the first compound NP complement. The ordering of the two complements is critical for the interpretation of this second complement: whereas the referents of the first complement, "I saw all the acquisition and success of work," are clear, the referent of היא in the second complement would be ambiguous without the first complement. As the information is ordered and processed, though, the referent of היא becomes contextually clear so that the sense of the verse is "I saw that acquisition and success is (due to) jealousy." For the use of מן to introduce a causal adjunct, see WO §11.2.11d; it is ambiguous whether the envy is the cause or result of human striving (so Seow 1997: 179).

גַּם־זֶה הֶבֶל וּרְעוּת רוּחַ. See comments at 1:2 for הבל, 1:14 for רעות, and 1:11 for גם.

4:5   הַכְּסִיל חֹבֵק אֶת־יָדָיו וְאֹכֵל אֶת־בְּשָׂרוֹ:

The fool folds his hands and eats his flesh

הַכְּסִיל חֹבֵק אֶת־יָדָיו. Participle ms Qal √חבק. The Qal of חבק elsewhere means "to embrace," but "embracing one's hands" makes little sense. The collocation of חבק and יד also appears in Prov 6:10 and 24:33 as חִבֻּק יָדַיִם "folding of hands," though the *qattūl* pattern of the noun חִבֻּק typically presents action associated with the Piel *binyan* (JM §88le). Even so, the meaning of the Qal חֹבֵק here is likely the same as חִבֻּק, except that the active participle makes the image more concrete by its progressive sense, lit. "(is) folding his hands." The image of folding hands transparently references lack of physical labor and so, by simple extension, laziness.

וְאֹכֵל אֶת־בְּשָׂרוֹ. Participle ms Qal √אכל. Many take this statement to say that even lazy fools may eat well (Lohfink, 69–70; cf. Murphy, 31 n. 5a). Seow protests, though, that the noun בשר occurs four other times in the book and all are in reference to the human body not food; moreover, even outside of Ecclesiastes, when בשר occurs with a possessive suffix, it refers to the human body not one's portion of food. Thus, we agree that "Qohelet is using the grotesque imagery of self-cannibalism to speak of self-destruction. Fools who are so lazy will end up devouring themselves" (1997: 179; so also Fox 1999: 220). The juxtaposing of the two generic activities—both expressed by the participle—highlights the grotesque reinterpretation of the relaxation of fools: though by all appearances the fool looks to be at ease (cf. Ps 73:12), "folding his hands," in reality he is in the process of "eating his (own) flesh."

4:6   טֹוב מְלֹא כַף נָחַת מִמְּלֹא חָפְנַיִם עָמָל וּרְעוּת רוּחַ:

The fullness of a palm (with) quietness is better than the fullness of a two handfuls (with) acquisition(s) and chasing wind.

טֹוב מְלֹא כַף נָחַת. A null copula clause with מלא as the subject and the adjective טוב as the copular complement. The form מְלֹא could be identified as either an Inf Constr Qal √מלא or the noun having the sense "fullness, filling." Semantically and syntactically, both options are possible; however, we think it best not to view the form as an infinitive since, out of 110 occurrences of the infinitive construct, Ecclesiastes almost always has a preposition with it. There are only seven or eight exceptions to this pattern (1:17; 3:4 [2×], 5; 6:10 [text uncertain]; 7:1, 25; 10:10 [text uncertain]; 12:12); as well, when the author employs an infinitive as the subject of a comparative טוב מן "better than" predicate, he uses the preposition (7:2, 5). As in v. 3, this טוב is the first component of the טוב מן comparative construction (MNK §39.14.8; WO §11.2.11e.3); see comment in v. 3 on the position of טוב. In contrast to Fox (1999: 221), Seow argues that נחת should be taken only as the adverbial use of the noun, thus "restfully, (with) rest" rather than as the second item in a construct phrase, "a handful of rest" since one "does not measure rest by handfuls" (1997: 180). While on the one hand this is simply imposing an extreme logic on the text, on the other hand the suggested syntax parallels the next clause nicely, where עמל is used adverbially. Seow also suggests that מלא כף "refers to a very small amount" and that "the emphasis is on the limited nature of a handful, not on the fullness" (1997: 180).

מִמְּלֹא חָפְנַיִם עָמָל וּרְעוּת רוּחַ. See comment on preceding clause in 4:6 on the identification of מלא as either a noun or an Inf Constr Qal √מלא. This מן-PP is the second half of the comparative טוב מן construction with the compound NPs עמל ורעות רוח used adverbially ("*with* acquisitions and wind-chasing"). As Seow notes, "[t]he comparison is not between an amount of rest and twice the amount of toil, but an amount of anything with peace vs. anything with toil" (1997: 180). On רעות, see 1:14.

4:7-12 Two Are Better Than One

Verses 7-12 shift to the worthlessness of working one's life away without someone with whom to share the benefits. Companionship may be life-saving. Although vv. 7-8 are often separated off as a distinct section, the thematic continuity (the issue of companionship in life) and some grammatical features (the use of the article on אחד and שני) suggest that it is all one section. As in the previous set (vv. 4-6), Qoheleth begins with his refrain statement about the absurdity of life, only to set within that framework what appear to be very conventional wisdom sayings.

4:7   וְשַׁבְתִּי אֲנִי וָאֶרְאֶה הֶבֶל תַּחַת הַשָּׁמֶשׁ׃

And I returned, I, and saw a הבל under the sun.

וְשַׁבְתִּי אֲנִי וָאֶרְאֶה. See comment* at v. 1.

הֶבֶל תַּחַת הַשָּׁמֶשׁ. See comment at 1:3.

4:8   יֵשׁ אֶחָד וְאֵין שֵׁנִי גַּם בֵּן וָאָח אֵין־לֹו וְאֵין קֵץ
לְכָל־עֲמָלֹו גַּם־עֵינָיו* לֹא־תִשְׂבַּע עֹשֶׁר וּלְמִי | אֲנִי
עָמֵל וּמְחַסֵּר אֶת־נַפְשִׁי מִטּוֹבָה גַּם־זֶה הֶבֶל וְעִנְיַן
רָע הוּא׃

There is one but no second (indeed no son or brother belongs to him), yet there is no end to all of his toil, nor will his eyes be sated (by) riches. "(So) for whom am I toiling and depriving myself of goodness?" This, too, is a הבל, and it is an unfortunate task.

יֵשׁ אֶחָד וְאֵין שֵׁנִי. A יש existential clause (see 1:10 on the syntax of יש) and an אין negative existential clause (see also the comment at 1:7). Note that both clauses lack complements (cf. אין in the following clause). In the יש clause, the cardinal אחד is the subject and is used in the sense of "one person alone." In the second clause, the ordinal numeral adjective שֵׁנִי is the subject and refers substantivally to "a second person," which is identified further in the next clause as an heir and successor.

גַּם בֵּן וָאָח אֵין־לֹו. An אין negative copula clause. The possessive ל-PP is the copular complement (JM §133d; MNK §39.11.1.3; WO §11.2.10d). The subject is the compound NP בן ואח and is both fronted (one expects אין to be in clause-initial position, as it is in the second and fourth clauses) and marked by גם for focus (see comment at 1:11 on גם). The focus on בן ואח isolates these entities out of a wide open membership set as the two that fit the intended reference of שני. The overlap of אין לו and the specification of שני as בן ואח suggest that this is a parenthesis used to clarify שני (see comment on 2:3 for a discussion of parenthesis).

וְאֵין קֵץ לְכָל־עֲמָלֹו. An אין negative copula clause with קץ as the subject and the ל-PP as the copular complement. Semantically, עמלו has the sense of acquisition (the product of toil); there is no end to what the man has achieved (as opposed to no end to his labor). This meaning works with the following clause: he has endless acquisition(s) and treasure, but his eyes are not filled/satisfied by the abundance.

גַּם־עֵינָיו* לֹא־תִשְׂבַּע עֹשֶׁר. Yiqtol 3fs √שבע. The גם is often taken as an adversative (so Seow 1997: 181; see HALOT), but Fox argues that it is the additive use, presenting a second factor in the man's behavior (1999: 222; for the additive function of גם, see MNK §41.4.5.2; van der Merwe). If the גם is additive (as we have taken it) and not a focus marker, the subject-negative-verb word order may reflect the typologically later profile of the book's language (see Introduction §§2D, 6). Note that the Ketiv עיניו (which would be vocalized as עֵינָיו) presents a lack of agreement with the singular verb (see GKC §145k; JM §150g); the marginal Qere has the singular noun עֵינֹו. The use of the yiqtol has the force of making the generic statement more forceful by casting it as a future prediction: not only does the present state of wealth not satisfy, which idea could be expressed by אין and the verbal adjective שָׂבֵעַ, but no matter how much wealth the man accumulates, his eyes will never be satisfied. The NP עֹשֶׁר presents an unmarked (i.e., without a preposition) complement for bivalent שבע, indicating the item(s) with which one is sated (see also 5:9).

וּלְמִי | אֲנִי עָמֵל וּמְחַסֵּר אֶת־נַפְשִׁי מִטּוֹבָה. Participle ms Piel √חסר. A null copula clause with עָמֵל as the adjectival complement compounded with the participle as the second complement. The verbal characteristics of עָמֵל (see comment at 2:18) and its compounding with a participle suggests both are to be interpreted progressively (lit. "toiling/

being anxious and depriving myself]. Though the ו syntactically marks
the front edge of this clause and, in this case, connects the two clauses as
a coordinating conjunction, the implication in this context is that it presents Qoheleth's frustrated conclusion, and so it is a discourse-determined
result clause.

גַּם־זֶה הֶבֶל וְעִנְיַן רָע הוּא. See comments at 1:2 for הבל, 1:11 for
גם, and 1:13 for ענין. These are two null copula clauses. In the first the
deictic demonstrative זה is the subject and הבל is the complement. In the
second, the NP וענין רע is the focus-fronted complement while the 3ms
pronoun serves as subject.

4:9   טוֹבִים הַשְּׁנַיִם מִן־הָאֶחָד אֲשֶׁר יֶשׁ־לָהֶם שָׂכָר
טוֹב בַּעֲמָלָם:

Two are better than one, who have a good wage in exchange for their toil.

טוֹבִים הַשְּׁנַיִם מִן־הָאֶחָד. Null copula clause. See comment in
v. 3 on the position of the complement טוב. The subject is the articular
cardinal numeral השנים and the מִן-PP, though an adjunct to the null
copula, is crucial to the comparative construction (MNK §39.14.8; WO
§11.2.11e.3). The cardinal האחד within the PP is the complement of
the preposition. Seow suggests that "the definite articles on the numerals
probably refer to those who are not solitary … and those who are solitary,
respectively" (1997: 181). More specifically, the article grounds the referents of שנים and אחד in the case study begun in v. 8: the man who *does*
have a son or brother (identified here as "the two") is now presented as
better off than "the one" who does not (v. 8). On the use of the article in
Ecclesiastes, see Baranowski, esp. p. 45 and the discussion of Ecclesiastes'
use of case studies.

אֲשֶׁר יֶשׁ־לָהֶם שָׂכָר טוֹב בַּעֲמָלָם. A יש copula clause with the
possessive PP להם as the complement (JM §133d; MNK §39.11.1.3;
WO §11.2.10d), the NP שכר טוב as the subject, and the PP בעמלם
as a copular adjunct (for the ב of price, see JM §133c; WO §11.2.5d).
The אשר clause is an extraposed relative (see Holmstedt 2001, 2016:
186–92). The relative head is השנים and the relative clause itself has
been moved lower than the comparative PP. Contra Seow (1997: 182),
the אשר is not causal (see Holmstedt 2016: 216–47). Semantically, this
relative clause is nonrestrictive; i.e., the relative adds the information that
the two in Qoheleth's mind earn a good wage, but this information itself

does not identify them in any way (e.g., over against "the two who do *not* earn a good wage").

כִּי אִם־יִפֹּלוּ הָאֶחָד יָקִים אֶת־חֲבֵרוֹ וְאִילוֹ הָאֶחָד ‎4:10
שֶׁיִּפּוֹל וְאֵין שֵׁנִי לַהֲקִימוֹ׃

*Because if they should fall, one can raise his companion, but woe to him,
the one that falls, and there is no second (person) to raise him up.*

כִּי אִם־יִפֹּלוּ. *Yiqtol* 3mp Qal √נפל. Seow suggests that the plural
verb was used distributively; i.e., "if either of them falls" (1997: 182).
Distributive semantics, though, would give the sense that *each* person
falls, which is not the same as *either* falls. The distributive notion is essentially correct, though: the plural verb likely has in its scope multiple situations in which one of the two falls on one occasion and then the other
falls on the next occasion. The כי marks the whole clause (both the protasis and apodosis) as a causal subordinate clause providing the reason for
the better-than evaluation of השנים in v. 9. The אם introduces this first
half as the subordinate conditional protasis to the next clause, rendered
appropriately by the English subjunctive "if ... should fall."

הָאֶחָד יָקִים אֶת־חֲבֵרוֹ. *Yiqtol* 3ms Hiph √קום. In the Qal, קום
is typically monovalent; correspondingly, in the Hiphil it is bivalent,
here with the NP את־חברו as its complement (and האחד as its subject).
Regardless which one might fall, the other can help him up. Such is the
nature of a truly reciprocal relationship. Within the larger כי clause, this
is the apodosis to the conditional אם clause. The irrealis *yiqtol* expresses
dynamic modality in this context: reciprocal friendship means that if one
happens to fall, the other is available to raise the one up again.

וְאִילוֹ הָאֶחָד. A null copula clause with אי as the subject and לו
as the PP complement of the null copula. The first word of the main
clause, אילו, seems to be a mixed form; the consonants suggest a (mistakenly) fully written form of the conditional אִלּוּ, which is common in
postbiblical Hebrew, whereas the vocalization of the final vowel suggests
a combination of אי "woe" and the possessive PP לו (see Schoors, 149;
Seow 1997: 182). If we choose the former analysis, we end up with a rare
one-part null copula clause introduced by a conditional (see Gen 13:9);
if the latter, then האחד is the head of a complex NP that is coreferential
with the suffix in the PP לו: "woe to him, the one who falls and there is
no second to raise him." This latter option, which we have adopted here,

is either a case of apposition (i.e., הָאֶחָד is appositive to the 3ms pronoun in לוֹ) or right-dislocation—the two constructions are often hard to distinguish when they occur at the end of a clause (see comments on the function of right-dislocation in 2:21). This clause is either contextually associated with the better-than statement in v. 9 but syntactically distinct, or it is within the syntactic domain of the initial כִּי in the verse (this relates to the overall status of v. 11; see comment there). If the אִילוֹ הָאֶחָד clause is within the domain of כִּי, it is likely a parenthesis relating to the conditional construction; this is suggested by the "if-then" structure of the clauses both before and after it (see 2:3 on identifying parentheses).

שֶׁיִּפּוֹל וְאֵין שֵׁנִי לַהֲקִימוֹ. *Yiqtol* 3ms Qal √נפל, אֵין negative copula clause and Inf Constr Hiph √קום with 3ms clitic pronoun (as its complement). This שֶׁ clause is not temporal (contra Seow 1997: 182); it is a relative that modifies הָאֶחָד restrictively—it identifies which "one person" among all possible "one persons" that Qoheleth has in mind. In this verse the membership set is obvious: {one who has a companion to help him up, one who does not have a companion to help him up}. Within the שֶׁ relative is a compound clause: יפול (monovalent with a null-subject that resumes the head הָאֶחָד) and אין שני להקימו (a null copula clause with the ordinal שֵׁנִי as the subject and the ל-PP/infinitive clause as the complement, with clitic 3ms pronoun resuming the head). On the use of ל-PP/infinitive in null copula or אֵין/יֵשׁ clauses with a modal nuance (here, of possibility), see WO §36.2.3f and 3:14.

4:11   גַּם אִם־יִשְׁכְּבוּ שְׁנַיִם וְחַם לָהֶם וּלְאֶחָד אֵיךְ יֵחָם:

Also, if two lie down, they will keep warm, but for one—how can he get/ keep warm?

גַּם אִם־יִשְׁכְּבוּ שְׁנַיִם וְחַם לָהֶם. *Yiqtol* 3mp Qal √שכב and *qatal* 3ms Qal √חמם. The אִם marks the first clause as a conditional protasis, for which the second clause is the apodosis. Both verbs are irrealis mood by virtue of the conditional context (i.e., conditional clauses talk about contingent events rather than "real" events). On the verb-subject order following the אם, see Introduction §2D. The initial גם is best understood in its additive sense (MNK §41.4.5.2; van der Merwe): it signals that this is an additional observation relating to the better-than assertion in v. 9. In fact, one could justifiably argue that this entire verse is a second reason within the syntactic domain of the כי that begins v. 10 (see comment on the אִילוֹ clause in v. 10). The Qal verb חמם "to be hot, grow warm" is stative and usually monovalent with the subject NP expressing the one who becomes warm/hot (e.g., Exod 16:21; Deut 19:6; 2 Kgs 4:34; Ps 39:4; Neh 7:3). However, in both occurrences here and several other instances (1 Kgs 1:1-2; Hag 1:6), the verb is avalent, and the one who experiences the heat is expressed by an adjunct לְ-PP. Not only is a subject NP absent here, but there is no semantic role for a subject. Compare expressions with "dummy" subject pronouns in non–pro-drop languages (i.e., those that require an overt expression of a syntactic subject), such as meteorological statements like "it is raining" (cf. *llueve* in Spanish, and *il pleut* in French; Ps 68:15 תשלג בצלמון "it snowed on Zalmon"). An additional clue to the avalent pattern here is the singular verb but the plural pronoun on the adjunct PP לָהֶם. Thus, lit. "there is warmth for them."

וּלְאֶחָד אֵיךְ יֵחָם. *Yiqtol* 3ms Qal √חמם (this verb reflects the Qal stative pattern for ע″ע prefix verbs; see JM §82b). As in the prior clause, the verb is avalent with the adjunct לְ-PP marking the experiencer (of warmth). The best interpretation of the semantics of the verb form is dynamic modality, given the rhetorical interrogative clause: lit. "How can there be warmth for him?" The initial PP is positioned higher than the interrogative אֵיךְ, but interrogatives typically take the highest position in the Hebrew clause, excepting only dislocated constituents and cases of extreme fronting. לְאֶחָד is a case of extreme fronting (see comment on 2:12).

וְאִם־יִתְקְפוֹ הָאֶחָד הַשְּׁנַיִם יַעַמְדוּ נֶגְדּוֹ וְהַחוּט   4:12
הַמְשֻׁלָּשׁ לֹא בִמְהֵרָה יִנָּתֵק׃

And if someone should overpower him—the one, the two can stand against him [i.e., the aggressor]. And a three-ply thread will not quickly be torn.

וְאִם־יִתְקְפוֹ הָאֶחָד. *Yiqtol* 3ms Qal √תקף with 3ms clitic pronoun as the complement. This *yiqtol* imperfective is irrealis in the conditional context and is used with a null-subject, impersonally, "if (some) one should overpower him." The form of the suffix is unusual, since the typical form is הו with a *ṣere* linking vowel, as in תִּתְקְפֵהוּ (Job 14:20). The וֹ in יִתְקְפוֹ presumably comes from the use of an *a*-class linking vowel followed by the syncopation of the -*h*- and the contraction of the resulting *au* diphthong: *-āhū > *-āū > -ô (see GKC §60d). The clitic pronoun וֹ is coreferential with the following noun, הָאֶחָד. Structurally, this is either an example of right-dislocation, where a pronominal reference is specified by a constituent on the right margin of the clause, or apposition (JM §146e; see also comment on 2:21; similarly, Seow 1997: 182). The sequence of a cataphoric pronoun specified by a noun that occurs later (rather than the typical order of a noun picked up by an anaphoric pronoun) is sometimes referred to as prolepsis or anticipation; this occurs much more regularly in Syriac and its use in Ecclesiastes (here and in 2:12) has been connected to the influence of "north Israelite" and the presence of colloquialisms (see Seow 1997: 137–38, 182). Although syntactically it is possible to take הָאֶחָד as the subject of the verb, "if the one overpowers him," it is awkward to leave the "him" unidentified; in contrast, there is nothing unusual about an unspecified, impersonal subject. Finally, some take אם to have a concessive sense, "even though" (JM §§167f, 171d), but a simple conditional also makes sense.

הַשְּׁנַיִם יַעַמְדוּ נֶגְדּוֹ. *Yiqtol* 3mp Qal √עמד. Again, dynamic modality semantics for this verb fits well in the series of qualifications of the ability of two people versus one person in this section. The verb עמד can be monovalent but is often bivalent with a locative complement, which is how we take נגד here (see comment at 2:9). The word נגד specifies "what is opposite" and is often used as a preposition, "opposite," or adverb "oppositely"; here it takes on the additional nuance of "against, opposed to" given the context of struggle. In this clause, נגדו seems to be a PP whose 3ms clitic pronoun refers back to the null-subject of the impersonal verb in the previous clause.

וְהַחוּט הַמְשֻׁלָּשׁ לֹא בִמְהֵרָה יִנָּתֵק. Participle ms Pual √שלש and *yiqtol* 3ms Niph √נתק (which as a passive is monovalent). The presence of a negative often results in both the negative and the verb combining as a complex constituent and raising above an overt subject (see Holmstedt 2009a, 2011); thus, the S-Neg-PP-V order here is rare. The position of the subject החוט המשלש likely reflects focus-fronting to contrast with not just the solitary person but also with the pair, utilizing a typical numerical trope: "If one is bad, and two is good, how much better is three!" (Longman, 143). It is not only the subject that is focus-fronted—the negative לֹא does not negate the clause in this case but is an item adverb and specifically negates the adjunct PP במהרה (see WO §39.3.2). Together the negative and PP are in a second focused position, highlighting that any eventual breaking of the three-ply thread is "not quickly." The definite article on the subject החוט is generic, denoting it as representative of the class of three-ply ropes (see WO §13.5.1f). In English it sounds more natural to use the indefinite article, as in our translation.

4:13-16 Wisdom Does Not Preserve
One's Station or Legacy

Verses 13-16 are not easy to connect to the preceding sections of this discourse (chap. 4). Fox titles it "Wisdom's Failure to Secure Enduring Fame" and suggests that the theme of the companion (שֵׁנִי) links this section with vv. 9-12 (1999: 217), but how this linking is built on anything more than simply the word itself (used in vv. 8, 10, and 15) is wholly opaque. Longman sees it as an anecdote on the meaninglessness of political power (144–45) and Seow sees Qoheleth using a reversal of fortune theme to support his conclusion that even the "better things" in life are not durable. Grammatically the ambiguity of the pronominal reference in this section makes determining the number of characters difficult. We take the sequence as a contrast between two individuals: the old, foolish king and the young, poor youth. This contrast plays out in a number of ways: the king apparently started in prison, which means he should have some awareness of poverty, yet in his old age he is foolish; the youth who is born poor nevertheless attracts the crowd, but he too will go the way of the old man—so even fame and power disappear. (Contrast Fox 1999: 224–28, who sees three distinct youths.)

4:13   טוֹב יֶלֶד מִסְכֵּן וְחָכָם מִמֶּלֶךְ זָקֵן וּכְסִיל אֲשֶׁר לֹא־
יָדַע לְהִזָּהֵר עוֹד:

A poor but wise youth is better than an old but foolish king, who still does not know to be careful,

טוֹב יֶלֶד מִסְכֵּן וְחָכָם מִמֶּלֶךְ זָקֵן וּכְסִיל. A null copula clause with טוב as the copular complement and the NP ילד מסכן וחכם as the subject. On the position of טוב, see the comment on v. 3. The comparative מן-PP (MNK §39.14.8; WO §11.2.11e.3) is an adjunct to the null copula.

מִסְכֵּן וְחָכָם ... זָקֵן וּכְסִיל. The comparison operates on three levels: age, wealth, and wisdom. The contrast between wise and foolish is expected and governs the second and third contrasts, between youth and old age and poverty and royalty (wealth), with the result that the normal order of preference is reversed. In other words, the expectation is that an old (and presumably rich) king would be better (in most ways) than a poor youth, but rather whoever possesses wisdom is better regardless of age or wealth. Thus, the normal youth-versus-age and poor-versus-wealthy contrasts are flipped in light of wisdom. Note the clear adjectival status of כסיל (see also note at 2:14)—it not only follows and modifies the noun מלך, but it also follows another adjective, זקן.

אֲשֶׁר לֹא־יָדַע לְהִזָּהֵר עוֹד. *Qatal* 3ms Qal √ידע and Inf Constr Niph √זהר. The ל-PP/infinitive clause is the complement and the adverb עוֹד is an adjunct for the bivalent verb ידע. Collocated with the infinitive, the sense of ידע here is "to know *how to do* X" (see also 4:17; 10:15; Amos 3:10; Jer 1:6; 6:15; 1 Kgs 3:7; Isa 50:4; 56:11 [2×]). The אשר introduces a third modifier (following the two adjectives זקן and כסיל) that specifies what it is about the foolish king that makes him foolish: "the point is that he disregards advice" (Seow 1997: 183). Rather than a restrictive relative, constraining the reference to not-knowing-how-to-speak kings, this relative is better understood as a nonrestrictive modifier, adding relevant but nondefining information.

4:14　　כִּי־מִבֵּית הָסוּרִים יָצָא לִמְלֹךְ כִּי גַּם בְּמַלְכוּתוֹ
　　　　נוֹלַד רָשׁ׃

because from the prison he [= old king] had come out to be king, even though a poor one [= youth] was born in his [= old king's] reign.

כִּי־מִבֵּית הָסוּרִים יָצָא לִמְלֹךְ. Participle mp Qal passive √אסר, *qatal* 3ms Qal √יצא, and Inf Constr Qal √מלך. The noun הסורים seems to represent the elision of the א in האסורים; HALOT suggests the path הָאֲסוּרִים* < הָאֲסוּרִים* < הָסוּרִים (see GKC §68i; BL §31f). The כי clause as a whole provides a reason for the better-than statement of v. 13. In our opinion the *qatal* perfective verb here carries past-perfect semantics, based on the overall logic of the discourse.

כִּי גַּם בְּמַלְכוּתוֹ נוֹלַד רָשׁ. *Qatal* 3ms Niph √ילד and Participle ms Qal √רוש. The participle רש is within a null-head, unmarked participial relative, "(one) (who) is poor." The verb-subject נולד רש word order is typical after an initial function word like כי. However, the position of the במלכותו above the verb and subject indicates that it has been focus-fronted within the כי clause. The combination of כי גם is troublesome. The order גם כי is often associated with introducing a concessive clause

(JM §171), while כִּי גַם is not a common collocation and Ecclesiastes contains six out of the twenty-two occurrences (Gen 35:17; Deut 12:31; 1 Sam 21:9; 22:17; 2 Sam 4:2; Isa 26:12; Jer 6:11; 12:6; 14:5, 18; 23:11; 46:21; 48:34; 51:12; Ezek 18:11; Hos 9:12; Eccl 4:14, 16; 7:22; 8:12, 16; 9:12). In all other instances besides this verse, the כִּי either has a causal or asseverative meaning and the גַם has an additive or focus function. No combination of these seems to make good sense here in v. 14, which is why we tentatively circle back to the concessive use, primarily based on what makes contextual sense.

4:15   רָאִ֙יתִי֙ אֶת־כָּל־הַ֣חַיִּ֔ים הַֽמְהַלְּכִ֖ים תַּ֣חַת הַשָּׁ֑מֶשׁ עִ֚ם הַיֶּ֣לֶד הַשֵּׁנִ֔י אֲשֶׁ֥ר יַעֲמֹ֖ד תַּחְתָּֽיו׃

I saw all the living who were walking under the sun (being) with the second youth, who will stand in his [= old king] place.

רָאִ֙יתִי֙ אֶת־כָּל־הַ֣חַיִּ֔ים הַֽמְהַלְּכִ֖ים תַּ֣חַת הַשָּׁ֑מֶשׁ. *Qatal* 1cs Qal √ראה and Participle mp Piel √הלך. The complement of the bivalent verb ראיתי is not merely the NP אֶת כל החיים, but the remainder of the verse following ראיתי, which is a small clause (see also 7:21). That is, the object of "I saw" is not "all the living" (who happen to be characterized as walking …), but the whole situation of all the living who walk being with the second/next youth. Fox (1999: 226) is nearly correct in his analysis, except that the עם PP is not an adjunct of the main verb ראיתי but of the reduced and covert verb within the small clause (reconstructed here as "being"; i.e., "being with" in the sense of companionship or loyalty).

עִם הַיֶּ֣לֶד הַשֵּׁנִ֔י אֲשֶׁ֥ר יַעֲמֹ֖ד תַּחְתָּֽיו. *Yiqtol* 3ms Qal √עמד. The verb עמד is bivalent here with the PP תחתיו as its locative complement. The ordinal שֵׁנִי denotes "second," but here likely connotes "next," as in the next in line (Seow 1997: 185; Fox 1999: 226; see HALOT, s.v.). The phrase "the next youth" does not need to imply a third character (contra Fox 1999); rather, this youth is the "second" figure in the comparison and the "second" in that he takes the king's place.

4:16   אֵֽין־קֵ֣ץ לְכָל־הָעָ֗ם לְכֹ֤ל אֲשֶׁר־הָיָה֙ לִפְנֵיהֶ֔ם גַּ֥ם הָאַחֲרוֹנִ֖ים לֹ֣א יִשְׂמְחוּ־ב֑וֹ כִּֽי־גַם־זֶ֥ה הֶ֖בֶל וְרַעְי֥וֹן רֽוּחַ׃

There is no end to all the people, that is, to all who he [= youth] was before them, yet those after will not be happy with him [= youth]. Indeed, this too is a הבל *and chasing wind.*

Despite the foolishness of the image of the old unheeding king, the youth is bound to that same fate through his reign; he, too, will become the old dotard with whom no one is pleased.

אֵין־קֵץ לְכָל־הָעָם. An אין negative copula clause with קץ as the subject and the ל-PP as the copular complement. The NP העם refers to the people under the rule of the king (the youth from v. 15).

לְכֹל אֲשֶׁר־הָיָה לִפְנֵיהֶם. *Qatal* 3ms Qal √היה. This ל-PP can be taken as the second part of the compound אין copular complement along with לכל העם or as an appositive PP clarifying the referent of העם. The first option, which results in two groups, "the people" versus "all who he was before," makes less sense than the second option, that העם refers specifically to the king's subjects. Within the אשר relative clause, the subject is a null pronoun that refers back to "the youth," and the copular complement is the PP לפניהם. This PP could be understood as temporal (so the Versions), but Seow rightly explains that it is locative here: "Kings are typically described as going before their subjects (1 Sam 18:16; 2 Chron 1:10). The author has in mind the king going before the vast multitudes to acknowledge their allegiance" (1997: 185).

גַּם הָאַחֲרוֹנִים לֹא יִשְׂמְחוּ־בוֹ. *Yiqtol* 3mp Qal √שמח. The initial גם appears to be concessive ("though, although") or adversative ("but, yet, however") since the context suggests a contrast between the two primary statements. If so, the subject NP האחרונים should likely be taken as carrying focus-fronting pragmatics and so in the higher focus-phrase of the clause. The verb שמח is monovalent (see 3:12; 8:15) and the ב-PP is an adjunct providing the object or occasion motivating the pleasure or joy. Fox cites Judg 9:19, שִׂמְחוּ בַּאֲבִימֶלֶךְ וְיִשְׂמַח גַּם־הוּא בָּכֶם, "be happy with Abimelech and also he will be happy with you," as a similar context regarding the people's pleasure with a ruler (1999: 227). Taking בו to refer to the youth of v. 15, the statement means that not even he, "though leader of limitless masses, would find favor with later people, because everyone is soon forgotten" (227). A similar sentiment is expressed in 9:13-15.

כִּי־גַם־זֶה הֶבֶל וְרַעְיוֹן רוּחַ. An asseverative כי followed by an additive גם (see comment on 1:11). On הבל, see 1:2; on רעיון, see 1:14.

4:17–5:6 Behave Properly Before God

Chapter 5 is not a distinct literary unit in the book. In fact, neither of
the discernible sections stand entirely on their own but are connected
to material from chapters 4 and 6, respectively. Verses 1-6 continues the
admonitions begun with 4:17. Note that this more "traditional wisdom"
section reflects Qoheleth's stance among the sages—he does not everywhere challenge the tradition (Fox 1999: 229).

4:17   שְׁמֹר רַגְלֶיךָ* כַּאֲשֶׁר תֵּלֵךְ אֶל־בֵּית הָאֱלֹהִים
וְקָרוֹב לִשְׁמֹעַ מִתֵּת הַכְּסִילִים זָבַח כִּי־אֵינָם
יוֹדְעִים לַעֲשׂוֹת רָע:

> *Watch your feet when you go to the house of God: to listen is more accept-*
> *able than fools giving a sacrifice because they do not know how to do bad.*

The last verse of chapter 4 appears to begin a new section of admonitions (a shift from the reflective discourse preceding it) that runs through
5:6 on the topic of behaving properly in cultic contexts.

שְׁמֹר רַגְלֶיךָ. Impv ms Qal √שמר. The NP רגליך is the complement
of bivalent שמר. The *Ketiv* רגליך reflects the plural form and would be
vocalized as רַגְלֶיךָ; the *Qere* reflects the singular, רַגְלְךָ.

כַּאֲשֶׁר תֵּלֵךְ אֶל־בֵּית הָאֱלֹהִים. *Yiqtol* 2ms Qal √הלך. The אשר
nominalizes the following clause so that it may serve as the complement
of the כ preposition used temporally ("when you go …"). On the כ in
its temporal or approximation uses, see WO §11.2.9; on the syntax of
כאשר, see Holmstedt 2016: 119–24. Within the כאשר clause, the אל-
PP is the locative complement of the motion verb.

וְקָרוֹב לִשְׁמֹעַ מִתֵּת הַכְּסִילִים זָבַח. A null copula clause, Inf
Constr Qal √שמע and √נתן. The initial word, קָרוֹב, can either be the
adjective "near" or an Inf Abs "being near." The former provides a simpler syntactic parsing: it is a comparative construction with קרוב as the
copular complement, לשמע as the subject, and the מן-PP/infinitive
clause as the adjunct that finishes the comparison (MNK §39.14.8;
WO §11.2.11e.3). Within the מתת infinitive phrase, the clitic host NP
הכסילים is the subject of the bound infinitive, and the NP זבח is one of
the complements of bivalent נתן (whose other complement in this case is
covert but recoverable, "to God"). The context suggests that the connotation indicated by קרוב is "acceptable" or "presentable," perhaps derived

from "near to God's favor" (Fox 1999: 230; Seow 1997: 194; Gordis 1968: 247; see Longman, 149 for an analysis of קרוב as an infinitive absolute used imperatively).

כִּי־אֵינָם יוֹדְעִים לַעֲשׂוֹת רָע. An אין negative copula, Participle mp Qal √ידע, and Inf Constr Qal √עשׂה. The participle is the complement of the negative copula אין, and the clitic 3mp pronoun on אינם is the subject. Within the embedded participial clause, the ל-PP/infinitive לעשׂות is the complement of the bivalent verb ידע. The bivalent עשׂה takes the NP רע as its complement. Grammatically this clause makes sense, contextually it does not. Seow's (1997: 193) interpretation "because they do not recognize that they are doing evil" goes beyond what the grammatical construction allows.

5:1   אַל־תְּבַהֵל עַל־פִּיךָ וְלִבְּךָ אַל־יְמַהֵר לְהוֹצִיא דָבָר
לִפְנֵי הָאֱלֹהִים כִּי הָאֱלֹהִים בַּשָּׁמַיִם וְאַתָּה עַל־
הָאָרֶץ עַל־כֵּן יִהְיוּ דְבָרֶיךָ מְעַטִּים:

Don't be hasty with regard to your mouth, and don't let your mind hurry to bring out a word before God because God is in the heavens and you are upon the earth. Therefore let your words be few.

אַל־תְּבַהֵל עַל־פִּיךָ. Jussive 2ms Piel √בהל. The imperative form cannot be negated in BH. Thus, the corresponding negative is expressed by the אַל with a second-person jussive or לא with a second-person *yiqtol* form (WO §34.2.1b). The על-PP is an adjunct of the verb תבהל narrowing the scope of the hastiness to the domain of things related to the mouth, i.e., speech. On the use of the preposition על in the sense of "concerning, with regard to," see WO §11.2.13g. Elsewhere this verb takes an NP complement (2 Chr 35:21) or an infinitive complement (7:9; Esth 2:9). Here we should probably understand a null complement as fulfilling the valency of this verb, and its contents are provided in the complementary infinitive of the following, synonymous verb מהר.

וְלִבְּךָ אַל־יְמַהֵר. Jussive 3ms Piel √מהר. Both the modal (jussive) verb and the negative would normally trigger verb-subject order. Thus, the subject-negative-verb order here reflects the further raising of the subject לבך for topic or focus. Contextually, it is less likely that לבך is being set over against פיך, so rather than focus-fronting, this appears to be a case of topic-fronting. That is, while the previous clause was about the speech in general (things of the פה), this one shifts to to a specific concern for intentional speech (thoughts of the לב that lead to speech). The following ל-PP infinitive clause, beginning with להוציא, is a complement expressing what one should not be in a hurry to do. Semantically it provides the content of the null complement of the previous verb, תבהל.

לְהוֹצִיא דָבָר לִפְנֵי הָאֱלֹהִים. Inf Constr Hiph √יצא. The Hiphil יצא is trivalent, requiring a complement of the thing moved (here דבר) and a complement indicating the locative goal (here the PP לפני האלהים). As with many infinitives, the subject is null and can be contextually identified as the subject of the main verb. Fox asserts that "to speak before God" is an Aramaism, equivalent to אמר (//אנפק) אמרא קדם, meaning "speak to." There are a number of examples in Daniel of speaking before (קדם) a king (Dan 2:9, 36; 4:4; 5:17; 6:13-14), but there are also numerous examples in Daniel of speaking to (ל) someone, including to a king (e.g., Dan 3:9, 16). Moreover, the expression "to speak before someone/ God" is attested elsewhere in BH: Deut 26:5, 13; 1 Sam 20:1; Neh 3:24; 6:19. Alternatively, "bringing out a דבר" can refer to raising a matter for consideration, as one often does in prayers of supplication. So, whether the collocation הוציא דבר in this context refers explicitly to speaking or more generally to directing God's attention to some matter, the context itself is almost certainly prayer.

כִּי הָאֱלֹהִים בַּשָּׁמַיִם וְאַתָּה עַל־הָאָרֶץ. Two null copula clauses. The כי clause is causal, providing Qoheleth's justification for asserting caution and restraint in speech to God. Each null coupula has a locative PP complement.

עַל־כֵּן יִהְיוּ דְבָרֶיךָ מְעַטִּים. Yiqtol or Jussive 3mp Qal √היה. The verb's form is ambiguous: it could be an imperfective yiqtol or a jussive. The verb-subject word order does not help since, while it may reflect the typical order with modal verbs, it may also simply reflect the inversion triggered by the initial PP על כן. Ambiguous morphology and syntax notwithstanding, the semantics are clearly modal because the statement is a resulting directive relating back to the clear negative jussives earlier in the verse. The collocation of the preposition על in its causal usage and the deictic adverb כן "thusly" results in a clausal adverb that specifies the effects of the action that has occurred or will occur, "therefore" (< "because of thus") (WO §§11.3.2a; 39.3.4e). Syntactically, the clause is not subordinate to the previous clause but stands on its own. The semantic connection (i.e., the sense of result) is made by the connection between deictic כן "thus" and its pointing back at the preceding context.

5:2   כִּי בָּא הַחֲלוֹם בְּרֹב עִנְיָן וְקוֹל כְּסִיל בְּרֹב דְּבָרִים:

Because "the dream comes in abundance of activity and a voice of a fool (comes) in abundance of words."

We essentially concur with Fox, who calls this "a parenthetical remark of proverbial character, motivating the advice in 5:1. The main point of this verse comes in the second line: it is foolish to talk too much" (1999: 231). However, rather than a true parenthesis, which breaks the flow of discourse to provide background information, we take this as a כִּי clause that grounds the assertion of the preceding verse by quoting a proverb.

כִּי בָּא הַחֲלוֹם בְּרֹב עִנְיָן. *Qatal* 3ms Qal √בוא. Although the morphology is ambiguous between a *qatal* and participle parsing, the triggered verb-subject order, due to the initial כִּי, suggests that בא is a finite verb (= *qatal*) since the participle does not exhibit triggered inversion to verb-subject order after function words (see Holmstedt 2002: 156–68; 2016: 48–49). The *qatal* form casts the proverb as (past-time) anecdotal (see Cook 2005: 130–31; 2013: 329–30); our translation, however, reflects the preference for general present tense in English proverbs. The כִּי is causal and so provides the reason for letting one's words be few from the preceding clause in v. 1. The specific sense of בא החלום ברב ענין "dreams coming in abundance of activity" has eluded most commentators. Seow builds upon the use of חלום within contexts that employ it for ephemerality and suggests that the "point of the aphorism, then, is that much preoccupation amounts to nothing more than a dream, and many words produce nothing more than the hollow sound of the loquacious fool" (1997: 200). According to Fox, the phrase בא ב means "come with," "come bringing," or "accompanied by," and he cites Lev 16:3 and Ps 66:13 as support (see also HALOT, s.v. Qal 2e; GKC §219n): "Just as a dream holds much empty 'activity,' so does the voice of the fool convey only a lot of vapid verbiage" (1999: 231–32). The use of the article on the NP חלום suggests either that this is a generic reference to an arbitrary member of a well-established kind (e.g., dreams are like this) or a specific reference that is grounded in an understood frame of reference outside the quoted proverb (and thus, also outside this passage). It is impossible to know which is correct. On the use of the article in BH, see Bekins; on the pattern of the article on Ecclesiastes, see Baranowski.

וְקוֹל כְּסִיל בְּרֹב דְּבָרִים. This clause is also governed by the כי at the beginning of the verse, and the verb is gapped from the previous clause, tying together the comparison. The verb tense may actually be "played with" between the two clauses, so that the *qatal* past sense is inverted to a future prediction in this verse. To paraphrase, "Because, (just as) the dream has been known to come in/with much activity, so the sound of the fool (will come) in/with abundance of words" (see Cook 2013: 330). The bound phrase קול כסיל lacks the article, which signals that the referent of the NP is nonspecific and unidentifiable—any voice of any fool represents too many words.

5:3 כַּאֲשֶׁר תִּדֹּר נֶדֶר לֵאלֹהִים אַל־תְּאַחֵר לְשַׁלְּמוֹ כִּי אֵין חֵפֶץ בַּכְּסִילִים אֵת אֲשֶׁר־תִּדֹּר שַׁלֵּם:

When you make a vow to God, do not delay in fulfilling it, because there is no delight in fools. (The thing) that you vow fulfill.

כַּאֲשֶׁר תִּדֹּר נֶדֶר לֵאלֹהִים אַל־תְּאַחֵר לְשַׁלְּמוֹ. *Yiqtol* 2ms Qal √נדר, Jussive 2ms Piel √אחר, and Inf Constr Piel √שלם with clitic 3ms pronoun. On the function of כאשר, see comment on 4:17. The כ-PP is a scene-setting adjunct in fronted (topic) position (contrast the position of the כאשר in 4:17). The verb נדר is bivalent (fulfilled here by a null-subject and the complement נדר). The ל-PP adjunct indicates the recipient of the vow. The main verb of the clause, תאחר, is bivalent and takes either an NP complement for the person or thing "delayed" or, as here, a ל-PP infinitive clause indicating the activity that is (not) delayed. The clitic 3ms pronoun on לשלמו is the complement of the bivalent Piel infinitive. On negating an imperative with the jussive, see 5:1.

כִּי אֵין חֵפֶץ בַּכְּסִילִים. An אין negative copula clause. The NP חפץ is the subject and the ב-PP is the (locative) complement. This might be an impersonal locution (so Fox 1999: 232): "no one delights in fools." Perhaps better, it is a slightly oblique reference to *God* not taking any delight in fools. The כי clause is causal, grounding the assertion to avoid fulfilling a vow to God by the rationale that not doing so would be foolish and would anger God.

אֵת אֲשֶׁר־תִּדֹּר שַׁלֵּם. *Yiqtol* 2ms Qal √נדר, Impv ms Piel √שלם. The את precedes the null head of the relative clause. As a whole, the null NP and its relative is the complement of bivalent Piel שלם. The null head of the relative can be reconstructed from the context as "vow." Within the relative, there is null resumption of the null head; the null resumptive is the syntactic complement of the bivalent verb נדר: "Pay the (thing/vow) which you vow (it)."

5:4   טוֹב אֲשֶׁר לֹא־תִדֹּר מִשֶּׁתִּדּוֹר וְלֹא תְשַׁלֵּם׃

That you do not vow is better than that you do and do not fulfill (it).

טוֹב אֲשֶׁר ... מִשֶׁ. *Yiqtol* 2ms Qal √נדר (2×), 2ms Piel √שלם. The first half of the verse is a null copula clause in which the nominalized אשר clause is the subject and the adjective טוב is the focus-fronted copular complement. The compound שׁ clause of the second half is the complement of the comparative preposition מן (MNK §39.14.8; WO §11.2.11e.3). Seow (1997: 195) makes a point of connecting this use of שׁ to the "that" usage of אשר and late BH; he lists the following parallels: Neh 2:5, 10; 7:65; 8:14, 15; 10:31; 13:1, 19, 22; Esth 1:19; 2:10; 3:4; 4:11; 6:2; 8:11; Dan 1:8 (cf. JM §157a; see also Holmstedt 2006: 10, where Neh 2:5 is omitted simply because of the complexity that the gapped verb from 2:4 creates). Here the אשר and שׁ nominalize their respective clauses so that the clauses may function as a clausal subject (אשר לא תדר) and prepositional complement (משתדור ולא תשלם), respectively. Contrast the use of אשר in the final clause of v. 3, where את אשר תדר is a null-head relative clause, "[the vow] that you vow." (See Introduction §4 for a discussion on אשר and שׁ in Ecclesiastes.)

5:5   אַל־תִּתֵּן אֶת־פִּ֫יךָ לַחֲטִיא אֶת־בְּשָׂרֶךָ וְאַל־תֹּאמַר
לִפְנֵי הַמַּלְאָךְ כִּי שְׁגָגָה הִיא לָמָּה יִקְצֹף הָאֱלֹהִים
עַל־קוֹלֶךָ וְחִבֵּל אֶת־מַעֲשֵׂה יָדֶיךָ׃

Do not let your mouth cause your flesh to sin, and do not say before the messenger, "Indeed, it is an error!" Why should God become angry at the sound of you and (so) destroy the work of your hands?

אַל־תִּתֵּן אֶת־פִּ֫יךָ לַחֲטִיא אֶת־בְּשָׂרֶךָ. Jussive 2ms Qal √נתן and Inf Constr Hiph √חטא. For the "permissive" sense of נתן, see HALOT, s.v. *Qal* #8. Note that the ה prefix in the Hiphil infinitive לחטיא has syncopated intervocalically (i.e., *la-hahfi' > *laahfi' > lahăfi'*). Although

this sound change occurs throughout BH morphology, it is rare within
the paradigm of the Hiphil infinitive, probably due to paradigm pressure
(GKC §53q; JM §54b). However, it does occurs more often in Mishnaic Hebrew (Segal, §143). Trivalent נתן takes here a complement of the
thing/person allowed (את־פיך) and a ל-PP/infinitive complement marking the activity allowed. The infinitive חטיא is itself bivalent and takes
the NP את־בשרך as its complement.

וְאַל־תֹּאמַר לִפְנֵי הַמַּלְאָךְ כִּי שְׁגָגָה הִיא. Jussive 2ms Qal √אמר
and null copula clause. The לפני PP is an adjunct indicating the addressee
of speech. The clause כי שגגה היא is the complement of the verb of speaking אמר and consists of the free 3fs pronoun as the subject and שגגה as
the focus-fronted complement. The focus-fronting שגגה signals that the
copular clause does more than assert that the referent of היא (whatever it
was) is erroneous, it isolates שגגה out of all the possible descriptors and
asserts that it is *only* שגגה and nothing else. Note that כי never introduces direct speech clauses but is contained within them, typically as an
asseverative כי (see Miller 1996: 116). Thus, if the complement of אמר
is construed as direct speech, then כי is asseverative (WO §§39.3.4e;
40.2.2b); if it is construed as indirect speech, then כי has its more common complementizer function (WO §38.8). Some commentators (e.g.,
Fox 1999) suggest that the Versions have the more accurate reading, with
האלהים instead of המלאך, and that the latter is a case of creating distance
from God. The objection to this is that God is mentioned throughout
the book, so why would it be changed only here? The better analysis is
that this refers to an intermediary, like the temple priest (so Seow 1997:
196, who cites Mal 2:7).

לָמָּה יִקְצֹף הָאֱלֹהִים עַל־קוֹלֶךָ וְחִבֵּל אֶת־מַעֲשֵׂה יָדֶיךָ. *Yiqtol*
(irrealis) 3ms Qal √קצף and *qatal* (irrealis) 3ms Piel √חבל. As Seow says,
this is "a rhetorical question used to introduce undesirable alternatives"
(1997: 196). Although קצף is sometimes monovalent (e.g., Esth 1:12;
2:21), much more often it is bivalent with the object of anger expressed
by an על-PP complement, as here (e.g., Gen 40:2; 41:10; Lam 5:22).
The *qatal* (irrealis) perfective חבל expresses the outcome of becoming
angry; the meaning of the *Piel* "to destroy" is typically postbiblical (Jastrow, 419), but HALOT lists it as "to ruin" here and in Isa 13:5; 32:7;
54:16; Song 2:15; Job 17:1; Mic 2:10. The complement of bivalent חבל
is the bound phrase את־מעשה ידיך.

5:6 כִּי בְרֹב חֲלֹמוֹת וַהֲבָלִים וּדְבָרִים הַרְבֵּה כִּי אֶת־
הָאֱלֹהִים יְרָא:

*Because in the abundance of vacuous visions and many words—indeed
fear God.*

כִּי בְרֹב חֲלֹמוֹת וַהֲבָלִים וּדְבָרִים הַרְבֵּה. Seow takes the initial כי
as causal, presumably providing a motivation to avoid the entire preceding scenario of being careless with words and so angering God. However,
he translates the first two phrases as null copula clauses without explaining how he arrives at this syntactic analysis: "for vacuous dreams are in
abundance and there are words aplenty" (1997: 193). Fox makes two
emendations: he reads ברב as כרב and omits the ו in the word ודברים,
thus making דברים הרבה a better candidate for the clausal subject, "For
much talk is <like> a lot of dreams" (1999: 229, 233). Alternatively, it is
possible that the first כי clause was meant to provide the motivation for
avoiding the scenario in v. 5 but that Qoheleth did not finish it. Rather,
he shifted midstream to provide a simpler (and more pious?) reason,
"Oh, just fear God!" This kind of interrupted syntax, where the author
switches abruptly from one (unfinished) statement to another is called
anacoluthon (GKC §167b).

חֲלֹמוֹת וַהֲבָלִים. Seow notes that, given the metaphorical use of
חלום for something that is illusory or ephemeral (see also 5:2), the collocation of חלום and הבל here is an instance of hendiadys and so he
translates it as "vacuous dreams" (1997: 197); perhaps the alliteration of
"vacuous visions" would be better.

כִּי אֶת־הָאֱלֹהִים יְרָא. Impv ms Qal √ירא. The complement of
the verb is אלהים. Some commentators follow the LXX and reconstruct
the 2ms pronoun אתה from the initial את, producing something like
Seow's "but as for you, fear God" (1997: 197). This can be done either
by redividing the words so that the ה on האלהים is suffixed to את, or
by suggesting that את is simply written defectively. However, the use of
the independent pronoun with an imperative is a marked structure, and
grammatically there is nothing wrong with the text as it stands if one
accepts that the verse is an example of anacoluthon.

5:7–6:9 Be Content, Not Greedy

In an extended section weaving together themes he has already addressed,
Qoheleth returns to the problem of money and working for a legacy in

life. His conclusion addresses both life and death—in life, the one set on gain is never satisfied; in death, everything is leveled anyway (*whatever* happens *after* life).

אִם־עֹ֣שֶׁק רָ֠שׁ וְגֵ֨זֶל מִשְׁפָּ֤ט וָצֶ֙דֶק֙ תִּרְאֶ֣ה בַמְּדִינָ֔ה   5:7
אַל־תִּתְמַ֖הּ עַל־הַחֵ֑פֶץ כִּ֣י גָבֹ֜הַּ מֵעַ֤ל גָּבֹ֙הַּ֙ שֹׁמֵ֔ר
וּגְבֹהִ֖ים עֲלֵיהֶֽם׃

If oppression of the poor and robbery of righteous judgment you see in the province, don't be amazed at the matter, because one high above (another) high one is watching, and ones higher than them (are also watching).

Verse 7 continues the instructional discourse but switches to the theme of greed. Fox characterizes vv. 7-8 as "an epigram on the ubiquity of social oppression and greed" (1999: 233).

אִם־עֹ֣שֶׁק רָ֠שׁ וְגֵ֨זֶל מִשְׁפָּ֤ט וָצֶ֙דֶק֙ תִּרְאֶ֣ה בַמְּדִינָ֔ה. *Yiqtol* (irrealis) 2ms Qal √ראה. The vocalization of the ו conjunction in וָצֶדֶק suggests that this and the previous word form a hendiadys "righteous judgment" or "just due" (so Fox 1999: 233). The initial אם establishes this clause as a conditional clause (subordinate to the following אל תתמה). Typically, due to triggered inversion, a verb follows the אם; here the compound NP complement has been raised above the verb so that it now follows the אם. In the context it seems that the raised complement reflects topic-fronting, indicating a shift in the discourse theme (רש, עשק, and משפט have all been invoked previously in the book, making them available as topics to reactivate; see 3:16, 4:1, 14). A locative adjunct ב-PP marks where one sees these things.

אַל־תִּתְמַ֖הּ עַל־הַחֵ֑פֶץ. Jussive 2ms Qal √תמה. The verb תמה (where final ה is a genuine consonant and not a *mater*) occurs only eight times in the Hebrew Bible (Gen 43:33; Isa 13:8; 29:9; Jer 4:9; Hab 1:5; Ps 48:6; Job 26:11; Eccl 5:7). When the source of the amazement is specified by an adjunct phrase, the phrase occurs twice with the preposition אל (Gen 43:33 and Isa 13:8), once with the preposition מן (Job 26:11), and once with the preposition על (here). The NP חפץ "matter" refers back to the situation mentioned in the conditional clause, עשק and גזל, and since it is an unnecessary reference (the clause would be grammatical without the PP על החפץ), it may serve to reinforce the gravity of the condition.

כִּי גָבֹהַּ מֵעַל גָּבֹהַּ שֹׁמֵר וּגְבֹהִים עֲלֵיהֶם. Two null copula clauses, Participle ms Qal √שמר. The first clause has a substantival adjective גָבֹהַ as the subject, followed by an NP-internal PP adjunct and then the participle as the copular complement. In the second null copula clause, a second mp substantival adjective וּגְבֹהִים is the subject and it is also modified by an NP-internal PP (with a clitic 3mp pronoun), and the participle שׁמר is gapped from the prior clause as the null complement. All readers have difficulty with this section. Seow disregards the accents and takes the ו from וּגְבֹהִים and suffixes it to שׁמר to make a 3cp perfect and translates it as "an arrogant one is above an arrogant one, (and) arrogant ones have watched over them all" (1997: 203); this analysis does not mesh with our NP-internal analysis of the two PPs. Longman has a slightly different assessment: "the preoccupation with other things means that no one is watching out for justice" (158; cf. Fox 1999: 233). Rather than a straightforward statement about injustice occurring because leaders are too consumed with watching each other, we take the verse to be highly sarcastic. Qoheleth instructs his listener not to be surprised at injustice because multiple levels of leaders have their eyes on it. Of course, if injustice continues to occur, then the watchful eyes of those in charge are highly ineffective, which is Qoheleth's point.

וְיִתְרוֹן אֶרֶץ בַּכֹּל הִיא* מֶלֶךְ לְשָׂדֶה נֶעֱבָד׃   5:8

And the profit of land—he is over everything, a king of an arable country.

וְיִתְרוֹן אֶרֶץ בַּכֹּל הִיא* מֶלֶךְ לְשָׂדֶה נֶעֱבָד. This is a notoriously difficult verse, which Seow describes as "hopelessly corrupt" and making "no sense" (1997: 204). Fox suggests that the gist is the "advantage a land possesses" and emends to arrive at a more specific sense, that "a country that has all of its fields cultivated has an advantage over others" (1999: 234). As the text stands, the first half appears to present a left-dislocation (יתרון ארץ) followed by a null copula clause with the complement (בכל, which resumes the dislocated יתרון by semantic coreference) and the subject, הוא (note that we read the 3ms pronoun of the *Qere*, not the 3fs pronoun, הִיא, of the *Ketiv*). Thus, in contrast to those who assume some positive resolution to the preceding in this verse (so Bartholomew, 217; Crenshaw, 119; Krüger, 115; Murphy, 51 et al.), with Longman, we take the clause to continue the theme of oppression from on high, "*even the king* himself takes advantage of his politically powerful position to get *the* *profit of the land*" (158, emphasis in original). But the first clause does not specify that the הוא, who is over everything (i.e., the profit of the land), is the king. This is specified by the right-dislocated NP מלך. The final PP לשדה נעבד we take to be internal to the structure of the NP מלך and thus to restrict the semantic domain of מלך from any מלך to only those kings who belonged to countries with arable land. Admittedly, the meaning of נעבד as "arable" is novel and so we suggest it tentatively. Moreover, the use of both left- and right-dislocation in the same clause is certainly grammatical but also rare (we are currently unaware of any other examples). Together with the difficulty of v. 7, the syntax in this verse may suggest that this epigram is highly oral in style and that only the added prosody (the pauses and intonational emphases) would make it easier to process.

5:9   אֹהֵב כֶּסֶף לֹא־יִשְׂבַּע כֶּסֶף וּמִי־אֹהֵב בֶּהָמוֹן לֹא
תְבוּאָה גַּם־זֶה הָבֶל׃

He who loves money will not be sated by money, and whoever loves abundance (will) not (be sated) by the product. This too is a הבל.

The theme of greed begun by the epigram in vv. 7-8 continues in v. 9 and does not end until 6:12. Structurally, we agree that "this unit comprises five loosely related sections treating the themes of greed and satisfaction" (Fox 1999: 235). Verse 9 itself is proverbial in character (parallelism and ellipsis, which are common in proverbs, are both present) and moves from the coordination of greed and oppression in vv. 7-8 to the never-ending (and never sated) nature of greed.

אֹהֵב כֶּסֶף לֹא־יִשְׂבַּע כֶּסֶף. Participle ms Qal √אהב and *yiqtol* 3ms Qal √שבע. The participle אהב is either used as an agentive noun, "a lover of" (see above, on 1:15), or within a relative clause structure, "(he who) loves." The latter analysis is the simpler since the participle encodes event predicates and is not restricted to a purely nominal bound expression. The lack of an article signals a nonspecific, arbitrary reference for the null head, "*any one* who loves." The relative clause analysis also aligns with our view that a participle with an internal modifier should not be treated as a substantive (see Holmstedt 2016: 74–77). Since in BH the negative with a verb typically results in word order inversion to verb-subject, the subject-verb order here suggests that the subject אהב כסף is either fronted for topic or focus or that the grammar of Ecclesiastes reflects a change so that the negative by itself does not trigger inversion (see Introduction §§2D, 6). The NP כסף is an NP complement of the bivalent stative verb שׂבע, indicating the source of the (desired but absent) satiation (see also 4:8; but cf. 1:8). The switch from participle (present state of loving) to *yiqtol* points to a strong future prediction: "will *never* be sated …" (see Cook 2005: 128).

וּמִי־אֹהֵב בֶּהָמוֹן לֹא תְבוּאָה. Participle ms Qal √אהב. The initial מִי presents this as a free-choice relative clause (see comment on 1:9). The root אהב never takes ב to mark its complement elsewhere; it may be a dittography from the final consonant of the verb, or it might be that the author's idiolect allowed him to mark the complement of אהב with ב. Fox (1999: 235) emends the ב away as a dittography (following BHS), while we retain it as possible dialectal variation (cf. Schoors, 59). The lack of an overt verb for this clause is due to verbal ellipsis or gapping: it is necessary to reconstruct a copy of ישׂבע from the preceding clause. Interestingly, while a verb and its negative are often taken as a bundle and so gapped together, here the negative is repeated and so only the verb is read into the second clause (see Miller 2005 for a study of ellipsis involving negation). As with the preceding clause, the NP תבואה is the complement to the gapped verb.

5:10   בִּרְבוֹת הַטּוֹבָה רַבּוּ אוֹכְלֶיהָ וּמַה־כִּשְׁרוֹן לִבְעָלֶיהָ
כִּי אִם־רְאִית* עֵינָיו:

When good things increase, those who consume it increase; and what benefit belongs to its owner except what his eyes see?

בִּרְבוֹת הַטּוֹבָה רַבּוּ אוֹכְלֶיהָ. Inf Constr Qal √רבה, *qatal* 3cp Qal √רבב, and Participle mp bound form Qal √אכל with 3fs clitic pronoun. The stative *qatal* expresses a present inchoative state in this gnomic expression: "become many." The PP-infinitive preceding the main verb is a common pattern for establishing the context of the assertion in the main clause. The subject of the infinitive is a singular, definite noun used generically: "the good (thing)," as in English "*the* good life." Most commentators interpret its use here and in 6:3 in reference to wealth or the enjoyable goods of life. The position before the verb and subject indicates that such adjuncts have been fronted as scene-setting topics. The fronting of the PP-infinitive adjunct has, in turn, triggered the inverted verb (רבו)-subject (אוכליה) order. The enclitic pronoun marks the complement of the participle and has הטובה as its antecedent. There are three common interpretations of this clause: (1) the wealthier one becomes, the more one must deal with leeches and sycophants; (2) an increase of wealth simply means an increase of taxes and expenses; or (3) increased wealth generates an increase of greed within those who earn it. All three make sense of the grammar and within the context of the book.

וּמַה־כִּשְׁרוֹן לִבְעָלֶיהָ כִּי אִם־רְאִית* עֵינָיו. A null copula clause with an embedded exceptive clause (also with null copula). The subject is מה כשרון (regarding the use of מה, see comment on 1:3); the copular complement is the ל-PP לבעליה. On כשרון, Fox notes, "as commonly recognized, [it] here means 'benefit,' 'prosper,' corresponding to *yikšar* 'succeed' in 11:6" (1999: 236); on לִבְעָלֶיהָ, even when this word is in the singular (as context suggests here, viz., the 3ms suffix on עֵינָיו), it often takes a plural form, especially with suffixes (see GKC §124i; JM §136d). The question "What benefit is [wealth] for its owner?" is rhetorical and sets up an automatic negative answer, "none," which is then qualified by the exceptive clause "except what his eyes can see" (WO §38.6). The interpretation of this clause depends, of course, on how one takes the preceding clause. If the first clause is about leeching relatives or abundant expenses, then "what his eyes see" may refer to the little that is left for the owner to enjoy, what has not slipped through his fingers. But if the first clause refers to the cycle of increasing greed that wealth often imposes upon the owner, then this second half pierces the futility of the cycle by asserting that wealth offers pleasure that can be experienced only in the present; it does not last.

*רְאִית. The *Ketiv* should likely be vocalized as רְאִיַּת, the bound form of רְאִיָּה "seeing, look, glance," a noun not attested in BH but well attested in rabbinic Hebrew (Jastrow, s.v.). The *Qere* appears to be רְאוּת, which is not attested in either BH or rabbinic Hebrew; it is presumably the bound form of a fs noun with a meaning similar to ראיה. With a small change in vocalization, the *Qere* could be read as רְאוֹת, the *Qal* Inf Constr. The result would be similar to the meaning of the bound noun "seeing of." Since none of the options present clear differences, Seow (1997: 205) is correct to draw on the similar phrase in 6:9, מראה עינים "a sight/vision of the eyes," which refers to "what the eyes see." Both here and in 6:9 the expression refers not merely to seeing, but "enjoying" (so Krüger, 120; Seow 1997: 220). Thus, the point of the כי אם contrastive clause is to underscore the absurdity of the increase of wealth apart from the immediate enjoyment of that wealth. Alternatively, in keeping with the theme of anxiety of the wealthy in the following verse, the owner can merely watch with consuming care (due to leeches, taxes, or his own greed) over his increasing wealth without ever enjoying it (so Bartholomew, 219; Whybray, 99).

5:11   מְתוּקָה֙ שְׁנַ֣ת הָעֹבֵ֔ד אִם־מְעַ֥ט וְאִם־הַרְבֵּ֖ה יֹאכֵ֑ל
וְהַשָּׂבָע֙ לֶֽעָשִׁ֔יר אֵינֶ֛נּוּ מַנִּ֥יחַֽ ל֖וֹ לִישֽׁוֹן:

The sleep of the worker is sweet whether he eats little or much, but the satisfaction of the rich—it does not allow him to sleep.

This verse presents a popular wisdom sentiment. Seow (1997: 220) cites a Sumerian proverb, "He who eats too much will not (be able) to sleep," while Fox (1999: 137) reminds us of the Mishnaic proverb from Gamliel: "He who increases property increases worry" (Avot 2:7).

מְתוּקָה֙ שְׁנַ֣ת הָעֹבֵ֔ד אִם־מְעַ֥ט וְאִם־הַרְבֵּ֖ה יֹאכֵ֑ל. Participle ms Qal √עבד. A null copula clause with the copular complement fronted for focus. The two אם phrases present a fronted compound complement for יאכל in the adjunct conditional clause. The subject העבד is an agentive noun using the participial *qotel* form (see comment on 1:15).

הָעֹבֵ֔ד. The versions reflect the NP הָעֶבֶד, "the servant, slave," which is consonantally identical to the MT הָעֹבֵד. The contextual difference in meaning between "the sleep of the one who works/worker" and "the sleep of the servant/slave," if there is a difference, is subtle. Seow (1997: 206) maintains the MT and suggests that "the worker does not have worry about all the 'increase' as the wealthy do." Fox (1999: 236) argues that the contrast between the rich man and the worker makes little sense, since "the rich man too works hard"; thus, he suggests that "slave" is more meaningful since then the contrast focuses on property ownership.

אִם־מְעַ֥ט וְאִם־הַרְבֵּ֖ה יֹאכֵ֑ל. *Yiqtol* (irrealis) 3ms Qal √אכל. In this conditional context the *yiqtol* is irrealis but may also express other modalities such as epistemic ("might") or dynamic ("is able to").

וְהַשָּׂבָע֙ לֶֽעָשִׁ֔יר אֵינֶ֛נּוּ מַנִּ֥יחַֽ ל֖וֹ לִישֽׁוֹן. An אין negative copula clause; Participle ms Hiph √נוח; Inf Constr Qal √ישׁן. The Hiph participle is the copular complement, and the clitic pronoun נו on אין is the subject. The initial NP, with the NP-internal PP לעשיר, is in a left-dislocated position and is resumed within the clause by the 3ms clitic pronoun attached to

אֵין (see also 1:7; 9:5, 16). The NP הַשָּׂבָע, "satisfaction; surfeit, (over) abundance," is likely in reference to either too much food or too much wealth, or both, which results in troubled sleep. The participle מַנִּיחַ is trivalent and takes both the PP לוֹ and the ל infinitival (Qal √ישׁן) clause as its complements. Typically the Hiphil of נוח means "to give rest" or "to set down," but in a few biblical contexts it is clearly used as a permissive: Ps 105:14; 1 Chr 16:21; Judg 16:26. The permissive connotation is also a common meaning in postbiblical Hebrew (Jastrow, 885–86).

5:12   יֵשׁ רָעָה חוֹלָה רָאִיתִי תַּחַת הַשָּׁמֶשׁ עֹשֶׁר שָׁמוּר
       לִבְעָלָיו לְרָעָתוֹ:

There is a sickly misfortune (that) I have seen under the sun: wealth is kept by its owner to his misfortune.

יֵשׁ רָעָה חוֹלָה רָאִיתִי תַּחַת הַשָּׁמֶשׁ. Participle fs Qal √חלה; *qatal* 1cs Qal √ראה. The main predicate is the existential יֵשׁ (see 1:10). The subject רעה חולה is modified by an unmarked (and thus restrictive) relative clause ראיתי תחת השמש; within the relative clause, the head is resumed as a null complement of ראיתי, "a sickly misfortune (which) I have seen (it)."

עֹשֶׁר שָׁמוּר לִבְעָלָיו לְרָעָתוֹ. Passive Participle ms Qal √שמר. A null copula clause that also functions as a clausal appositive to the subject רעה חולה. The subject is עשר, and the copular complement is the passive participle.

לִבְעָלָיו. Seow suggests that the ל here indicates agent with the passive predicate (see JM §132f; WO §11.2.10g), thus "by its owner" (1997: 206).

לְרָעָתוֹ. An adjunct phrase expressing the outcome of the wealth being kept.

5:13   וְאָבַד הָעֹשֶׁר הַהוּא בְּעִנְיַן רָע וְהוֹלִיד בֵּן וְאֵין בְּיָדוֹ
       מְאוּמָה:

When that wealth perished in an unfortunate business and he had begotten a son, there was nothing in his [i.e., the son's] hand.

וְאָבַד הָעֹשֶׁר הַהוּא בְּעִנְיַן רָע. *Qatal* (irrealis) 3ms Qal √אבד. The verb אבד is monovalent. The subject העשר ההוא and the ב-PP is an adjunct. Contrary to Seow, it is not the וֹ that indicates the explicative nature of this verse, but the context; the וֹ simply marks the clause edge. The irrealis clause shows the expected verb-subject word order.

וְהוֹלִיד בֵּן. *Qatal* (irrealis) 3ms Hiph √ילד. The Hiphil of ילד is bivalent; the complement is בן. The series of irrealis *qatal* forms points to a protasis-apodosis dependency construction. How precisely the three clauses are to be construed is uncertain. Although a conditional idea "if … then" is possible, the previous verses set this up as an observation of something that actually took place not simply a possible misfortune. A temporal idea with the irrealis *qatal* maintaining its default past temporal reference makes good sense, with the protasis beginning with ואבד ("when that wealth perished") and the apodosis starting with either והוליד ("then he begat a son") or ואין ("then there was nothing"). In either case the past temporal reference carries over into the אין negative copular clause.

וְאֵין בְּיָדוֹ מְאוּמָה. An אין negative copula clause with מאומה as the subject and the PP בידו the copular complement. The clitic 3ms pronoun on בידו renders the expression ambiguous: it may refer to the man's lack of wealth to hand on (so Murphy, 47) or the son's lack of inheritance from his father (so Longman, 161).

5:14   כַּאֲשֶׁר יָצָא מִבֶּטֶן אִמּוֹ עָרוֹם יָשׁוּב לָלֶכֶת כְּשֶׁבָּא
וּמְאוּמָה לֹא־יִשָּׂא בַעֲמָלוֹ שֶׁיֹּלֵךְ בְּיָדוֹ:

Like he came out from the womb of his mother, naked he will again go, like he came. Nothing will he be able to take in exchange for his toil that he may bring into his [= his son's] hand.

כַּאֲשֶׁר יָצָא מִבֶּטֶן אִמּוֹ. *Qatal* 3ms Qal √יצא. The DSS ms 4QQoh[a] has כיא (= BH כי "because") instead of MT כאשר. The MT makes more sense with the comparative, particularly given the following comparative כשבא. See 4:17 for the use of כאשר. Within this embedded clause, the PP מבטן אמו is the complement of bivalent יצא. The subject of the coming and going in this verse is ambiguous (perhaps intentionally so; Krüger, 121): the son may be in view here, particularly if the pronoun in the PP בידו in the previous verse is taken in reference to him; however, the pronoun in בעמלו later in this verse requires reference to the man rather than his son (after all, the son was set to inherit, not anxiously work, for his wealth), which suggests that the man is to be understood as the subject throughout (according to most commentators; see Fox 1999: 238; Murphy, 47).

עָרוֹם יָשׁוּב לָלֶכֶת. *Yiqtol* 3ms Qal √שׁוב; Inf Constr Qal √הלך. The Masoretic accents make it clear that עָרוֹם is an adjunct to יָשׁוּב rather than the preceding clause; although it is morphologically ms (as is the verb), עָרוֹם is not the subject of the clause (the null-subject representing the man from the preceding verses is). The fronted position of this modifying adjunct focuses on the state of that man's naked departure. On the adverbial function of שׁוב with the infinitive ("again"), see 1:7.

כְּשֶׁבָּא. *Qatal* 3ms Qal √בוא. Although morphologically identical with the participle, the parallel with יצא in the earlier comparative clause points to the *qatal* here. Both compare the way he came (past) with how he will go (future) (see Cook 2013: 337 n. 96). This clause seems redundant with the initial comparative clause, but it serves to reinforce the idea that *precisely* in the state of his coming the man departs this life under the sun.

וּמְאוּמָה לֹא־יִשָּׂא בַעֲמָלוֹ שֶׁיֹּלֵךְ בְּיָדוֹ. *Yiqtol* 3ms Qal √נשׂא and Hiph √הלך. The negated *yiqtol* in this context implies a dynamic sense: the inability and not simply the inevitability of not taking anything with him when he dies. The complement of לֹא־יִשָּׂא is the focus-fronted מאומה, underscoring man's inability to take *anything* with him when he departs. In the PP בעמלו the preposition ב is best interpreted as the *beth pretii* (GKC §119p; WO §11.2.5d) and not with the meaning "from," as Crenshaw (123) takes it (see 1:3).

שֶׁיֹּלֵךְ בְּיָדוֹ. A relative clause modifying the head מאומה, which is resumed within the relative by the null complement of Hiph הלך. In exchange for all his toil/acquisitions, he cannot take/retain *anything which he can bring (it) into his hand.* The *yiqtol* has an epistemic sense: "that he may/might … ." The meaning of the Hiphil verb here is uncertain, depending on how the PP בידו is interpreted: the expression either refers to the man's hand and what he cannot take with him when he departs (so Fox 1999: 237; Seow 1997: 201) or what he brings into his possession more generally (so Longman, 161); or it refers to what he is unable to hand on to his son (i.e., "his hand" = the son's hand; so Krüger, 116–17). The latter interpretation keeps the father-son dual focus in view in the verse.

5:15 וְגַם־זֹה רָעָה חוֹלָה כָּל־עֻמַּת שֶׁבָּא כֵּן יֵלֵךְ וּמַה־ יִּתְרוֹן לוֹ שֶׁיַּעֲמֹל לָרוּחַ:

And this also is a sickly misfortune: like he came—so he will go. What is profit for him who toils for wind?

וְגַם־זֹה רָעָה חוֹלָה. Participle fs Qal √חלה. A null copula clause with זה as subject and רעה חולה as complement. As in 5:12, the participle חולה has an attributive function. The וגם and repetition of the opening phrase connect this with v. 12, so that while it is an *additional* misfortune, it is one connected with the previous one. In the previous verses the focus is on the loss of wealth so that one has nothing to pass along to one's offspring; here the additional observation is that the toiling man himself does not even have an advantage, let alone something to leave to his son. This focus argues for keeping the dual (ambiguous) focus on father and son in the preceding verses.

כָּל־עֻמַּת שֶׁבָּא כֵּן יֵלֵךְ. *Qatal* 3ms Qal √בוא, and *yiqtol* 3ms Qal √הלך. The premise in both cases is that, just as one is born, one dies—expressed here for the third time in the span of two verses. Given the parallel with the expressions in v. 14, the verb בָּא is a *qatal*, though morphologically the form is identical to the participle. The phrase כל־עמת שבא is a כ-PP adjunct (see comments in next paragraph) that is left-dislocated and resumed within the core clause by the focus-fronted adverb כן (see also 3:19; 7:6).

כָּל־עֻמַּת שֶׁ. Schoors (146) summarizes the issues for this phrase very nicely. Though some have considered it to be an Aramaism (a calque of כל־קבל די), Schoors follows those who point out the Hebrew nature of the expression. He argues that the כל should be understood as the prepositions כ and ל both prefixed to the bound form of עמה and translates it as "just as he came," by which he presumably intends the more mimetic "like concerning the nearness that he came, so he will leave."

וּמַה־יִּתְרוֹן לוֹ שֶׁיַּעֲמֹל לָרוּחַ. A null copula clause and *yiqtol* 3ms Qal √עמל. Seow's (1997: 201) and Fox's (1999: 237) translations reflect a purpose clause analysis of the שׁ, but a relative analysis is simpler and contextually acceptable. The head of the relative clause is the clitic 3ms pronoun on לו; see Holmstedt 2016: 112 for more examples. For the ambiguity of the syntactic structure of this null copula clause, see 1:3.

גַּם כָּל־יָמָיו בַּחֹשֶׁךְ יֹאכֵל וְכָעַס הַרְבֵּה וְחָלְיוֹ   5:16
וָקָצֶף׃

Also, all his days he shall eat in darkness, that is, (with) great anger, his
sickness, and wrath!

גַּם כָּל־יָמָיו בַּחֹשֶׁךְ יֹאכֵל. *Yiqtol* 3ms Qal √אכל. The initial גם is
additive and the quantified NP כל־ימיו is topic-fronted to be a scene-setting temporal phrase. The PP בחשך is focus-fronted in order to underscore that the manner of human eating is in darkness. The scene pictured
here fills out the description of "toils for wind" in the previous verse.

וְכָעַס הַרְבֵּה וְחָלְיוֹ וָקָצֶף. We read וכעס as the noun כַּעַס rather
than the *qatal* Qal verb (so the Versions and most commentators; see
Seow 1997: 208; Fox 1999: 237). How these three constituents fit into
the clause is a bit of a puzzle, since there is no preposition to make its
syntactic role more explicit. It makes no sense as the subject of יאכל,
or as the complement (particularly with the ו intervening between the
verb and כעס). We have analyzed them as a compound verbal adjunct
describing further circumstances of how the person might "eat" and thus
in apposition to חשך. Following the Versions, both Seow (1997: 208)
and Fox (1999: 238) (the former citing WO §11.4.2 and the latter citing
König §419l and JM §132g) suggest that the ב on חשך does double (or
quadruple!) duty and governs all the nouns. However, the notion that a
preposition may do "double-duty" is misguided; rather, a single preposition may govern a compound complement (i.e., more than one coordinated noun). Here, rather than four coordinated nominal complements
of ב, we see one NP complement, which is itself modified by a compound (three coordinated NPs) in apposition. Note also that the appositive is extraposed from its anchor, resulting in the verb יאכל intervening.

וְחָלְיוֹ. Seow suggests that the suffix is a case of dittography with
the following conjunction ו (1997: 208); this accords with the Versions.

הִנֵּה אֲשֶׁר־רָאִיתִי אָנִי טוֹב אֲשֶׁר־יָפֶה לֶאֱכוֹל־   5:17
וְלִשְׁתּוֹת וְלִרְאוֹת טוֹבָה בְּכָל־עֲמָלוֹ | שֶׁיַּעֲמֹל
תַּחַת־הַשֶּׁמֶשׁ מִסְפַּר יְמֵי־חַיָּו* אֲשֶׁר־נָתַן־לוֹ
הָאֱלֹהִים כִּי־הוּא חֶלְקוֹ׃

Look, (the thing) that I saw, I, is good—that to eat and to drink and to see goodness in all his toil that he does under the sun, (for) the number of the days of his life that God has given him, because it is his lot, is good.

הִנֵּה אֲשֶׁר־רָאִיתִי אָנִי טוֹב. Null copula and *qatal* 1cs Qal √ראה inside the null-head relative clause. The null copula of the main clause has as its subject the null head of the relative clause and as its complement the adjective טוֹב; within the relative clause, the null head is resumed as the complement of bivalent רָאִיתִי: "(the thing) that I saw (it) is good, namely … ." The טעמים suggest the break at אני, but with Seow (1997: 208) we think this makes less grammatical sense, particularly for the following אשר clause (Fox: "It is a good thing that is beautiful to eat and drink …"; 1999: 238). It is preferable to make the break at טוב, and take this second אשר clause as a nominalized clause in apposition to the null head of the prior אשר relative clause, specifying "what" is good. On the use of the 1cs pronoun without לב, see 1:17.

אֲשֶׁר־יָפֶה לֶאֱכוֹל־וְלִשְׁתּוֹת וְלִרְאוֹת טוֹבָה בְּכָל־עֲמָלוֹ | שֶׁיַּעֲמֹל תַּחַת־הַשֶּׁמֶשׁ. Inf Constr √אכל, √שתה, and √ראה, and *yiqtol* 3ms Qal √עמל. See above for the syntactic role of this אשר clause. As an appositive, semantically it clarifies more precisely what it was that Qoheleth saw to be good. This embedded clause consists of a null copula clause, with the triple infinitives serving as the compound subject, and the adjective יפה as the focus-fronted copular complement. Although rare, note the lack of concord between the compound subject and the singular adjective (see JM §148b; GKC §§145 and esp. 146f). The PP בכל־עמלו serves as an adjunct to the third infinitive clause. Within the NP עמלו, the noun עמל is itself further modified by the שׁ relative clause, which contains a null-subject "he" (coreferential with the clitic 3ms pronoun on עמלו); the head of the relative clause ("toil") is resumed as the null complement of bivalent יעמל. The PP תחת־השמש is a locative adjunct.

מִסְפַּר יְמֵי־חַיָּו* אֲשֶׁר־נָתַן־לוֹ הָאֱלֹהִים כִּי־הוּא חֶלְקוֹ. *Qatal* 3ms Qal √נתן and null copula clause. This unmarked temporal complex adjunct could modify the closer verb יעמל, but in the context it fits better as a qualifier for the further, higher-level לראות and by extension the other ל-PP infinitive clauses לאכל and לשתות. The *Ketiv* חיו reflects the singular form of the noun with the 3ms clitic pronoun (חָיוֹ), but this noun is almost always plural, especially with an attached pronoun, hence the *Qere* form, חַיָּיו (see 8:15 for the fully written form in an almost identical expression). Within the relative clause, the valency of trivalent נתן

is satisfied by the subject הָאֱלֹהִים, the null complement that resumes the head ("the number of the days of his life"), and the PP לֹו marking the recipient. The final כִּי clause adds the rationale/explanation for Qoheleth's assessment of what is good; it consists of a null copula clause with the 3ms pronoun as subject and the NP חֶלְקֹו as the copular complement.

גַּם כָּל־הָאָדָם אֲשֶׁר נָתַן־לֹו הָאֱלֹהִים עֹשֶׁר   5:18
וּנְכָסִים וְהִשְׁלִיטֹו לֶאֱכֹל מִמֶּנּוּ וְלָשֵׂאת אֶת־חֶלְקֹו
וְלִשְׂמֹחַ בַּעֲמָלֹו זֹה מַתַּת אֱלֹהִים הִיא:

Also, the whole (portion) of man is that God has given him wealth and possessions and has given him the power to eat from it and to bear his portion and to be happy in his toil. This—it is a gift of God,

גַּם כָּל־הָאָדָם אֲשֶׁר נָתַן־לֹו הָאֱלֹהִים עֹשֶׁר וּנְכָסִים. *Qatal* 3ms Qal √נתן. As in 3:13 and 12:13, the initial NP כל האדם is likely elliptical for כל חלק האדם and stands as the subject of a null copula, whose complement is the אשר nominalized clause. Contra Fox, this does not qualify as anacoluthon (1999: 239). Within the אשר clause, the subject הָאֱלֹהִים, the complement PP לֹו, and the compound NP עשׁר ונכסים fulfill the trivalency of נתן.

וְהִשְׁלִיטֹו לֶאֱכֹל מִמֶּנּוּ וְלָשֵׂאת אֶת־חֶלְקֹו וְלִשְׂמֹחַ בַּעֲמָלֹו. *Qatal* 3ms Hiph √שלט+ 3ms clitic pronoun; Inf Constr Qal √אכל, √נשׂא, and √שׂמח. The Hiphil of שלט occurs here and in 6:2. In both cases the verb is trivalent in contrast to the bivalent Qal (see 2:19). The first complement is the attached pronoun, and the second is the compounded infinitives. HALOT (s.v.) paraphrases as "grants him the opportunity to …," but the more literal rendering retains the basic idea of power or ability to do something. We depart from Seow (1997: 208–9) and take this to be an independent statement rather than a second example of what is "good" from v. 17. He has to present a forced analysis of the initial כל האדם for his treatment to work.

זֹה מַתַּת אֱלֹהִים הִיא. A null copula clause. The deictic pronoun זה both points back to the previous assertion as a whole and stands in a left-dislocated position; it is resumed in the clause by the 3fs pronoun הִיא. The copular complement is the NP מתת אלהים, which has been focus-fronted within the core clause (i.e., fronted before the subject היא but situated after the left-dislocated זה).

כִּי לֹא הַרְבֵּה יִזְכֹּר אֶת־יְמֵי חַיָּיו כִּי הָאֱלֹהִים 5:19
מַעֲנֶה בְּשִׂמְחַת לִבּוֹ:

*because he will not much call to mind the days of his life, because God
keeps (him) busy with the joy of his mind.*

The כִּי clauses together provide motives for the last clause of v. 18,
the second כִּי clause being syntactically subordinate to the first.

כִּי לֹא הַרְבֵּה יִזְכֹּר אֶת־יְמֵי חַיָּיו. *Yiqtol* 3ms Qal √זכר. The adverb
הרבה is morphologically a Hiphil infinitive absolute from רבה. But it
has been grammaticalized as an adverb of quantity, "much, many," and
rarely functions infinitivally. The verb זכר means "call to mind," a type
of "remembering": "The man blessed with pleasure, Qohelet says, will
not often think of the days of his life, that is to say, brood about how
few they are" (Fox 1999: 240). The complement of bivalent זכר is the
bound NP אֶת־יְמֵי חייו.

כִּי הָאֱלֹהִים מַעֲנֶה בְּשִׂמְחַת לִבּוֹ. Participle ms Hiph √ענה. The
participle is the copular complement of a null copula clause (having
האלהים as the subject) and has a generic (gnomic) sense here. Note that
the participial clause does not undergo inverted word order following
the כִּי. The Qal verb of ענה is bivalent, taking a ב-PP complement marking the thing that one is troubled/occupied with (see Eccl 1:13; 3:10).
The Hiphil verb increases the valency to a trivalent pattern with a ב-PP
complement of what one is occupied with (בשׂמחת לבו) and a complement of who is occupied (transitive). The latter is null in this context
and recoverable as "him" referenced by the clitic pronoun on the other
complement בשׂמחת לבו. Thus the LXX makes the implicit complement
explicit by its rendering περισπᾷ αὐτόν.

יֵשׁ רָעָה אֲשֶׁר רָאִיתִי תַּחַת הַשָּׁמֶשׁ וְרַבָּה הִיא 6:1
עַל־הָאָדָם:

*A misfortune that I have seen under the sun exists, and it is severe upon
the human.*

יֵשׁ רָעָה אֲשֶׁר רָאִיתִי תַּחַת הַשָּׁמֶשׁ. A יש existential clause and
qatal 1cs Qal √ראה. The subject of the existential יש is רעה. The word
order in יש and אין clauses is often existential-subject, which may either
reflect that, when the particles are existential (and not copular), they are
raised to the front of the clause, or it may reflect HNPS of the subject,

which is often a much "heavier," complex constituent (here it is an NP modified by a relative clause).

וְרַבָּה הִיא עַל־הָאָדָם. A null copula clause. The subject is the 3fs pronoun הִיא and the complement is רבה. For the rendering of the adjective רב as "severe," see HALOT s.v. sense #5 ("numerous, varied, much"). This adjective is used prototypically for *quantity* ("many, much"), but it has been applied in many instances to the *quality* of something that is not counted or quantified (so *"great* guilt," Ps 25:11; *"serious* sin," Ps 19:14; *"ample* reward," Ps 19:12; *"abundant* honor," Prov 28:12; *"heavy* defeat," Num 11:33; *"heavy* slaughter," Isa 30:25). Regarding word order, typically the complement follows the subject; in this case it has been raised from its more normal position, in front of any adjunct (here the PP עַל האדם) to the front of the clause for focus. The focus-fronting indicates the force and conviction of Qoheleth's conclusion: the hypothetical but realistic scenarios he describes in the following verses are, above all, *severely* wrong.

6:2   אִישׁ אֲשֶׁר יִתֶּן־לֹו הָאֱלֹהִים עֹשֶׁר וּנְכָסִים וְכָבֹוד
וְאֵינֶנּוּ חָסֵר לְנַפְשֹׁו ׀ מִכֹּל אֲשֶׁר־יִתְאַוֶּה וְלֹא־
יַשְׁלִיטֶנּוּ הָאֱלֹהִים לֶאֱכֹל מִמֶּנּוּ כִּי אִישׁ נָכְרִי
יֹאכְלֶנּוּ זֶה הֶבֶל וָחֳלִי רָע הוּא׃

A man to whom God has given riches and possessions and wealth—he does not lack for his appetite anything that he craves, but God does not authorize him to eat from it because a "foreign" man will eat it. This is a הבל *and it is a severe sickness.*

אִישׁ אֲשֶׁר יִתֶּן־לֹו הָאֱלֹהִים עֹשֶׁר וּנְכָסִים וְכָבֹוד. *Yiqtol* 3ms Qal √נתן. The restrictive אשר relative defines what kind of אישׁ Qoheleth will discuss. Within the relative clause, the verb-subject order reflects the typical inversion after a function word and the light PP complement לו has raised with the verb. The compound NP עשר ונכסים וכבוד is the second complement of the trivalent verb נתן. The noun כבוד commonly has the sense of "honor, prestige," but here it seems to have the sense of "wealth" (see also Gen 31:1; Isa 10:3, where respectively כבוד is something that Jacob "makes" or that is left somewhere) and, along with the other two nouns, is the referent of the 3ms clitic pronoun functioning as the object of "eat" later in this verse. The אישׁ NP as a whole is left-dislocated and is resumed by the 3ms clitic pronoun attached to אין in אֵינֶנּוּ. In verse 1 the existence of *a misfortune* is introduced in the first clause, and a comment is added about its severity in the second clause. However, the identity of that misfortune has been held in abeyance. Now in v. 2, the left-dislocation is used to orient the reader to the topic that specifies the particular misfortune Qoheleth is pointing out.

וְאֵינֶנּוּ חָסֵר לְנַפְשׁוֹ | מִכֹּל אֲשֶׁר־יִתְאַוֶּה. An אין negative copula clause, Participle ms Qal √חסר, and *yiqtol* 3ms Hith √אוה. The 3ms clitic pronoun in אֵינֶנּוּ resumes the left-dislocated constituent אִישׁ (with its relative clause). Note the ו that marks the left edge of the clause proper— a common strategy to distinguish the edge constituent from the clause proper (see Holmstedt 2014). The pronoun is also the subject of the אין copula clause with the stative participle חסר as the complement. For-mally the ms participle of stative verbs (as well as stative 3ms *qatal*) and related adjectives can be identical; hence, the form חָסֵר could be parsed as a participle or an adjective. However, since it is doubtful that normal adjectives are used as predicates along with the copular particles יש/אין (see Cook 2008: 10 n. 13), we prefer to analyze this form as the parti-ciple (contrary to HALOT). The ל-PP is an adjunct to the participle, while the partitive מן-PP is a complement to it (when governed by a negated verbal, the partitive מן-PP is no longer rendered as "some of" but as "not ... any of"; see Sir 51:24). When the Qal of חסר is monovalent, the (typically) inanimate subject is construed as "lacking" in terms of itself undergoing diminishing (so in Gen 8:3 the waters *decrease*; in 1 Kgs 17:14, 16 the jar of oil does not *run out/become empty*; in Isa 51:14 the bread *is lacking/runs out*). When bivalent, an (typically) animate subject experiences the diminishing of some complement, as here (see also Deut 2:7; 8:9).

וְלֹא־יַשְׁלִיטֶנּוּ הָאֱלֹהִים לֶאֱכֹל מִמֶּנּוּ. *Yiqtol* 3ms Hiph √שלט plus 3ms clitic pronoun as the complement, Inf Constr Qal √אכל. The nega-tive triggers word order inversion to verb-subject. The verb שלט in the Hiphil is either bivalent (see Ps 119:133) or, as here, trivalent, with both a complement of the patient (the person authorized) and a complement of the goal (the action authorized); see also 5:18.

כִּי אִישׁ נָכְרִי יֹאכֲלֶנּוּ. *Yiqtol* 3ms Qal √אכל plus 3ms clitic pronoun as the complement. The כי can be analyzed in one of two ways. Either it introduces a causal adjunct clause that is subordinate to the verb ישליט and provides the reason that God does not allow the owner to consume his own wealth (JM §170d–da; MNK §40.9.1.3; WO §38.4a), or it introduces an adversative (or restrictive) clause following the prior negative statement ("not X, but/rather Y"): God does not allow him to eat it; rather, a foreigner eats it! (see MNK §40.9.2.3; JM §172c; WO §39.3.5d).

זֶה הֶבֶל וְחֳלִי רָע הוּא. Two null copula clauses. In the first, the subject is the deictic זה, which points back to the absurd situation just described—that God would give wealth to a man but not allow him to partake from it, instead giving it to another. In the second, the copular complement is focus-fronted before the pronominal subject הוא. The focus-fronted complement communicates Qoheleth's exasperation at the futility of even God-given wealth.

6:3 אִם־יוֹלִיד אִישׁ מֵאָה וְשָׁנִים רַבּוֹת יִחְיֶה וְרַב | שֶׁיִּהְיוּ יְמֵי־שָׁנָיו וְנַפְשׁוֹ לֹא־תִשְׂבַּע מִן־הַטּוֹבָה וְגַם־קְבוּרָה לֹא־הָיְתָה לּוֹ אָמַרְתִּי טוֹב מִמֶּנּוּ הַנָּפֶל:

If a man begets a hundred and lives many years and complains* that the days of his years would occur but his appetite would not be sated by goodness and he would not have a (proper) burial, I say, "The stillborn is better than him!"

אִם־יוֹלִיד אִישׁ מֵאָה. *Yiqtol* (irrealis) 3ms Hiph √ילד. The Hiphil ילד is bivalent; here the subject is אישׁ and the complement is the bare numeral מאה, which given the context needs no clarification by a noun: it is clear that it refers to "a hundred (children)." The אם signals the protasis of a conditional clause, which continues through the next four clauses before the main clause/apodosis with אמרתי. The compound protasis sets up the hypothetical but realistic situation that Qoheleth uses to present yet another absurdity.

וְשָׁנִים רַבּוֹת יִחְיֶה. *Yiqtol* (irrealis) 3ms Qal √חיה. The subject of the monovalent Qal חיה is null (the referent of the 3ms inflection is the אישׁ of the prior clause), and the NP שנים רבות is an adjunct quantifying the temporal extent of the verbal situation (JM §126i; MNK §33.3.1b; WO §10.2.2c).

וְרַב | שֶׁיִּהְיוּ יְמֵי־שָׁנָיו. *Qatal* (irrealis) 3ms Qal √ריב and *yiqtol* 3mp Qal √היה. We adopt Seow's suggestion (1997: 211) to emend וְרַב, which the Leningrad Codex has as a ms adjective "many," to וְרָב and thus taking it to be an irrealis *qatal* within the conditional protasis "and (if) he complains." Assuming that ורב is a verb of speaking, שׁ functions as a complementizer introducing indirect speech, the content of his complaint. The subject of the monovalent occurrence of היה is יְמֵי־שָׁנָיו ("that the days of his years *were occurring/coming about*").

וְנַפְשׁוֹ לֹא־תִשְׂבַּע מִן־הַטּוֹבָה. *Yiqtol* 3fs Qal √שׂבע. The NP נפשו is the subject of the bivalent שׂבע, and the complement PP מן הטובה specifies the source of the (lack of) satisfaction (cf. 4:8; 5:9 where the source of satisfaction is unmarked, i.e., nonprepositional). The clause as a whole continues the שׁ complement clause for the verb רב. The relationship between this clause and the first clause of the שׁ clause is adversative: this man complains that his days were unfolding *but* he was not being satisfied. The subject-negative-verb order, however, does not reflect fronting, but the later typological profile of the book (see Introduction §§2D, 6).

וְגַם־קְבוּרָה לֹא־הָיְתָה לּוֹ. *Qatal* 3fs Qal √היה. The subject of היה is קבורה; the copular complement is the possessive ל-PP (JM §133d; MNK §39.11.1.3; WO §11.2.10d). This is the third and last clause within the שׁ complement of the verb רב. It completes the picture of a life of tragically unfulfilled potential: the man who has a hundred children is not even buried properly. Fox notes that "concern for proper interment was … a deep-rooted attitude in Jewish society," and thus it should be no surprise that Qoheleth voices such a concern, particularly given his mention of similar issues in 8:10 and 6:4 (1999: 242).

אָמַרְתִּי טוֹב מִמֶּנּוּ הַנָּפֶל. *Qatal* 1cs Qal √אמר and a null copula clause within the direct speech. The *qatal* verb is best interpreted as a performative, introducing the content of his verdict on the situation (also 8:14; see Cook 2013: 319). The copular complement is the adjective טוב and the מן-PP adjunct is critical to the overall semantics since it signals the comparison. In this apodosis/main clause of the second hypothetical scenario, Qoheleth varies his conclusion. Rather than repeating the judgments that this is הבל or רע, here he concludes by using a stark and dark comparison: such a man's life is worse than a stillborn child's.

6:4   כִּי־בַהֶבֶל בָּא וּבַחֹשֶׁךְ יֵלֵךְ וּבַחֹשֶׁךְ שְׁמוֹ יְכֻסֶּה:

because in a breath he would have come and into the darkness he would go and in the darkness his name would be covered.

Whether this verse refers to the tragic man or the stillborn child is unclear. Seow (1997: 212) and Longman (171), for example, take it to describe the stillborn, while Fox argues for the man (1999: 243). We find it more compelling that the description keeps the stillborn in view to set up the final contrast between the stillborn and the long-lived man at the end of v. 5.

כִּי־בַהֶבֶל בָּא. *Qatal* 3ms Qal (or Participle ms) √בוא. The form of בָּא is ambiguous—it could be 3ms *qatal* or ms participle. However, the conjoined *yiqtol* (ילד and יכסה) forms suggest a past-future contrast and so a *qatal* form here. The statement is in reference to no particular stillborn, hence, it portrays a hypothetical arrival (past) and its departure (future): "it would have come … and would go." The ב-PP adjunct indicates the manner of entering the world (for ב used to indicate manner, see MNK §39.6.3.5; WO §11.2.5d–e), though the precise nuance is unclear: does Qoheleth mean that the birth is quick or futile (see Seow 1997: 212; Longman, 171 translates it both ways)? Regardless which is intended, the focus-fronting is clear: Qoheleth does not stress the birth itself but its manner.

וּבַחֹשֶׁךְ יֵלֵךְ. *Yiqtol* 3ms Qal √הלך. As with the preceding clause, the adjunct PP בחשך is focus-fronted. In this case it highlights the obscurity toward which the stillborn would have proceeded in life, if he had been born living.

וּבַחֹשֶׁךְ שְׁמוֹ יְכֻסֶּה. *Yiqtol* 3ms Pual √כסה. The subject of the monovalent passive verb is שמו, and בחשך is a focus-fronted adjunct, again to contrast the normal expectation for the beginning of life and reputation versus Qoheleth's view of the stillborn's lack of both. Rather than a proper course and end to life, including a legacy (hence the use of שֵׁם), the stillborn's life and legacy are cut brutally short (see 1:11).

6:5   גַּם־שֶׁמֶשׁ לֹא־רָאָה וְלֹא יָדָע נַחַת לָזֶה מִזֶּה:

Not even the sun has he seen or known—more rest belongs to this one [the stillborn] than the other one [the aged, unsatisfied man]!

גַּם־שֶׁמֶשׁ לֹא־רָאָה וְלֹא יָדָע. *Qatal* 3ms Qal √ראה and √ידע. The first half of the verse consists of two simple clauses with the complement in the first clause, שמש, both focus-fronted and focus-marked by גם. The null-subject for both verbs is the same as the primary referent in the previous verse (presumably, the stillborn child), and the complement of the second bivalent verb, יָדַע, is a null pronoun referring back to שֶׁמֶשׁ. See Fox 1999: 243 for a creative alternate analysis (though one that we do not find grammatically compelling).

נַחַת לָזֶה מִזֶּה. A null copula clause. The first demonstrative points directly back to the one described there (i.e., the stillborn child). The second demonstrative points to the other entity that has been invoked and already compared to the stillborn—the tragic man. Note that BH indicates a set of alternatives or reciprocal relationships by the repetition or pairing of the same near demonstrative זה ... זה, while other languages like English choose different demonstrative forms for the second item: "this one ... that one" or "the one ... the other" (WO §17.3c; 17.4.2d; MNK §36.2.2.4). The NP נחת is the subject of the copular clause, and the possessive ל-PP is the copular complement (JM §133d; MNK §39.11.1.3; WO §11.2.10d). The adjunct מן-PP signals the comparison. Qoheleth in this verse reinforces his observation from v. 4—if the stillborn goes in darkness and its name is covered in darkness, then it clearly never sees or knows the sun. The implication, then, is that the stillborn will never know the absurdity of life under the sun, something that Qoheleth knows all too poignantly (see 6:1). That is why he says that "rest belongs to it more than to the other"—it never has to toil for nothing like those who survive the womb, see life under the sun, and toil, only to fail to enjoy it!

וְאִלּוּ חָיָה אֶלֶף שָׁנִים פַּעֲמַיִם וְטוֹבָה לֹא רָאָה   6:6
הֲלֹא אֶל־מָקוֹם אֶחָד הַכֹּל הוֹלֵךְ׃

And if he lived a thousand years, twice, he would not have seen goodness. Doesn't everything go to one place?

This verse may be an example of anacoluthon: Qoheleth starts by commenting on "the conditions for desirable life but suddenly gives up and just exclaims [הלא] in despair or frustration upon the universality of death's power" (Fox 1999: 244). But it also may be, as translated above, a conditional clause with a negative apodosis, followed by a separate rhetorical question. The despair remains (experiencing goodness is elusive and everyone dies anyway), though the syntax differs.

וְאִלּוּ חָיָה אֶלֶף שָׁנִים פַּעֲמַיִם. *Qatal* 3ms Qal √חיה. The conditional אִלּוּ (perhaps reflecting the contraction of אִם and לוּ; see GKC, §159l) occurs only here, possibly in 4:10, and Esth 7:4. It presents an irrealis (hypothetical) event (a man living a thousand years) in order to set up the result clause, which carries the rhetorical "punchline" (he still would not have seen goodness). The NP שנים אלף is a temporal adjunct to the verb indicating the extent of time the verbal activity occurs (WO §10.2.2c; JM §126i; MNK §33.3.1b). The word פעמים is a dual form of פַּעַם. Since the lexeme here is multiplicative (JM §102f; GKC §134r), having the sense of "time, occasion" (rather than "step, foot"), this form is to be understood as an adjunct: "live a thousand years, twice/two times/twice over."

וְטוֹבָה לֹא רָאָה. *Qatal* 3ms Qal √ראה. The verb ראה is bivalent; here its complement is the noun (homophonous with the fs adjective) טובה. The complement is focus-fronted in order to drive home the point that of all that a two-thousand-year-old person would see, טובה would not be one of them! The collocation of ראה and complements that are not typically "seen" (i.e., processed by the visual sense) result in the connotation of "experiencing" or "enjoying" the item (DCH, s.v. Qal 1a; cf. HALOT, s.v. Qal 13).

הֲלֹא אֶל־מָקוֹם אֶחָד הַכֹּל הוֹלֵךְ. Participle ms Qal √הלד. The interrogative ה plus negative לא often introduces a rhetorical question, the answer to which is assumed to be "yes, of course!"; i.e., rhetorical questions do not set up the context for a content answer but merely the consent of the audience. The אל-PP is fronted for focus and so returns to a drum that Qoheleth beats throughout (see 2:14-15; 9:2-3)—whether good or bad, everyone receives the same end (the focus-fronting contrasts "ONE place" with the implied and expected "TWO places" for the righteous and wicked).

6:7   כָּל־עֲמַל הָאָדָם לְפִיהוּ וְגַם־הַנֶּפֶשׁ לֹא תִמָּלֵא:

All of man's labor is for his mouth, and yet his appetite is never filled.

כָּל־עֲמַל הָאָדָם לְפִיהוּ. A null copula clause with כל עמל האדם as the subject and the PP לפיהו the copular complement. The ל preposition in לפיהו marks the entity that *benefits* from כל עמל (WO §11.2.10d; JM §133d).

וְגַם־הַנֶּפֶשׁ לֹא תִמָּלֵא. *Yiqtol* 3fs Niph √מלא. The initial גם may be concessive (see HALOT, s.v. #8, WO), but since this is not a function typically assigned to גם, it is more likely that the use here is as an overt focus word reinforcing the focus-fronting of the NP הנפש. The point of the focus-fronting is to contrast all the food (the connotation of כל עמל in light of לפיהו) produced with the never-satisfied appetite.

6:8   כִּי מַה־יּוֹתֵר לֶחָכָם מִן־הַכְּסִיל מַה־לֶּעָנִי יוֹדֵעַ
לַהֲלֹךְ נֶגֶד הַחַיִּים:

Indeed, what profit belongs to the wise more than the fool? What belongs to the poor (who) knows how to walk before the living?

Just as there is no advantage to the wise (more than the fool), who might through wisdom hold their desires in check, neither is their any advantage to the poor, who through lack of means are unable to seek fulfillment of their desires, even though they may have the ability to get along or lead people. The fool, the wise, and the poor all suffer from the insatiability of human desire (see Krüger, 128–29).

כִּי מַה־יּוֹתֵר לֶחָכָם מִן־הַכְּסִיל. Null copula clause. On the syntax of מה יותר ל, see comment on מה יתרון ל in 1:3. On יתר, see discussion at 2:15. Within the PP לֶחָכָם, the article ה has undergone syncopation, but its vowel is present under ל (for the vowel change from *pataḥ* to *segol* and the lack of *dagesh forte* due to the guttural consonant, see GKC §35c–k). The מִן PP is a comparative adjunct of the null copula clause, comparing not adjectival qualities, but how much יותר "advantage" belongs to the wise over the fool. Even though the wise may control their desires and have loftier aims, such as the acquisition of wisdom, such desires remain as insatiable as those more base desires of the fool (1:16-18), and hence there is not advantage to the wise (Krüger, 128; Fox 1999: 245).

מַה־לֶּעָנִי יוֹדֵעַ לַהֲלֹךְ נֶגֶד הַחַיִּים. Null copula, participle ms Qal √ידע, and Inf Constr Qal √הלך. Though the more common form of the infinitive construct for √הלך is לֶכֶת (GKC §69x; even in Ecclesiastes, see 1:7; 5:14; 7:2; 10:15), here and in v. 9 the strong verb paradigm form is used (the reason for the variation is inscrutable and cannot be interpreted as a sign of lateness, contra GKC §69x). The subject of the null copula is the interrogative מה, and the complement is the entire possessive ל-PP stretching to the end of the verse. Since the PP לעני contains a definite noun (see comment above on לחכם) without a definite participle following, one should not analyze this as what is traditionally called an attributive participle. Instead, we take יודע להלך נגד החיים to constitute an unmarked relative clause modifying the head עני. Within the relative clause, the null-subject resumes the head, and the participle יודע is the complement of a null copula ("the poor [who] [he] knows …"). The ל-PP infinitive clause is the complement of the bivalent verb ידע, and the PP נגד החיים is the locative PP complement for הלך.

6:9   טוֹב מַרְאֵה עֵינַיִם מֵהֲלָךְ־נָפֶשׁ גַּם־זֶה הֶבֶל וּרְעוּת רֽוּחַ:

A vision of the eyes is better than a walk of the appetite. This, too, is a הבל *and chasing wind.*

טוֹב מַרְאֵה עֵינַיִם מֵהֲלָךְ־נָפֶשׁ. Null copula clause and Inf Constr Qal √הלך (on this form, see comment on v. 8). The subject is מראה עינים, and the complement of the null copula is the focus-fronted ms adjective טוב. The comparative מן-PP is an adjunct (MNK §39.14.8; WO §11.2.11e.3), and the monovalent infinitival complement (הלך) of the preposition מן has נפש as its subject. The contrast Qoheleth draws here is between accepting what lies before one in life ("vision of the eyes") and pursuing unrealistic expectations from life ("walk of the appetite"; see Krüger, 129). It is better to come to terms with the absurdity of life than to become "obsessed" with some object of desire, which will never be sated (Fox 1999: 246).

גַּם־זֶה הֶבֶל וּרְעוּת רֽוּחַ. See comments at 1:2 (for הבל), 11 (for גם), and 14 (for רעות).

6:10-12 The Limits of Human Knowledge

These verses are a reflection on what humanity can and cannot know.

6:10   מַה־שֶּׁהָיָה כְּבָר נִקְרָא שְׁמוֹ וְנוֹדָע אֲשֶׁר־הוּא אָדָם וְלֹא־יוּכַל לָדִין עִם שֶׁהַתַּקִּיף* מִמֶּֽנּוּ:

Whatever has been—its name has already been called. That he is man is known, but he is not able to contend with the one who is mightier than he.

מַה־שֶּׁהָיָה כְּבָר נִקְרָא שְׁמוֹ. *Qatal* 3ms Qal √היה and Niph √קרא. On the free choice relative מה שֶׁ, see 1:9. The entire מה שֶׁ relative is a left-dislocated constituent, which is resumed by the 3ms clitic pronoun ו attached to the NP שם in שמו. The NP שמו is the subject of the mon-ovalent Niphal verb נקרא, whose *qatal* 3ms form is homonymous with the particle ms due to the quiescence of final aleph (GKC §§27g, 74a).

וְנוֹדָע אֲשֶׁר־הוּא אָדָם. Participle ms Niph √ידע and null copula. Two clauses are present here. In the matrix clause, the participle is the copular complement of a null copula clause, while the subject is an embedded אשר clause. The אשר nominalizes the following null copula clause (whose subject is הוא and complement is אדם) so that the proposition "he is a man" may function as the subject of the monovalent Niphal verb נודע.

וְלֹא־יוּכַל לָדִין עִם שֶׁהַתַּקִּיף* מִמֶּנּוּ. *Yiqtol* 3ms Qal √יכל (see comment on 1:8 for a discussion of the form and *binyan* of this verb) and Inf Constr Qal √דין. The ל-infinitive construction is the complement of the bivalent verb יכל and the עם PP is the complement of the bivalent דין. The שׁ relative clause modifies a null head, which is the complement of the preposition עם, "with (one) who ... ." Within the שׁ relative, the consonantal *Ketiv* התקיף is an ambiguous form: (1) it may be a definite, substantival adjective from √תקף; i.e., הַתַּקִּיף "the strong one" (see JM §88lb on the *qattīl* adjective pattern); (2) it may be a Hiphil infinitive construct, הַתְקִיף, "making strong" (though this makes no sense in this context); or (3) it may be a *qatal* 3ms Hiph √תקף (with internal causative semantics; see WO §27.2f), עִם שֶׁהִתְקִיף "with (one) who is strong ... ." The omission of the ה in the *Qere* indicates a tradition in which the adjective was unambiguous, עִם שֶׁתַּקִּיף "with (one) who is strong ... ." Since the first option for the *Ketiv* matches the *Qere*, we follow this option in our analysis. The מן-PP adjunct turns the statement into a comparative, "with (one) who is stronger than him" (MNK §39.14.8; WO §11.2.11e.3).

6:11   כִּי יֵשׁ־דְּבָרִים הַרְבֵּה מַרְבִּים הָבֶל מַה־יֹּתֵר לָאָדָם:

Indeed, many words are increasing הבל. What advantage belongs to man?

כִּי יֵשׁ־דְּבָרִים הַרְבֵּה מַרְבִּים הָבֶל. A יש copula clause, with the NP הרבה דברים as the subject and the participle (ms Hiph √רבה) as the copular complement. The NP הבל is the complement of the bivalent participle מרבים. It does not make any sense to take כי as a reason for the last clause of the previous verse; instead, we take it as an asseverative כי. For discussion of הרבה, the Inf Abs Hiph √רבה, see 1:16.

מַה־יֹּתֵר לָאָדָם. A null copula clause; see comment on מה יתרון ל in 1:3. On יתר, see discussion at 2:15.

כִּ֣י מִֽי־יוֹדֵעַ֩ מַה־ט֨וֹב לָֽאָדָ֜ם בַּֽחַיִּ֗ים מִסְפַּ֛ר יְמֵי־חַיֵּ֥י　6:12
הֶבְל֖וֹ וְיַעֲשֵׂ֣ם כַּצֵּ֑ל אֲשֶׁ֣ר מִֽי־יַגִּ֣יד לָֽאָדָ֔ם מַה־יִּהְיֶ֥ה
אַחֲרָ֖יו תַּ֥חַת הַשָּֽׁמֶשׁ׃

*Because who knows what is good for man in life, that is, the number of
the days of his life of* הבל *(and he spends them like a shadow)? Because who
can tell man what will be after him under the sun?*

כִּ֣י מִֽי־יוֹדֵעַ֩ מַה־ט֨וֹב לָֽאָדָ֜ם בַּֽחַיִּ֗ים מִסְפַּ֛ר יְמֵי־חַיֵּ֥י הֶבְל֖וֹ. Participle ms Qal √ידע and two null copula clauses. This כי clause is causal in
that it grounds the second question of v. 11 by providing a reason for its
asking. The interrogative מי is the subject of the null copula clause that
takes the participle יודע as its complement. The participle, in turn, takes
the (unmarked) nominalized null copula clause מה טוב "what is good
…" as its complement. The indirect interrogative מה is the subject of the
null copula clause, the adjective טוב is its complement, and the ל-PP is an
adjunct indicating benefit (WO §11.2.10d; JM §133d). The PP בחיים is
a temporal adjunct, and the complex NP following it is an appositional,
four-member bound phrase adding what Qoheleth means by בחיים. The
final member of the bound phrase, הבלו, functions attributively in relation to חיי (a הבל "life"; see WO §9.5.3a–b; MNK §25.4.4.5); as well,
due to the normal constraints of Hebrew syntax, the clitic 3ms pronoun
properly belongs to חיי ("his life") but is attached to the final member of
the bound construction (MNK §25.3.1.4d).

וְיַעֲשֵׂ֣ם כַּצֵּ֑ל. *Yiqtol* 3ms Qal √עשה plus 3mp clitic pronoun as the
complement. The PP כצל appears to be an adjunct indicating a manner of behavior by way of a comparison. Wise argues that כצל in this
verse (and in 7:14 and 8:13) is a calque (a loan translation) of Aramaic
בטלל, which, unlike the Hebrew phrase, went through a series of semantic shifts: "in the shadow (of)" > "with the help (of)" > "because (of)."
For this verse (and 8:13), Wise suggests that the calque is of בטלל זי and
means "because, for" (256). He divides the verse against the טעמים (note
the אַתְנָחְתָא on כצל) and translates the clause starting with כצל, "For
who is able to tell a man what will happen under the sun after him?"
(257). While we agree that the book of Ecclesiastes was written at a time
in which Aramaic had a significant influence on Hebrew, Wise's solution
lacks sense. It provides a linguistic process by which an arguably more
suitable meaning for כצל can be identified, but it leaves unaddressed

a host of salient questions. For example, if a causal function word was needed, why did the author not simply choose כִּי, as at the beginning of the verse, or perhaps even אֲשֶׁר (see next comment)? How did the later tradition, which was also highly influenced by Aramaic, miss this calque so that the tradition the Masoretes encoded in the טעמים treats כְּצֵל as a PP taken with the preceding verb יַעֲשֶׂה? And why would the calque exist in Hebrew, anyway? Languages borrow for a discrete number of reasons, primarily need or prestige, and since there was clearly no need for another way to say "because," can this plausibly be a prestige borrowing?

אֲשֶׁר מִי־יַגִּיד לָאָדָם מַה־יִּהְיֶה אַחֲרָיו תַּחַת הַשָּׁמֶשׁ. *Yiqtol* 3ms Hiph √נגד and Qal √היה. How we take this אֲשֶׁר clause depends on what we do with כְּצֵל (see previous note): if we take כְּצֵל to be associated with the אֲשֶׁר, then the אֲשֶׁר simply nominalizes the following clause so that it may be functioning as the complement of צֵל, thus "because that" (following Wise); if we do not associate the כְּצֵל with the אֲשֶׁר clause, this is perhaps the only clear example of a causal אֲשֶׁר in Ecclesiastes (or the Hebrew Bible). See Holmstedt 2006; 2013: 303–7. As a causal clause, it would parallel the כִּי clause at the beginning of the verse and provide a second reason motivating v. 11.

7:1-24 What Is Better?

Verses 1-24 focus on the question, What is better? Verses 1-14 consist of a string of individual proverbs, many in the "better-than" form (vv. 1, 2, 3, 5, 8, 11), brought to a conclusion in vv. 13-14. Verses 15-22 depart from the "better-than" structure, excepting v. 18, but they expand on the conclusion Qoheleth draws in v. 14 by turning to the relationship between wisdom and righteousness. Verses 23-24 provide a conclusion to this stage of the investigation.

Although stylistically, vv. 1-24 appear to be a distinct unit, it does follow nicely from the question posed in 6:12, מִי־יוֹדֵעַ מַה־טּוֹב לָאָדָם בַּחַיִּים. While that question is rhetorical, expecting a negative answer "no one!," this section reflects Qoheleth's pragmatism: while humans cannot discern what is really good, some things do appear to be better than others (or, at least they give greater satisfaction).

טוֹב שֵׁם מִשֶּׁמֶן טוֹב וְיוֹם הַמָּוֶת מִיּוֹם הִוָּלְדוֹ:   7:1

A name is better than fine oil, and the day of death better than the day of one's birth.

טוֹב שֵׁם מִשֶּׁמֶן טוֹב. A null copula clause with the טוב מן comparative construction "better is X than Y" (for comparative מִן, see MNK §39.14.8; WO §11.2.11e.3). As in most of these comparisons, the copular complement (the adjective טוב) is fronted, although there is no discernible topic or focus features; it is possible that the order simply reflects the convention of the idiom, which may have a poetic origin (see also comment at 4:3). As far as poetic features go, note the alliteration of שם משמן as well as the hint of chiasm (any chiasm is purely on the level of the lexemes since the syntax of the clause excludes any formal chiasm) (contra Seow 1997: 234). The noun שם probably means more than simply "reputation" here; it also connotes "a lasting name … of someone who has died"; i.e., a "legacy" (Seow 1997: 234–35; Longman, 180 n. 17).

וְיוֹם הַמָּוֶת מִיּוֹם הִוָּלְדוֹ. A null copula clause and Inf Constr Niph √ילד + 3ms clitic pronoun indicating the subject, "his being born." This clause continues the comparison from the preceding clause. The comparative adjective טוב is elided and assumed from the preceding clause, though comparative מן is repeated overtly. Though awkward in English, the article on מות indicates that the day of death refers not to dying generally, but specifically to the death of the person referred to by the clitic pronoun (see WO §13.5.1b). For the infinitive הולדו, it is much smoother in English to use a genitive NP construction, "his birth" or even the impersonal "one's birth."

7:2   טוֹב לָלֶכֶת אֶל־בֵּית־אֵבֶל מִלֶּכֶת אֶל־בֵּית מִשְׁתֶּה
בַּאֲשֶׁר הוּא סוֹף כָּל־הָאָדָם וְהַחַי יִתֵּן אֶל־לִבּוֹ:

To walk into the house of mourning is better than to walk into the house of feasting because it is the end of every man, and the living should pay attention.

טוֹב לָלֶכֶת … מִלֶּכֶת …. A null copula clause and Inf Constr Qal √הלך twice. The subject of the null copula clause is the ל-infinitive phrase (WO §36.2.3b). Frequently, infinitives functioning as subjects occur without a prefixed preposition, but one also finds this type of construction: the ל has none of the semantics of the normal preposition and serves to mark the form as an infinitive (compare the function of English "to" as marking infinitives with no prepositional semantics). The clause presents a comparative טוב מן saying, "doing X is better than doing Y."

בַּאֲשֶׁר הוּא סוֹף כָּל־הָאָדָם. A null copula clause. The ב-PP is a causal adjunct to the null copula of the main clause (on the causal use of ב, see WO §11.2.5e) and the אשר simply nominalizes the following clause so that it may function syntactically as the complement of the preposition ב, which otherwise requires a nominal complement (see Holmstedt 2016: 119–28, 354; see also Gen 39:9, 23 for the identical construction). The referent of the subject pronoun הוא is the house of mourning, though in turn it refers by metonymy to death: the סוף thus refers to the end of a human life span (Seow 1997: 236), which is associated with the mourning house.

וְהַחַי יִתֵּן אֶל־לִבּוֹ. Yiqtol (irrealis) 3ms Qal √נתן. The word order is subject-verb even though the semantics of the verb appears irrealis (a realis value for יתן makes little sense, e.g., "the living will pay attention" or "the living pays attention"). The word order, therefore, reflects focus-fronting for the subject החי, "the living should pay attention" (in contrast to the dead who are being mourned, and who, presumably, cannot pay attention to anything!). The idiom נתן אל לב parallels שים אל לב, which is often taken to be the standard idiom, while the former one is the "late" idiom. See comment at 1:13. Trivalent נתן lacks an overt complement, but Hebrew frequently allows a null complement if it is easily recoverable from the context (here, the situation of impending death for all is what the living should pay attention to).

7:3　טוֹב כַּעַס מִשְּׂחֹק כִּי־בְרֹעַ פָּנִים יִיטַב לֵב:

Anger is better than laughing because in gloominess the mind will be good.

This verse stands in apparent contrast to other verses which advocate enjoyment (e.g., 2:24, 3:13, 5:18, 19, 8:15, 9:7) or warn against anger (7:9, 11:10), although it does fit the perspective of 2:2 on laughter. Rather than reflecting a sage "who is struggling with the traditions of his people and, thus, contradicts himself at times" (Longman, 183–84), there is a basic coherence behind vv. 2-4 that matches Qoheleth's argument throughout. See the comment on v. 4.

טוֹב כַּעַס מִשְּׂחֹק. A null copula and Inf Constr Qal √שחק. This is another טוב מן comparative clause (MNK §39.14.8; WO §11.2.11e.3), with the noun כעס as the first component of the comparison and the infinitive construct שחק as the second (standard) component.

כִּי־בְרֹעַ פָּנִים יִיטַב לֵב. *Yiqtol* 3ms *Qal* √יטב. The כי clause provides the motivation for the previous statement (see WO §38.4; MNK
§40.9; JM §170d). The position of the PP ברע פנים within the כי clause
is notable. First, the normal order for PP adjuncts is following the subject and verb. Here the PP is raised to the front of the clause. If the PP
is topic-fronted, then it serves simply to orient the reader to the context
in which the event יטב לב applies. If, however, it is focus-fronted, then
it is asserting that it is in this state, the רע פנים (i.e., in the consideration
of serious events such as visiting the house of mourning), and only this
state, that the assertion יטב לב applies. The V-S order of יטב לב reflects
the triggered raising of the verb over the subject, which would have been
triggered by either the כי or the fronting of the PP. See Gen 40:7 and
Neh 2:2-3 for phrases similar to ברע פנים; for יטב לב, see 11:9 and also
Ruth 3:7; Judg 19:6, 9, 22; 1 Kgs 21:7.

7:4   לֵב חֲכָמִים בְּבֵית אֵבֶל וְלֵב כְּסִילִים בְּבֵית שִׂמְחָה:

*The mind of the wise (ones) is in the house of mourning, while the mind
of the fools is in the house of feasting.*

This verse provides the key for understanding vv. 2-3 within Qoheleth's thought: the wise man should enjoy what he can in life, as he states
elsewhere in the book, but there is a qualitative difference between taking advantage of ephemeral pleasures (what the חכמים do) and center-
ing one's life around such activities or experiences (what the כסילים do).
For Qoheleth, what keeps the חכמים from succumbing to the behavioral
excesses of the כסילים is their perspective: they keep the sobering truths
of the human existence, such as human mortality, in mind.

The entire verse consists of two null copula clauses. In both cases
the ב-PP is the (locative) complement of the null copula. The content of
the two statements suggests that the conjoined clauses should be taken as
a comparison between the חכמים and the כסילים. Both are in the plural,
representing classes of persons, hence the leading bound element, לב, is
singular. As generic classes, they are least awkwardly rendered into English with a definite article: "the wise (ones)" versus "wise (ones)" and "the
fools" versus "fools."

7:5   טוֹב לִשְׁמֹעַ גַּעֲרַת חָכָם מֵאִישׁ שֹׁמֵעַ שִׁיר כְּסִילִים:

To listen to the rebuke of a wise man is better than a man who listens to the song of fools,

This verse is thematically distinct from the preceding one, but it does pick up on the use of כסילים in v. 4 in a proverb comparing the wise and foolish.

טֹוב לִשְׁמֹעַ ... מֵאִישׁ שֹׁמֵעַ. A null copula, Inf Constr Qal √שמע and Participle ms Qal √שמע. The entire verse is a null copula clause with the טוב מן comparison. The two halves are syntactically asymmetrical since the comparison is between an action, "to listen" and a type of person "a man who listens." Thus, Fox emends מאיש שמע to מִשְּׁמֹעַ, since "the infinitive construction is typically used in the second half of 'better than' comparisons" (1999: 252–53). Yet the comparison makes sense as it stands. Moreover, variety is the essence of poets and creative writers, and we find it questionable to emend a grammatical, sensible construction due to fairly narrow (and nonnative) expectations. According to Seow, the parallelism of גערה and שיר suggests that שיר here connotes a song of praise, contrasting it with the rebuke in the first colon (1997: 236).

אִישׁ שֹׁמֵעַ שִׁיר כְּסִילִים. A null copula clause and Participle ms Qal √שמע. The participle is the complement of the null copula and the whole is an unmarked relative clause modifying איש (on the relative status of these so-called attributive participles, see Holmstedt 2016: 74–77). The verb שמע takes either NP complements or PP (typically with ל) complements. Based on the usage in the Hebrew Bible, it is not possible to distinguish neatly between the connotations "hearing" and "listening" in terms of the type of complement the verb takes. Thus, while שמע לשיר could indicate "listens to a song," so could the construction used in this verse, with the NP complement.

7:6 כִּי כְקֹול הַסִּירִים֙ תַּחַת הַסִּיר כֵּן שְׂחֹק הַכְּסִיל
וְגַם־זֶה הָבֶל׃

because, like the sound of thorns under the cooking-pot—so is the laughter of fools (this too is a הבל),

The image of thorns under the cooking pot is one of an an irritating sound from a relatively worthless source: "Thistles provide quick flames, little heat, and a lot of unpleasant noise. The singing of fools is equally cacophonous" (Crenshaw, 135).

כְּי כְקוֹל ... כֵּן שְׂחֹק הַכְּסִיל. A null copula clause, in which the
subject is שְׂחֹק הַכְּסִיל and the focus-fronted predicate is the adverb כֵּן.
The כי clause loosely provides the reason for the assertion in the preceding verse. The כ/כאשר ... כן structure is one way to form a comparison.
WO §38.5 points out that in this pattern, the item compared is marked
by כן in the apodosis, and the thing to which is it is compared (the standard) is marked by כ/כאשר in the protasis. So marked, the two halves
normally occur in a protasis-apodosis order, but the reverse order is also
possible (e.g., Gen 18:5). In this case, as in 3:19 and 5:15, the initial unit
forming the standard of comparison, כקול ... הסיר, is left-dislocated and
resumed by the focus-fronted adverb כן in the main clause.

קוֹל הַסִּירִים תַּחַת הַסִּיר. The PP תחת הסיר is a case of an "NP-
internal" PP. The modification of nouns is normally carried out by adjectives and the bound construction (the "construct chain"); a minority NP
modification strategy is to embed a PP within the NP (see Holmstedt
and Screnock 2016: 84–85). Here there is no verb for the PP to modify,
so it can only modify the NP הסירים. The NP-internal PP strategy allows
something more complex than an adjective to modify the noun and, as
such, is similar to a relative clause. It is also by nature a semantically
restrictive modification; i.e., the PP helps to define or identify the noun.
In this case, it is the "under-the-pot thorns" (not any other thorns that
might be lying around) that are at issue. The author's choice of lexemes
in this phrase and the preceding clause is an artful play on words and
sounds: שִׁיר "song"; סִירִים "thorns"; and סִיר "cooking pot."

שְׂחֹק הַכְּסִיל. The exchange of שיר כסילים with שחק הכסיל here
further defines what the שיר referred to in the last verse means: it is not
likely a "song of praise," as Seow (1997: 236) suggests, but the inane discourse of the fool. The item שחק has the same form as the Qal infinitive;
it is taken here as the homophonous noun "laughter" (see HALOT, s.v.;
DCH, s.v.). The definite, singular הכסיל equally denotes a generic class
of persons as the indefinite, plural כסילים in v. 4.

וְגַם־זֶה הָבֶל. A null copula clause with the additive גם to connect
it to the הבל theme that runs throughout the book (MNK §41.4.5.2;
van der Merwe). Though the subject זה does point back to something in
the preceding context, the entirety of the comparison, it does not logically continue within the כי clause. This interruptive shift, as well as the
fact that this is a thematic statement in the book, suggests that this is a
parenthesis.

7:7   כִּי הָעֹשֶׁק יְהוֹלֵל חָכָם וִיאַבֵּד אֶת־לֵב מַתָּנָה:

because oppression makes a wise man a fool, and a gift destroys the mind.

כִּי הָעֹשֶׁק יְהוֹלֵל חָכָם. *Yiqtol* 3ms Piel (Polel) √הלל. This verb, which is the third lexical entry for הלל in HALOT, means "to make X look like a fool" in the Polel (= Piel semantics). Note the subject-verb order even inside the כי clause. As in v. 2, the S-V order reflects a focus-fronting, "the oppression [in contrast to something else] makes a wise man irrational." The כי here is causal, providing the evidence for the conclusion in v. 6 (so Seow 1997: 237; Longman, 186). Alternatively, it provides a second motive for the assertion in v. 5.

הָעֹשֶׁק. Lit. "the oppression." While the article in Hebrew is often used in the same context that the English definite article is, it does not always neatly correspond to the English definite article in usage (see Bekins), and the article in Ecclesiastes has often befuddled interpreters (see Baranowski). The article in העשק signals a generic reference in a clear proverbial context, "oppression makes a fool of a wise man." Bekins summarizes the generic usage succinctly:

> Generics are typically associated with definiteness since the kind as a whole is identifiable based on general-encyclopaedic knowledge, and generic noun phrases are, therefore, generally restricted to "well-established" kinds. Generics are typically found in characterizing sentences, which make predications concerning the kind as a whole, but in certain repeated or stereotypical situations a generic noun phrase can be used to refer to an arbitrary member of the kind. (238)

וִיאַבֵּד אֶת־לֵב מַתָּנָה. *Yiqtol* 3ms Piel √אבד. The pointing of the simple ו conjunction is the result of attaching it to a word beginning with a י. The י loses the *sheva* and the ו is pointed with a *hiriq* (see GKC §28a; JM §104c). Seow reads ויעוה "twists, perverts" with 4QQoh^a, taking ויעוה as the *lectio difficilior* (1997: 238); the MT is supported by the LXX, Vulgate, Peshitta, Targum, and the textual lemma of Jerome's commentary. There are three possible syntactic analyses of this clause: verb-complement, verb-complement-adjunct, and verb-complement-subject. The question is whether the final word, מתנה, functions as the feminine subject of the 3ms verb ויאבד, "a gift destroys," as an adjunct of means with העשק from the prior clause as the subject of ויאבד, "oppression ... destroys the mind with a gift," or as the host of the bound form of לב, "mind of a gift (?)." The latter option is the syntax reflected in most of the

Greek and Latin traditions (but not Symmachus' Greek version, which follows the former option, according to Jerome). Moreover, Scott (234) and Whitley (63) take the noun to be a form of מתנים "loins"; Scott thus emends to לב מתניו, which he takes to be figurative for "his courage" (supported in part by LXX εὐτονίας αὐτοῦ, possibly reading the text as if pointed מְתְנֹה, according to Goldman [90*]). In support of the first option, there are other instances of the lack of subject-verb agreement in Ecclesiastes (see comment on 1:10; see Fredericks, 187–88). The word order reflects the poetic inversion of the two lines: subject-verb-complement and verb-complement-subject.

מַתָּנֶה. This noun refers to not "just any gift, but a 'gift' that is exacted by oppressors, namely, a bribe" (Seow 1997: 237; cf. מַתָּנֶה in Prov 15:27, and related מַתָּן in Prov 18:16; 21:14).

7:8   טֽוֹב אַחֲרִ֥ית דָּבָ֖ר מֵֽרֵאשִׁית֑וֹ ט֥וֹב אֶֽרֶךְ־ר֖וּחַ
מִגְּבַהּ־רֽוּחַ׃

The end of a matter is better than its beginning; patience is better than arrogance.

Both clauses are null copula comparative clauses using the טוב מן construction (MNK §39.14.8; WO §11.2.11e.3).

אֶֽרֶךְ־ר֖וּחַ. Lit. "long of spirit." This phrase seems to be a near synonym for the more common phrase אֶרֶךְ אַפַּיִם "long of nostrils" (Exod 34:6; Num 14:18; Jonah 4:2), which is figurative for "patience." The meaning for ארך רוח also here seems clear from the context and is supported by the expression קְצַר רוּחַ "shortness of spirit" = "impatience" (Prov 14:29).

גְּבַהּ־ר֖וּחַ. Lit. "tall of spirit," to which we may compare גֹּבַהּ רוּחַ "height of spirit" in Prov 16:18 and postbiblical רוּחַ גְּבֹהָה "tall spirit." All variations seems to connote "arrogance," which is supported by the contrast with שְׁפַל רוּחַ "low of spirit" = "humble" (Isa 57:15; Prov 16:19; 29:23).

7:9   אַל־תְּבַהֵ֥ל בְּרֽוּחֲךָ֖ לִכְע֑וֹס כִּ֣י כַ֔עַס בְּחֵ֥יק כְּסִילִ֖ים
יָנֽוּחַ׃

Don't be hasty with your spirit to become angry because anger settles in the lap of fools.

אַל־תְּבַהֵ֤ל בְּרֽוּחֲךָ֙ לִכְע֔וֹס. Jussive 2ms Piel √בהל and Inf Constr Qal √כעס. The PP בְּרוּחֲךָ is an adjunct to the verb תבהל, and the ל infinitive phrase is the verb's complement. Although in form תְּבַהֵל could be either jussive or imperfect, the presence of the negator אל signals the jussive (WO §34.2.1b).

כִּ֣י כַ֔עַס בְּחֵ֥יק כְּסִילִ֖ים יָנֽוּחַ. *Yiqtol* (realis) 3ms Qal √נוח. The verb נוח has a sense of "rest" or "wait" when monovalent (e.g., Exod 23:12; 1 Sam 25:9), but when accompanied by a locative PP complement (either ב or על) as here, it has the sense of "settle in/upon" or "alight upon" (e.g., Isa 7:19; 11:2). The כי clause provides the evidence for the preceding assertion; i.e., why it is not good to be quick to anger. The word order within the כי clause is subject-PP-verb. Even if the grammar of Ecclesiastes allowed for subject-verb basic order within subordinate clauses, like a כי clause (see Holmstedt 2011 on word order variation in BH), subject-PP-verb order can only reflect the raising of both the subject to the topic position and the PP to the focus position. That is, the כעס is a topic, orienting the audience to the fact that the agent of the verb has shifted, from them (i.e., the second-person addressee in the preceding clause) to "anger." It is unlikely to be fronted for focus, since there is nothing in the context suggesting a contrast, i.e., anger versus what? The PP בחיק כסילים, though, does present focus, and the intended membership set for the contrast likely includes just two entities, {fools, you [the audience]}. Thus, the focus on the PP is concentrated on כסילים and serves to make the warning clear: if you are quick to anger, you're nothing but a fool!

7:10 אַל־תֹּאמַר֙ מֶ֣ה הָיָ֔ה שֶׁהַיָּמִ֥ים הָרִאשֹׁנִ֖ים הָי֣וּ טוֹבִ֣ים מֵאֵ֑לֶּה כִּ֛י לֹ֥א מֵחָכְמָ֖ה שָׁאַ֥לְתָּ עַל־זֶֽה׃

Don't say, "What has happened?"; that is, that the former days have been better than these because you do not ask about this out of wisdom.

אַל־תֹּאמַר֙. Jussive 2ms Qal √אמר. The complement of this verb of speaking is the reported speech that follows.

מֶה הָיָה. *Qatal* 3ms Qal √היה. This clause may be analyzed in two ways, depending on how one construes the interrogative מה. First, the clause could consist of the interrogative subject מה and the copular verb היה, "what has been?" or "what has happened?" The most common meaning of the verb היה is simply "to be, become, happen" (HALOT, s.v.; BDB, s.v.), for which it requires an NP or PP complement. In Ecclesiastes, though, we have seen a number of the one-place predicate uses of היה (see 1:9-11; 3:15)—i.e., of the existential use of היה that is similar to the Shakespearean "to be or not to be." In this verse היה seems to be a one-place predicate, i.e., it does not require any complement. Secondly, one could take מה to function, not as the interrogative subject "what?," but as an interrogative of manner or reason, "how/why?"

שֶׁהַיָּמִים֙ הָרִאשֹׁנִ֔ים הָי֥וּ טוֹבִ֖ים מֵאֵֽלֶּה. *Qatal* 3cp Qal √היה. If the first option above is taken, then the שׁ introduces a nominalized appositive clause to the first speech complement of the verb תאמר. The true rhetorical, negative thrust of the question מה היה is then clarified by the appositive clause—that the imagined speaker has taken the posture that life has become worse over time, whereas it should have become progressively better. If the second option is taken, then the שׁ clause is functioning as the subject of מה היה, "How/Why has [it] happened that the former days have been better?" (English prefers a dummy-it subject in such constructions where embedded clauses function as the subject: "It is delightful to meet you" = "To meet you is delightful").

כִּ֣י לֹ֥א מֵחָכְמָ֖ה שָׁאַ֥לְתָּ עַל־זֶֽה. *Qatal* 2ms Qal √שאל. The כי clause provides the reason for the prohibition on asking the question. The order within the כי clause is negative-PP-verb-PP. Negatives can modify a single constituent or the whole predicate, although the latter option is by far the dominant pattern in Hebrew (WO §39.3.2a). The position of the negative לא at a distance from the verb שאלת in this clause indicates that this is an example of לא negating a single constituent, the PP מחכמה. So the clause does not mean that the prohibited question has not been asked (the semantics of the predicate negation) but that when it was asked it was not out of wisdom (the semantics of constituent negation). The position of the לא מחכמה before the verb also signals its status as a focus constituent, thus "because not out of wisdom have you asked about this." This may be taken to mean it is a foolish question that a wise person would not ask (i.e., the wise would know that the assumption that life should become progressively better is facile) or perhaps that the question is not really prompted by concern for an answer but is merely a complaint about the way life is and, therefore, foolish. The PP על זה is an adjunct for שאלת, indicating the domain of the inquiry (for the function of על to mark specification or topic, "about, concerning, regarding," see WO §11.2.13g, MNK §39.19.4i).

7:11   טוֹבָ֥ה חָכְמָ֖ה עִֽם־נַחֲלָ֑ה וְיֹתֵ֖ר לְרֹאֵ֥י הַשָּֽׁמֶשׁ׃

Wisdom is good with an inheritance and (it is) an advantage for those who see the sun.

טוֹבָ֥ה חָכְמָ֖ה. This is a null copula clause that keeps the טוב but departs from the comparative construction (there is no מן). The order is predicate (טובה)-subject (חכמה), which reflects the raising of טובה for focus: wisdom is *good*. In the face of this strong assertion, though, the value of wisdom is not really the point. Rather, the thrust of this statement lies in the PP עם נחלה. That is, while everyone accepts the value of wisdom (it benefits everyone who sees the light of day), "it is especially good if one also has a material inheritance" (Fox 1999: 256).

עִֽם־נַחֲלָ֑ה. This comitative PP (WO §11.2.14; MNK §39.20.1) is an adjunct to the null copula and specifies what accompanies חכמה to complete the assertion. It is also possible that the preposition is used comparatively (see above, 2:16; WO §11.2.14c; DCH s.v. #10), which would suggest that wisdom and an inheritance are equally good.

וְיֹתֵ֖ר לְרֹאֵ֥י הַשָּֽׁמֶשׁ. Null copula clause; participle mp bound form Qal √ראה. This second half of the verse continues the assertion about חכמה. As such, the syntactic subject is a null pronoun anaphoric with חכמה and, like the first clause, the copula is also null, with the noun יתר functioning as the copular complement and the PP לראי השמש as an adjunct to the copula, specifying the beneficiary of the advantage provided by חכמה (WO §11.2.10d). Note that participles, representing the nominal takeover of event predication (see Cook 2008), may be morphologically cliticized to their verbal complements; this is the case with ראי השמש. Even so, the syntax and semantics of the construction are of a null-head, unmarked participial relative in which the participle has a complement. On יתר, see discussion at 2:15.

7:12   כִּ֛י בְּצֵ֥ל הַֽחָכְמָ֖ה בְּצֵ֣ל הַכָּ֑סֶף וְיִתְר֣וֹן דַּ֔עַת הַֽחָכְמָ֖ה תְּחַיֶּ֥ה בְעָלֶֽיהָ׃

Although "(living) in the shadow of wisdom is (living) in the shadow of money," the advantage of knowledge is (that) wisdom keeps its owner alive.

Both the grammar and the sense of this verse present difficulty. The grammatical crux rests on the meaning of בצל, which we take to be a

metaphor for protection (so Fox 1999). The overall sense depends on
how one understands the relationship of the two halves of the verse. On
this, Wise summarizes what we find to be the most compelling literary
analysis:

> Qoheleth quotes a well-known proverb which cynically claimed that there
> were two equally good ways to assure success in life, wisdom, and money.
> He counters that although both may lead to the same results, the way of
> wisdom has an advantage over wealth and bribery. It enriches the inner life
> in a way that money cannot (256).

כִּי בְּצֵל הַחָכְמָה בְּצֵל הַכָּסֶף. The כי is concessive (JM §171) and
so indicates that the first null copula clause is "a circumstance that might
be expected to preclude the action of the main clause, but does not"
(*New Oxford American Dictionary*). That is, one might think that the
proverb cited encapsulates a truism that qualifies the value of wisdom—
the advantage of wisdom lies in the success it brings (similar to the sentiment of v. 11). This proverb stands in contrast to the assertion in the
main clause that the real value of wisdom is not affluence but life. The
grammatical difficulty in the verse is how to take the NP צל in the cited
proverb. Fox takes צל metaphorically as shelter and protection and keeps
the ב (some argue for emending to כ based on the Versions): "The MT
implies causality, meaning that wisdom brings with it the protection of
wealth" (1999: 256). A completely different approach is taken by Wise,
who argues the בצל in this verse (and in 6:12 and 8:13) is a calque on
Aramaic בטלל, which, unlike the Hebrew phrase, went through a series
of semantic shifts: "in the shadow (of)" > "with the help (of)" > "because
(of)." For this verse, Wise translates "For 'With the help of wisdom or
with the help of money'—but the advantage of the knowledge of wisdom is that it vivifies those who possess it" (256). The literary explanation, with the proverbial background, can be provided without accepting
Wise's questionable grammatical analysis (see comment on 6:12).

וְיִתְרוֹן דַּעַת הַחָכְמָה תְּחַיֶּה בְעָלֶיהָ. *Yiqtol* 3fs Piel √חיה. The
טעמים indicate that the Masoretes did not take דעת החכמה as a bound
phrase; instead, החכמה is the subject of the verb תחיה and the referent
of the 3fs anaphoric clitic pronoun on בעליה. The syntactic problem,
then, is what to do with יתרון דעת, which is simply hanging out at the
front of the clause. If this is a case of left-dislocation, which requires the
resumption of the dislocated constituent (e.g., "my brother—I left him
at the airport"), the resumptive constituent is not an anaphoric pronoun

or a copy of the dislocated NP (יתרון דעת), but what appears to be a synonym (החכמה). But since "wisdom" is not a synonym for "the advantage of knowledge," we propose that this whole sequence is a null copula clause with an unmarked nominalized clause in the second half: "the advantage of knowledge is (that) wisdom keeps its master alive."

7:13　רְאֵה אֶת־מַעֲשֵׂה הָאֱלֹהִים כִּי מִי יוּכַל לְתַקֵּן אֵת
אֲשֶׁר עִוְּתוֹ:

See the work of God, that who is able to straighten (the thing) that he has twisted?

This verse moves from the collection of proverbs in vv. 1-12 to Qoheleth's summary. Here he makes a statement about God's creation with a backhanded compliment regarding God's power: humans cannot change what he has done, but what he has done is to "twist" things around. This serves as a dim reminder, coming on the heels of generally positive statements about wisdom, that Qoheleth's opinion of the wisdom that humans can attain is critically limited.

רְאֵה אֶת־מַעֲשֵׂה הָאֱלֹהִים. Impv ms Qal √ראה. The NP following the verb is its NP complement. The verb itself denotes "seeing," but the connotation here is similar to the English "look" or "consider" (see BDB, s.v.; HALOT, s.v.). Qoheleth instructs the audience not simply to take in God's work visually but to understand its nature. And the feature of God's work that concerns Qoheleth here is its immutability— what God does cannot be undone.

כִּי מִי יוּכַל לְתַקֵּן אֵת אֲשֶׁר עִוְּתוֹ. *Yiqtol* 3ms Qal √יכל (on this verb, see comment on 1:8), Inf Constr Piel √תקן, and *qatal* 3ms Piel √עוה + 3ms clitic pronoun for the verbal complement. The כי clause provides either Qoheleth's reason (with his point included) for instructing the audience to consider God's works or a second, appositional complement of the verb ראה. The former "reason" option or an asseverative ("indeed") interpretation is adopted by most commentators, although the latter "complement" option is simpler and presents no syntactic or semantic difficulties. The form לתקל is the infinitival complement of יוכל, while the complement of לתקל is a null head modified by an אשר-relative clause in which the clitic 3ms pronoun on עותו resumes the null head: "to straighten (the thing) that he has twisted it."

7:14   בְּיוֹם טוֹבָה הֱיֵה בְטוֹב וּבְיוֹם רָעָה רְאֵה גַּם אֶת־
זֶה לְעֻמַּת־זֶה עָשָׂה הָאֱלֹהִים עַל־דִּבְרַת שֶׁלֹּא
יִמְצָא הָאָדָם אַחֲרָיו מְאוּמָה:

On the day of goodness, be in good, and on the day of adversity, consider
that, indeed, God made this one (day of goodness) like (he has made) that one
(day of adversity), for the purpose that man does not find anything after him.

Qoheleth draws a logical conclusion from his observations: given
that even the wise cannot discern the order of creation (v. 13), which
makes good look like bad and vice versa (14a), it can only be that God
had designed it to be so.

בְּיוֹם טוֹבָה הֱיֵה בְטוֹב. Impv ms Qal √היה. The PP ביום טובה has
been fronted as a topic, to establish the salient temporal setting (for temporal use of the ב preposition, see WO §11.2.5c; MNK §39.6.2; JM
§133c). The feminine טובה signals that the referent is abstract, "goodness"; on the feminine used for abstract nouns, see WO §6.4.2. The PP
בטוב is the copular complement of היה.

וּבְיוֹם רָעָה רְאֵה. Impv ms Qal √ראה. As with the preceding clause,
the PP ביום רעה is topic-fronted to situate the assertion temporally. The
verb ראה is bivalent, and here the complement is the entire remainder
of the clause, which is, syntactically speaking, an unmarked nominalized
compound clause.

גַּם אֶת־זֶה לְעֻמַּת־זֶה עָשָׂה הָאֱלֹהִים. *Qatal* 3ms Qal √עשׂה. The
initial גם is a focus adverb that lexically, and thus explicitly, marks the
focus. Here the focus signals a contrast between the first זה and the second זה, which we have taken to point back to the two days just mentioned, יום טובה and יום רעה (see discussion in 3:19 for the use of זה to
indicate both sets of contrasting alternatives). Even if the גם were absent,
the focus-induced contrast between the two זה demonstratives would be
clear from their fronted position, which has triggered the verb עשׂה to
raise over the subject האלהים. In terms of the clause structure, the NP
את־זה לעמת־זה is the complement of bivalent עשׂה; within the NP, the
complex preposition לעמת signals correspondence: "God has made this
one *like (he has made)* the other."

עַל־דִּבְרַת שֶׁלֹּא יִמְצָא הָאָדָם אַחֲרָיו מְאוּמָה. *Yiqtol* 3ms Qal
√מצא. Seow takes this as a purpose clause linking God's activity with
intentionality in obscuring man's future from himself (1997: 240). He

also suggests that עַל דברת שׁ is a calque on Aramaic עַל דברת דִי (Dan 2:30; 4:14). Whether or not this is an Aramaism, the שׁ clause is best understood grammatically as a noun-complement (lit. "on the matter *that* ..."); it is not the שׁ (which simply nominalizes the following clause), but the preposition עַל or perhaps the collocation עַל דברת that provides either a causal or purpose nuance. See discussion in Schoors, 147. On the function of עַל, see WO §11.2.13e. Within the שׁ clause, bivalent מצא has האדם for its subject and מאומה as its complement; the PP אחריו (with clitic 3ms suffix) is a temporal adjunct ("after him" = in the future).

אֶת־הַכֹּל רָאִיתִי בִּימֵי הֶבְלִי יֵשׁ צַדִּיק אֹבֵד בְּצִדְקוֹ   7:15
וְיֵשׁ רָשָׁע מַאֲרִיךְ בְּרָעָתוֹ:

I have seen all sorts in my הבל *days. A righteous person perishes in his righteousness and a wicked person prolongs (his days) in his evilness.*

אֶת־הַכֹּל רָאִיתִי בִּימֵי הֶבְלִי. *Qatal* 1cs Qal √ראה. The complement of bivalent ראה is the focus-fronted אֶת־הכל; the בּ PP is a temporal adjunct. Although Seow suggests that כל can refer to just two things (1997: 252), neither HALOT nor WO lists such a use. Ecclesiastes' use of כל establishes that the variety of what he has seen (cf. Gen 24:10 כל־ טוב "all sorts of goods" and Gen 40:17 מכל מאכל פרעה "some of all kinds of Pharaoh's food"; see HALOT, s.v.) he considers a representation of all life's absurdities, though he proceeds to list only two as examples.

יֵשׁ צַדִּיק אֹבֵד בְּצִדְקוֹ. Participle ms Qal √אבד. In this clause and the next, the יֵשׁ is not existential but copular, linking the subject צדיק to the participial copular complement אבד. The PP בצדקו is an adjunct to the participle. See WO §11.2.5d, e for the various circumstantial functions of the preposition בּ; here the preposition seems to indicate a state of being, "while being righteous," during which the person is affected (so also Fox 1999: 259).

וְיֵשׁ רָשָׁע מַאֲרִיךְ בְּרָעָתוֹ. Participle ms Hiphil √ארך. The subject רשע is the subject of the יֵשׁ copula, and the participle מאריך is the complement (itself modified by another בּ-PP adjunct). The phrase מאריך here is elliptical for the idiom מאריך ימים "to lengthen days." Both participles in these final two clauses have gnomic semantics (see discussion in 1:4).

7:16   אַל־תְּהִי צַדִּיק הַרְבֵּה וְאַל־תִּתְחַכַּם יוֹתֵר לָמָּה
תִּשּׁוֹמֵם:

*Don't be a very "righteous" man nor consider yourself excessively wise.
Why should you be shocked?*

This seems to be a striking statement—don't be very righteous or
overly wise? Though many scholars accept this as Qoheleth's statement
of the golden mean, we find the parallel with אל תהי סכל in v. 17 and
Whybray's essential argument compelling: this is a warning not "against
the excess of righteousness nor against an excess of striving after it but
against *self*-righteousness" (191; contra Fox 1999: 260).

אַל־תְּהִי צַדִּיק הַרְבֵּה. Jussive 2ms Qal √היה. The jussive form is
morphologically distinct here from the *yiqtol* תִּהְיֶה. The complement of
תהי is צדיק; for the functions of הרבה, see discussion in 1:16. The adjective צדיק is used substantivally here to refer to a person characterized by
the quality צדיק, or in the context of vv. 16-17, one whose identify or
time is consumed with being an extreme צדיק.

וְאַל־תִּתְחַכַּם יוֹתֵר. Jussive 2ms Hithpael √חכם. The Hithpael of
this root occurs only here and in Exod 1:10; in the latter, the nuance
seems to concern behaving wisely, while here we sense a subtle reflexive
idea, "consider (oneself) wise." On יותר (functioning here adverbially),
see discussion at 2:15.

לָמָּה תִּשּׁוֹמֵם. *Yiqtol* (irrealis) 2ms Hithpael (Hithpoel) √שׁמם.
The Hithpael exhibits the assimilation of the infix -*t*- instead of the
expected metathesis, e.g., תִּשְׁתּוֹמֵם* (see JM §53e). According to Seow
(1997: 254), the verb in the Hithpael typically means "be shocked" or
"be dumbfounded," which is what HALOT lists for other occurrences,
although HALOT also lists "bring oneself to ruin" for this verse. Being
shocked is the result of considering oneself very wise and eventually real-
izing one's limits.

7:17   אַל־תִּרְשַׁע הַרְבֵּה וְאַל־תְּהִי סָכָל לָמָּה תָמוּת
בְּלֹא עִתֶּךָ:

*Don't be very wicked nor be a fool. Why should you die in (what is) not
your time?*

אַל־תִּרְשַׁע הַרְבֵּה. Jussive 2ms Qal √רשע; for the functions of הרבה, see discussion in 1:16.

וְאַל־תְּהִי סָכָל. Jussive 2ms Qal √היה. On the form, see comment on v. 16. The copular complement is סכל.

לָמָּה תָמוּת בְּלֹא עִתֶּךָ. *Yiqtol* (irrealis) Qal 2ms √מות. Notice here that the negator לא is within the domain of the ב preposition; hence, it functions as an item adverb to negate the constituent functioning as the NP complement of the preposition ("in not your time") rather than the entire predicate (as is typical); see also 7:10. Note that the Hebrew ("in not your time") is difficult to render closely in grammatical English and so we have translated with a different syntactic structure, "in what is not your time." The point seems to be premature death, which is what foolish behavior all too often results in.

7:18 טוֹב אֲשֶׁר תֶּאֱחֹז בָּזֶה וְגַם־מִזֶּה אַל־תַּנַּח אֶת־יָדֶךָ
כִּי־יְרֵא אֱלֹהִים יֵצֵא אֶת־כֻּלָּם׃

That you grab ahold of this is good, but also do not rest your hand from that, because a God-fearer fulfills all of them.

טוֹב אֲשֶׁר תֶּאֱחֹז בָּזֶה. *Yiqtol* 2ms Qal √אחז. A null copula clause with an adjective functioning as the copular complement, טוב, and an אשר nominalized clause as subject. The copula-subject order reflects the HNPS of the אשר clause (see also 2:7, 17; 3:14; 7:20, 26; 9:11, 14, 15; 11:7)—when a long and often complex constituent is moved down the clause for processing ease. The verb אחז is bivalent in the Qal and takes either an NP or ב-PP complement (see also 2:3); here the PP בזה is the complement of the verb.

וְגַם־מִזֶּה אַל־תַּנַּח אֶת־יָדֶךָ. Jussive 2ms Hiph √נוח. The Hiphil of נוח can be bivalent, "put X to rest" or trivalent, "put X in Y [place]." The bivalent option fits this context best, with את ידך as the complement and the PP מזה as an adjunct providing the activity or event from which the rest is given. The PP מזה is fronted as a topic, to signal the shift from זה in the previous clause to the (other) זה in this clause. The demonstratives זה refer most naturally back to being muchly righteous (v. 16) and muchly wicked (v. 17). See also discussion at 3:19; 7:14 for similar uses of the paired demonstrative זה.

כִּי־יָרֵא אֱלֹהִים יֵצֵא אֶת־כֻּלָּם. *Yiqtol* 3ms Qal √יצא. Following a function word such as כִּי, we typically find and so expect verb-subject order. Here the subject appears to be fronted within the כִּי clause in order to mark it with focus: this is what *the one who fears God* does (with the contextually implied contrast to *the one who does not fear God*). The אֵת is not the object marker but the homophonous preposition "with." The PP אֵת כֻּלָּם is an adjunct to יצא and adds what Qoheleth deems to be an important manner of movement—that the wise person goes out in life with a firm grasp of both righteousness and wickedness. This does not necessarily imply that Qoheleth advocates wickedness, but that one must be able to understand and discern both extremes of behavior. The referent of כֻּלָּם is ambiguous. If Qoheleth intended to refer to both overly righteous (v. 16) and overly wicked (v. 17) behavior, why did he not use the expected שְׁנֵיהֶם? We can only suggest that Delitzsch (followed by, e.g., Gordis 1955; Crenshaw, 142; Fox 1999: 262) might be correct in reading this as an elliptical idiom that is also found in the Mishnah:

> Already Jerome, with his vague *nihil negligit*, is right as to the meaning. The Bible says יָצָא אֶת־הָעִיר *egressus est urbem* Gen. 44,4, cf. Jer. 10,20 and the Mishna יָצָא אֶת־יְדֵי חוֹבָתוֹ "he has escaped his obligation"; i.e., he has rid himself of his obligation, he is quit (by fulfilling) of it. In most cases, one simply says יָצָא, "he has satisfied his duty," and לֹא יָצָא, "he has not satisfied it," e.g., Berachoth II,1. Accordingly, since אֶת־כֻּלָּם relates to ποιεῖν ταῦτα κάκεῖνα μὴ ἀφιέναι, Matt 23:23, here יָצֵא means "the God-fearer will set himself free from all," that is, he will acquit himself of the one as well as of the other, will perform both, and thus preserve the golden middle way. (1875: 321; Holmstedt transl.)

יָרֵא אֱלֹהִים. The bound phrase ירא אלהים illustrates the often blurry boundary between the morphological class adjective and the (normally verbal) semantics of events. The bound relationship expresses what is traditionally termed an objective genitive, in which the second element expresses the complement of the action encoded in the adjective. Hence, a periphrastic equivalent of the adjectival bound construction is the relative clause with a verbal predication: "the one that fears God."

7:19   הַחָכְמָה תָּעֹז לֶחָכָם מֵעֲשָׂרָה שַׁלִּיטִים אֲשֶׁר הָיוּ בָּעִיר:

(Wisdom gives strength to the wise more than ten rulers who were in the city.)

As Barton (144) observed, it is difficult to identify the explicit connection between this verse and either the preceding or following verses. It may be a parenthesis that presents, as Gordis speculates, "a conventional proverb, extolling wisdom as giving a man the self-assurance he needs" (1955: 268). Fox, in contrast, emends this verse to deal with "wealth" (see below) and moves it to follow v. 12 (256–57).

הַחָכְמָה תָּעֹז לֶחָכָם. *Yiqtol* 3fs Qal √עזז. The verb עזז presents some problems, since few modern commentators think that "gives strength" makes sense in this context. Barton asserts, "It is impossible to find any intelligent connection for this verse with the preceding context. It is undoubtedly an interpolation by the glossator who was interested in proverb" (144). Though it is elsewhere intransitive (i.e., monovalent) Gordis (1955: 269) and Whitley (67), for example, assert that the Qal עזז can only be transitive (i.e., bivalent), "Wisdom strengthens the wise." The textual evidence contributes to the complexity, since one of the fragmentary texts from Qumran (4QQoh^a) reads תעזר "she helps," which is the reading reflected in the LXX βοηθήσει. Fox follows the Qumran variant as the likelier reading (1999: 257), while Seow keeps the text of the MT but suggests that תעז is from a homonymous root עזז, "to be honored, be cherished" (i.e., "wisdom is dearer to the wise than 10 rulers ..."; see Seow 1997: 256). Murphy simply accepts the MT as the *lectio difficilior* (69) and opts for the intransitive analysis (contra Whitley), "wisdom is stronger for the wise." This analysis (and the English translation) makes poor sense to us. Finally, Goldman (editor of Ecclesiastes for BHQ) proposes the reading תָּעֵז, a revocalization to the Hiphil stem, such that the clause should read: "Wisdom makes bold (haughty, self assured) the wise more than ten governors who were in the city." Goldman argues, "The only certain attestations of עזז for the meaning 'to make audacious' are *Hiphil* (Prov 7:13; 21:29). In these occurrences the *Hiphil* is transitive, both with an object complement פנים, but the verb is also found in the *Hophal* for a man in Ben Sira (10:12). The ל before חכם is a complement marker. The only other attestation of the root in Ecclesiastes is עז פנים [in 8:1] ... 'boldness, haughtiness'" (2004: 93*–94*). If this is the original reading, how are the variants in MT and 4QQoh^a/LXX to be explained? Goldman suggests that the original reading is a warning to the disciples of wisdom (coming on the heels of the prior saying, not to be muchly wise), while these other readings are attempts to rehabilitate the instruction so as to give wisdom a more positive spin. While we have retained the MT above, in line with the goals of this series, we see no way to decide conclusively between the ancient variants: the Qal vocalization תעז of the MT, the Hiphil vocalization of Goldman's emendation, and the תעזר of the Qumran text and the LXX witness.

מֵעֲשָׂרָה שַׁלִּיטִים אֲשֶׁר הָיוּ בָּעִיר. *Qatal* 3cp Qal √היה. The מִן-PP is a comparative phrase adjunct to the verb תעז (MNK §39.14.8; WO §11.2.11e.3). The numeral עשרה is the prepositional complement and the quantified item שליטים is in apposition to the numeral and specify restrictively the identity of the quantification. In BH the numeral "ten" behaves like the digits three through nine, in that the grammatical gender marking of the numeral is the opposite of the gender of the noun being quantified (JM §100d; §GKC 97a–b; WO §15.2.2; MNK §37.2.2.3). The numeral עשרה is also the head of the אשר relative clause, which restrictively defines the עשרה שליטים as those in the city (versus some unknown number of rulers not in the city). The restrictive relative with the *qatal* היו suggests the comparison is with those who have been (i.e., have ruled) in the city in the past. Both Seow (1997: 256) and Fox (1999: 257) read מֵעֹשֶׁר (i.e., "more than wealth of the proprietors") by supposing a mis-divided text and a mistaken sibilant—i.e., מעשר השליטים was corrupted to מעשרה שליטים.

7:20   כִּי אָדָם אֵין צַדִּיק בָּאָרֶץ אֲשֶׁר יַעֲשֶׂה־טּוֹב וְלֹא יֶחֱטָא:

Because, man—a righteous one does not exist in the land, who does good and does not sin.

This verse may be an expansion of 1 Kgs 8:46, כִּי אֵין אָדָם אֲשֶׁר לֹא־יֶחֱטָא. If v. 19 is a parenthesis, then this כי clause could provide the delayed reason for v. 18 and the instruction to walk via media. Alternatively, this verse may continue the parenthesis and provide a contrasting quotation to the effect that "perfect goodness is never attainable to man" (Gordis 1955: 268). If so, then the כי is not causal but concessive ("although") or adversative ("but").

כִּי אָדָם אֵין צַדִּיק בָּאָרֶץ. An אין copula clause. Beside the role of אין as the negative copula, the structure of the clause following the כי is not transparent. אדם may be the subject, אין the negative copula, and

צדיק the complement, though the resulting proposition, "a man is not righteous in the land," makes little contextual sense. Instead, it appears that אדם is left-dislocated and resumed by the coreferential, substantive adjective צדיק; the אין remains the negative copula, but in this analysis בארץ is the copular complement. The latter analysis seems to provide slightly better sense and so is reflected in our translation. (Gordis' idea that צדיק בארץ "has been 'anticipated' from the subordinate clause" [1955: 269] is both ad hoc and grammatically questionable.)

אֲשֶׁר יַעֲשֶׂה־טּוֹב. *Yiqtol* 3ms Qal √עשה. This relative clause modifies the substantivized adjective צדיק. The placement of the relative, with the copular complement בארץ intervening between it and the relative head, is the result of relative clause extraposition, which is similar to HNPS (a complex constituent is moved down the clause, over simpler constituents, in order to facilitate the mental processing of the entire structure; see comment above on v. 18). The head צדיק has a relativized function within the relative clause as the null-subject of both bivalent יעשה (whose complement is טוב) and monovalent יחטא.

וְלֹא יֶחֱטָא. *Yiqtol* 3ms Qal √חטא. This clause continues within the scope of the אשר relative.

גַּם לְכָל־הַדְּבָרִים אֲשֶׁר יְדַבֵּרוּ אַל־תִּתֵּן לִבֶּךָ אֲשֶׁר 7:21
לֹא־תִשְׁמַע אֶת־עַבְדְּךָ מְקַלְלֶךָ:

Also, don't pay attention to any of the words that they speak; (in order) that you don't hear your servant cursing you.

This verse follows v. 20 only loosely, as a practical corollary (Gordis 1955: 269)—since no man is perfect and so one is likely to encounter unjustified criticism or disparagement or otherwise troubling speech toward himself, one must be prepared to ignore it (see Fox 1999: 263).

גַּם לְכָל־הַדְּבָרִים אֲשֶׁר יְדַבֵּרוּ אַל־תִּתֵּן לִבֶּךָ. *Yiqtol* 3mp Piel √דבר and Jussive 2ms Qal √נתן. This גם is additive (see 1:11; MNK §41.4.5) and connects v. 21 with the preceding verse as further relevant information. The main verb is תתן, which is trivalent. The first complement, the thing given, is לבך (ms לב with a clitic 2ms pronoun); the second complement, the recipient or goal, is the PP לכל הדברים. The PP לכל הדברים has been fronted as a topic, to switch the discourse attention from character (v. 20) to behavior in speech by those same types of people (v. 21). The אשר introduces a relative clause that

modifies הדברים, and with a null-subject of the plural verb within the
relative, ידברו, it expresses an impersonal, generic subject, e.g., "people
talk."

אֲשֶׁר לֹא־תִשְׁמַע אֶת־עַבְדְּךָ מְקַלְלֶךָ. *Yiqtol* 2ms Qal √שמע and
Participle ms Piel √קלל + 2ms clitic pronoun. This אשר clause reflects
the basic nominalizer role of אשר. It is not only used for relative clauses
or verbal complement clauses but can also be used to nominalize a
clause to fill any noun role, including prepositional complements or
the complements of function words like למען. As the complement of
למען, a nominalized verbal clause may be marked as such overtly by
אשר (see Gen 18:19; Lev 17:5; Num 17:5; Deut 20:18, 27:3; Josh 3:4;
2 Sam 13:5; Jer 42:6; Ezek 20:26, 31:14; 36:30; 46:18), or unmarked
and so lacking אשר (e.g., Gen 12:13, לְמַעַן יִיטַב־לִי). A third variation,
in which the למען is assumed and the אשר is present, also exists, though
rarely: Deut 4:40, 6:3 and here. The final constituent את־עבדך מקללך
is either a noun with an unmarked participial relative, "your servant
(who) is cursing you," or a small clause, "your servant cursing you."
Syntactically, there is no way to determine which option is correct;
however, semantically, there is a significant difference. The question is
whether what is (not) to be heard is a *thing*, the servant (who happens
to be cursing), or an *event*, the servant cursing. The latter makes better
contextual sense and so the small clause analysis is preferred.

7:22   כִּי גַּם־פְּעָמִים רַבּוֹת יָדַע לִבֶּךָ אֲשֶׁר גַּם־אַתָּ*
קִלַּלְתָּ אֲחֵרִים:

*Because, also, many times your mind has known that even you have
cursed others.*

This כי clause grounds v. 21 by providing the basis for the advice in
the first place—the listener should expect his slave to curse him simply
because he himself has acted that way in the past. Murphy's summary of
the way vv. 20-22 operate is succinct and clear:

> One can understand this admonition as an illustration of the truth con-
> tained in v. 20. No one is free from sin, and this should have an effect on
> the way one responds to reports. ... If one hears rumors and discovers a
> curse that has been uttered, one should not respond foolishly; rather, one
> should look at one's own failings. (71)

כִּי גַם־פְּעָמִים רַבּוֹת יָדַע לִבֶּךָ. *Qatal* 3ms Qal √ידע. The verb-subject order is triggered by the כי as well as the fronted adjunct. The גם associates the action of cursing expressed in this clause with that in the previous clause. The manner adjunct פעמים רבות is focus-fronted to highlight the near-normalcy (and so expectedness) of the activity—it is *common*, not *rare*. The subject of bivalent ידע is לבך, while the verbal complement is the אשר nominalized clause.

אֲשֶׁר גַּם־אַתָּ* קִלַּלְתָּ אֲחֵרִים. *Qatal* 2ms Piel √קלל. The אשר nominalizes the verbal clause so that it may function syntactically as the complement of the verb ידע. Though verb-subject order is normally triggered after a function word like אשר, an overt subject pronoun with a finite verb always carries focus and so is fronted. The focus-marking is signaled by the word order as well as the presence of גם, which here is a focus particle. The verbal complement is the substantivized adjective אחרים. Note the *Qere-Ketiv* with the 2ms pronoun אַתָּ—the *Ketiv* lacks the expected final ה resulting in a form that is consonantally identical to the 2fs pronoun אַתְּ. Context, though, suggests that the intended pronoun is more likely to be 2ms, the marginal *Qere*.

7:23   כָּל־זֹה נִסִּיתִי בַחָכְמָה אָמַרְתִּי אֶחְכָּמָה וְהִיא רְחוֹקָה מִמֶּנִּי׃

All this I have tested with wisdom. I said, "I shall become wise," but it is too distant for me.

This verse is a fitting conclusion to this stage of Qoheleth's investigation, which has unfolded in vv. 1-22 (כל זה). The conclusion continues through v. 24. The unconquerable distance of wisdom, or better here, attaining a deeper wisdom (see v. 24) in order to understand the operation of creation, echoes the hymn to wisdom in Job 28 and the words of Agur in Proverbs 30 (see, e.g., Murphy, 72).

כָּל־זֹה נִסִּיתִי בַחָכְמָה. *Qatal* 1cs Piel √נסה. The complement of bivalent נסה is fronted as a topic, indicating a switch from "cursing" in vv. 21-22 to כל זה, which refers back to the entirety of the discussion in vv. 1-22. The PP בחכמה is an adjunct providing the instrument by which the testing was performed.

אָמַרְתִּי אֶחְכָּמָה. *Qatal* 1cs Qal √אמר and Jussive 1cs Qal √חכם. The one-word clause אחכמה (the verb חכם is monovalent) serves as the direct speech complement of bivalent אמרתי, expressing a volitive sense—Qoheleth's intent. (See 2:1 for the use of the term "jussive" here.)

וְהִיא רְחוֹקָה מִמֶּנִּי. A null copula clause with היא the subject and the adjective רחוקה the copular complement. The PP ממני is the comparative construction (MNK §39.14.8; WO §11.2.11e.3) with the ground for the comparison the 1cs clitic pronoun that is the prepositional complement. The assertive part of the comparison is elided from the preceding clause, "being wise."

7:24   רָחוֹק מַה־שֶּׁהָיָה וְעָמֹק | עָמֹק מִי יִמְצָאֶנּוּ׃

Distant is whatever has happened and most deep. Who can find it?

Qoheleth explains precisely what he meant by concluding that wisdom had eluded him. The adjective רחוק provides the connection and "wisdom" is identified as מה־שהיה; i.e., the rhyme and reason for what happens in life.

רָחוֹק מַה־שֶּׁהָיָה. *Qatal* 3ms Qal √היה. The main clause is a null copula clause with a fronted copular complement, the adjective רחוק, and a complex subject phrase, which is headed by the free-choice relative מה־ש (see comment on 1:9).

עָמֹק | עָמֹק. This null copula clause reflects the ellipsis of the subject from the preceding clause מה־שהיה and replaces רחוק with another adjective as the copular complement, עמק. The repetition of the adjective is a Hebrew grammatical strategy for presenting a superlative (GKC §133k–l; WO §7.2.3; JM §141k).

מִי יִמְצָאֶנּוּ. *Yiqtol* 3ms Qal √מצא + 3ms clitic pronoun as the complement. The subject is the interrogative מי, and the subject-verb word order reflects the basic word order when no other syntactic phenomena are present to complicate and trigger a word order inversion. The clause presents a rhetorical question, and the intended answer is obvious and functions as a negative assertion: if Qoheleth cannot find it, *no one* can find it.

7:25-29 Seeking Wisdom Is Like Understanding the "Women"

After the long consideration of the impenetrability of wisdom, Qoheleth shifts to a new section in vv. 25-29. The transition is signaled grammatically by returning to his overarching "I-and-my-לב" investigative strategy (on this, see Introduction §3). Wisdom remains in view, though it is related to Qoheleth's experience with women (likely here allusions to characters founds in Proverbs 1–9: Lady Wisdom, חָכְמוֹת, and the Strange Woman, אִשָּׁה זָרָה, representing folly). In short, Qoheleth concludes that if man cannot avoid "the woman" (folly), finding "a woman" (wisdom) is hopeless.

7:25   סַבּוֹתִי אֲנִי וְלִבִּי לָדַעַת וְלָתוּר וּבַקֵּשׁ חָכְמָה
וְחֶשְׁבּוֹן וְלָדַעַת רֶשַׁע כֶּסֶל וְהַסִּכְלוּת הוֹלֵלוֹת:

I turned around, I and my לב, to understand and to investigate and seek wisdom and accounting and to understand irrational wickedness, stupidity, and foolishness.

Though v. 25 primarily orients the audience to what follows, it has a Janus-quality. Coming on the heels of the negative assessments of his conclusion in vv. 23 and 24, a subtle implication lingers—that by both avenues of investigation, he is consistently failing to find the wisdom to tally all his observations with the assumption of a rational, ordered world.

סַבּוֹתִי אֲנִי וְלִבִּי. *Qatal* 1cs Qal √סבב. The lack of agreement between the 1cs verb סבותי and the 1cp coordinate phrase אני ולבי indicates the coordinate phrase is not the syntactic subject. Rather, the subject is null and expanded upon by the appositive coordinate phrase אני ולבי. By this strategy Qoheleth is able to reinforce his role as the instigator and primary reporter of the experiment while at the same time indicating that he was not alone in his quest. See the Introduction on the "I-and-my-לב" strategy.

לָדַעַת וְלָתוּר וּבַקֵּשׁ חָכְמָה וְחֶשְׁבּוֹן וְלָדַעַת רֶשַׁע כֶּסֶל וְהַסִּכְלוּת הוֹלֵלוֹת. Inf Constr Qal √ידע (2×) and √תור and Piel √בקש. The infinitive clauses are purpose adjuncts to the verb סבותי. Those within ל-PPs are distinct adjuncts while the near synonyms תור and בקש are a compound predicate within the scope of a single ל-PP (see WO §11.4.2a for "preposition override"). Both bivalent verbs share the compound complement חכמה וחשבון. The preceding verb ידע is also bivalent, though its syntactic complement is null and is reconstructed during processing as a copy of the complement of תור ובקש. The second occurrence of לדעת has an overt complement, the compound רשע כסל והסכלות הוללות. See 1:17 for a similar statement.

7:26　וּמוֹצֶא אֲנִי מַר מִמָּוֶת אֶת־הָאִשָּׁה אֲשֶׁר־הִיא
מְצוֹדִים וַחֲרָמִים לִבָּהּ אֲסוּרִים יָדֶיהָ טוֹב לִפְנֵי
הָאֱלֹהִים יִמָּלֵט מִמֶּנָּה וְחוֹטֵא יִלָּכֶד בָּהּ:

*I find more bitter than death "the woman," who is snares, and her mind
is nets, her hands are fetters. (The one) pleasing before God will escape from
her, but the offensive one will be captured by her.*

וּמוֹצֶא אֲנִי מַר מִמָּוֶת אֶת־הָאִשָּׁה. Participle ms Qal √מצא. The
vocalization of מוצא, with the *segol* in the final syllable rather than the
expected *ṣere* of the paradigm form (i.e., מוֹצֵא), reflects the normal pattern for III-ה roots. Although there is no clear diachronic pattern in the
Hebrew Bible, according to Mishnaic Hebrew, III-א verbs commonly
have the vowel pattern of III-ה verbs (see JM §78e–g). Note the participle-subject order, מוצא אני. The word order of participial clauses is
strongly subject-participle (see comment on 1:6); this is especially true
with pronominal subjects: pronoun-participle order is favored over participle-pronoun by five-to-one. Yet, here (with אני) and in 8:12, Qoheleth
uses the less common, grammatically marked order, with the participle
preceding an overt subject pronoun. The participle מוצא, then, must
be focus-fronted. This fronting serves to contrast with Qoheleth's earlier
confession in vv. 23-24 that he could not find wisdom: "Who can find
it?" (v. 24) versus "Look what I *did find*!" Note that the complement of
the bivalent מוצא, the NP את האשה, follows the comparative phrase מר
ממות (for comparative מן, see MNK §39.14.8; WO §11.2.11e.3). Since
complements normally precede adjuncts, the position of את האשה suggests that it has been moved down the clause toward the end. That the
NP את האשה is followed by a long, complex אשר clause provides the
clue—HNPS (see above, vv. 18, 20). The syntactic analysis of the adjectival phrase מר ממות is more complicated that it initially appears. It is
not simply an adjunct of the verb מוצא since semantically the notion that
"one finds X bitter" fails. Rather, "one finds [X (to be) bitter]." That is,
the entire proposition that "the woman (is) more bitter than death" is the
clausal complement of the מוצא. This is similar to nominalized clauses
introduced by אשר, ש, or כי. The one significant difference in the type
of construction in this verse is that the subject of the clausal complement
(האשה) is also marked by את as a complement of the higher verb מוצא.
This is a rare example of exceptional case-marking (ECM) in a small
clause in BH (cf. GKC §117i–m; JM §125j). Though Schoors does not

use the labels "small clause" or ECM, he is on the right track in his analysis (188, 191; he is followed by Pahk, though Pahk misunderstands the syntax and function of the אשר).

מַר מִמָּוֶת אֶת־הָאִשָּׁה. Note that the ms adjective מר does not agree in gender with the noun with which it is linked, האשה, in the small clause. Though the normal rules of grammatical agreement between a subject noun and an adjective that is the copular complement (i.e., a predicate adjective) requires the two to match in gender and number, here the grammar has been stretched. Rather than positing some grammatical rule for this, we propose that Qoheleth placed the adjective first and left it as the default masculine gender in order to delay revealing the point of his assertion, which is contrary to his audience's expectations (contra Schoors, 188).

אֲשֶׁר־הִיא מְצוֹדִים וַחֲרָמִים לִבָּהּ אֲסוּרִים יָדֶיהָ. Three null copula clauses are strung together within this relative clause, which modifies את האשה restrictively (there is no justification for Fox's assertion that the אשר forces a nonrestrictive relative and so makes the passage misogynistic; 1999: 266–69). On determining relative restrictiveness, see Holmstedt 2016: 209–14. We take the relative as restrictive and so the statement about a particular type of woman, not all women. The first clause has the order subject (היא)–null copula–complement (מצודים), while the following two clauses exhibit the fronting of their complements, חרמים and ידיה, as topics, signaling the switch from snares to nets to fetters. The 3fs clitic pronouns on the subjects לבה and ידיה provide the anaphoric connection with היא; all three are anaphorically connected to the relative head האשה.

טוֹב לִפְנֵי הָאֱלֹהִים יִמָּלֵט מִמֶּנָּה. Yiqtol 3ms Niph √מלט. The subject of the monovalent ימלט is the adjective טוב, which has been substantivized and is also modified internally by the compound preposition לפני and its complement האלהים. The PP ממנה is an adjunct to ימלט and indicates movement away from a specified source, in this case the dangerous woman (WO §11.2.11b; MNK §39.14.1).

וְחוֹטֵא יִלָּכֶד בָּהּ. Participle ms Qal √חטא and yiqtol 3ms Niph √לכד. Since the participle חוטא has no internal modifiers, it can be analyzed as a substantive here, "sinner, offender" (see discussion at 1:15). The substantive participle is the subject of the monovalent Niphal ילכד, and the adjunct PP בה adds the agent of the activity (WO §11.2.5d; MNK §39.6.3.1b).

7:27 רְאֵה֙ זֶ֣ה מָצָ֔אתִי אָמְרָ֖ה קֹהֶ֑לֶת אַחַ֥ת לְאַחַ֖ת לִמְצֹ֥א חֶשְׁבּֽוֹן׃

See, this I found—said Qoheleth—, one to one to find a conclusion.

The third-person reference to Qoheleth reflects the intrusive voice
of the book's narrator. As we suggested in the Introduction (§1 Structure), we take this to signal the midpoint of the book, dividing the first
half from the second half.

רְאֵה֙ זֶ֣ה מָצָ֔אתִי ... אַחַ֥ת לְאַחַ֖ת לִמְצֹ֥א חֶשְׁבּֽוֹן. Impv ms Qal
√ראה and *qatal* 1cs Qal √מצא. The imperative ראה here functions similarly to the deictic exclamative הנה. If it still requires a complement
(since ראה is normally bivalent) the following clause זה מצאתי would
be the nominalized clausal complement, "see (that) I found this." The
verb מצאתי is also bivalent and the demonstrative זה is the complement
(there is no grammatical reason to follow Seow in taking the זה as a relative; 1997: 264). The demonstrative is cataphoric, pointing forward to
"what" Qoheleth found, which is delayed until v. 29: אשר עשה האלהים
את־האדם ישר והמה בקשו חשבנות רבים. The phrase at the end of this
verse, אחת לאחת, is an adjunct of manner for מצאתי (so also Seow 1997:
264) and describes Qoheleth's inductive method (and the use of the feminine אחת, following on the heels of v. 26, may be a subtle allusion to
his investigations in the arena of "women"; Gordis 1955: 274; Fox 1999:
270). The ל-PP/infinitive clause is a purpose adjunct to מצאתי, having
חשבון as its complement.

אָמְרָ֖ה קֹהֶ֑לֶת. *Qatal* 3fs Qal √אמר. The fs verb bothers commentators, and many suggest that the words were misdivided (see, e.g., GKC
§122r and Gordis 1955: 274; Fox 1999: 269). In light of אמר הקהלת
in 12:8, we tentatively agree. If so, the article on הקהלת reflects the narrator's overt intrusion into the text, in which he refers to Qoheleth as
a third party. The complement of the speech verb (ה)אמר is the clause
that surrounds it, ראה זה מצאתי ... אחת לאחת למצא חשבן. The placement of the quotative frame in the middle of the direct speech is rare but
attested (see comment on 1:2).

7:28 אֲשֶׁ֛ר עֽוֹד־בִּקְשָׁ֥ה נַפְשִׁ֖י וְלֹ֣א מָצָ֑אתִי אָדָ֞ם אֶחָ֤ד מֵאֶ֙לֶף֙ מָצָ֔אתִי וְאִשָּׁ֥ה בְכָל־אֵ֖לֶּה לֹ֥א מָצָֽאתִי׃

(The one) whom my soul sought continually I did not find. One man out of a thousand I found but "a woman" among all these I did not find.

Qoheleth does not specify what kind of person he is seeking. Fox (1999: 270–71) surveys the proposals and argues that the key is the use of אדם (vs. איש) and the contrast is between humans and beasts. That is, Qoheleth is searching for a "real human," but finds only one in every thousand, the remainder being nothing more than "dumb beasts." Seow argues that a misogynistic meaning is hard to avoid (1997: 273). If האשה in v. 26 is a personified allusion to folly, we would reasonably also expect an allusion to wisdom personified at this point. And yet, it would be folly for us to say that we see clearly how all the pieces fit together in Qoheleth's argument here.

אֲשֶׁר עוֹד־בִּקְשָׁה נַפְשִׁי וְלֹא מָצָאתִי. *Qatal* 3fs Piel √בקש and 1cs Qal √מצא. Seow takes this as two disjunctively coordinated clauses, "the one whom ... but I didn't find" (1997: 251, 264); however, this produces a sentence fragment. Thus, it is better to take this as an instance of topic-fronting, with the null-head relative clause functioning as the fronted complement of the verb מצאתי. The ו simply marks a phrasal edge and in such cases aids in the processing of the fronted phrase by demarcating it from the rest of the clause (see, e.g., 2 Kgs 16:14 וְאֶת־הַמִּזְבַּח הַנְּחֹשֶׁת אֲשֶׁר לִפְנֵי יְהוָה וַיַּקְרֵב מֵאֵת פְּנֵי הַבַּיִת, where the fronted complement ... את המזבח is separated from the clause to which it belongs by the ו on ויקרב; see Holmstedt 2013d, 2014; cf. JM §176g–l). There is no good reason to emend the אשר to אשה with Fox (1999: 270; 2004: 52; see also Fox and Porten), since the null head can be reconstructed from the following context. Within the relative clause, the adverb עוד is an adjunct to the bivalent בקשה. Its subject is נפשי, and the missing complement is null and coreferential with the null relative head. Similarly, the null relative head is also the null complement of bivalent מצאתי in the clause ולא מצאתי, which continues within the scope of the relative אשר.

אָדָם אֶחָד מֵאֶלֶף מָצָאתִי. *Qatal* 1cs Qal √מצא. The NP אדם אחד, which is the complement of the bivalent מצאתי, is focus-fronted in order to contrast the results of Qoheleth's search (presumably for a worthy man) with natural expectations—only one out a thousand? Qoheleth has set his bar high. Following the אדם אחד is a second focus-fronted constituent, the PP מאלף. This follows the highly constrained quantified phrase, "1 X," with the startlingly high pool, "out of 1000 X." Finding one worthy man out of 10 or 100 would not be so bad, but only 1 out of 1000 is a discouraging result. (On multiple focus-fronting, see Holmstedt 2009: 135–37.)

וָאִשָּׁה בְכָל־אֵלֶּה לֹא מָצָאתִי. *Qatal* 1cs Qal √מצא. As in the
preceding clause, the initial NP אשה is the fronted complement of the
bivalent verb מצאתי. However, this NP is not fronted for focus, but as
a topic, to signal the switch from discussing אדם to אשה. The contrast,
and so the high point of the assertion, is presented with the focus-fronted
PP בכל אלה. One might expect that for the worthy men that Qoheleth
discovered, there was an equal number of worthy women, But not so!,
says Qoheleth, and he drives this home by the focused בכל אלה and the
negated identical verb.

7:29   לְבַד רְאֵה־זֶה מָצָאתִי אֲשֶׁר עָשָׂה הָאֱלֹהִים אֶת־
       הָאָדָם יָשָׁר וְהֵמָּה בִקְשׁוּ חִשְּׁבֹנוֹת רַבִּים:

*Only, see—this I found, that God made man (to be) straightforward but
they seek many schemes.*

Qoheleth ironically notes that the conclusion he has drawn at this
stage of his investigation is that God did not create man to carry out
investigations like this. This also fits into the notion that some types or
forms of knowledge have been withheld from humans (e.g., Job 28; Prov
30; and Gen 2–3).

לְבַד רְאֵה־זֶה מָצָאתִי. Impv ms Qal √ראה and *qatal* 1cs Qal √מצא.
The adverbial PP לבד "alone, only" is most often combined with a clitic
pronoun, e.g., לבדו "by himself"; when it is used without a clitic pronoun, it is bound to a following PP (e.g., Isa 26:13 לְבַד־בְּךָ; though it is
more commonly followed by מן for the sense of "apart from, except").
When לבד is used in its free form (e.g., Judg 7:5 תַּצִּיג אוֹתוֹ לְבָד "you shall
set him aside"), it is an adjunct to the verb indicating resultative manner.
Only here does לבד begin a clause and appear not to be bound. But what
verb does it modify? It makes little sense with ראה, since "only see" or
"see alone" is hard to decipher here. But it does make some sense with the
clause that contains מצאתי, either as a restrictive adverb for the subject,
"I alone found this," or, more likely in this context, as an adverb restrict-
ing the complement זה, "I have found this alone." However, it is syntactically impossible to jump over ראה to connect לבד with the following
clause. Gordis (1955: 170) translates לבד as a conjunction, "Besides, …,"
but he gives no support. Similarly, Fox (1999: 265; 271–72) notes the
unique usage and translates לבד as "Only, see, …"; this suggests לבד is
an adversative or exceptive conjunction, similar to "but" or "except" (so

also Seow 1997: 265, though the verse references Seow provides for לבד
are irrelevant for this example). Given that the use of לבד in this verse is
unique in the Hebrew Bible, and since it makes little sense as an adjunct
in either clause, we hesitantly follow the conjunctive analysis of Fox and
Seow. The imperative ראה functions less as a verb and more like the
deictic exclamative הנה (see also v. 27); as such, its bivalency goes unfulfilled. The demonstrative זה is the complement of the bivalent מצאתי;
moreover, זה is focus-fronted ("*this* I have found …") and cataphorically
points to Qoheleth's conclusion (the conclusion that was pointed to by
the זה in v. 27 but delayed until here).

אֲשֶׁר עָשָׂה הָאֱלֹהִים אֶת־הָאָדָם יָשָׁר. *Qatal* 3ms Qal √עשׂה.
The אשר clause is appositional to זה; the אשר nominalizes the clause
so that it can stand in apposition to the demonstrative, which fills a
nominal syntactic position (see also 8:11, 12; 9:1). Within the אשר
clause, the complement of the bivalent עשׂה is a small clause, "God
made [man (to be) straight]," with ECM on the first complement,
את האדם (see above, v. 26). Fox argues that ישׁר here is not a moral
quality ("upright") but "intellectual directness or simplicity" (1999:
272); however, in wisdom literature ישׁר frequently bears moral connotations, and even in the context of chapter 7, there is much moral
language—vv. 15-17, 20, 25, 26.

וְהֵמָּה בִקְשׁוּ חִשְּׁבֹנוֹת רַבִּים. *Qatal* 3cp Piel √בקשׁ. The pronoun
is for focus and contrasts the intentions of God (for man to be upright)
with the desires and actions of humans (to seek solutions or explanations). Though the noun חשׁבון has a feminine ending in the plural, the
singular form and the modification here by mp רבים indicate that it is a
masculine noun for agreement purposes. It is not uncommon to find the
plural ending ות- on nouns that are otherwise masculine (GKC §87p;
JM §90d).

8:1-15 On Human Power

Thematically, chapter 8 is held together by its reflection on human power
over other humans (v. 9). Verses 1-9 treat kingly power and vv. 10-15
discuss the problem of retribution expected for evil people. Nevertheless,
the chapter is connected with the preceding discussion of knowledge at
both the beginning (v. 1) and the conclusion (vv. 16-17).

Verse 1a is treated as concluding the preceding chapter by some (so
Whybray, 128; Fox 1999: 272) and as introducing the section on royal

power (vv. 1-9) by others (e.g., Crenshaw, 149). The chapter begins with
an irony (that though wisdom is illuminating, some things cannot be
illumined), and it proceeds to test cases: how to deal with monarchs can
be figured out (vv. 2-6), but little else can.

$$\text{מִי כְּהֶחָכָם וּמִי יוֹדֵעַ פֵּשֶׁר דָּבָר חָכְמַת אָדָם} \quad 8{:}1$$
$$\text{תָּאִיר פָּנָיו וְעֹז פָּנָיו יְשֻׁנֶּא:}$$

Who is like the wise, and who knows a matter's interpretation? A man's
wisdom will illumine his face, and the "strength" of his face will be (thus)
changed.

The first half of this verse connects to the problem of what can be
known (chap. 7), while the second part, though not entirely clear, points
to the positive benefits of wisdom. The metaphorical meaning of illumination of a king's face as his favor (Prov 16:15) helps create a connection
between the illumination of a wise man's face here and the challenge of
negotiating the presence (lit. "face") of the king that follows.

מִי כְּהֶחָכָם. A null copula interrogative clause with subject-complement order. As it stands the text reads "Who is like the wise man?" Some
commentators prefer to redivide the Hebrew consonants to read מי כה
חכם "Who is thus wise?," still a null copula clause but with an adverb
between the copula and subject (Seow 1997: 277; Fox 1999: 272). This
proposed, very slight emendation avoids the unusual nonsyncopation
of the ה after the preposition כ; however, the ה is not syncopated in a
number of examples, especially in texts typically dated to the later Second Temple period (see GKC §35n; JM §35e).

מִי יוֹדֵעַ פֵּשֶׁר דָּבָר. A null copula and Participle ms Qal √ידע as the
copular complement. The interrogative מי is the subject and the bound
phrase פשר דבר is the NP complement of the participle. The lack of an
article is only a problem if one thinks that the bound phrase in English—
i.e., "an interpretation of a matter," is not as contextually appropriate as
"the interpretation of a matter." In contrast to English, it is not grammatical to have a cliticized noun marked for definiteness without marking the host noun; to do this in Hebrew requires using the possessive ל
rather than the bound construction; i.e., הַפֵּשֶׁר לְדָבָר (see WO §9.7; JM
§130). The noun פשר occurs only here in the Hebrew texts of the Bible;
it also occurs thirty-four times in the Aramaic sections of Daniel (Dan
2:4-7, 9, 16, 24-26, 30, 36, 45; 4:3-4, 6, 15-16, 21; 5:7-8, 12, 15-17,

26; 7:16). The Hebrew cognate פתר is used nine times in the Joseph
narrative (Gen 40:8, 16, 22; 41:8, 12-13, 15). The noun פשר becomes a
prominent literary-hermeneutical type in the Dead Sea Scrolls.

חָכְמַת אָדָם תָּאִיר פָּנָיו. *Yiqtol* (realis) 3fs Hiph √אור. The subject-verb order is expected for a main, realis clause. The NP פניו is
the complement of the bivalent verb (in BH the word "face" is always
morphologically plural; consequently, the clitic 3ms pronoun is the
one attached to plural forms). The imperfective *yiqtol* is generic. As it
frequently functions in Proverbs (see Cook 2005), the *yiqtol* presents a
predictive perspective, generic sense here: wisdom holds promise to illu-
minate the face of a wise person (cf. English *Boys will be boys*).

וְעֹז פָּנָיו יְשֻׁנֶּא. *Yiqtol* (realis) 3ms Pual √שנא (a by-form of שנה).
The final א for the expected final ה also occurs with this root in 2 Kgs
25:29 and Lam 4:1 and also in Ben Sira 13:25. The vocalization of the
final syllable suggests that the Masoretes also understood the form to be a
variant spelling of שנה: the *segol* is appropriate to the III-ה root, whereas
a true III-א root would have a *qames*. Confusion between III-ה and III-
א roots in the writing conventions (GKC §§23, 75nn–rr) becomes more
common in the later Second Temple period (see Sáenz-Badillos 1993:
124, 129; JM §§24fa, 79l). Some argue for emending the verb ישנא to
a Piel and adding the 3ms pronominal suffix (יְשַׁנֶּאנּוּ) by moving the difficult אני from the beginning of v. 2 and taking the א as dittography. The
reconstructed phrase would be עֹז פָּנָיו יְשַׁנֶּאנּוּ "the 'strength' of his face
will change him" (see, e.g., Seow 1997: 278–79; Fox 1999: 276; others
translate as a Piel but do not note it, e.g., Crenshaw, 148–49; Longman,
209). The phrase עז פנים "strong of face" is idiomatic for impudence;
although here in Ecclesiastes the noun עז is used instead of the adjective
עַז, the context suggests the same meaning.

אֲנִי פִּי־מֶלֶךְ שְׁמֹור וְעַל דִּבְרַת שְׁבוּעַת אֱלֹהִים: 8:2

*As for me, a king's command obey, that is, according to the manner of an
oath (to) God.*

In this verse Qoheleth intrudes with his own perspective, indicating
that while much in life is not discernible, appropriate behavior toward
the king is. One must obey his commands with the same diligence that
one fulfills one's oaths to God.

אֲנִי פִּי־מֶלֶךְ שְׁמוֹר. Impv ms Qal √שמר. The initial 1cs pronoun
is out of place. It cannot be the subject of the imperative, which encodes
only second-person deixis. Moreover, the sequence אני פי־מלך cannot be
a null copula clause for two reasons: (1) "I am the mouth of the king"
is contextually nonsensical, and (2) פי־המלך is the only available NP
to be the complement of bivalent שמור. Some take אני as a scribal mistake, suggesting that it be moved and rewritten as the clitic pronoun on
the verb ישנא in v. 1 or as the object marker את (see comment above;
see Seow 1997: 278–79 for a summary of proposals). Gordis suggests
that a parallel exists in rabbinic literature "where the first-person pronoun introduces a statement without a verb," and so he takes אני here as
short for "I *declare*" (1955: 278). Seow objects that the Talmud passage
requires the pronoun to specify one speaker ("I") among many in the
context, whereas this passage in Ecclesiastes lacks that need; however, his
objection is founded upon the failure to recognize the "I-and-my-לב"
framework (see Introduction). The לב has been most recently invoked
in 7:25 and will be mentioned again in 8:9. Thus, we take Gordis to be
fundamentally correct in his interpretation, though rather than assuming
a verb of speaking, we take the syntax to be that of a fronted adjunct orienting the speaker to the perspective from which the following opinion
proceeds. On the use of פי (lit. "mouth of") as "command," see Num
14:41; 22:18; 24:13; Deut 1:26, 43; 9:23; 1 Sam 12:14, 15; 15:24;
1 Kgs 13:21, 26; see also HALOT, s.v.

וְעַל דִּבְרַת שְׁבוּעַת אֱלֹהִים. This PP is in apposition to the fronted
NP complement פי המלך. It is a type of apposition that could not
replace the anchor noun but rather clarifies it. The preposition על here
is used to express a norm, "in accordance with" (WO §11.2.13e; MNK
§39.19.4ii), and the bound NP דברת refers to the "manner" of its clitic
host שבעת אלהים. On the use of cliticization (i.e, the construct relation)
in שבעת אלהים for the "genitive of a mediated object" (i.e., "oath [made
to] God"), see WO §9.5.2; MNK §25.4.5.

8:3　אַל־תִּבָּהֵל מִפָּנָיו תֵּלֵךְ אַל־תַּעֲמֹד בְּדָבָר רָע כִּי
כָּל־אֲשֶׁר יַחְפֹּץ יַעֲשֶׂה׃

Don't panic because of him—leave! Don't stand (around) during a bad
word, because everything that he desires he does.

Verses 3-4 are an exhortation to respond appropriately to the king because his power is absolute and unquestionable (like God's). Although one cannot know how the powerful monarch will ultimately wield his authority, one can behave wisely in his presence when he is angry.

אַל־תִּבָּהֵל מִפָּנָיו תֵּלֵךְ. Jussive 2ms Niph √בהל; *yiqtol* 2ms Qal √הלך. In the Niphal the verb בהל normally means "to be horrified, dismayed, or panicked," although HALOT also provides a second sense for the Niphal, "to make haste" (however, the only places cited are Eccl 8:3 and Prov 28:22; see HALOT, s.v.; DCH, s.v.). For this verse, then, one might consider emending to Piel or simply taking the Niphal of בהל to be semantically equivalent to the Piel (as in 5:1; 7:9), i.e., "don't *hurry* concerning … ." However, since this verbal root already occurs in Ecclesiastes twice in the Piel, with the sense of "hurry," one wonders why the Niphal stem should be used here with that same sense. As well, in the context of advice concerning how to deal with a king, "being panicked" makes fine sense, since it is natural to feel anxiety or even fear in the presence of such power (see Seow 1997: 280). The compound preposition מפני introduces an adjunct that provides the source of anxiety—in this case, the king himself (as the antecedent of the 3ms clitic pronoun). The semantics of the prefix form תֵּלֵךְ are volitional or modal: "Leave!/You should/shall leave!"

אַל־תַּעֲמֹד בְּדָבָר רָע. Jussive 2ms Qal √עמד. The verb עמד (normally with the sense "to stand up" but here "to stand still, stay, stick around") is typically bivalent, with a locative NP or PP complement. Here the complement appears to be the ב-PP, though it is not strictly locative but temporal. On the temporal use of ב, see WO §11.2.5c; MNK §39.6.2. The expression of the time frame in which this event is positioned is best expressed by English "during." The denotation of דבר רע is clear, "a bad word," but its connotation may be something more along the lines of a king's negative response to an event, report, or official's poor performance, hence more like "a (king's) angry response." This also fits the context of דבר רע in v. 5. The point of this caution, then, is that it is not wise to hang around while a king chastises another official in case you are accidentally caught within the scope of the king's anger.

כִּי כָּל־אֲשֶׁר יַחְפֹּץ יַעֲשֶׂה. *Yiqtol* (realis) 3ms Qal √חפץ and √עשה. The כי clause provides the motivation for the preceding two negative instructions. Within the כי clause, the second verb יעשה is the main verb and the preceding verb יחפץ is within the embedded אשר clause headed

by the quantifier כל, all of which is the complement of bivalent יעשה
(so "he does x" where x = "all that he desires"). As a restrictive relative
clause, the אשר יחפץ crucially narrows the referent for the כל that the
king does; i.e., he does not do everything *simpliciter*, but "everything
that he desires." The saying clearly implies that one should avoid any
confrontation involving a king, not only because one does not know how
the king will respond but also because his position of power allows him
to respond severely, and because such a response may well spill over to
include those who are simply bystanders.

8:4   בַּאֲשֶׁר דְּבַר־מֶלֶךְ שִׁלְטוֹן וּמִי יֹאמַר־לוֹ מַה־
תַּעֲשֶׂה:

Because a king's word is power, and who dares to say to him, "What are
you doing?"

The power of the king is described here in terms reminiscent of
God's power and sovereignty (see Job 9:12; Sir 39:17, 21). Such realities
provide the motivation to exercise great caution in the king's presence.

בַּאֲשֶׁר דְּבַר־מֶלֶךְ שִׁלְטוֹן. A null copula clause that begins with a
causal ב (WO §11.2.5e) and a nominalizer אשר, which allows the ב to
take as its clitic host a full clause (whereas it typically requires a noun
phrase, infinitive construct, or pronominal suffix as its host). The subject
is the bound NP דבר־מלך, and the copular complement is שלטון. The
causal ב continues the motivation for the negative instructions in the
preceding verse. Why the causal ב is used instead of a second כי clause
is unclear, unless one should read with LXX כַּאֲשֶׁר (καθὼς). For discussion of the difficulty in transmission of באשר/כאשר in Ecclesiastes, see
Goldman's comments in the BHQ *Megilloth* fascicle (82*). The indefinite bound NP דבר־מלך might be better rendered "the word of a king"
instead of "a word of a king," but see comment at 8:1 regarding how it
is not grammatical in Hebrew to have a (semantically) definite cliticized
noun without marking the host noun as definite.

וּמִי יֹאמַר־לוֹ מַה־תַּעֲשֶׂה. *Yiqtol* (irrealis) 3ms *Qal* √אמר and *yiqtol*
(realis) 2ms *Qal* √עשׂה. In the higher clause, the interrogative מי is the
subject and the PP לו is an adjunct providing the speech recipient. The
clause מה תעשה is the unmarked direct speech complement of יאמר. In
the subordinate speech clause, the interrogative מה is the complement
of bivalent תעשה, and the subject is the null addressee (marked by the

2ms inflection and contextually supplied as the king). The verb יאמר in the higher interrogative clause is best interpreted as irrealis, but the precise nuance is ambiguous: it may express dynamic modality ("who can say") or more likely a sense closest to the English semi-modal "dare" (see Cook 2013: 337). The irrealis mood of the verb notwithstanding, the subject-verb order is required by the interrogative, since interrogatives are almost always fronted for focus. The verb within the reported speech clause appears realis and reflects the durative semantics of the imperfective (Cook 2013: 336–37).

8:5   שׁוֹמֵר מִצְוָה לֹא יֵדַע דָּבָר רָע וְעֵת וּמִשְׁפָּט יֵדַע
לֵב חָכָם:

He who keeps a commandment will not know a bad word, and a wise mind knows a time and a judgment,

The point of this verse is that, while the order of creation may not be accessible, figuring out how monarchs behave is (contra Seow 1997: 281). The observant and intelligent person should be able to determine when, where, and how to speak (or not!).

שׁוֹמֵר מִצְוָה לֹא יֵדַע דָּבָר רָע. Participle ms Qal √שמר and *yiqtol* (realis) 3ms *Qal* √ידע. The participle שׁוֹמֵר is often substantivized as an agentive noun "guard"; however, such an analysis is prohibited here since the participle has a complement, the NP מצוה, which fulfills the bivalency of שמר (see comment at 1:15). Thus, the syntax is that of a null-head, unmarked relative clause, in which the null copula takes the participle as its complement, "(he who is) keeping ... ." The word order is subject-negative-verb, which departs from the norm of most BH. The subject may be fronted for focus: it is *this type* of person (and *only* this type) that will be able to escape life's messes on a regular basis. Or the subject-negative-verb order reflects a further shift in the subject-verb typology of the book's language (see Introduction §§2D, 6). The meaning of ידע here probably reflects the sense of "to know through experience" (see also 1:17; 6:5; 7:25; 8:16; and possibly the second occurrence in 9:5). The meaning of דבר רע is likely the same as in v. 3—a negative (if not angry) response from a ruler. The implicit advice of the gnomic statement is clear and simple—if you do what you are told, you will not get in trouble with the king. The generic ידע both here and in the following clause can be rendered by an English future or present construction (our translation illustrates the ambiguity), since in Ecclesiastes the *yiqtol* and participle are used more frequently than the *qatal* with stative predicates to express present states (see Cook 2012).

וְעֵת וּמִשְׁפָּט יֵדַע לֵב חָכָם . *Yiqtol* (realis) 3ms *Qal* √ידע. The complement-verb-subject order reflects the focus-fronting of the NP complement (contra Seow 1997: 281) followed by the triggered raising of the verb over the subject. The focus-marking reinforces all that has just been said—if nothing else, the wise man should know עת ומשפט! Fox interprets this expression to be a hendiadys, likely with the sense of "the time and the right way" or "the right time" (see Fox 2004: 55). Seow, however, rightly points out that in the other four occurrences of משפט in Ecclesiastes (3:16; 5:7; 11:9; 12:14), it has the sense of "judgment" or "justice," and that Qoheleth, rather than stating that one knows the proper time of things (he avers that we cannot), asserts "that everyone knows that there is 'time and judgment' (v 6), but no one knows when and how God will act (v 7)" (Seow 1997: 281). The complement עת ומשפט consists of two coordinated NPs, which are further explicated by the four appositional complement clauses in vv. 6-7 (so also Seow 1997: 281).

כִּי לְכָל־חֵפֶץ יֵשׁ עֵת וּמִשְׁפָּט כִּי־רָעַת הָאָדָם רַבָּה עָלָיו: 8:6

that for every matter there is a time and a judgment; that the man's evil is severely upon him;

Verses 6-8 present four clarifying appositives to what the לב חכם knows in v. 5 (עת ומשפט).

כִּי לְכָל־חֵפֶץ יֵשׁ עֵת וּמִשְׁפָּט. A יש copula clause. The initial ל-PP complement is fronted for focus to assert that there is עת ומשפט for *everything* (nothing is excepted). The coordinated subject NPs עת ומשפט repeat the fronted complement of v. 5b and provide the explicit lexical link supporting the analysis of this and the following three כי clauses as appositional. Thus כי functions as a complementizer (or nominalizer) in all four clauses in vv. 6-7 (WO §38.8; JM §157a, c–ca).

כִּי־רָעַת הָאָדָם רַבָּה עָלָיו. The second appositional complement clause—a null copula clause with normal subject-complement order.

The subject is the bound NP רעת האדם, the copular complement is the fs adj רבה, and the על PP with clitic 3ms pronoun is an adjunct.

8:7 כִּי־אֵינֶנּוּ יֹדֵעַ מַה־שֶּׁיִּהְיֶה כִּי כַּאֲשֶׁר יִהְיֶה מִי יַגִּיד לֽוֹ׃

that he does not know whatever will be; that when it will be who can tell him?

This verse transitions from the specific, discernible case of dealing with monarchs back to the rest of life, for which patterns are generally opaque.

כִּי־אֵינֶנּוּ יֹדֵעַ מַה־שֶּׁיִּהְיֶה. An אין negative copula clause, Participle ms Qal √ידע, and *yiqtol* 3ms Qal √היה. In the אין clause, the clitic 3ms pronoun is the subject and the participle ידע is the copular complement. The verb ידע is bivalent and takes the free relative clause as its complement (on שׁ מה free relatives, see discussion at 1:9). The verb היה here (and in v. 7b) does not function as a copula (as it typically does, in which case it would be bivalent); rather it is existential and monovalent.

כִּי כַּאֲשֶׁר יִהְיֶה מִי יַגִּיד לֽוֹ. *Yiqtol* (realis) 3ms *Qal* √היה and *yiqtol* (irrealis) Hiph √נגד. The fourth appositional complement clause. Within the כי clause, the initial כאשר, which represents a temporal כ with a nominalizing אשר (see comment on באשר in v. 4), presents a temporal clause that appears to be a complement of the verb יגיד within the following interrogative clause. Normally interrogatives like מי are at the front of clauses since the open variables they present often carry focus-marking. However, here the כאשר clause is higher than the interrogative מי. This suggests a topic-focus structure (all within the domain of the כי)—the topic כאשר clause orients the listener to the relevant variable (when) and the focus follows with the assertive and rhetorically contrastive מי. The question is rhetorical since the wise person understands that *no one* can provide this information. The כאשר is the complement of יגיד, indicating the content of the report. The irrealis יגיד expresses dynamic (ability) modality here. The PP לו is the second complement of trivalent יגיד, specifying the recipient of the report.

אֵין אָדָם שַׁלִּיט בָּרוּחַ לִכְלוֹא אֶת־הָרוּחַ וְאֵין   8:8
שִׁלְטוֹן בְּיוֹם הַמָּוֶת וְאֵין מִשְׁלַחַת בַּמִּלְחָמָה וְלֹא־
יְמַלֵּט רֶשַׁע אֶת־בְּעָלָיו:

No man is a ruler over the wind in order to contain the wind, and control over the day of death does not exist, nor does release in war exist, and wickedness cannot save its owner.

This verse follows logically from the observation of the previous verse, that one does not know what the future holds: lack of knowledge translates into lack of control over one's life. The use of שׁלטון only here and in v. 4, in reference to the king, suggests that the subject אדם includes both the wise man (the focus of vv. 5-7) and the king: despite his power, the king is no different from the rest of mortals, who have no control over the future (see Krüger, 156).

אֵין אָדָם שַׁלִּיט בָּרוּחַ לִכְלוֹא אֶת־הָרוּחַ. An אין negative copula clause, Inf Constr Qal √כלא. The subject is אדם and the copular complement is שׁליט. The ב-PP is an NP-internal adjunct to the adjective שׁליט and so narrows what type of שׁליט activity is under discussion. The ל-PP/ infinitive clause is a purpose adjunct.

וְאֵין שִׁלְטוֹן בְּיוֹם הַמָּוֶת. Another אין negative existential clause with שׁלטון as the subject and the PP ביום המות as a NP-internal adjunct for שׁלטון. The existential clause indicates what kind of man does not exist. The ב-PP should be understood as having a metaphorical-locative sense in conjunction with שׁלטון: "power/control over." There is an implicit comparison with the preceding אין clause by their juxtaposition: one can as well have power to restrain the wind as have control over the day of one's death (so Fox 1999: 280).

וְאֵין מִשְׁלַחַת בַּמִּלְחָמָה. A third אין clause, and the second existential clause, with the same structure as the preceding one. The ב-PP should be understood temporally: in/at (the time) of battle" (WO §11.2.5c; JM §133c). Most commentators interpret מׁשלחת etymologically (i.e., as "dispatch"; "release" from שלח "to send"), and relate the passage to the Deuteronomic legislation about release from battle (Deut 20:5-7) and the curse of being denied that release to enjoy one's wife, house, and vineyard (Deut 28:30; so Whybray, 133; Crenshaw, 152; Longman, 214; Fox 1999: 281). Seow (1997: 282) argues that מׁשלחת,

which occurs only here and Ps 78:49, should be understood as "deputa-
tion" based on the LXX rendering ἀποστολή in both instances. Hence,
one cannot send a "substitute" in one's place on the day of battle, as
Seow argues was a common practice in the Persian period. Gordis (1955:
291) interprets the expression as elliptical "sending forth (the hand)" as
an alternative expression of power. We follow the majority approach,
interpreting משלחת as "dismissal," though all these views amount to the
unavoidability of battle on its day, best understood as an allusion to the
battle against death (Murphy, 84; Bartholomew, 283).

וְלֹא־יְמַלֵּט רֶשַׁע אֶת־בְּעָלָיו. *Yiqtol* 3ms Piel √מלט. The verb-subject order is triggered by the negative. The Piel מלט is bivalent and so the
NP בעליו is the complement. The switch from the אין copula clauses is
motivated by the need/desire to describe an event rather than a quality
or characteristic. The NP בעליו has a clitic 3ms pronoun, which is coreferential with the subject רשע. In Hebrew the expression "master of x"
refers to a person characterized by the quality of the second NP, as in בעל
החלמות "master of dreams, dreamer" (Gen 37:19). So here, "the master
of it (wickedness)" implies the "one who is wicked." The point is in keeping with Proverbs, where the consequences of wickedness are inescapable
(Prov 1:19), but righteousness and wisdom save one from (premature)
death (Prov 10:2; 11:4).

8:9   אֶת־כָּל־זֶה רָאִיתִי וְנָתוֹן אֶת־לִבִּי לְכָל־מַעֲשֶׂה
אֲשֶׁר נַעֲשָׂה תַּחַת הַשָּׁמֶשׁ עֵת אֲשֶׁר שָׁלַט הָאָדָם
בְּאָדָם לְרַע לוֹ:

I have seen all of this (while) setting my לב *to every deed that happens*
under the sun, a time when the man rules over (another) man—to his
misfortune.

This verse ties together the first portion of this chapter (vv. 1-9) in
a reflection on the bad result of humans having power over one another,
exemplified in the power of a king.

אֶת־כָּל־זֶה רָאִיתִי. *Qatal* 1cs Qal √ראה. The complement of ראיתי
is fronted for focus as a summary reflection on the preceding observations (כל־זה).

וְנָתֹ֫ון אֶת־לִבִּ֫י לְכָל־מַעֲשֶׂה. Inf Abs Qal √נתן. The infinitive absolute functions almost as a serial verb with an adverbial sense of accompanying activity: "(while) giving …" (see Cook 2013: 322 and notes on infinitive absolute in 4:2 and 9:11; see also Screnock and Holmstedt on Esth 9:1). In the course of his investigation, Qoheleth observes the preceding (vv. 1-8) with respect to humans having power over each other. The trivalent נתן takes two complements: here the first is marked by אֶת and the other marked by ל.

אֲשֶׁר נַעֲשֶׂה תַּחַת הַשֶּׁמֶשׁ. *Qatal* 3ms Niph √עשׂה. The head of the relative clause is the preceding לְכָל־מעשׂה, which functions as the resumptive null-subject of נעשׂה. On this verb, see 1:9, and on the phrase, cf. 1:13-14; 4:3; and 9:6.

עֵת אֲשֶׁר שָׁלַט הָאָדָם בְּאָדָם לְרַע לֹו. *Qatal* 3ms Qal √שלט. The עת is appositional to the preceding PP תחת השמשׁ, identifying "under the sun" as "a time" when one human has power over another to a bad end. The PP באדם is the complement of שלט, and the לרע PP is an adjunct of purpose or result. The final PP לו modifies the preceding לרע, designating precisely for whom this situation is a misfortune. The pronoun on the final לו PP is ambiguous, however, and could refer to האדם, who has power, or the באדם, who is under that power. A reference back to האדם may allude to the just retribution one may receive from one's actions (see Prov 1:19), but the latter option is more likely given the commonsense understanding that those under another's power are more likely to suffer ill, and that Qoheleth does not specifically denounce having power over another as an evil for which to receive retribution.

8:10 וּבְכֵ֫ן רָאִיתִי רְשָׁעִים קְבֻרִים וָבָ֫אוּ וּמִמְּקֹום קָדֹושׁ
יְהַלֵּ֫כוּ וְיִשְׁתַּכְּחוּ בָעִיר אֲשֶׁר כֵּן־עָשׂוּ גַּם־זֶה הָבֶל׃

And then I saw wicked people buried, and they used to come and go from a place of a holy one. But they would be forgotten in the city, who have acted justly. This, too, is a הבל,

This verse introduces a section on injustices (vv. 11-15), which reaches its climax in v. 14 with the repetitive reference to absurdity. Both the text and the interpretation of this verse are uncertain, but within the broader context of this section it is evident that the wicked are honored in life and death while the just are forgotten.

וּבְכֵן רָאִיתִי רְשָׁעִים קְבֻרִים. *Qatal* 1cs Qal √ראה and Participle mp Qal passive √קבר. The conjunction ובכן transitions to a new topic. This construction consisting of כֵּן (HALOT, כֵּן II; DCH כֵּן I) + ב + ו occurs here and in Esth 4:16 with a temporal sense "and then" or "and thereupon." The complement of ראיתי is the small clause רשעים קברים, in which רשעים is subject, and the passive participle is predicate but without a supporting copula (see 4:15; 7:21, 26, 29 for other "small clauses" in Ecclesiastes). The wicked were given "proper burial" (see above on 6:4).

וָבָאוּ וּמִמְּקוֹם קָדוֹשׁ יְהַלֵּכוּ. Irrealis *qatal* 3cp Qal √בוא and irrealis *yiqtol* 3mp Piel √הלך. The word order is awkward but not ungrammatical; the PP ממקום קדוש goes with both verbs and thus must be gapped from the first clause. Some commentators take the first word ובאו with the previous, emending to קְבָרִים מוּבָאִים "brought to (their) graves" based on the LXX (so Fox 1999: 282; Krüger, 158). Though this avoids the awkward word order in this clause, it does not substantially add to the idea of the wicked receiving proper burial in the previous, and so we retain the MT. The irrealis *qatal* and *yiqtol* convey habitual modality here (see Cook 2013: 337). The PP ממקום קדוש may refer to the temple or synagogue. It does not seem necessary (contra Krüger, 158) to emend to מְמָקוֹם to avoid the bound form before the adjective קדוש: the adjective modifies a null head "a holy (one)" = a deity. Some commentators see a connection to the possibility that high-status individuals may have been eulogized in either place before being carried to their burial (so Seow 1997: 285). However, interpreting in light of the larger context, it may be a reference to the impunity of the wicked even in the presence of the holy during their lifetime, which is followed by their proper burial. Thus a contrast is made with those mentioned in the following clause.

וְיִשְׁתַּכְּחוּ בָעִיר אֲשֶׁר כֵּן־עָשׂוּ. *Yiqtol* 3mp Hith √שכח and *qatal* 3cp Qal √עשׂה. Some emend וישתכחו "they would be forgotten" to וישתבחו "they would be praised" based on the LXX and other ancient versions (Crenshaw, 154; Longman, 218). We retain the MT with *yiqtol* functioning as future-in-the past expression (e.g., Gen 43:7, כִּי יֹאמַר "that he would say …"; if emended the *yiqtol* must be habitual "they would be praised"). The subject of the main verb וישתכחו is the null-head relative אֲשֶׁר כֵּן־עָשׂוּ, in which the complement of עשׂו precedes it (unlike the first occurrence of כן in v. 10, this is the adjective כן "right, just, correct"; HALOT כֵּן I, DCH כֵּן II). Thus, the contrast is between the wicked, who are remembered in burial, and those who act justly, who are forgotten. The wise man is similarly forgotten in the city (9:14), thus suggesting that the בעיר PP, adjunct to the main verb וישתכחו, merely identifies the geographic area where all this occurs, thus suggesting just censure of amnesia toward the just ones.

גַּם־זֶה הָבֶל. A null copula clause with זה as subject and הבל as complement introduced by the additive גם (see note in 1:11). The clause syntactically anchors the following, vv. 11-12a.

8:11   אֲשֶׁר אֵין־נַעֲשָׂה פִתְגָם מַעֲשֵׂה הָרָעָה מְהֵרָה עַל־
כֵּן מָלֵא לֵב בְּנֵי־הָאָדָם בָּהֶם לַעֲשׂוֹת רָע:

> *that a decision is not made quickly (regarding) the deed of evil, therefore
> the mind of humans is full within them to do evil;*

Verses 11-12a present two clauses that are in apposition to זה at the end of v. 10.

אֲשֶׁר אֵין־נַעֲשָׂה פִתְגָם מַעֲשֵׂה הָרָעָה מְהֵרָה. An אין negative and *qatal* 3ms Niphal √עשה. Since לא is the normal negative used with the perfect and אין with copular expressions, commentators suggest reading נעשה as the Niphal participle fs or repointed as the Niphal participle ms נַעֲשֶׂה (Murphy, 81; Seow 1997: 287; Fox 1999: 285). The subject of the verb is פתגם, a Persian loan word that occurs here and in Esth 1:20, suggesting a royal or court setting for the "decision." The adjunct phrase מעשה הרעה describes the matter with which the decision is made (see MNK §33.3iii; WO §10.2.2e for the so-called "accusative of specification"), but it does not seem necessary to read פתגם as a bound form (so in Esth 1:20, without any change in vocalization) to make sense of the adjunct phrase. The adverbial מהרה, despite the word order, modifies the main verb נעשה in its usual adverbial sense "quickly" (see Murphy, 81). The אשר nominalizes the clause in order to allow it to function as an appositive to clarify the intended content of the deictic זה in the phrase גם־זה הבל (see Holmstedt 2016: 380). Both here and in v. 12, the אשר appositions provide additional examples (related, of course, to the initial example in each context) of what is called הבל at the end of Eccl 8:10. Additional examples of אשר clauses in apposition to זה occur in Eccl 7:29; 9:1.

עַל־כֵּן מָלֵא לֵב בְּנֵי־הָאָדָם בָּהֶם לַעֲשׂוֹת רָע. *Qatal* 3ms Qal √מלא and Inf Constr Qal √עשה. The עַל־כֵּן introduces this as a conclusion that follows from the preceding remark about delayed decision/decree. The word order after the initial עַל־כֵּן is verb-subject, with the subject being the entire bound phrase לֵב בְּנֵי־הָאָדָם. The PP בָּהֶם, though redundant, makes the best sense referring back to the בְּנֵי־הָאָדָם of the subject phrase. The ל-PP infinitive clause לַעֲשׂוֹת רָע is the theme complement of מלא by metonymy: doing evil stands for *thoughts* about doing evil. The predicate complement of the bivalent infinitive is the substantival adjective רָע.

8:12 אֲשֶׁר חֹטֶא עֹשֶׂה רָע מְאַת וּמַאֲרִיךְ לוֹ כִּי גַם־
יוֹדֵעַ אָנִי אֲשֶׁר יִהְיֶה־טּוֹב לְיִרְאֵי הָאֱלֹהִים אֲשֶׁר
יִירְאוּ מִלְּפָנָיו:

*that a sinner does evil a hundred (times) and prolongs himself. Yet I also
know that wellness belongs to those who fear God—whom they should be
afraid of!*

This verse begins with an additional appositional clause to זֶה in v. 10, but the second portion, beginning with adversative כִּי, shifts to drawing a conclusion from the preceding observations (vv. 9-12a) on the fates of the just and unjust.

אֲשֶׁר חֹטֶא עֹשֶׂה רָע מְאַת וּמַאֲרִיךְ לוֹ. Two null copulas and Participles ms Qal √עשה and Hiph √ארך. The subject of both clauses is חטא, which shows the participle pattern, but functions as an agentive noun (see comment on 1:15). The noun רע is complement of עשה and the numeral מאה is an adverbial adjunct. The form מְאַת "is either a construct" (with פַּעַם "times" omitted), "or it may be an archaic absolute (cf. דַּעַת, יִרְאַת), and modify רָע" (Gordis 1968: 297). The second participle וּמַאֲרִיךְ has לוֹ as its complement here (similarly, Ps 129:3), referring back to the subject חטא. Most of the time, however, this verb has יום as a complement (see next verse) or an implied reflexive sense of "one's days" (see 7:15).

כִּי גַם־יוֹדֵעַ אָנִי. A null copula and Participle ms Qal √ידע. The כי is adversative, introducing an antithesis, and the fronted participle bears focus, which is signaled by the unexpected participle-pronoun word order as well as by the presence of the focus גם (כי) itself does not trigger inversion of copula clauses, including predicative participle clauses). Thus the clause sets up a stark contrast between what Qoheleth has *seen* (vv. 9-12a; note רָאִיתִי in v. 9) and what he *knows* (following). Isaksson (67), followed by Seow (1997: 288), and Longman (219) argue that Qoheleth uses the participle of ידע to cite other views, while retaining the *qatal* form to refer to his own found knowledge. While it is clear that Qoheleth uses the *qatal* with an inchoative sense "I have come to know" in some instances (see 1:17 and notes there), this view does not adequately address the 3ms *qatal* forms (4:13; 6:5; 7:22; 10:15), which constitute half the *qatal* forms in the book (the other four are 1cs, in 1:17; 2:14; 3:12, 14), nor the presence of *yiqtol* ידע in the book (8:5 [2×]; 9:12; 10:14; 11:2, 5), all which overlap in sense in some instances (i.e., a present state). Instead, the variation of present state encodings of ידע seems to be diachronically motivated (see Cook 2012). The contrast here need not be a contradiction to be solved by treating the statement as an "orthodox gloss" or understood as an admittance of counterexamples to his earlier observations (see Krüger, 160). Rather, Qoheleth struggles with what he knows (his expectations) and what he observes (see Bartholomew, 291), which often ends with his "coming to know" other truths (e.g., 1:17).

אֲשֶׁר יִהְיֶה־טּוֹב לְיִרְאֵי הָאֱלֹהִים. *Yiqtol* 3ms Qal √היה. The אשר marks the complement clause of the participle יודע. The word order is verb-subject following the אשר, and the complement of יהיה is לירִאי הָאלהים, expressing a possessive relationship. The stative adjective ירא functions as an agentive noun here, though its adjectival character is seen in the complementary relationship it has with האלהים, to which it is bound. As typical of generic expressions with *yiqtol* (see Cook 2005), this generic statement refers to eventualities.

אֲשֶׁר יִירְאוּ מִלְּפָנָיו. Irrealis *yiqtol* 3mp Qal √ירא. The head of the relative clause is the immediately preceding האלהים, resumed by the clitic 3ms pronoun on מלפניו. The subject is null, though inferred to be the earlier ירא, and the compound PP מלפניו is complement of the preceding verb. The irrealis sense suggests here deontic obligation: "whom they *ought* to fear."

8:13   וְטוֹב לֹא־יִהְיֶה לָרָשָׁע וְלֹא־יַאֲרִיךְ יָמִים כַּצֵּל אֲשֶׁר
אֵינֶנּוּ יָרֵא מִלִּפְנֵי אֱלֹהִים:

And wellness will not belong to the wicked person and he will not lengthen
days, as a shadow—(he) who does not have fear before God!

This verse presents a complementary view to the previous statement. Though grammatically not subordinated to the יודע אני of the
previous verse, the parallels with v. 12 suggest understanding this as the
continuation of Qoheleth's knowledge of how the world works (i.e.,
should work), over and against his observation to the contrary.

וְטוֹב לֹא־יִהְיֶה לָרָשָׁע. *Yiqtol* 3ms Qal √היה. This is the same structure with inverted meaning of the positive יהיה clause in the previous
verse: the subject is טוב and the complement לרשע, denoting ownership.
The verb is generic as in the previous verse, referring to eventualities.

וְלֹא־יַאֲרִיךְ יָמִים כַּצֵּל. *Yiqtol* 3ms Hiph √ארך. The subject is null,
understood to be the רשע in the previous clause. As per the usual pattern
for ארך, the complement is ימים here (cf. 8:12), with the PP כצל a comparative adjunct to the verb that underscores the negative dimension of
the expression (i.e., he will *not* lengthen his days just as a shadow does *not*
lengthen endlessly but disappears), in keeping with the consistent comparison of life with "shadow" to express transience of life (Pss 102:12;
109:23; 144:4; Job 14:2; Eccl 6:12; 1 Chr 29:15).

כַּצֵּל. As with 6:12 and 7:12, Wise argues that כצל in this verse is
again a calque on Aramaic בטלל. He divides the verse contrary to the
Masoretic טעמים, since כצל here has an אֶתְנַחְתָּא, and suggests that כצל
אשר functions like the conjunction "because, for": "The wicked man
will not experience good, nor will he have a long life, because he does
not fear God" (256). For the reasons given above at 6:12, we do not follow Wise here; the semantics of צל as "shadow" is entirely appropriate
without having to resort to his questionable analysis.

אֲשֶׁר אֵינֶנּוּ יָרֵא מִלִּפְנֵי אֱלֹהִים. An אין negative copula clause with
stative adjectival complement ירא. The relative has a null head implied
as the רשע, which is also the subject of יאריך, and is resumed in the
relative by the 3ms clitic pronoun on איננו. The entire null-head relative
clause, "he who does not have fear before God," could be analyzed as
a right-dislocation on the clausal edge, resuming רשע from the main
clause to make explicit the participant that was implicit in the immediately prior clause (see 2:21 for discussion of the function of right-
dislocation). The stative adjective ירא governs the complementary PP
מלפני אלהים, illustrating the fuzzy line between state and action/event
with stative verbs.

יֵשׁ־הֶבֶל אֲשֶׁר נַעֲשָׂה עַל־הָאָרֶץ אֲשֶׁר | יֵשׁ   8:14
צַדִּיקִים אֲשֶׁר מַגִּיעַ אֲלֵהֶם כְּמַעֲשֵׂה הָרְשָׁעִים וְיֵשׁ
רְשָׁעִים שֶׁמַּגִּיעַ אֲלֵהֶם כְּמַעֲשֵׂה הַצַּדִּיקִים אָמַרְתִּי
שֶׁגַּם־זֶה הָבֶל:

There is a הבל *that has happened on the earth, that there are righteous
people who (a thing) befalls them just like the deed of the wicked, and there
are wicked people who (a thing) befalls them like the deed of the righteous. I
say that this, too, is a* הבל!

The bookending of this verse with the repeated statement that this
is an absurdity suggests it is the central focus of this section (vv. 9-15),
with the focus turning to pleasure in the following verse over and against
the pursuit of, or concern with, justice in vv. 9-14.

יֵשׁ־הֶבֶל אֲשֶׁר נַעֲשָׂה עַל־הָאָרֶץ. A יש existential clause and *qatal*
3ms Qal √עשׂה. The subject is הבל, which is modified by the following
restrictive relative clause.

אֲשֶׁר | יֵשׁ צַדִּיקִים אֲשֶׁר מַגִּיעַ אֲלֵהֶם כְּמַעֲשֵׂה הָרְשָׁעִים. A יש
existential clause and Participle ms Hiph √נגע. The אשר nominalizes the
two following יש clauses so that they may be in apposition (as a compound nominalized NP) to the subject of the preceding יש clause, the
NP הבל. The two יש clauses that follow אשר are monovalent existential
clauses: "righteous people exist ... and wicked people exist." Each is then
modified by the following relative clauses. The אשר clause modifying
צדיקים has a null copula with complement participle מגיע. The 3mp
clitic pronoun on the PP אלהם refers back to the head of the relative
clause, צדיקים, while the subject is null ("a thing"). The final PP bound
phrase in the clause is adjunct to the participle, defining the standard of
"thing" that encounters the righteous. We can paraphrase it: "righteous
people exist upon whom befalls a thing according to what a deed of the
wicked people deserves."

וְיֵשׁ רְשָׁעִים שֶׁמַּגִּיעַ אֲלֵהֶם כְּמַעֲשֵׂה הַצַּדִּיקִים. A יש existential
clause and Participle ms Hiph √נגע. The structure is the same as the
previous clause, except the relative modifier of רשעים here is שׁ instead
of אשׁר (see Introduction §4). The focus in this and the preceding clause
is the existence of righteous and wicked people who meet with situations out of keeping with the expectations of the traditional retribution
principle.

אָמַ֫רְתִּי שֶׁגַּם־זֶה הָ֑בֶל .Qatal 1cs Qal √אמר. Given the present-
time predicates in this verse, the *qatal* is better interpreted as a present-
time performative judgment by Qoheleth (see also 6:3), as opposed to a
past-time report of his verdict, as in, for example, 9:16, which appears at
the end of a past-time anecdote. The שׁ marks the following null copula
clause as the complement of אמרתי with זה as subject and הבל as copular
complement. The גם functions as a conjunctive adverb, joining "this"
(זה) situation to previous ones that he has classified as הבל.

וְשִׁבַּ֫חְתִּי אֲנִי֙ אֶת־הַשִּׂמְחָ֔ה אֲשֶׁ֤ר אֵֽין־טוֹב֙ לָֽאָדָ֣ם   8:15
תַּ֣חַת הַשֶּׁ֗מֶשׁ כִּ֚י אִם־לֶאֱכֹ֣ל וְלִשְׁתּ֣וֹת וְלִשְׂמ֔וֹחַ
וְה֞וּא יִלְוֶ֣נּוּ בַעֲמָל֗וֹ יְמֵ֤י חַיָּיו֙ אֲשֶׁר־נָתַן־ל֣וֹ הָאֱלֹהִ֔ים
תַּ֖חַת הַשָּֽׁמֶשׁ׃

*I praised, I, happiness, (namely), that there is no good thing for man
under the sun but to eat and drink and be happy! It will accompany him in
his labor (during) the days of his life, which God has given him under the
sun.*

In the face of the absurdity of the known retribution principle and
the observed miscarriage of it in the world, Qoheleth turns to praise
pleasure in this verse. Similar to his conclusion to other sections (e.g.,
2:24; 6:12), Qoheleth's affirmation of pleasure reinforces the idea that he
cannot make sense out of the preceding topic: power and justice.

וְשִׁבַּ֫חְתִּי אֲנִי֙ אֶת־הַשִּׂמְחָ֔ה אֲשֶׁ֤ר אֵֽין־טוֹב֙ לָֽאָדָ֣ם תַּ֣חַת הַשֶּׁ֗מֶשׁ.
Qatal 1cs Piel √שבח and an אין negative copula clause. Though the verb-
subject order would normally signal that the verb was in a focus position,
here the postverbal 1cs pronoun is part of the "I-and-my לב" strategy
(see Introduction §3); thus, the 1cs pronoun is in a postverbal focus
phrase and signals that it is Qoheleth, not his לב, that is praising pleasure.
The complement of the verb follows, marked by את. The complement
"happiness" is elucidated by the אשר nominalized clause standing in
apposition to it. Within the אשר clause is a copula-subject-complement
order. The טוב subject and לאדם complement give a sense similar to the
negative-possessive construction in 8:13 (which, however, uses לא־יהיה
as copula). Here אין is more appropriate since eventualities are not being
referred to, but the current existence of certain things for man. The final
PP תחת השמש is adjunct to the copula אין.

כֵּי אִם־לֶאֱכֹל וְלִשְׁתּוֹת וְלִשְׂמֹחַ. Inf Constr Qal √אכל, √שתה, and √שמח. The construction is similar to 2:24, except that here infinitive clauses are used after the exceptive construction כי אם: "except to eat … ." This clause is still under the domain of the אשר from the preceding clause.

.וְהוּא יִלְוֶנּוּ בַעֲמָלוֹ יְמֵי חַיָּיו אֲשֶׁר־נָתַן־לוֹ הָאֱלֹהִים תַּחַת הַשָּׁמֶשׁ. *Yiqtol* 3ms Qal √לוה + 3ms clitic pronoun and *qatal* 3ms Qal √נתן. The subject of the *yiqtol* is the initial 3ms pronoun הוא, which most commentators take as referring to the pleasure of eating, drinking, and being happy, just enumerated. The fleeting opportunities for pleasure will accompany one in one's labor. Both the PP בעמלו and the NP ימי חייו are adjuncts to the main verb. The latter is best interpreted as temporal, denoting the time of this accompaniment. The relative clause introduced by אשר modifies the head חייו, which is resumed as the first null complement of trivalent נתן. The second complement is the indirect object PP לו, and האלהים is subject of נתן. The final PP תחת השמש is a locative adjunct to נתן.

8:16-17 A Reflection on the Experiment

Qoheleth reflects upon his experiment and the human condition in such a way that commentators are split on whether to connect the passage with the preceding material as a concluding reflection, or the following (chap. 9) as an introductory idea.

8:16   כַּאֲשֶׁר נָתַתִּי אֶת־לִבִּי לָדַעַת חָכְמָה וְלִרְאוֹת אֶת־
הָעִנְיָן אֲשֶׁר נַעֲשָׂה עַל־הָאָרֶץ כִּי גַם בַּיּוֹם וּבַלַּיְלָה
שֵׁנָה בְּעֵינָיו אֵינֶנּוּ רֹאֶה:

At (the time) that I set my לב to understand wisdom and to consider the business that has happened on the earth, indeed even during day and night he sees no sleep in his eyes,

Verse 16 is subordinate to the following verse, making a unit of the two.

כַּאֲשֶׁר נָתַתִּי אֶת־לִבִּי לָדַעַת חָכְמָה וְלִרְאוֹת אֶת־הָעִנְיָן אֲשֶׁר נַעֲשָׂה עַל־הָאָרֶץ. *Qatal* 1cs Qal √נתן, Inf Constr Qal √ידע and √ראה, and *qatal* 3ms Qal √עשה. The initial כאשר subordinates this verse to the following, specifically וראיתי in v. 17. The temporal sense comes from the כ preposition, whose complement is the null head of the relative אשר. The main verb of the relative clause is the trivalent נתתי, whose complements are the את-marked לבי and the coordinated infinitive clauses, each of which are bivalent with their complement immediately following. The second אשר modifies the immediately preceding הענין, which is resumed as the null-subject of נעשה.

כִּי גַם בַּיּוֹם וּבַלַּיְלָה שֵׁנָה בְּעֵינָיו אֵינֶנּוּ רֹאֶה. An אין negative copula clause and Participle ms Qal √ראה. This clause is parenthetical and introduced by an asseverative כי. The compound PP is fronted for focus (explicitly marked for focus not only by the word order but also by the function word גם) and highlights the lack of sleep both day and night; hence the placement of the two PPs at the front of the clause (see van der Merwe, 330) The expression to "see sleep in the eyes" is unique in the Bible but is paralleled by expressions in ancient Latin literature (see Murphy, 81). The pronoun on איננו is subject of the negative copula clause, and refers to the לב and its experience during the experiment. This understanding solves the dilemma of the referent of איננו addressed in less satisfying ways by the commentators: Fox (1999: 287–88) emends בעיניו to עיני to serve as subject of the clause ("my eyes see not sleep"); most understand the subject to be humanity generally or anticipating specifically האדם in the following verse as the subject; others transpose the clause into v. 17 (Seow 1997: 289; Lohfink, 110–11) or move ראיתי before the clause (Gordis 1955: 298).

וְרָאִיתִי אֶת־כָּל־מַעֲשֵׂה הָאֱלֹהִים כִּי לֹא יוּכַל   8:17
הָאָדָם לִמְצוֹא אֶת־הַמַּעֲשֶׂה אֲשֶׁר נַעֲשָׂה תַחַת־
הַשֶּׁמֶשׁ בְּשֶׁל אֲשֶׁר יַעֲמֹל הָאָדָם לְבַקֵּשׁ וְלֹא יִמְצָא
וְגַם אִם־יֹאמַר הֶחָכָם לָדַעַת לֹא יוּכַל לִמְצֹא:

I saw the whole work of God, that man is not able to "find out" the deed that has happened under the sun, because man toils to seek but does not find. Even if the wise man intended to understand, he could not "find (it) out."

Verse 16 is subordinate to this verse, which reflects on the human condition. Lohfink (110–11) argues for the importance of this verse in interpreting Ecclesiastes because it appears to equate the "whole work of God" with "the deed that has happened under the sun." However, according to our analysis (i.e., the כי-clause is appositional to the "whole work of God"), the two are not equated; rather the inability of humanity to "'find out' the deed what has happened under the sun" is simply one part of God's work, and specifically the part that Qoheleth has undertaken to investigate.

וְרָאִ֫יתִי֙ אֶת־כָּל־מַעֲשֵׂ֣ה הָאֱלֹהִ֔ים. *Qatal* 1cs Qal √ראה. This is the main clause to which the preceding v. 16 is the subordinate temporal protasis. The bound phrase marked by את is the complement of וראיתי.

כִּ֣י לֹ֤א יוּכַל֙ הָאָדָ֔ם לִמְצ֖וֹא אֶת־הַֽמַּעֲשֶׂה. *Yiqtol* 3ms Qal (?) √יכל (see comment at 1:8) and Inf Constr Qal √מצא. A complement clause in apposition to מעשה האלהים, defining what aspect of God's work that Qoheleth saw in his experiment. After the כי and לא the order is verb-subject, the האדם being subject of יוכל. The infinitive למצוא is complement of יוכל. The singular determined המעשה, the complement of the infinitive, refers collectively to the sum of activities in life. Qoheleth's concern is not with all that is done under the sun here, but what humanity's plight is in the midst of it

אֲשֶׁ֤ר נַעֲשָׂ֙ה תַֽחַת־הַשֶּׁ֔מֶשׁ. See comments at 1:3, 14; 4:1.

בְּ֠שֶׁל אֲשֶׁ֤ר יַעֲמֹ֙ל הָאָדָ֛ם לְבַקֵּ֖שׁ. *Yiqtol* 3ms Qal √עמל; Inf Constr Piel √בקש. The conjunction בשל אשר is often taken to be a calque of the Aramaic ד בדיל "so that" (see Dalman, §51; Jastrow, 421), which is used in Targumic Aramaic to render Hebrew למען. The same Hebrew construction occurs in 4QMMT and a Bar Kokhba letter (see Qimron, 89) and so appears earlier in Hebrew than the Targumic Aramaic construction, making it an unlikely Hebrew calque of an Aramaic phrase (Gordis 1949: 107; Seow 1997: 289; contra Fox 1999: 289; Schoors, 146–46; Krüger, 163). If it is not a calque of the Aramaic phrase, the redundancy of של and אשר is unlikely to be grammatical (see Holmstedt 2015: 25–26, esp. n. 5). We take the ב to be causal and, ignoring the של as textually and/or grammatically suspect, the following אשר clause to nominalize the clause as the prepositional complement. After the conjunction the word order is verb-subject with an adjunct ל-PP infinitive clause לבקש qualifying what "the man" labors to accomplish. The infinitive is bivalent and requires a complement, which is elided here but inferred from the previous את־מעשה.

וְלֹ֥א יִמְצָ֖א. *Yiqtol* 3ms Qal √מצא. The verb might be interpreted as irrealis dynamic modality "he cannot discover," but given the overt lexical marking of dynamic modality in the following clause, this is better understood as simply a generic statement about the failure of the search.

As with the previous לבקש, the complement of bivalent ימצא is inferred as the previously mentioned את־מעשה.

וְגַם אִם־יֹאמַר הֶחָכָם לָדַעַת. Irrealis *yiqtol* 3ms Qal √אמר; Inf Constr Qal √ידע. This clause is a second appositional complement to מעשה האלהים, introduced by the focus גם as a conjunctive adverb. The order is verb-subject after אם. In a conditional clause, the *yiqtol* is irrealis, denoting a hypothetical here. The complement of יאמר is the לדעת infinitive. The same situation applies to the bivalent לדעת as ימצא and לבקש: the required but elided complement is understood as את־מעשה.

לֹא יוּכַל לִמְצֹא. *Yiqtol* 3ms Qal √יכל (see comment on 1:8) and Inf Constr Qal √מצא. In contrast to the earlier generic expression ולא ימצא, here the dynamic modality (the inability) of the wise person to succeed where others have failed is lexically indicated by יוכל with the complementary ל-PP infinitive clause למצא. The complement of the infinitive is elided but inferred from the earlier את־מעשה.

9:1-12 Live Life Fully

Verses 1-12 provide an extended argument focused on the exhortations in vv. 7-10 that one should live life fully in the face of its vicissitudes as well as the certainty of death.

כִּי אֶת־כָּל־זֶה נָתַתִּי אֶל־לִבִּי וְלָבוּר אֶת־כָּל־זֶה   9:1
אֲשֶׁר הַצַּדִּיקִים וְהַחֲכָמִים וַעֲבָדֵיהֶם בְּיַד הָאֱלֹהִים
גַּם־אַהֲבָה גַּם־שִׂנְאָה אֵין יוֹדֵעַ הָאָדָם הַכֹּל
לִפְנֵיהֶם:

Indeed, all of this I set to my לב, that is, in order to examine all of this: that the righteous and the wise and their works are in the hand of God; whether love or hate, no man knows everything before them.

Qoheleth describes the next subject that he and his לב investigated—how even the wise and righteous, who may be thought to determine their own fate through their wisdom and behavior, are under God's control (Fox 1999: 291). The phrase "in the hand of God" occurs in Wis 3:11, where it refers to God's protection of the souls of the righteous. Here Qoheleth turns that idea to a less comforting perspective: God is in control of the fate of the righteous and wise, but they are ignorant of precisely what that fate is (see the similar idea in 3:11).

כִּי אֶת־כָּל־זֶה נָתַתִּי אֶל־לִבִּי וְלָבוּר אֶת־כָּל־זֶה. *Qatal* (realis)
1cs Qal √נתן and Inf Constr Qal √בור (*hapax legomenon*). The כי is
exclamative, not causal, since there is no claim to ground. The כל זה
could point back to the "absurdity" noted in the previous verse (8:17);
however, it makes better sense of the entire clause if זה is cataphoric and
thus points forward to the clarification ולבור. The complement quantifier phrase את כל זה is fronted for focus, e.g., "*all this* I set ... ." The
second complement of the trivalent verb is the PP אל־לבי. The use of
the ו to mark the edge of the ל-PP/infinitive clause ולבור here signals the
appositive status of the phrase (WO calls this the "epexegetical" use of ו;
see §39.2.4; also GKC §154a n. 1; MNK §40.8); as an appositive, the
לבור PP clarifies the first occurrence of כל־זה.

אֲשֶׁר הַצַּדִּיקִים וְהַחֲכָמִים וַעֲבָדֵיהֶם בְּיַד הָאֱלֹהִים. A null copula
complement clause. The אשר is used here to nominalize the clause as
an appositive for the second occurrence את כל זה, the NP complement
of bivalent בור (see also 7:29; 8:11, 12). The vocalization of the noun
עֲבָדֵיהֶם, which lacks the reduction of the /a/ vowel in the antepenul-
timate syllable, reflects Aramaic, not Hebrew, morphophonology (see
Introduction §6).

גַּם־אַהֲבָה גַם־שִׂנְאָה אֵין יוֹדֵעַ הָאָדָם הַכֹּל לִפְנֵיהֶם. An אין negative copula and Participle ms Qal √ידע. The participle is the complement
of the אין copula and, within the participial clause, the quantifier הכל is
the complement of the verb ידע and the PP לפניהם is an NP-internal
adjunct, that is a spatial or temporal modifier to הכל (not the verb). The
two senses (spatial and temporal) blend together, however, as the ability to discern the working of God's favor and displeasure in the world
(Fox 1999: 291) plays out temporally as ignorance of what "awaits them"
(Bartholomew, 299) We follow the טעמים in taking the גם-גם phrase as a
topic-fronted (i.e., orienting) adjunct to the following participial clause
rather than with the preceding clause, against the טעמים (see, e.g., Seow
1997: 296, 98). The גם ... גם adjunct limits the range or scope of the
following assertion (an adverbial "accusative of limitation" or perhaps
"specification," in the undesirable Latinate framework, WO §10.2.2).
The repetition of the גם on a compound phrase creates a double conjunction, analogous to English "both X and Y" or "either X or Y" (van
der Merwe, 216; see also MNK §41.4.5, §41.4.5.2ii). The word order in
this clause appears unique with only a partial parallel (לא instead of אין
and no fronted adjunct) in Zeph 3:5: וְלֹא־יוֹדֵעַ עַוָּל בֹּשֶׁת "and the sinner

does not know shame." Neither context, here or in Zeph 3:5, suggests that focus on the negative, participle, or both together is warranted, leaving the specific reason for the position of the participle before the subject opaque.

הַכֹּל כַּאֲשֶׁר לַכֹּל מִקְרֶה אֶחָד לַצַּדִּיק וְלָרָשָׁע   9:2
לַטּוֹב וְלַטָּהוֹר וְלַטָּמֵא וְלַזֹּבֵחַ וְלַאֲשֶׁר אֵינֶנּוּ זֹבֵחַ
כַּטּוֹב כַּחֹטֶא הַנִּשְׁבָּע כַּאֲשֶׁר שְׁבוּעָה יָרֵא:

Everything is like (that) which belongs to everyone. One fate belongs to the righteous and the wicked, to the good <and the bad>, to the clean and the unclean, to him who sacrifices and him who does not sacrifice; (so too) the good person is like the sinner (and) he who makes an oath is like (the one) who is afraid of an oath.

Building on his argument from v. 1, Qoheleth affirms that among the uncertainties of life, one certainty remains for all: they all share a single fate regardless of their character or actions (see 2:14-15; also 3:19, on humans and animals sharing one fate).

הַכֹּל כַּאֲשֶׁר לַכֹּל. A null copula clause. The טעמים suggest that the first three words constitute a prosodic unit, an analysis we follow: הכל is the subject and the comparative כ-PP is the copular complement (similarly, Seow 1997: 299; Krüger, 166). The null-head אשר relative is the complement of the כ preposition. Note that Fox emends הכל to הֶבֶל and takes it with the preceding verse, "everything one sees is absurd" (1999: 287–91).

מִקְרֶה אֶחָד לַצַּדִּיק וְלָרָשָׁע לַטּוֹב וְלַטָּהוֹר וְלַטָּמֵא. A null copula clause with the NP מקרה אחד, the subject and a long, compound copular complement consisting of the pairs of ל-PP. The ל-PPs fall into natural pairs of opposites: צדיק and רשע, טוב and רע, and טהור and טמא. In the MT the adjective טוב stands alone. This awkwardness leads many commentators to follow the LXX and understand ולרע to have fallen out by a scribal error (so, among others, Seow 1997: 299; Fox 1999: 292); others omit טוב as an erroneous intrusion (see, e.g., Longman, 225 n. 7).

וְלַזֹּבֵחַ וְלַאֲשֶׁר אֵינֶנּוּ זֹבֵחַ. Null copula, אין negative copula, and two Participles ms Qal √זבח. These two ל-PPs finish the appositive list of opposites. Whereas the first three pairs list behavioral attributes (and so use adjectives), this pair turns to an activity that represents behavior, which explains the shift to participles. Both clauses consist of a null-head complement to the ל preposition; each null head is then modified by a null copula participial relative clause. Most participial relatives do not show an overt relative word and many lack an overt head, so the first clause of the pair is not unusual. For negation (and thus the presence of an overt negator like אין), it is also possible to omit the relative word, though the reader/listener processing ease is increased by the simple addition of the overt relative אשר.

כַּטּוֹב כַּחֹטֶא. A null copula comparative clause, "the good (is) like the bad" (see WO §38.5).

הַנִּשְׁבָּע כַּאֲשֶׁר שְׁבוּעָה יָרֵא. Participle ms Niph √שבע and Qal √ירא. A second null copula comparative clause juxtaposed to the first. הנשבע is a null-head relative with the ה-relative, "(he) who swears," and the כאשר introduces a comparative PP within which the אשר clause is a null-head relative, "like (he) who fears an oath." The complement שבועה appears before the verb it modifies, perhaps for the poetic effect of keeping the cognate noun close to the counterpart participle הנשבע.

9:3   זֶה | רָע בְּכֹל אֲשֶׁר־נַעֲשָׂה תַּחַת הַשֶּׁמֶשׁ כִּי־
מִקְרֶה אֶחָד לַכֹּל וְגַם לֵב בְּנֵי־הָאָדָם מָלֵא־רָע
וְהוֹלֵלוֹת בִּלְבָבָם בְּחַיֵּיהֶם וְאַחֲרָיו אֶל־הַמֵּתִים:

This is a tragedy in all that has happened under the sun, that there is one fate for everything and also the mind of humans is full of evil and lack of reason is in their mind during their lives and he who is after each (is joined) to the dead.

The shared fate being lamented is here explicitly identified as death by the last word of the verse. To Qoheleth it is a tragedy that both the good and bad die in the same way. In the second half of the verse, Qoheleth takes what may have been a typical explanation for man's shared fate—that all are evil in some way—and turns it on its head by implying that the evil, irrational behavior is a product of the shared fate. The not-so-subtle complaint is that, if there was a clear distinction between the righteous and wicked, there would be a reason for being righteous! (See also 7:15; 8:11; Seow 1997: 304.)

זֶה | רָע בְּכֹל אֲשֶׁר־נַעֲשָׂה תַּחַת הַשֶּׁמֶשׁ. A copula clause and a *qatal* 3ms Niph √עשה. The subject of the null copula is the deictic

זֶה, which is cataphoric, pointing ahead to the appositive כִּי clause. The locative בְּ-PP, in which the head כל is modified by a relative clause, is an adjunct to the null copula.

כִּי־מִקְרֶה אֶחָד לַכֹּל וְגַם לֵב בְּנֵי־הָאָדָם מָלֵא־רָע וְהוֹלֵלוֹת בִּלְבָבָם בְּחַיֵּיהֶם. Two null copulas and Participle mp Qal √מות. All three clauses are governed by the initial כִּי, which nominalizes them all as a compound phrase appositional to the initial זֶה. The adverbial conjunction וגם helps imply the evil and irrational behavior as attaching to and resulting from humanities shared fate.

וְאַחֲרָיו אֶל־הַמֵּתִים. This sequence of words is difficult. Many commentators emend אחריו to אחריהם, so that the clitic pronoun matches the plural בני האדם and the 3ms pronouns on בלבבם and בחייהם, "after them—to the dead"; others emend to אחריתם, "their end is to the dead" (so HALOT, s.v.; Fox 1998: 287); Krüger (166) maintains the 3ms pronoun and argues that it refers back distributively to each human. Given the mention of כל החיים in the next verse, we understand the *Qere* יחבר to be either implied or formally gapped back into this clause, thus creating a contrast between "being joined to the dead" and "being joined to the living." The PP אחריו, then, is within a null-head, unmarked relative clause, "(he who is) after him."

9:4 כִּי־מִי אֲשֶׁר יְבֻחַר* אֶל כָּל־הַחַיִּים יֵשׁ בִּטָּחוֹן כִּי־לְכֶלֶב חַי הוּא טוֹב מִן־הָאַרְיֵה הַמֵּת:

Indeed, whoever is joined (Qr) to all the living has confidence, because, even as a dog, life is better than a lion that is dead,

Even if the righteous and wicked share one fate, Qoheleth maintains that some things are clearly better than others. On the topic of fate and death, he asserts that life, even as the lowest on the social scale, is better than death, even if one had prestige or strength in life.

כִּי־מִי אֲשֶׁר יְבֻחַר אֶל כָּל־הַחַיִּים יֵשׁ בִּטָּחוֹן. *Yiqtol* 3ms Pual √בחר (*Ketiv*)/√חבר (*Qere*) and יש copula. The *Ketiv* presents the verb בחר while the *Qere* presents חבר. The variants almost certainly stem from a case of metathesis regarding the first two consonants. The difficulty is determining which form was intended. In the case of the *Ketiv*, this would be a *hapax* since בחר nowhere else appears in the Pual (which is why most who choose the *Ketiv* point the form as a Niphal); moreover, it is not easy to see how "is chosen" makes contextual sense (contra Seow 1997: 300). The *Qere* חבר does occur in the Pual, with the sense of "to be joined together, attached" (DCH, s.v.; HALOT, s.v.), which fits with the following אל-PP to produce "whoever is joined to (or associated with) the living … ." The syntax of the clause seems simple but is not. First, the clause appears to be introduced by an asseverative כי since there is no clear way to connect it causally or concessively to the preceding or following context. Second, the initial מי אשר free choice relative (see comment on מה שֶׁ in 1:9) appears to be the subject of the יש copula, but the result is nonsense: "whoever … is confidence." Rather, בטחון must be the subject and the מי אשר free choice relative is either an unmarked (recipient/possessor) adjunct in a possessive statement (as if it had a ל attached to מי; i.e., למי אשר …), "(to) whomever … belongs confidence," or the מי אשר clause is left-dislocated and there is an assumed resumptive PP, לו, "whoever is joined …—confidence belongs (to him)."

כִּי־לְכֶ֤לֶב חַי֙ ה֣וּא ט֔וֹב מִן־הָאַרְיֵ֖ה הַמֵּֽת. Copula clause with הוא as the pronominal copula and Participle ms Qal √מות. The כי provides support for the preceding statement by providing Qoheleth's rationale: even a dog's life is better than a lion's death. The PP לכלב is fronted for focus in order to isolate and contrast the bottom end of the social scale with the high end mentioned toward the end in the comparative PP. The ל on כלב is neither emphatic (contra Gordis 1955: 304; Seow 1997: 301) nor signals benefit (contra Fox 1999: 292); rather, the ל indicates the function, status, or role in which the subject חי acts or experiences (WO §11.2.10d, ##42–44). The NP חי is the subject of the copular clause with הוא serving as the pronominal copula and the adjective טוב as the copular complement. The comparative מן-PP is an adjunct to the copula; it combines with the adjective טוב to produce the comparative idiom "better X than Y" (MNK §39.14.8; WO §11.2.11e.3). The participle מת is the complement of the null copula clause within the ה relative that modifies האריה.

9:5   כִּ֣י הַֽחַיִּ֤ים יוֹדְעִים֙ שֶׁיָּמֻ֔תוּ וְהַמֵּתִ֖ים אֵינָ֣ם יוֹדְעִ֣ים
מְא֑וּמָה וְאֵֽין־ע֤וֹד לָהֶם֙ שָׂכָ֔ר כִּ֥י נִשְׁכַּ֖ח זִכְרָֽם׃

because the living know that they will die, but the dead—they do not know anything, and they have no more reward because memory of them has been forgotten.

Qoheleth drives his point home: even though the living recognize that they will eventually face death, at least they know *something*! In contrast, the dead know nothing, experience nothing, and are forgotten.

כִּי הַחַיִּים יוֹדְעִים שֶׁיָּמֻתוּ. Null copula, Participle mp Qal √ידע, and *yiqtol* 3mp Qal √מות. The כִּי indicates that this is a second causal clause modifying the initial assertion in v. 4.

וְהַמֵּתִים אֵינָם יוֹדְעִים מְאוּמָה. An אין negative copula and Participle mp Qal √ידע. The NP המתים is left-dislocated and resumed by the 3mp clitic pronoun attached to the negative copula אין (see also 1:7; 5:11; 9:16). The left-dislocated NP unambiguously switches the informational topic to החיים and the resumptive pronoun also marks "the dead" for focus, contrasting it to החיים from the preceding clause.

וְאֵין־עוֹד לָהֶם שָׂכָר כִּי נִשְׁכַּח זִכְרָם. An אין negative copula and *qatal* 3ms Niph √שכח. Either the entire predicate, אין עוד להם, has been fronted (for focus?) or the subject, שכר, has been extraposed (for delayed focus); we prefer the latter analysis in this context, since the lack of a reward (defined by the following כי clause as a legacy) adds insult to injury to their inability to know anything—the dead do not even know that they have been forgotten! The verb-subject order within the כי clause reflects the normal verb raising over the subject in the presence of a trigger, such as כי.

9:6 גַּם אַהֲבָתָם גַּם־שִׂנְאָתָם גַּם־קִנְאָתָם כְּבָר אָבָדָה
וְחֵלֶק אֵין־לָהֶם עוֹד לְעוֹלָם בְּכֹל אֲשֶׁר־נַעֲשָׂה
תַּחַת הַשָּׁמֶשׁ:

Their love, hate, and jealousy have already perished, and a portion no longer belongs to them forever in all that happens under the sun.

This verse concludes the section reflecting on the common fate of death for all (vv. 1-6), focusing on the loss of "interpersonal communications" (Lohfink, 113) in life, which have been mentioned previously (see 3:8; 4:4; 9:1). In the process of the argument, Qoheleth has adroitly shifted the valuation of things: from lamenting life's common fate of death, he ends up promoting a new appreciation of life for those who are yet alive.

גַּם אַהֲבָתָם גַּם־שִׂנְאָתָם גַּם־קִנְאָתָם כְּבָר אָבָדָה. *Qatal* 3fs Qal √אבד. The repetition of the גם on a compound phrase functions together as a multiple conjunction, analogous to English "both X and Y" or "either X or Y" (van der Merwe, 216; see also MNK §41.4.5, §41.4.5.2ii), except that this string of three conjoined NPs demonstrates that גם in Hebrew is not limited to two members (as English "both-and" is). The preverbal position of the adverb כבר indicates that it is likely focus-fronted (see discussion of כבר in 1:10), which means that the compound subject is also fronted, either for a first focus or as a topic. Here the compound subject—"their love, hate, and jealousy"—makes better sense as a fronted topic, since the subject before this was "their memory" (or, if subordinate clauses do not factor into information structuring with regard to topics, the last main clause agent was "the dead"). The focus status of כבר drives home the fact that, in Qoheleth's opinion, upon death, all aspects of a person's interpersonal behavior, personality, and character are immediately nullified.

וְחֵלֶק אֵין־לָהֶם עוֹד לְעוֹלָם בְּכֹל אֲשֶׁר־נַעֲשָׂה תַּחַת הַשָּׁמֶשׁ. An אֵין negative copula and *qatal* 3ms Niph √עשׂה. The NP חלק is the subject and the PP להם is the copular complement. The adverb עוד modifies the copula as an adjunct, as does both the ל-PP לעולם and the ב-PP. On תחת השמש, see discussion at תחת השמים in 1:13.

9:7   לֵךְ אֱכֹל בְּשִׂמְחָה לַחְמֶךָ וּשֲׁתֵה בְלֶב־טוֹב יֵינֶךָ כִּי
        כְבָר רָצָה הָאֱלֹהִים אֶת־מַעֲשֶׂיךָ:

Go, happily eat your food and gladly drink your wine because God has already accepted your deeds.

The shift to imperatives signals Qoheleth's advice to enjoy life as springing from the lessons of his preceding observations as to the common fate of death for all humans (vv. 1-3) along with the undeniable preference for being alive over being dead (vv. 4-6). Despite the uncertainties of life (v. 1), the certainty of its finitude should motivate one to make the most of it.

לֵךְ אֱכֹל בְּשִׂמְחָה לַחְמֶךָ וּשֲׁתֵה בְלֶב־טוֹב יֵינֶךָ. Impv ms Qal √הלך, √אכל, and √שתה. For the verb אכל, the complement is the NP לחמך; for שתה, the complement is יינך. However, in both clauses, the normal order for most adjuncts (here, the manner PPs בשמחה and בלב טוב) is to follow the complement (for the "ב of manner," see MNK §39.6.3.5; WO §11.2.5d–e). It may be that there is a class of adverbs (like עוד or PPs that function in specific ways) that normally precede the complement; such word order nuances remain a desideratum in BH studies.

רצה√ Qal 3ms *Qatal*. כִּי כְּבָ֫ר רָצָה הָאֱלֹהִים אֶת־מַעֲשֶׂיךָ. Within the subordinate כי clause, note the focus-fronted position of כבר (see comment above on v. 6). The כי triggers verb-subject order, with the subject האלהים following the verb רצה. Fox argues that כבר and רצה work together to convey a future perfective sense, as "at that time (in the future when you enjoy life) he will have accepted" (though he translates with a present perfective, "he has already accepted"; 1999: 294). This interpretation is motivated by Fox's view that the opportunity to enjoy life itself is demonstration of God's favor. Although, עתה can function in this way (i.e., "at that time"—a reference time established by the context), כבר, which only occurs in Ecclesiastes (8×), *never* functions in this way; it always establishes an event as having occurred before the speaker's reference time ("already"). Further, the immediately succeeding context suggests that simply remaining "under the sun," alive, is indication that God has bestowed a certain degree of favor. Qoheleth never seems to struggle greatly over whether one *cannot* enjoy life in his "carpe diem" passages; he simply recommends one choose to enjoy life as one is able.

9:8   בְּכָל־עֵת יִהְי֣וּ בְגָדֶ֫יךָ לְבָנִ֑ים וְשֶׁ֖מֶן עַל־רֹאשְׁךָ֣ אַל־
        יֶחְסָֽר׃

At every time let your clothes be white, and do not let oil be lacking on your head.

This verse reinforces the idea in the preceding, that one should *choose* to enjoy life: wearing white clothes and anointing one's head with oil both indicate festival and joyful occasions in contrast to a mournful approach to life in the face of death (see 2 Sam 12:20; 14:2).

בְּכָל־עֵת יִהְי֣וּ בְגָדֶ֫יךָ לְבָנִ֑ים. היה√ *Yiqtol* (jussive) 3mp Qal. The ב-PP is fronted as a temporal-setting topic. The fronting of the PP triggers verb-subject order, making it difficult to determine whether the morphologically ambiguous יהיו is indicative/realis (normally subject-verb, but often triggered to verb-subject) or irrealis (the irrealis mood triggers verb-subject order). The parallel with the next clause, in which the jussive status of the verb is signaled by the use of the negative אל, supports the jussive analysis of יהיו.

וְשֶׁמֶן עַל־רֹאשְׁךָ אַל־יֶחְסָר. *Yiqtol* (jussive) 3ms Qal √חסר. The
verb חסר may be either monovalent (e.g., Ps 23:1 לֹא אֶחְסָר) or bivalent
(e.g., Isa 51:14 וְלֹא יֶחְסַר לַחְמוֹ); here it is monovalent and the על-PP is
a locative adjunct. Typically negation (as well as irrealis mood) results in
verb-subject order. Here the initial position of the subject, not to mention the following על-PP, reflect the double-fronting of both constituents, the subject as a topic (orienting the reader to the shift from בגדים to
שמן) and the adjunct PP as a focus (absolutely limiting the location by
contrasting על ראשך with the implied likely alternatives).

9:9　　רְאֵה חַיִּים עִם־אִשָּׁה אֲשֶׁר־אָהַבְתָּ כָּל־יְמֵי חַיֵּי
הֶבְלֶךָ אֲשֶׁר נָתַן־לְךָ תַּחַת הַשֶּׁמֶשׁ כֹּל יְמֵי הֶבְלֶךָ
כִּי הוּא חֶלְקְךָ בַּחַיִּים וּבַעֲמָלְךָ אֲשֶׁר־אַתָּה עָמֵל
תַּחַת הַשָּׁמֶשׁ:

Enjoy life with the woman whom you love all the days of your הבל *life,*
whom he has given to you under the sun all your הבל *days, because it is your*
lot in life and in exchange for your labor that you did under the sun.

Qoheleth urges further that, in the face of the absurdity of life,
one should choose enjoyment—namely, of human relationships
between the sexes. He suggests that whatever enjoyment one obtains is
in exchange for the labor of one's life, as opposed to the vain hope of
escaping death.

רְאֵה חַיִּים עִם־אִשָּׁה אֲשֶׁר־אָהַבְתָּ כָּל־יְמֵי חַיֵּי הֶבְלֶךָ. Impv ms
Qal √ראה and *qatal* 2ms Qal √אהב. On the collocation of ראה and
an abstract NP complement, see comment on ראה טובה in 6:6; see
also 2:1. The verb ראה develops the sense of experience (see > experience) in Ecclesiastes, which in this immediate context gives the sense of
"enjoy." The עם PP is an adjunct to the verb ראה, narrowing the notion
of "enjoying life" down to the aspect that involves one's wife. The אשר
relative clause clearly modifies אשה. However, the syntactic position of
the complex NP כל ימי חיי הבלך is ambiguous: it could refer to the duration of אהבת within the relative clause or it could belong to the higher
clause as a temporal adjunct to ראה, adding reinforcement in the sense
of "as long as your הבל life lasts." We have left the translation ambiguous,
though we prefer the main clause adjunct analysis.

אֲשֶׁר נָתַן־לְךָ תַּחַת הַשֶּׁמֶשׁ כֹּל יְמֵי הֶבְלֶךָ. The head of a אשר relative is typically the closest available antecedent, which here would appear to be כל ימי חיי הבלך. However, Hebrew strongly disprefers a full copy of the relative head as the resumption within the relative (see Holmstedt 2016: 171–72, esp. n. 46). Thus, it is more likely a second, stacked relative modifying the further אשה. On the near repetition of כל ימי הבלך, Seow follows those who suggest that this phrase is a dittography of the earlier כל ימי חיי הבלך (1997: 302). Longman (226) notes that the text makes sense as it stands, though his translation reflects a reordering of the second part of this phrase and the preceding אשר clause. We take it as a virtual repetition of כל ימי חיי הבלך used to reinforce the fatalism with which Qoheleth is toying—a man's life leaves no permanent mark and so is, in the long view, הבל (on הבל, see comment at 1:2).

כִּי הוּא חֶלְקְךָ בַּחַיִּים וּבַעֲמָלְךָ אֲשֶׁר־אַתָּה עָמֵל תַּחַת הַשֶּׁמֶשׁ. Two null copula clauses (on the adjective עמל as a copular complement with its own internal arguments, see comment at 2:18). The כי clause provides the reason or motivation for following Qoheleth's advice to enjoy life with a wife—it is probably the only (or perhaps the best) product of one's toil in life. On the function of the ב in בעמלך, as marking the entity given in exchange for something else (the so-called ב *pretii*), see 1:3; 2:22; 3:9; 4:9; 5:14.

כֹּל אֲשֶׁר תִּמְצָא יָדְךָ לַעֲשׂוֹת בְּכֹחֲךָ עֲשֵׂה כִּי אֵין 9:10
מַעֲשֶׂה וְחֶשְׁבּוֹן וְדַעַת וְחָכְמָה בִּשְׁאוֹל אֲשֶׁר אַתָּה
הֹלֵךְ שָׁמָּה: ס

All that your hand finds to do with your strength, do, because no deed or accounting or knowledge and wisdom exists in Sheol, where you are going.

Rounding out his series of instructions on how to behave in the face of the certainty of death and absurdity of life, Qoheleth urges the reader to make the most of life because despite the absurdities the opportunities afforded the living are not afforded the dead. The focus here is particularly on "intellectual activity" that is lacking in death (Whybray, 145), which balances the previous "carpe diem" statements: Qoheleth does not advocate blind hedonism in the face of death and absurdity but rather that one make the most out of life, finding enjoyment in relationships,

satisfaction in one's labor, and exercising all one's capacity for thought
and wisdom within life's inescapable confines.

כֹּל אֲשֶׁר תִּמְצָא יָדְךָ לַעֲשׂוֹת בְּכֹחֲךָ עֲשֵׂה. *Yiqtol* 3fs Qal √מצא,
Inf Constr, and Impv 2ms Qal √עשׂה. The entire כל quantifier phrase is
the fronted complement of the imperative עשׂה. The כל quantifies a null
noun that is defined by the following restrictive אשׁר relative. Within
the relative, the אשׁר has triggered verb (תמצא)-subject (ידך) order. The
complement of the bivalent תמצא is the ל-PP/infinitive clause לעשׂות.
In the infinitive clause, the bivalent עשׂות has a null complement which
is coreferential and thus the (doubly embedded) resumption of the null
relative head: "every (thing) that your hands find to do (it)." The ב-PP is
a manner adjunct for לעשׂות (for the "ב of manner," see MNK §39.6.3.5;
WO §11.2.5d–e).

כִּי אֵין מַעֲשֶׂה וְחֶשְׁבּוֹן וְדַעַת וְחָכְמָה בִּשְׁאוֹל אֲשֶׁר אַתָּה הֹלֵךְ
שָׁמָּה. An אין copula clause and Participle ms Qal √הלך. The subject is
the compound NP מעשׂה וחשבון ודעת וחכמה and the copular complement is the ב-PP בשׁאול. The אשׁר relative clause modifies שׁאול nonre-
strictively and so serves not to define שׁאול but simply to drive home the
point that everyone dies and goes to a place where nothing done in life
matters.

9:11   שַׁבְתִּי וְרָאֹה תַחַת־הַשֶּׁמֶשׁ כִּי לֹא לַקַּלִּים הַמֵּרוֹץ
וְלֹא לַגִּבּוֹרִים הַמִּלְחָמָה וְגַם לֹא לַחֲכָמִים לֶחֶם
וְגַם לֹא לַנְּבֹנִים עֹשֶׁר וְגַם לֹא לַיֹּדְעִים חֵן כִּי־עֵת
וָפֶגַע יִקְרֶה אֶת־כֻּלָּם:

I again considered under the sun that the race is not to the swift nor the
battle to the mighty, nor even food to the wise, riches to the discerning, or
favor to the skillful, because time and change happen to them all,

Though some treat vv. 11-12 as a separate unit (so Longman, 232)
or with the following verses (so Seow 1997: 306), their connection with
the preceding is evident in how they serve as a bookend with vv. 1-6,
drawing the focus to Qoheleth's advice to live life fully in vv. 7-10 (see
Krüger, 167). These verses do not merely repeat the earlier reflections,
however; rather, alongside the affirmation that life is uncertain (vv. 1, 11)
and death is certain (vv. 2-6), Qoheleth adjoins the further motivation to
enjoy life by observing that while death is certain for all, the time of each
one's own death ("his time") is uncertain (v. 12).

שַׁבְתִּי וְרָאֹה תַחַת־הַשָּׁמֶשׁ. *Qatal* 1cs Qal √שוב and Inf Abs Qal
√ראה. On the use of the infinitive absolute as a finite verb, see comment on 4:2, 8:9 and Cook 2013: 322. Here the infinitive absolute
occurs in a verbal hendiadys coordinated with the *qatal* of שוב. On
the similar coordination of שוב with another finite verb in which שוב
provides the adverbial notion "again," see comment on 1:7. The verb
ראה is bivalent and the following כי clause is its complement. The תחת
PP is a locative adjunct for ראה; on the position of the adjunct before
the "heavy" כי complement, see 2:7, 17; 3:14, 22; 7:18, 20, 26; 9:14,
15; 11:7.

כִּי לֹא לַקַּלִּים הַמֵּרוֹץ וְלֹא לַגִּבּוֹרִים הַמִּלְחָמָה וְגַם לֹא לַחֲכָמִים
לֶחֶם וְגַם לֹא לַנְּבֹנִים עֹשֶׁר וְגַם לֹא לַיֹּדְעִים חֵן. Five null copula clauses,
all within the domain of the initial כי. In each the ל-PP copular complement is fronted for focus, as is the clausal negative לא. The focus contrasts not only the NP within the ל-PP with likely alternatives, but also
the negative, since the expected proposition is, for example, the positive
"the race goes to the swift."

כִּי־עֵת וָפֶגַע יִקְרֶה אֶת־כֻּלָּם. *Yiqtol* 3ms Qal √קרה. This כי clause
is an adjunct to ראה. It provides the reason that Qoheleth draws his
conclusion about the race not going to the swift, and so on—because,
apart from the ultimately leveling influence of death, the fact is that
some set of circumstances inevitably occurs to negate the results of life's
achievements.

> 9:12   כִּי גַם לֹא־יֵדַע הָאָדָם אֶת־עִתּוֹ כַּדָּגִים שֶׁנֶּאֱחָזִים
> בִּמְצוֹדָה רָעָה וְכַצִּפֳּרִים הָאֲחֻזוֹת בַּפָּח כָּהֵם
> יוּקָשִׁים בְּנֵי הָאָדָם לְעֵת רָעָה כְּשֶׁתִּפּוֹל עֲלֵיהֶם
> פִּתְאֹם:

*because, indeed, man does not know his time. Like fish that are caught in
a bad net and like birds that are snagged in a trap—like them humans are
ensnared at a time of misfortune, when it falls upon them suddenly.*

This verse extends from v. 11 the uncertainty observed in life to the
time of one's death, providing further motivation to enjoy life (vv. 7-10).

כִּי גַם לֹא־יֵדַע הָאָדָם אֶת־עִתּוֹ. *Yiqtol* 3ms Qal √ידע. This כי may
be exclamative (so Fox 1999: 297), creating a bookend of this verse with
v. 1 (כי ... גם ... אין יודע; see Murphy, 89). However, it makes more sense

to us that this כִּי clause is a second כִּי clause complement to רָאָה. The conjunctive adverb גַם highlights Qoheleth's extension of the idea of uncertainty in life in v. 11 to his reflection on the uncertainty of the time of one's death.

כַּדָּגִים שֶׁנֶּאֱחָזִים בִּמְצוֹדָה רָעָה וְכַצִּפֳּרִים הָאֲחֻזוֹת בַּפָּח כָּהֵם יוּקָשִׁים בְּנֵי הָאָדָם. Participles, mp Niph and fp Qal passive √אחז and mp Pual √יקש. The initial, complex כְּ-PP is left-dislocated and resumed by the כְּ-PP within the clause proper, כהם. Though the focus-fronting of the resumptive כהם would trigger verb-subject order with finite verbal clauses, it does not trigger inversion with participles. Thus, the position of the subject NP בני אדם after the participle suggests that the subject has been extraposed for secondary focus, a mostly literary strategy for delaying and thus heightening a climactic element. The result is a double contrast: כהם is focus-fronted to contrast the positive "like them" with the logical negative alternative, "NOT like them"; the NP בני אדם is extraposed for focus because the comparison of humans to fish and birds is contrary to expectations.

לְעֵת רָעָה כְּשֶׁתִּפּוֹל עֲלֵיהֶם פִּתְאֹם. *Yiqtol* 3fs Qal √נפל. Both the לְ-PP and the כְּ-PP are temporal adjuncts to the participle יוקשים. The שֶ within כשתפול is not a relative word, but a nominalizer that recategorizes the following clause so that it may be the "nominal" complement of the preposition כְּ. The implied null-subject of the nominalized clause is the fs עֵת, which matches the 3fs תפול. The PP עליהם is an adjunct to נפל, which, though monovalent, is often accompanied by a locative phrase. The adverb פתאם is a manner adjunct to תפול.

9:13–10:19 Diverse Reflections on Wisdom

Verse 13 introduces a series (9:13–10:20) of reflections on the excellence but limited value of wisdom among life's uncertainties. The first section in this series, 9:13-18, is held together by the dialectal statements regarding the relative valuation of wisdom and war or power of a ruler/king. The large section in 10:1-20 is woven together by the comparison between folly and wisdom (vv. 1-3, 12-15) and the affect of folly on the social order and ruling class (vv. 4-7, 16-20). Between these two pairs of discussion, wisdom is portrayed as useful to everyday life, which does not exhibit an intrinsic retribution principle at work (vv. 8-10); however, wisdom is no panacea for life's uncertainties (v. 11).

9:13 גַּם־זֶה רָאִיתִי חָכְמָה תַּחַת הַשָּׁמֶשׁ וּגְדוֹלָה הִיא
אֵלָי:

Also this I saw (about) wisdom under the sun. And it was impressive to
me.

This verse introduces a short parable about wisdom (on anecdotal
wisdom, see Cook 2005: 130–31), which stands at the head of a section
of various reflections on wisdom that extends through 10:19, at which
point Qoheleth shifts back to offering advice to the reader (10:20–11:6).
The story and subsequent sayings illustrate both the excellence of wisdom and its limitations in life. At the same time, the mention that the
poor wise man is "forgotten" (זכר) links this section with the preceding
concern with death, which takes even the "memory" (זכרם) of those who
die (9:5).

גַּם־זֶה רָאִיתִי חָכְמָה תַּחַת הַשָּׁמֶשׁ. *Qatal* 1cs Qal √ראה. The
complement of bivalent ראה is the demonstrative זה, which is fronted
to signal a switch of topics from the preceding discussion of death to
the following parable about wisdom. With Seow (1997: 308–9; also
Longman, 233), we do not omit חכמה (contra Fox 1999: 298) but take
it as an unmarked adjunct limiting the scope or reference of זה, i.e.,
"with regard to wisdom" (see the so-called accusative of limitation, WO
§10.2.2e; JM §126g).

וּגְדוֹלָה הִיא אֵלָי. Null copula clause, interpreted as past tense in the
context of the preceding *qatal*. The subject היא refers back to fs זה (cf.
the more frequent form זאת). The copular complement גדולה is fronted
for focus, allowing Qoheleth to emphasize the impact of the following
parable on his own thinking (i.e., it was not simply *banal* or even *effec-*
tive, but *impressive*!).

9:14 עִיר קְטַנָּה וַאֲנָשִׁים בָּהּ מְעָט וּבָא־אֵלֶיהָ מֶלֶךְ גָּדוֹל
וְסָבַב אֹתָהּ וּבָנָה עָלֶיהָ מְצוֹדִים גְּדֹלִים:

A small city (people are in it, a few)—a great king came to it and sur-
rounded it and built against it great towers,

Verses 14-15 present Qoheleth's anecdote about the king, a besieged
city, and a poor, wise man. Though the poor wise man saves the whole
city because of his wisdom, even he is not remembered.

עִיר קְטַנָּה וַאֲנָשִׁים בָּהּ מְעָט וּבָא־אֵלֶיהָ מֶלֶךְ גָּדוֹל. *Qatal* 3ms
Qal √בוא. Note the ו marking the front edge of the clause proper, thus
separating the dislocated constituent, עיר קטנה ואנשים בה מעט, from
the clause to which is it connected by the resumptive 3fs clitic pronoun in אליה. Although the word order would suggest irrealis *qatal*
forms here and in the following verse, the most natural reading of
the two verses is as a realis narrative of a succession of events (... ובא
וסבב ... ובנה ... ומצא ... ומלט), for which the *wayyiqtol* conjugation
would be expected (cf. the anecdote in Prov 21:22 and discussions in
Cook 2005: 130–31; 2013: 315). This passage is a strong argument
that infrequency of *wayyitol* in Ecclesiastes is not attributable to the
literary character of the book but is probably diachronically significant. Further, the ו prefixing and verb-subject order of these realis *qatal*
forms appear to mimic the syntax of *wayyiqtol* purposely, and together
with the other *waw*-prefixed, clause initial *qatal* forms in the book,
indicate a decline in the use of the irrealis *qatal*, which these features
served to distinguish from realis *qatal* (see Introduction §5). Though
a compound, complex NP could be resolved as a singular entity for
agreement reasons (see Holmstedt 2009c), here it is unlikely that עיר
and אנשים are considered a single entity. Rather, the NP אנשים בה מעט
is better understood as a parenthetical phrase that does not contribute to the agreement features of the dislocated constituent, which is fs
and resumed by the 3fs clitic pronoun in the PP אליה. The noun מעט
modifies אנשים as an extraposed appositive, "people, a few."

וְסָבַב אֹתָהּ. *Qatal* 3ms Qal √סבב. The bivalent סבב takes the clitic
pronoun attached to את as its complement.

וּבָנָה עָלֶיהָ מְצוֹדִים גְּדֹלִים. *Qatal* 3ms Qal √בנה. Though it is
more normal to find the complement of a bivalent verb preceding an
adjunct, here the light PP עליה stands before the more complex NP complement מצודים גדלים due to HNPS (see also 2:7, 17; 3:14, 22; 7:18, 20,
26; 9:11, 15; 11:7).

9:15   וּמָצָא בָהּ אִישׁ מִסְכֵּן חָכָם וּמִלַּט־הוּא אֶת־הָעִיר
בְּחָכְמָתוֹ וְאָדָם לֹא זָכַר אֶת־הָאִישׁ הַמִּסְכֵּן הַהוּא:

*but he found a poor wise man in it and he saved—he!—the city by his
wisdom. But no one remembered that poor man!*

This verse completes the anecdote begun in v. 14, ending with the negative description of the poor deliverer of the city as forgotten.

וּמָצָא בָהּ אִישׁ מִסְכֵּן חָכָם. *Qatal* 3ms Qal √מצא. The PP בה is an adjunct to מצא and precedes the complex NP complement איש מסכן חכם. On this order due to HNPS, see 2:7, 17; 3:14, 22; 7:18, 20, 26; 9:11; 11:7. The subject of the verb is most naturally taken as the king, but Longman (234) treats it as impersonal passive ("a poor but wise man was found in it"). However, the discovery of the man by the king need not be taken literally: the king "discovered" the poor wise man in the city through the deliverance performed by the man (Fox 1999: 299).

וּמִלַּט־הוּא אֶת־הָעִיר בְּחָכְמָתוֹ. *Qatal* 3ms Piel √מלט. An independent pronoun is not required with finite verbs (Holmstedt 2013b); thus, when it is present, it is almost always fronted before the verb for topic or focus. Here the pronoun is present for focus, but it follows the realis *qatal*, which order seems to mimic intentionally the *wayyiqtol* (see comment on 9:14). The reference of הוא in this clause is formally ambiguous: it could refer to the closer איש מסכן חכם or the more distant מלך. The question is whether it is the king who saves the city because of something the wise man does, or the wise man who is credited with the city's deliverance. Due to the closer position of איש מסכן חכם and the context, we associate the focus marking on הוא with the surprise agency of the poor wise man, and so the contrast drives home why Qoheleth finds this parable impressive and explains the motivation for the use of the focus pronoun—the switch agency in the series of the *qatal* verbs.

וְאָדָם לֹא זָכַר אֶת־הָאִישׁ הַמִּסְכֵּן הַהוּא. *Qatal* 3ms Qal √זכר. The NP את האיש המסכן ההוא is the complement of bivalent זכר. The subject is אדם, which is positioned at the front of the clause even though a negative typically triggers inversion to verb-subject order. The NP אדם may be topic-fronted to signal the shift from the poor wise man to the unnamed אדם, who here stands for the witness of posterity. Or the subject-negative-verb order may reflect the later typological profile of the book (see Introduction §§2D, 6).

9:16 וְאָמַרְתִּי אָנִי טוֹבָה חָכְמָה מִגְּבוּרָה וְחָכְמַת
הַמִּסְכֵּן בְּזוּיָה וּדְבָרָיו אֵינָם נִשְׁמָעִים:

So I said, I, wisdom is better than might: the wisdom of the poor is despised, and his words—they are not heeded.

After his mini-parable, Qoheleth does not leave its interpretation to chance, but makes his conclusion explicit: wisdom is better than power, as demonstrated by the anecdote. At the same time, the fact that the poor wise man is nevertheless forgotten proves the rule that wisdom of the poor is generally despised and his words unheeded (Prov 19:7; Ben Sira 13:22). Thus the story still stands over and against the traditional perspective of the sages that wisdom actually outweighs or compensates for poverty (Prov 8:11; 16:16; Ben Sira 11:1).

וְאָמַרְתִּי אָנִי טוֹבָה חָכְמָה מִגְּבוּרָה. *Qatal* 1cs Qal √אמר. With the use of the postverbal 1cs pronoun, Qoheleth returns to the "I-and-my-לב" rhetorical device, thereby asserting that what follows is his, and not his לב's, conclusion (for the "I-and-my-לב" framework, see the Introduction). On the "better-than" saying and the initial position of טובה, see comments at 4:3 and 7:1.

וְחָכְמַת הַמִּסְכֵּן בְּזוּיָה. A null copula clause with its complement Participle fs Qal passive √בזה. This statement would appear to contradict the success of the poor wise man in saving the city. For this reason Seow (1997: 306) reads the previous verse as a counterfactual conditional ("might have delivered … but no one gave thought"). Harmonizing the two verses requires recognizing that המסכן here is generic rather than referring to the specific wise man in the story. The separation of this statement from the anecdote by the generic better-than statement supports this reading.

וּדְבָרָיו אֵינָם נִשְׁמָעִים. An אין negative copula and Participle mp Niph √שמע. The subject is the 3mp clitic pronoun attached to אין, which resumes the left-dislocated NP, דבריו. The point of the dislocation structure is to signal a switch of topics from חכמת to דבריו and also allow the topic NP דבריו to carry focus. The shift in topic clarifies what constitutes despised wisdom and sets up the observation about words in the following verse. On the אינם structure, see also 1:7; 5:11; 9:5.

9:17   דִּבְרֵי חֲכָמִים בְּנַחַת נִשְׁמָעִים מִזַּעֲקַת מוֹשֵׁל
בַּכְּסִילִים:

The words of the wise in calm are heeded more than the shout of a ruler among fools.

The contradictory character of this verse with the preceding might suggest a dialectic in Qoheleth's thinking (so Fox 1999: 300), or he is suggesting that the words of the wise are *worthy* of heeding even if they are not always actually heeded (so Whybray, 149). Though neither the wise nor the ruler in this verse are equated with the poor wise man and king in vv. 14-15, there is an implicit connection: though the poor wise man was successful, thus illustrating the inherent superiority of quiet wisdom to power or a shouting ruler (vv. 15-16a), the usual way of the world is that the wisdom of the poor is despised and his words unheeded because of his poverty (v. 16b), nevertheless, wisdom retains its superiority (v. 17).

דִּבְרֵי חֲכָמִים בְּנַחַת נִשְׁמָעִים. A null copula clause with a Participle ms Niph √שמע as the copular complement. The PP בנחת is not felicitous as an adjunct to either the null copula or the participle נשמעים. Instead, it appears to modify the NP (on NP-internal PPs, see comment on 1:1). Thus, it is not just the words of the wise that are in view, but the words of the wise spoken calmly or quietly. The NP-internal status of the PP explains its position before the null copula or the participle. (Fox, who understands the role of בנחת similarly, suggests that the disjunctive טעם, the זָקֵף קָטֹן, should be moved to בנחת [1999: 300]; but since Dresher 1994 argues convincingly that the טעמים do not always match syntax, we need not make such a change to accept the NP-internal analysis.)

מִזַּעֲקַת מוֹשֵׁל בַּכְּסִילִים. Participle ms Qal √משל, used as an agentive NP, "ruler" (see comment on 1:15). The comparative מִן-PP (MNK §39.14.8; WO §11.2.11e.3) is an adjunct of the participle נשמעים and so qualifies what it means that that quiet words of the wise are heard— they are heard more than the shout of a ruler. The PP בכסילים could modify the NP זעקת or the agentive participle מושל: if so, the question is whether the cry is among fools or the ruler is among fools. But better than either option is ellipsis of נשמעים from the main clause into the lower clause and taking בכסילים as an adjunct of the participle; hence, "than the shout of a ruler (is heeded) among fools" (Fox 1999: 300).

9:18   טוֹבָה חָכְמָה מִכְּלֵי קְרָב וְחוֹטֶא אֶחָד יְאַבֵּד טוֹבָה
הַרְבֵּה:

Better is wisdom than instruments of war; one offender destroys much goodness.

The dialectic of Qoheleth's thinking in this section (vv. 13-18) is carried further along: no matter how good wisdom may be, a single offender can negate its positive effects.

טוֹבָה חָכְמָה מִכְּלֵי קְרָב. A null copula clause with the copular complement, טובה, in initial position. This is typical of the "better than" sayings (see comments on 4:3 and 7:1). The comparative מִן-PP is an adjunct to the null copula.

וְחוֹטֶא אֶחָד יְאַבֵּד טוֹבָה הַרְבֵּה. Participle ms Qal √חטא (used as an agentive noun; see comment at 1:15) and irrealis *yiqtol* 3ms Piel √אבד, expressing dynamic modality. Rather than the expected verb-subject word order, the subject is focus-fronted: despite the vastness of the armies that take up the instruments of war, it takes just one offender to destroy much goodness.

10:1   זְבוּבֵי מָוֶת יַבְאִישׁ יַבִּיעַ שֶׁמֶן רוֹקֵחַ יָקָר מֵחָכְמָה מִכָּבוֹד סִכְלוּת מְעָט:

Dead flies stink, (it) putrefies a perfumer's oil. More weighty than wisdom, than honor is a little foolishness.

This verse illustrates the general principle given in 9:18b: something as small as a dead fly can ruin a lot of goodness wrought by wisdom such as the skillfully mixed perfumer's oil. The asyndetic structure (between the two verbal clauses in the first half, the two PPs in the second, and between the two halves) of the saying makes the syntax somewhat awkward but the comparison stark.

זְבוּבֵי מָוֶת יַבְאִישׁ. *Yiqtol* (realis) 3ms Hiph √באש. Note the apparent lack of agreement between the formally mp זביבי מות and the ms verb. It is likely that, rather than syntactic lack of agreement, the morphologically plural זביבים was perceived as a collective (see JM §150g for more examples). The subject-verb order is basic; there appears to be no reason for any topic- or focus-fronting; the realis *yiqtol* expresses the generic/gnomic idea. The Hiphil verb is intransitive (see WO) in all but two instances, in which the NP complement is personal ("me" in Gen 34:30; "our aroma" in Exod 5:21), suggesting that it is likely intransitive here, and not a case of verbal asyndeton ("make a perfumer's oil stink and ferment") as suggested by most commentators (see Longman, 238 n. 3). For the clitic phrase זבובי מות, the meaning would appear to be "flies of death," i.e., flies that bring death. Fox argues that the context requires "dead flies" and suggests an emendation (by a simple redivision of the words) to זבוב ימות, "a fly dies (and) spoils ..." (1999: 297, 301). Yet, in WO's discussion (§9.5.3a) of the construct, the "c[onstruct] is characterized by g[enitive]" category would produce for this collocation "flies characterized by death," which is ambiguous enough to refer to (1) "flies that are affected by death" or (2) "flies that bring death," or even (3) "flies associated with death." The first and third both fit the context and so there is no need for emendation.

יַבִּיעַ שֶׁמֶן רוֹקֵחַ. Yiqtol (realis) 3ms Hiph √נבע. The subject is the same as in the preceding clause זבובי מות, and the following NP שמן רוקח is the complement. It is difficult to discern the precise sense of the expression because all nine other instances (Pss 19:3; 59:8; 78:2; 94:4; 119:171; 145:7; Prov 1:23; 15:2, 28) have a NP complement that relates the basic sense of "emit" to speech. HALOT suggests "ferment" in a bad sense as the meaning, presumably on the idea that "cause to bubble" is an effect of fermentation (see BDB; cf. DCH, which provides a separate entry for this occurrence). Since ferment is ambiguously positive or negative, it is better to render it "putrefy" or similarly. Emending the verb to the noun גביע "chalice" to avoid the lexical problem (so Seow 1997: 312; Fox 1999: 297–98) is unlikely to be correct given the dominant intransitive pattern of יבאיש.

יָקָר מֵחָכְמָה מִכָּבוֹד סִכְלוּת מְעָט. The null copula, comparative clause has the order predicate-subject, which reflects the focus-fronting of the predicate. The two comparative מן-PPs (MNK §39.14.8; WO §11.2.11e.3) are juxtaposed without a conjunction as a compound adjunct to the null copula. The NP יקר typically means "precious," and if that is the sense here, the statement must be ironic (see Longman, 238–39). However, יקר also takes on the sense of "weighty" in Aramaic (*Comprehensive Aramaic Lexicon*, s.v.; Payne-Smith, s.v.) and postbiblical Hebrew (Jastrow, s.v.), a meaning which would fit the context of this verse, producing the sense that a little foolishness easily outweighs wisdom.

10:2 לֵב חָכָם לִימִינוֹ וְלֵב כְּסִיל לִשְׂמֹאלוֹ:

The mind of a wise man (goes) to his right, but the mind of a fool (goes) to his left.

The לֵב of the wise and the fool go in diametrically opposed direction. The right and the left are associated with decision making (Gen 24:49), and the right is superior to the left (Gen 48:18). Thus the association of the wise with the right and the fool with the left implies an ethical nuance beyond simply diametric opposition: right represents the good and left the bad (Seow 1997: 312–13; Longman, 240).

Both clauses are null copula clauses in which the directional PPs לִימִינוֹ and לִשְׂמֹאלוֹ force a movement interpretation of the copula, thus our translation "goes." The point of the juxtaposed clauses is that the wise and the fool go in opposite directions.

10:3   וְגַם־בַּדֶּרֶךְ כְּשֶׁהַסָּכָל* הֹלֵךְ לִבּוֹ חָסֵר וְאָמַר לַכֹּל
סָכָל הוּא׃

And also, on the road, when the fool is walking, his mind is lacking, so that he says to everyone (that) he is a fool!

The directional means of drawing the moral contrast between the wise and the fool in v. 2 suggests a connection with the saying in this verse about the fool "on the road." The adverbial conjunction גַם here makes the connection between the verses explicit.

וְגַם־בַּדֶּרֶךְ כְּשֶׁהַסָּכָל הֹלֵךְ לִבּוֹ חָסֵר. Participle ms *Qal* √הלך. The additive גַם indicates that the following information adds to the preceding (MNK §41.4.5.2; van der Merwe), drawing the PP בדרך to the front for focus: even when the fool has started going (left), along the way his foolishness remains evident. The כ-PP, which includes a participial clause that has been nominalized (so that it can be the complement of the preposition כ), is either in a second fronted position, also for focus, or is to be understood simply as appositional to the PP בדרך. The subject לבו and predicate חסר of the main (null copula) clause are finally provided at the end. The comment about lacking his לֵב would appear to be at odds with his לֵב tending left in v. 2. Combining the two verses, however, suggests that the לֵב of the fool sends him on a bad way, and he continues along without any sense to change course or get off (Prov 5:23; Krüger,180). Note that the fronting does not trigger any change in the subject-predicate order in the null copula clause. The *Ketiv* form כְּשֶׁהַסָּכָל is noted in the margin (יתיר ה׳) as having a superfluous ה, resulting in a virtual *Qere* of כְּשֶׁסָּכָל, which we follow.

וְאָמַר לַכֹּל סָכָל הוּא. *Qatal* (irrealis) 3ms *Qal* √אמר. The irrealis *qatal* is well understood as expressing a final (result) nuance here: the lacking mind results in his foolishness being evident to passers-by. The PP לכל is an adjunct specifying the addressee of the verb of speaking. The complement is the null copula clause סכל הוא. Commentators are divided on whether the complement represents direct or indirect speech (see Seow 1997: 313). If it represents direct speech, the fool must be calling passers-by "fools" ("He says to everyone, 'He is a fool!'") and thereby illustrates his foolishness (see Prov 12:15). If סכל הוא is indirect speech—i.e., "he says (that) he is a fool"—then it refers to the fool himself, and what the nature of his foolish actions is is not provided. The connection made by the irrealis *qatal* to the preceding לבו חסר suggests the latter option is more likely: the fools lack of sense as he walks along a bad path is evident to all so that they recognize his folly (Prov 13:16), and if they are wise, they avoid him along the way (Prov 17:12).

סָכָל הוּא. The predicate-subject order of the null copula clause reflects the focus-fronting of the predicate. Thus, if the clause is direct speech, the fool is asserting that each person he calls a fool is nothing but a fool. If the clause is indirect speech (and so about the fool himself), the narrator is asserting the same but about the fool: he is showing himself to be nothing but a fool.

10:4   אִם־רוּחַ הַמּוֹשֵׁל תַּעֲלֶה עָלֶיךָ מְקוֹמְךָ אַל־תַּנַּח כִּי מַרְפֵּא יַנִּיחַ חֲטָאִים גְּדוֹלִים:

If the spirit of the ruler rises against you, don't leave your place because healing/calmness sets aside great offenses.

This verse has a conceptual link with 8:2-3, and verbal links (מושל and נחת/יניח) with 9:17. In contrast to the earlier advice to get out of the way of the king's wrath (8:3), here the value of wisdom is extolled for its ability to assuage the wrath of a ruler (see Prov 16:14), similar to the efficacy of the "calm" words of the wise versus the "shout" of the ruler in 9:17.

אִם־רוּחַ הַמּוֹשֵׁל תַּעֲלֶה עָלֶיךָ. Participle (agentive noun; see 1:15) ms *Qal* √משל; *yiqtol* (irrealis) 3fs *Qal* √עלה. This clause is the protasis of a conditional statement. The function word אם typically triggers verb-raising over the subject (see Holmstedt 2009a, 2011). The subject-verb order in this clause reflects, then, either a change in grammar from other

biblical books or the additional focus-fronting of רוח המושל, which
would suggest that the advice in this verse applies only in the case that a
ruler (not anyone else) is angry with you (in contrast, the advice given in
8:2-9 was about being in the presence of a ruler that is mad in general or
at someone else). Since in Hebrew one's wrath "rises against" someone
(Pss 78:21, 31), the רוח here is elliptical for a wrathful spirit.

מְקוֹמְךָ אַל־תַּנַּח. *Yiqtol* (jussive) 2ms Hiph √נוח. The form תַּנַּח
reflects the "Aramaising" morphology of some II-ו verbs (JM §80p),
although it is more common for II–III verbs (i.e., Geminate verbs). This
clause is the apodosis of the conditional statement. The focus-fronted
PP makes it clear that the person is in their rightful place, hence the
angry spirit is undeserved, which may explain the apparent contradictory
advice between this verse and 8:3, which suggests running away at a bad
word (בדרב רע) from the king.

כִּי מַרְפֵּא יַנִּיחַ חֲטָאִים גְּדוֹלִים. *Yiqtol* 3ms Hiph √נוח. This כי
clause provides the reason or motivation that supports the preceding
advice not to leave. As with אם, the function word כי triggers verb-
raising over the subject in the grammar of most biblical books. So again,
the subject-verb order here either reflects a change in grammar or the
focus-fronting of the subject, presumably to isolate the only thing that
is effective in such situations, a soothing and pacifying response. The
NP מרפא may be either from √רפא and thus "healing" or √רפה and
thus "calmness." It is likely, as Seow (1997: 313–14) suggests (with many
others), that regardless of the etymology, the similarity of form and root
has lead to a multivalent lexeme and that, at least here, the word has
both meanings. The verb יניח in this context admits several nuances (see
Krüger, 183), but the parallels in Prov 16:14 and Ben Sira 20:28 suggest
the sense of "assuage" or "appease" (Fox 1999: 304; Longman, 239).
It can be interpreted either generically (gnomic) or dynamic (ability):
"is capable of," since the word order is no aid in distinguishing realis
(generic) or irrealis (dynamic) here.

10:5   יֵשׁ רָעָה רָאִיתִי תַּחַת הַשֶּׁמֶשׁ כִּשְׁגָגָה שֶׁיֹּצָא
       מִלִּפְנֵי הַשַּׁלִּיט:

*There is a tragedy that I saw under the sun, like a mistake that proceeds
from the ruler.*

Verses 5-7 present related examples of the sort of reversal of proper social place that is objected to in wisdom literature (see Prov 19:10; 30:22).

יֵשׁ רָעָה רָאִיתִי תַּחַת הַשָּׁמֶשׁ. *Qatal* 1cs Qal √ראה. An existential יֵשׁ clause (see 2:21) with predicate-subject order. The subject רעה is modified by an unmarked relative clause consisting of the verb ראיתי and its PP complement תחת השמש.

כִּשְׁגָגָה שֶׁיֹּצֵא מִלִּפְנֵי הַשַּׁלִּיט. Participle fs Qal √יצא. The PP כשגגה is adjunct to the main predicate יש and modified by the following relative clause. The כ preposition has been treated as asseverative "indeed" (Gordis 1955: 319; Longman, 241), but a comparative reading is possible since the specifics of the comparison are ambiguous: for example, it may be that the tragedy is of an equivalent magnitude to a mistaken decision made by one in power.

10:6 נִתַּן הַסֶּכֶל בַּמְּרוֹמִים רַבִּים וַעֲשִׁירִים בַּשֵּׁפֶל יֵשֵׁבוּ:

The fool/folly is set in many high places, and the rich dwell in humility.

This verse specifies what the tragedy mentioned in v. 5 is: namely, the improper reversal of the social standing of the fool/folly and the rich or upper class.

נִתַּן הַסֶּכֶל בַּמְּרוֹמִים רַבִּים. *Qatal* 3ms Niph √נתן. The clause is appositionally related to רעה in the previous verse. The verb-subject word order reflects the irrealis use of the *qatal* verb in generic or anecdotal statements (see Cook 2005; Holmstedt 2009a, 2011). The *hapax* סֶכֶל is presumed to be the abstract "foolishness" as opposed to סָכָל (see 10:3). The locative PP "in high places" in the context is best understood as social position.

וַעֲשִׁירִים בַּשֵּׁפֶל יֵשֵׁבוּ. *Yiqtol* 3mp Qal √ישב. This clause is coordinated with the preceding as appositionally modifying רעה in v. 5. The *yiqtol* is best interpreted as the irrealis imperfective used for genericity like the *qatal* in the previous clause. The subject-PP-verb word order indicates that the subject has been fronted as a topic (to signal the switch from הסכל to עשירים) and the PP is fronted for focus (to create an implied contrast with where one might expect the wealthy to sit, in high and honored places).

10:7   רָאִיתִי עֲבָדִים עַל־סוּסִים וְשָׂרִים הֹלְכִים כַּעֲבָדִים
עַל־הָאָרֶץ:

I saw servants on horses and princes walking like servants on the ground.

The initial רָאִיתִי separates this verse somewhat from the previous two, though it treats a related issue: the improper reversal of social position.

רָאִיתִי עֲבָדִים עַל־סוּסִים. *Qatal* 1cs Qal √ראה. The NP complement עבדים is modified by the NP-internal PP עַל־סוּסִים.

וְשָׂרִים הֹלְכִים כַּעֲבָדִים עַל־הָאָרֶץ. Participle mp Qal √הלך. The שׂרים is coordinated with עבדים as the complement of רָאִיתִי, and modified by the relative-participle clause. The comparative adjunct כ-PP makes the reversal explicit: princes are in the place of servants.

10:8   חֹפֵר גּוּמָץ בּוֹ יִפּוֹל וּפֹרֵץ גָּדֵר יִשְּׁכֶנּוּ נָחָשׁ:

(He who) digs a pit will fall into it, and (he who) breaks down/through a wall—him a snake will bite.

This verse begins with a motif commonly used to characterize the retribution principle (see Pss 7:16; 57:7; Prov 26:27; Ben Sira 27:26). However, Qoheleth alters the sense of the motif by placing it at the head of a series of everyday activities that culminate in the observation that humans cannot know what is in store for them (v. 14). There is no explicit retribution principle here (cf. Ps 7:16-17); rather, there is simply an inherent uncertainty and danger for those who engage in these everyday activities, such as digging a hole (e.g., for hunting animals; so Seow 1997: 316) and demolishing a wall.

חֹפֵר גּוּמָץ בּוֹ יִפּוֹל. Participle ms Qal √חפר and *yiqtol* 3ms Qal √נפל. The subject is the null head of the relative participle. The NP complement of the participle is the Aramaic calque גמוץ (cf. Heb. שׁחת). The second clause has the PP בו fronted for focus: into *the same* he will fall. Both predicates are generic, but as is often the case in Proverbs (see Cook 2005), the participle is more apt to describe habitual actions whereas *yiqtol* tends to refer to eventualities. We can paraphrase the effect as: "He who is wont to dig a hole, into the same he is bound to fall!"

וּפֹרֵץ גָּדֵר יִשְּׁכֶנּוּ נָחָשׁ. Participle ms Qal √פרץ and *yiqtol* 3ms Qal √נשך + enclitic נ plus 3ms clitic pronoun. The syntactic structure of this maxim is slightly different from the preceding. The first expression constitutes of a left-dislocated null-head relative participle followed by an NP complement. The main clause is in verb-subject order to focus-front the resumptive clitic NP complement: "*Him* will a snake bite." Amos 5:19 also refers to the dangers of snakes hidden in walls.

מַסִּיעַ אֲבָנִים יֵעָצֵב בָּהֶם בּוֹקֵעַ עֵצִים יִסָּכֶן בָּם: 10:9

He who uproots (= quarries) rocks may be hurt by them; he who splits wood may be endangered by them.

The list of everyday activities and the dangers they pose to those engaged in them continues. In contrast to the implied retribution principle in the familiar motif in v. 8a, here the dangers have no moral overtones. This fact along with the lack of any over focus-fronting in this verse, in contrast to v. 8, leads to a reinterpretation of the series of verses: one who quarries stone or splits wood will not *inevitably* be hurt by the stone and wood, though they pose a danger (i.e., the *yiqtol* verbs express irrealis epistemic modality); in turn, this interpretation overturns the initial inevitable-generic expression of the *yiqtol* verbs in v. 8, instigated by the association of v. 8a with the retribution principle.

מַסִּיעַ אֲבָנִים יֵעָצֵב בָּהֶם. Participle ms Hiph √נסע and irrealis *yiqtol* 3ms Niph √עצב. The syntax is identical with v. 8a, except that there is no focus-fronting in the second clause. The *yiqtol* verb here is irrealis, expressing epistemic modality within the generic expression.

בּוֹקֵעַ עֵצִים יִסָּכֶן בָּם. Participle ms Qal √בקע and irrealis *yiqtol* 3ms Niph √סכן. The syntax is identical with the preceding, as are the verbal semantics. The shift to passive Niphal and lack of animate agency in this verse contributes to reading it as a description of everyday dangers in which one finds oneself rather than a characterization of the retribution principle.

אִם־קֵהָה הַבַּרְזֶל וְהוּא לֹא־פָנִים קִלְקַל וַחֲיָלִים   10:10
יְגַבֵּר וְיִתְרוֹן הַכְשֵׁיר* חָכְמָה:

If one has blunted the iron and he has not sharpened (its) edges, then he must exert (his) power; that is, an advantage to working skillfully is wisdom.

Despite some grammatical uncertainties, this verse follows quite naturally on the previous clause, dealing with the issue of a blunt

instrument and the advantage wisdom provides. Krüger (185) notes that
this verse presents another reversal of expectations, as is the case in the
previous two verses: we expect the observation of the dull blade to lead
to a comment on the increased dangers, but instead we find a comment
on the need for more effort and the wisdom of sharpening the blade.

אִם־קֵהָה הַבַּרְזֶל. *Qatal* 3ms Piel √קהה. The NP הברזל is either
the subject or complement of the Piel verb (see HALOT). Since the verb
occurs only here (the Qal verb appears in Jer 31:29 and Ezek 18:2), it
is best to expect a transitive valency pattern in keeping with most Piel
verbs, though the impersonal null-subject makes the difference between
the two analyses slight (i.e., "one has blunted the iron" vs. "the iron is
blunted"). It seems unnecessary to repoint according to Seow's (1997:
317) suggestions of a Qal 3ms קָהָה or the adjective קֵהֶה. The "iron"
stands for the iron tool, presumably an axe in the context of the preceding verse (so elsewhere, 2 Kgs 6:5), though iron tools would also have
been used in rock quarrying.

וְהוּא לֹא־פָנִים קִלְקַל. *Qatal* 3ms Pilpel (= Piel) √קלל. The subject
is expressed overtly by the pronoun, which also appears in the fronted
position, ahead of the negative. It is entirely unclear why the pronoun is
used and why the agent (assuming it is the same unexpressed agent from
the previous clause) is either a topic or focus. Moreover, the position of
the negative, before the complement and not juxtaposed to the verb, suggests that the לא is an item adverb, "he sharpened not edges (but something else)." But this is nonsense. Why would one blunt a piece of iron
and sharpen part of it that are not edges? The noun פנים is understood
as either temporal "previously" (so Gordis 1955: 322; but the expected
form is the preposition לְפָנִים) or the two "faces" of the axe head that
must be ground in sharpening it (cf. the usual Hebrew idiom for blade
edge as פֶה "mouth"; e.g., Job 1:17 et al.). The verb only appears here and
in Ezek 21:26 of shaking arrows. Murphy (98) therefore suggests it refers
in this context to the quickly moving sharpening instrument. Alternatively, Seow (1997: 317) suggests this verb here is a denominative from
קָלָל "smooth, shiny" used to describe bronze in Ezek 1:7 and Dan 10:6.

וַחֲיָלִים יְגַבֵּר. Irrealis *yiqtol* 3ms Piel √גבר. The word order is complement-verb, and the null-subject is identical with the previous clause.
The irrealis *yiqtol* is best understood as expressing deontic (necessity)
modality here. A similar idiom appears in Job 21:7 with the Qal form
of the root גבר (intransitive) followed by an adjunct חיל "increase (with

respect to) strength." The plural form is difficult to convey with "power" or "strength"; Longman (243) translates "his efforts."

וְיִתְרוֹן הַכְשִׁיר חָכְמָה. The first and third words are familiar from the rest of the book, but the middle word and the word order are problematic. The *Ketiv* הַכְשִׁיר is the Hiphil infinitive construct; the *Qere* הַכְשֵׁר is the Hiphil infinitive absolute. The *Ketiv* is noted in the margin of B19a (יתיר י) as containing a superfluous י, implying a *Qere* reading of הַכְשֵׁר. Several interpretations have been advanced: (1) "the advantage of the skilled (man) is wisdom," by repointing the infinitive as an adjective הַכָּשֵׁר (so Fox 1999: 306); (2) "to appropriate/improve in wisdom is an advantage," reading the *Ketiv* with חכמה as the complement and the infinitive clause the subject of the null copula clause (so Seow 1997: 318; Krüger, 177); (3) reading the *Qere* infinitive absolute as a verbal noun, "an advantage of being skillful/for succeeding is wisdom" (see Crenshaw, 173; Whybray, 154; Murphy, 97); and (4) treat יתרון and חכמה as a broken construct chain, "the advantage of wisdom is skill/preparation (Longman, 245). We follow the third approach here, treating חכמה as subject and the bound phrase ויתרון הכשיר as the predicate of the null copula: sharpening the blade (wisdom) is an advantage to being successful (chopping wood). Wisdom is defined in this verse as the practical wisdom of the skilled worker. The whole clause is appositive to the previous metaphor and essentially translates it.

10:11 אִם־יִשֹּׁךְ הַנָּחָשׁ בְּלוֹא־לָחַשׁ וְאֵין יִתְרוֹן לְבַעַל הַלָּשׁוֹן:

If the snake bites without a charm, then there is no advantage to the charmer.

As soon as the relative advantage of wisdom is commended (v. 10), it is relativized by the everyday occupational hazard of the snake charmer (note the verbal link of יתרון in both verses): wisdom to charm a snake is useless if something prompts the snake to bite before it is charmed.

אִם־יִשֹּׁךְ הַנָּחָשׁ בְּלוֹא־לָחַשׁ. *Yiqtol* (irrealis) 3ms Qal √נשך. The protasis of the conditional clause calls for an irrealis verb form, which shows verb-subject inverted order after אם. The PP בלוא־לחש (the preposition ב is prefixed to the negative לוא) can be taken as either a NP-internal modifier of the subject ("a charmless snake") or an adjunct to the verb (see Seow 1997: 318). The different syntactic options lead to only slightly different statements. If the PP is a verbal adjunct, the point is that the snake bites before it is charmed; if the PP is NP-internal, the snake is identified as an uncharmed snake. The functional difference in meaning is nil. See Jer 8:17, in which God threatens to send snakes "for which no charm exists for" (אֲשֶׁר אֵין־לָהֶם לָחַשׁ).

וְאֵין יִתְרוֹן לְבַעַל הַלָּשׁוֹן. An אין negative copula clause. The subject is יתרון and the ל-PP phrase expresses advantage or ownership. The PP "master of the tongue" in this context refers to the snake charmer, who is referred to more usually as a מְלַחֵשׁ (e.g., Ps 58:6). Seow (1997: 318) compares this phrase with the Akkadian *bēl lišāni* "master of the tongue" in reference to people knowledgable in a foreign language: the snake charmer is thus knowledgeable in the language of snake charms. Crenshaw (173) and Murphy (102) summarize the point as that wisdom (skill) is of no advantage if unused or wasted, implying that the snake charmer should have used his skills to prevent the bite. Longman demurs that "it is not about unused skill; it is about wisdom that is useless in practical situations [i.e., after the snake has bitten] … . Basically, the skill of a snake charmer is good for shows but not for practical everyday living, where snakebites are a matter of life and death" (246). However, this seems a gratuitous denigration of the snake charmer's "wisdom," which is not evidenced in this context, in which Qoheleth makes no distinction moral or otherwise between different everyday activities, but rather points out that they all equally hold uncertain dangers in store for those who engage in them.

10:12 דִּבְרֵי פִי־חָכָם חֵן וְשִׂפְתוֹת כְּסִיל תְּבַלְּעֶנּוּ:

The words of the mouth of the wise (are) gracious, but the lips of the fool will swallow him.

This verse returns to the wise-fool contrast in previous verses (e.g., 10:2), but also picks up on the topic of speech (see 9:17; 10:4). The ideas echo those found elsewhere in the wisdom literature: e.g., Prov 14:3; 18:7; 13:4; Ben Sira 6:5.

דִּבְרֵי פִי־חָכָם חֵן. A null copula clause. The subject is the bound phrase דברי פי־חכם, and the predicate complement is חן.

וְשִׂפְתוֹת כְּסִיל תְּבַלְּעֶנּוּ. *Yiqtol* 3fs Piel √בלע + energic נ + 3ms clitic pronoun. The subject is the bound phrase ושפתות כסיל, even though we expect a plural verb with the dual head וְשִׂפְתוֹת (see GKC §145n). The clitic pronoun refers back to כְּסִיל.

10:13   תְּחִלַּת דִּבְרֵי־פִיהוּ סִכְלוּת וְאַחֲרִית פִּיהוּ הוֹלֵלוּת רָעָה:

The beginning of the words of his mouth are foolishness, and the end of his mouth is evil inanity.

This verse continues from the previous, elaborating on the character of the fool's speech that leads to his self-destruction.

תְּחִלַּת דִּבְרֵי־פִיהוּ סִכְלוּת. A null copula clause. The predicate complement is סכלות. The pronoun on פיהו refers to the כסיל of the previous verse.

וְאַחֲרִית פִּיהוּ הוֹלֵלוּת רָעָה. A null copula clause. The subject is ואחרית פיהו with the pronoun referring back to כסיל as in the previous clause. The predicate complement הוללות (on which see note on 1:17) is modified by the adjective רעה. The beginning-afterwards distinction may be understood temporally, describing the fool as going from bad to worse, or the "after affect" or outcome of his speech (so Fox 1999: 307; see Prov 5:4). We have translated so as to retain the ambiguity, though it is somewhat awkward with the metonymy "mouth" for "speech" (or elliptical for "words of his mouth").

10:14   וְהַסָּכָל יַרְבֶּה דְבָרִים לֹא־יֵדַע הָאָדָם מַה־שֶׁיִּהְיֶה וַאֲשֶׁר יִהְיֶה מֵאַחֲרָיו מִי יַגִּיד לוֹ:

But the fool will multiply words! Man cannot know what will happen, and what will happen after him—who can tell him?

Ignorance about the future has already been expressed in the book (e.g., 6:12; 8:17). Lohfink (130) explains that if the wise cannot foresee the future, then a fortiori the fool cannot. The אחרית in v. 13 suggests the focus on the future here, even as the ambiguity of the term מאחריו "after him" plays off of the earlier form.

וְהַסָּכָל יַרְבֶּה דְבָרִים. *Yiqtol* 3ms Hiph √רבה. A subject-verb-complement generic clause. The vanity of multiplying words appears in 6:11.

לֹא־יֵדַע הָאָדָם מַה־שֶׁיִּהְיֶה. *Yiqtol* (irrealis) 3ms Qal √ידע and √היה. The negative (and irrealis *yiqtol*) explain the verb-subject word order. The *yiqtol* here is generic but also dynamic: one is unable to know the future (see Cook 2013: 338).

וַאֲשֶׁר יִהְיֶה מֵאַחֲרָיו מִי יַגִּיד לוֹ. *Yiqtol* 3ms Qal √היה and Hiph √נגד. The null-head אשר clause is a left-dislocation before the clause-initial מי interrogative, which is resumed by the PP לו. The focused dislocation contrasts with the previous מה־שׁיהיה, suggesting that the previous clause has do to with what will happen in the future of one's life versus what will happen after one's death in this verse. At the same time, מאחריו plays on the אחרית פיהו in the previous verse: Is the concern with the outcome of one's life or events after one dies? The *yiqtol* is here, as in the previous clause, a generic dynamic

10:15   עֲמַל הַכְּסִילִים תְּיַגְּעֶנּוּ אֲשֶׁר לֹא־יָדַע לָלֶכֶת אֶל־עִיר:

> *The toil of the fools will weary him—he who does not (even) know (how) to get to town!*

Expanding further on the ignorance of fools, their lack of knowledge about the future is unsurprising (v. 14) given that despite their toiling to know (as suggested by 6:11-12), they do not even attain to the practical knowledge of directions to town.

עֲמַל הַכְּסִילִים תְּיַגְּעֶנּוּ. *Yiqtol* 3fs Piel √יגע + energic נ + 3ms clitic pronoun. The word order is subject-verb, as expected for the realis generic *yiqtol* clause. The clause lacks agreement, however: (1) the feminine verb תיגענו does not agree with the masculine subject עמל; and (2) the clitic pronoun does not agree in number with its antecedent הכסילים, which is treated as a generic collective. Some emend (see Fox 1999: 307); others suggest that perhaps the verb is masculine, as is sometimes found in Ugaritic (so Seow 1997: 320).

אֲשֶׁר לֹא־יָדַע לָלֶכֶת אֶל־עִיר. *Qatal* 3ms Qal √ידע and Inf Constr √הלך. The clitic pronoun on תיגענו is the head of the relative clause. The stative ידע has a present state meaning here with an infinitival complement clause.

10:16   אִי־לָךְ אֶרֶץ שֶׁמַּלְכֵּךְ נָעַר וְשָׂרַיִךְ בַּבֹּקֶר יֹאכֵלוּ:

> *Woe belongs to you, O Land, whose king is a servant, and your princes feast in the morning.*

This and the following verse clearly belong together by their contrastive אי and אשרי expressions. This verse reads as a twin thought to

Prov 30:22: "[21 under three things the earth quakes …] 22 under a slave if/when he becomes a king, and a fool when he is sated with bread." Fox (1999: 308) argues that they belong also with vv. 18-20 and that all of them deal with the "virtues and vices of the ruling class." The return to royal ideas in v. 20 would appear to substantiate treating them as a unit, which helpfully gives context to vv. 18-19 (see Krüger, 188; cf. Longman, 248).

אִי־לָךְ אֶרֶץ שֶׁמַּלְכֵּךְ נָעַר. A null copula clause. The subject is אִי "woe," and the predicate PP complement expresses ownership: woe is the lot for the land whose king is a child. The anarthrous ארץ is vocative and serves as the head of the null copula relative clause marked by שׁ. The noun נער is rendered by most as "a minor," "boy," "youth" or the like (e.g., Murphy, 104; Seow 1997: 328; Krüger, 177). However, as Fox (1999: 309) points out, understanding the term as referring to social standing rather than age creates a more fitting contrast with בן־חורים in the following verse (חורים "nobles" is contrasted with עבד "servant" in Ben Sira 10:25; so HALOT). Hence he translates נער as "lackey." Either interpretation implies weak leadership, though not necessarily for the same reasons.

וְשָׂרַיִךְ בַּבֹּקֶר יֹאכֵלוּ. Yiqtol 3mp Qal √אכל. The relative שׁ has scope over the second clause, too. This is not only suggested by the parallelism but also by Miller's (2010) analysis of vocative syntax. She argues that unmarked relative clauses following vocatives only show agreement in the third person (e.g., Isa 44:1). The second-person agreement within a relative can only be used when the relative is overtly introduced by a relative word, as in the first clause in this verse. Thus, the second-person suffix on שׂריך, which refers back to the vocative ארץ, indicates that the second clause must be contained within the domain established by the שׁ. The word order suggests a double focus-fronting of both the PP בבקר (they feast in the morning rather than at the proper time) and ושׂריך (your princes and not simply your lackey king). The yiqtol could be interpreted as a present imperfective ("are feasting"), but better as an irrealis expressing habituality ("are wont to feast"). The parallel with Prov 30:22 and contrast with the following verse suggest more than just timing is in question with the term יאכל. The all-day overindulgence in wine is condemned in Isa 5:11, 19.

10:17 אַשְׁרֵיךְ אֶרֶץ שֶׁמַּלְכֵּךְ בֶּן־חוֹרִים וְשָׂרַיִךְ בָּעֵת
יֹאכֵלוּ בִּגְבוּרָה וְלֹא בַשְּׁתִי:

Fortunate are you, O Land, whose king is a noble and whose princes eat
at the (proper) time—with manliness and not with drinking!

The contrast with the previous verse is quite complete: woe versus
happiness; the son of a noble versus a servant; at the (proper) time versus
in the morning. Even the syntax matches closely between the two.

אַשְׁרֵיךְ אֶרֶץ שֶׁמַּלְכֵּךְ בֶּן־חוֹרִים. A null copula clause with אשר as
complement and the clitic pronoun as subject. The noun ארץ is vocative,
as in v. 16, and head of the following relative clause modifier. The term
חורים occurs twelve other times with clear reference to the noble class
(1 Kgs 21:8, 11; Isa 34:12; Jer 27:20; 39:6; Eccl 10:17; Neh 2:16; 4:8,
13; 5:7; 6:17; 7:5; 13:17).

וְשָׂרַיִךְ בָּעֵת יֹאכֵלוּ בִּגְבוּרָה וְלֹא בַשְּׁתִי. *Yiqtol* 3mp Qal √אכל.
With the realis generic *yiqtol*, a subject-verb word order is expected.
However, the PP בעת intervenes unexpectedly between the subject ושריך
and the verb יאכלו, suggesting a double focus-fronting of the subject and
PP. Thus the word order matches exactly the last clause in the preceding
verse, and the focus fronting contributes to the contrast between one
land's princes and the time of their feasting and the other. The definite article on בָּעֵת suggests a particular time is in mind: the *proper* time
for such behavior. The last two adjunct phrases present more difficulty:
"in/for strength but not in/for drunkenness." Krüger's (188) connection
of "in strength" with Isa 5:22 הוֹי גִּבּוֹרִים לִשְׁתּוֹת יָיִן "woe (you) heroes
at drinking wine," making this verse somehow an ironic censure of the
aristocratic ideal, is unconvincing. Rather the PP בגבורים refers to the
"manly" manner of drinking with restraint, as clarified by the negative
counterpart "not in drunkenness" (for the "ב of manner," see MNK
§39.6.3.5; WO §11.2.5d–e).

10:18 בַּעֲצַלְתַּיִם יִמַּךְ הַמְּקָרֶה וּבְשִׁפְלוּת יָדַיִם יִדְלֹף
הַבָּיִת:

Through laziness the (roof) beams will become sagged, and through slack-
ness of hands the house will leak.

The dissolute life of the ruling נער and princes is to be understood
as the context for this criticism of the lazy. In this case the reference to

"the house" takes on political overtones as it has elsewhere (e.g., 2 Sam 7:11; Isa 7:2; et al.).

בַּעֲצַלְתַּיִם יִמַּךְ הַמְּקָרֶה. *Yiqtol* 3ms Niph √מכך. The clause begins with a focus-fronted PP followed by the verb and its subject. The prepositional complement עצלתים is a *hapax* noun and dual in form. The traditional "intensive dual" explanation (see HALOT) is unconvincing, as is the idea that this dual anticipates the dual ידים in the following clause (so Longman, 251). We find the most suitable explanation to be that the -ים is a dittography of the following word ימך, and we should read בעצלות, which appears in Prov 31:27. The subject המקרה is a *hapax*, though there is general agreement that it is equivalent to the more common קוֹרָה used in reference to the beamwork of the roof. The beams of the roof sink or collapse due to laziness (cf. Qal form in Ps 106:43 "sink low[er] in their iniquities").

וּבְשִׁפְלוּת יָדַיִם יִדְלֹף הַבָּיִת. *Yiqtol* 3ms Qal √דלף. The lead PP is again focus-fronted. The noun שפלות is a *hapax*, though its sense is clear enough from the equation of low hands (שפל√) with slackness. The verb "leak" substantiates the understanding of מקרה in the previous clause as specifically roof beams. The *yiqtol* verbs in both clauses are realis generic forms, which suggest that the dilapidation of the "house" is inevitable in lazy hands.

10:19 לִשְׂחוֹק עֹשִׂים לֶחֶם וְיַיִן יְשַׂמַּח חַיִּים וְהַכֶּסֶף יַעֲנֶה אֶת־הַכֹּל:

For laughter they make food, and wine will gladden life; and money answers everything.

This verse is read as either positive and negative: (1) it is a criticism of the dissolute and lazy nobles in vv. 16-18 (so Krüger, 188–89); (2) it is an affirmation of eating and drinking, which is found throughout the book (Longman, 251; Fox 1999: 310). The positive reading is more in keeping with Qoheleth's overall theme of joy in food and drink as well as the pattern of relativizing previous statements particularly found in this chapter: though debauchery and laziness will ruin the society, this does not mean that food and wine should be abandoned.

לִשְׂחוֹק עֹשִׂים לֶחֶם. Participle mp Qal √עשה. The PP is focus-fronted to isolate laughter as the only activity that will reap such benefits. The participle is complement of a null predicate and is plural to express

the impersonal agent. The formulation "prepare food" has been identified as an Aramaism, represented in the Aramaic portion of Daniel (עֲבַד
לְחֶם, Dan 5:1) in contrast to the Hebrew עשׂה משׁתה (Gen 21:8; so Seow
1997: 333; Fox 1999: 309).

וְיַיִן יְשַׂמַּח חַיִּים. *Yiqtol* 3ms Piel √שׂמח. Subject-verb-complement
order with a generic *yiqtol*. The choice of *yiqtol* instead of the participle
may suggest the promise of wine is in view.

וְהַכֶּסֶף יַעֲנֶה אֶת־הַכֹּל. *Yiqtol* 3ms Qal √ענה. Another subject-
verb-complement clause with generic *yiqtol*. We parse the verb as Qal,
"answers everything," as in providing for all (contingencies) (so also
Longman, 251; Küger 2004: 177–78; Bartholomew, 326). The form
may also be parsed as Hiphil, carrying the sense of "preoccupies everyone," which is paralleled by the same verb in 5:19, in which God keeps
people preoccupied with enjoyment (so Seow 1997: 332; Fox 1999:
310). In this case, and given the parallel with 5:19, the statement must
be interpreted as elliptical: "the money (necessary for food and wine)
preoccupies everyone." This seems a strained interpretation to us. The
more natural reading would be a negative counterpart to the preceding:
food and wine make life happy, but everyone is preoccupied with money
(see 4:8; 5:9-19). But this makes poor sense of the proverb overall, so we
follow the Qal parsing.

10:20 גַּם בְּמַדָּעֲךָ מֶלֶךְ אַל־תְּקַלֵּל וּבְחַדְרֵי מִשְׁכָּבְךָ
אַל־תְּקַלֵּל עָשִׁיר כִּי עוֹף הַשָּׁמַיִם יוֹלִיךְ אֶת־הַקּוֹל
וּבַעַל הַכְּנָפַיִם* יַגֵּיד דָּבָר׃

*Also, in your thinking do not insult a king, or in the rooms of your bed do
not insult a rich man, because the birds of the skies carry the sound, and the
winged creature reports a word.*

The advice in this verse is against the foil of the preceding critical remarks. Fox (1999: 310–11) suggests it is an "afterthought" since
Qoheleth recognizes he has just insulted the king and the rich! The shift
from generic realis verbs to the second-person jussives in this verse create a segue to the imperatival advice in the opening of chapter 11, with
which Murphy (105) treats the latter portion of chapter 10.

גַּם בְּמַדָּעֲךָ מֶלֶךְ אַל־תְּקַלֵּל. *Yiqtol* (jussive) 2ms Piel √קלל. The
additive גם suggests that this verse is connected in some way, perhaps (as

Fox takes it) as an adjustment to address a potential inference from the preceding passage. The initial PP is topic-fronted, to orient the listener to what the speaker's subsequent proposition will address or to what it will pertain. The complement of the negative jussive, the NP מלך, must be focus-fronted since both complements and adjuncts normally follow the verb (see Introduction §2D). The focus on מלך isolates this NP as the entity above all others that should not be insulted. The caution is that one cannot be too careful about guarding one's view especially of kings, who can do what they please (8:4).

וּבְחַדְרֵי֙ מִשְׁכָּבְךָ֔ אַל־תְּקַלֵּ֖ל עָשִׁ֑יר. *Yiqtol* (jussive) 2ms Piel √קלל. In poetic parallelism with the previous clause, this clause warns equally about reviling the wealthy. The PP is focus-fronted ahead of the irrealis negative jussive, but the complement of the verb appears after it, as expected. The "rooms of your bed" express the next most private place to "thinking."

כִּ֤י ע֣וֹף הַשָּׁמַ֙יִם֙ יוֹלִ֣יךְ אֶת־הַקּ֔וֹל. *Yiqtol* 3ms Hiph √הלך. After the causal כי, we expect verb-subject order here, so that the subject must be focus-fronted to highlight the unlikelihood that a bird, who cannot talk, would carry news of one's thoughts to the concerned parties. The metaphor appears also in proverbs of Aḥiqar, whose sense is conveyed by the modern saying "the walls have ears":

> [My] son, do not d[a]mn the day until you see [nig]ht.
> Do n[ot] let it come into your mind that in every place
>   are their e[yes] and their ears.
> But (as regards) your mouth, watch yourself; let it not be
>   [their] prey.
> More than all watchfulness watch your mouth and over
>   what you h[eard] harden (your) heart. For a bird is
>   a word and he who sends it forth is a person of no
>   hea[rt]. (Translation based on Porten and Yardeni
>   1986: III.1.1.80–83)

וּבַ֤עַל הַכְּנָפַ֙יִם֙* יַגֵּ֣יד דָּבָ֑ר. *Yiqtol* 3ms Hiph √נגד. Note the *Ketiv* form includes the article ה, which is absent from the *Qere* form. Either are possible, as the article on generic nouns is frequent in BH (see WO §13.5.1.f; JM §137m). The "owner of wings" can refer to a bird or possibly insect. The generic *yiqtol* here and in the previous clause conveys the inevitability of the sound/word getting out.

11:1-6 Hedge Your Bets

Since Qoheleth argues that discerning life is, at best, seeing through a glass darkly, he promotes a two-pronged approach to living daily—keep busy (don't waste time speculating!—an obviously ironic piece of advice) and hedge your bets. If Qoheleth worked in pithy sayings, this section would simply be "keep your nose to the grindstone" and "don't put all your eggs in one basket."

11:1   שַׁלַּח לַחְמְךָ עַל־פְּנֵי הַמָּיִם כִּי־בְרֹב הַיָּמִים
תִּמְצָאֶנּוּ׃

Cast your bread upon the surface of the water because in a number of days you will find it.

Verses 1-2 are about taking risks in doing good, for even the smallest of good deeds may return surprising (and unlooked for) rewards. As Fox says, "wager on charitable and gracious deeds, even if this seems like a long shot, because the unexpected may happen and your deeds pay off" (1999: 312; similarly Seow 1997: 341–43). Although the dominant modern interpretation of this verse sees it as a reference not to charity but to business ventures (see, e.g., Delitzsch, 379; Gordis 1955: 319–20; Murphy, 106), there is a nice parallel in Egyptian instructional literature that supports the charitable deed interpretation: "Do a good deed and throw it in the water; when it dries you will find it" (Instruction of Ankhsheshonq 19.10; Lichtheim, 174).

שַׁלַּח לַחְמְךָ עַל־פְּנֵי הַמָּיִם. Impv ms Piel √שלח. The verb שלח in both Qal and Piel is bivalent; here the subject is null and the complement is the NP לחמך. The PP על פני המים is a locative adjunct.

כִּי־בְרֹב הַיָּמִים תִּמְצָאֶנּוּ. *Yiqtol* 2ms Qal √מצא + 3ms clitic pronoun as the complement. The כי clause provides the motive for the preceding imperative. It can be interpreted as a realis generic statement "you will find it" or irrealis epistemic "you may find it." Within the כי clause, the fronted PP ברב הימים is a topic, establishing the temporal setting.

11:2   תֶּן־חֵלֶק לְשִׁבְעָה וְגַם לִשְׁמוֹנָה כִּי לֹא תֵדַע מַה־
יִּהְיֶה רָעָה עַל־הָאָרֶץ׃

Give one portion to seven or even to eight, because you cannot know what will be calamitous on the earth.

תֶּן־חֵלֶק לְשִׁבְעָה וְגַם לִשְׁמוֹנָה. Impv ms Qal √נתן. The NP חלק is the first complement (the patient, or thing "given") of bivalent נתן, and the compound PP לשמונה גם לשבעה is the second complement (the recipient or goal of the "giving"). The גם on the second conjunct is additive (MNK §41.4.5.2; van der Merwe).

כִּי לֹא תֵדַע מַה־יִּהְיֶה רָעָה עַל־הָאָרֶץ. Yiqtol 2ms Qal √ידע and 3ms Qal √היה. The verb is irrealis dynamic. The מה phrase is the complement of תדע. Within the embedded interrogative, מה is the subject, and the NP רעה is the complement of יהיה, "what will be a calamity." Notice that the verb is masculine while רעה is feminine, strongly suggesting that it is not the subject as so many commentaries take it to be (i.e., "what misfortune will happen"; see, e.g., Seow 1997: 328; Longman, 254).

אִם־יִמָּלְאוּ הֶעָבִים גֶּשֶׁם עַל־הָאָרֶץ יָרִיקוּ וְאִם־   11:3
יִפּוֹל עֵץ בַּדָּרוֹם וְאִם בַּצָּפוֹן מְקוֹם שֶׁיִּפּוֹל הָעֵץ
שָׁם יְהוּא:

If the clouds are filled with rain, they will empty (it) out on the earth, and if a tree falls in the south or in the north, the place that the tree falls—there it remains.

This verse seems to be about the inevitability of natural phenomena, hence the preference for *yiqtol* generic predicates: one may not know when such events will occur, but one can be sure that they will indeed happen at some time. Moreover, humans have no control over when or where, thus reinforcing Qoheleth's previous statement about the inability of humans to discern much (a theme he returns to in v. 5). The mention of south and north is a geographic merism to indicate "everywhere" (Fox 1999: 314).

אִם־יִמָּלְאוּ הֶעָבִים גֶּשֶׁם עַל־הָאָרֶץ יָרִיקוּ. Yiqtol 3mp Niph √מלא and Hiph √ריק. The first clause is the protasis in the conditional statement, with העבים the subject of the bivalent Niphal מלא and the NP גשם the complement specifying the content with which the clouds are filled. The second clause is the apodosis, with a focus-fronted PP על הארץ, indicating that the point of this statement is the constancy of the natural process of rain: if the clouds are full, there is nowhere else but the

earth for the rain to fall upon. Note that there is no need to ignore the
טעמים and take גשם with the apodosis (as Seow does, 1997: 336); this
NP can be assumed as the complement of bivalent יריקו in the second
clause—it is a case of null anaphora, which is common in Hebrew (see
Creason; Holmstedt 2013b).

וְאִם־יִפּוֹל עֵץ בַּדָּרוֹם וְאִם בַּצָּפוֹן מְקוֹם שֶׁיִּפּוֹל הָעֵץ שָׁם יְהוּא.

Yiqtol 3ms Qal √נפל and √הוה. This clause is a second conditional
statement that is much more syntactically complex. In the protasis (note the verb-subject order after אם), the PP בדרום is a locative
adjunct for יפול, but it is then continued by an alternative אם בצפון;
given the initial conditional אם, the second אם likely cannot be taken
as a simple "or X" but instead reflects the ellipsis of the subject and
verb, e.g, "or if (a tree falls) in the north." In the apodosis, the initial
NP מקום, with the restrictive relative clause שיפול העץ, is left-dislocated and resumed by the locative adverb שם in the clause (the relative
clause is unambiguously marked as restrictive by the bound form of
the head, מְקוֹם; see Holmstedt 2008b and 2016: 209–14). The verb
יהוא is a *hapax* form, though the root is apparently used once more:
the imperative הֱוֵא appears in Job 37:6. In Job it is a command to the
snow (הֱוֵא אָרֶץ), which is typically understood as a by-form of הוה "to
fall" and so translated as "fall (to) the earth." The occurrence here is
sometimes also connected to הוה (DCH, s.v.), thus "the place that the
tree falls, there it falls," though this results in a banal tautology. Taking
יהוא as a by-form of היה (HALOT, s.v.) results in a slightly less tau-
tologous statement, "the place that a tree falls, there it remains," which
reflects an established minority connotation of היה (HALOT, s.v. היה;
Exod 34:23; Judg 17:12; Ruth 1:2). A good explanation for using the
by-form הוא for היה remains elusive.

11:4   שֹׁמֵר רוּחַ לֹא יִזְרָע וְרֹאֶה בֶעָבִים לֹא יִקְצוֹר:

*He who observes wind will not sow, and he who watches clouds will not
harvest.*

This verse follows on the inevitability of natural phenomenon
described in the previous verse. As Fox explains, "A farmer who con-
stantly frets about the weather will never get around to doing his tasks"
(1999: 314). The implied lesson of this seemingly trivial maxim is
unpacked in the following two verses.

שֹׁמֵ֤ר ר֙וּחַ֙ לֹ֣א יִזְרָ֔ע. Participle ms Qal √שמר and *yiqtol* 3ms √זרע. Normally, a negative like לֹא would trigger verb-subject order. So, here either the subject-verb order reflects the fronting of the subject for focus or topic (although neither pragmatic function seems felicitous) or the grammar of Ecclesiastes reflects a step further in the shift to a more strongly subject-verb typology (see Introduction §2D). The participle has an NP complement and thus cannot be a simple agentive noun, "a guard" (see comment on 1:15). Rather, it is the complement of a null copula within a null-head, unmarked relative clause structure, "(he who is) observing the wind." The whole participial relative clause is the subject of the verb. The verb זרע is normally bivalent and takes a NP complement, often its cognate זֶרַע "seed" but also sometimes the effected object, e.g., the field being sown. The lack of a complement here does not mean that the verb is monovalent, rather, the verb has an implicit complement suggested by the activity itself: "seed" or "field." Similarly, the implied complements of "bake" is "bread" or "cake." The preference for *yiqtol* in the negative generic statements here, as in the previous verse, points toward a focus on the inevitability of the outcome: one who is so paralyzed by uncertainties in life will *never* realize the positive outcome of taking action.

וּרֹאֶ֥ה בֶעָבִ֖ים לֹ֥א יִקְצֽוֹר. Participle ms Qal √ראה and *yiqtol* 3ms Qal √קצר. As with the previous clause, the participle here has a PP complement and as such is the complement of a null copula within a null-head, unmarked relative clause structure, "(he who is) watching the clouds." (Note the same subject-negative-verb order as in the preceding clause; see comment above.) As with זרע in the previous clause, the verb here, יקצור, is typically bivalent, though here the complement is implicit in the verb itself.

11:5   כַּאֲשֶׁ֨ר אֵֽינְךָ֜ יוֹדֵ֗עַ מַה־דֶּ֙רֶךְ֙ הָר֔וּחַ כַּעֲצָמִ֖ים בְּבֶ֣טֶן הַמְּלֵאָ֑ה כָּ֗כָה לֹ֤א תֵדַע֙ אֶֽת־מַעֲשֵׂ֣ה הָֽאֱלֹהִ֔ים אֲשֶׁ֥ר יַעֲשֶׂ֖ה אֶת־הַכֹּֽל׃

Just as you do not know what the path of the wind is, (which is) like bones in the belly of the pregnant woman, so you cannot know the work of God, who does everything.

In this verse and the following, Qoheleth draws the broader lesson from the maxim of v. 4. Here watching the weather for the "best" time to sow is shown to be pointless because despite the appearances, one cannot discern future weather patterns any more than one can discern the growth of life in a pregnant woman's belly. Both of these comparable cases point to the broader conclusion of human ignorance of all God's work.

כַּאֲשֶׁר אֵינְךָ יוֹדֵעַ מַה־דֶּרֶךְ הָרוּחַ כַּעֲצָמִים בְּבֶטֶן הַמְּלֵאָה. Participle ms Qal √ידע. The כ initiates a comparative clause and the אשר both serves as a clitic host for the preposition and nominalizes the following clause so that it is a suitable nominal complement. The complement of the verb יודע is the indirect question מה דרך הרוח. The second כ is the PP complement of the null copula inside an unmarked relative clause, "(which is) like the bones … ." The phrase בבטן המלאה can either be an adjective-relative construction, "in a belly that is full" (on the lack of "article" agreement in adjectival constructions, see Holmstedt 2016: 69–77) or a bound construction with a substantive adjective, "in the belly of the full (one)." The resulting image in the same and Fox (1999: 315) cites 11QT 50:10, m. Yeb 17:1, and b. Bek 20b as examples of מלאה in reference to a pregnant woman.

כָּכָה לֹא תֵדַע אֶת־מַעֲשֵׂה הָאֱלֹהִים אֲשֶׁר יַעֲשֶׂה אֶת־הַכֹּל. Yiqtol 2ms Qal √ידע and 3ms Qal √עשׂה. The adverb ככה picks up the protasis, "so, in this way, similarly" to begin the comparative apodosis. The switch from the participle יודע in the previous verse to yiqtol תדע here points to a shift from generic to dynamic modality: you *do not know* the wind; so you *cannot know* the works of God. The obvious ignorance in the one case is broadened to affirming the impossibility of finding out the rest of God's works. The relative clause modifies האלהים not the head of the phrase מעשה האלהים. As Fox notes, "The 'work of God' … is not creation …, but God's ongoing governance of the world, manifest in his causation of processes, such as a misfortune, the clouds emptying, [or] a tree falling" (1999: 315).

בַּבֹּקֶר זְרַע אֶת־זַרְעֶךָ וְלָעֶרֶב אַל־תַּנַּח יָדֶךָ כִּי 11:6
אֵינְךָ יוֹדֵע אֵי זֶה יִכְשָׁר הֲזֶה אוֹ־זֶה וְאִם־שְׁנֵיהֶם
כְּאֶחָד טוֹבִים:

*In the morning sow your seed, and in the evening don't let your hand rest,
because you do not know which will prosper, whether this or that, or if both
of them are equally good.*

Qoheleth rejects paralysis in the face of human ignorance, urging
instead that humans are free to take initiative. The overall conclusion is
that action in the face of ignorance is preferable to inactivity, since the
latter will inevitably bring one nothing (v. 4), while action *may* produce
a good result.

בַּבֹּקֶר זְרַע אֶת־זַרְעֶ֫ךָ. Impv ms Qal √זרע. The initial temporal
adjunct PP בבקר is topic-fronted to establish the temporal setting and
make the contrast with the succeeding clause clear. The complement of
the verb is its "cognate accusative" זֶרַע.

וְלָעֶרֶב אַל־תַּנַּח יָדֶ֫ךָ. Jussive 2ms Hiph √נוח (the form תַּנַּח reflects
the "Aramaising" morphology of some II-ו verbs; see JM §80p). The 2ms
subject of the clause is null and ידך is the NP complement of the verb,
and the topic-fronted PP לערב is a temporal adjunct. On the temporal
use of ל, see WO §11.2.10c.

כִּי אֵינְךָ יוֹדֵע אֵי זֶה יִכְשָׁר הֲזֶה אוֹ־זֶה. Participle ms Qal √ידע
and *yiqtol* 3ms Qal √כשר. This כי clause provides the motivation for the
preceding imperative and negative jussive.

וְאִם־שְׁנֵיהֶם כְּאֶחָד טוֹבִים. This null copula conditional clause
presents a second option within the scope of the כי clause. The syntactic
question for the clause itself is whether כאחד or טובים is the complement of the null copula (leaving the other as an adjunct); i.e., "both of
them are like one (with respect to being) good" or "both of them, like
one, are good." If the former, the meaning is that they are similar with
respect to goodness; if the latter, the meaning is that they are good when
they are together (taking כאחד to be a calque of Aramaic כַּחֲדָה, parallel
to Hebrew יַחְדּו "together"). In light of the use of כאחד in Isa 65:25 and
Ezra 6:20, where the PP seems to be an adjunct, we have adopted the latter analysis, taking the PP כאחד to be similar but not identical with יחדו
"together." Rather than the notion of accompaniment, as with יחדו, the
nuance of כאחד is equivalence. Thus, both of them "(are) equally good."

11:7–12:8 Enjoy Life While You're Young

This is the final substantive unit in the book before the epilogue and
concludes the advice of the book by encouraging enjoyment of life while
one is young. The tone begins positively, urging enjoyment in contrast

to paralysis in the face of inevitable ignorance of life (vv. 4-6) but quickly introduces the motivation of the brevity of life in the face of the certain prospect of death (v. 9; 12:118).

11:7   וּמָת֥וֹק הָא֑וֹר וְט֥וֹב לַֽעֵינַ֖יִם לִרְא֥וֹת אֶת־הַשָּֽׁמֶשׁ׃

The light is sweet, and for the eyes to see the sun is good.

This verse initiates the new unit (11:7–12:8) and establishes an initially positive tone.

וּמָת֥וֹק הָא֑וֹר. A null copula clause with predicate-subject order due to the focus-fronting of the predicate: "*sweet* is the light!"

וְט֥וֹב לַֽעֵינַ֖יִם לִרְא֥וֹת אֶת־הַשָּׁמֶשׁ. Inf Constr Qal √ראה. The infinitive is not the primary verb in this clause; rather, it is a null copula clause in which the infinitival clause is the subject (see, e.g., Gen 2:18). The copular complement could be understood as fronted for focus, just as מתוק was fronted in the previous clause, but this would demand that לעינים is also fronted, for which we can think of no good discourse explanation. Thus, it is more plausible to us that the complex and "heavy" PP-infinitival subject is shifted down the clause for processing ease (i.e., a form of HNPS; see 2:7, 17; 3:14, 22; 7:18, 20, 26; 9:11, 14, 15).

11:8   כִּ֣י אִם־שָׁנִ֥ים הַרְבֵּ֛ה יִחְיֶ֥ה הָאָדָ֖ם בְּכֻלָּ֣ם יִשְׂמָ֑ח וְיִזְכֹּר֙ אֶת־יְמֵ֣י הַחֹ֔שֶׁךְ כִּֽי־הַרְבֵּ֥ה יִהְי֖וּ כָּל־שֶׁבָּ֥א הָֽבֶל׃

Indeed—if a man lives many years, in all of them he should be happy, and he should remember the days of darkness, that they will be many. All that is coming is ephemeral.

Basing his advice on the maxim in v. 7 (similarly, 11:4-6), Qoheleth urges one to be happy every day of one's life, because darkness will follow this life and everything in one's future is ephemeral.

כִּ֣י אִם־שָׁנִ֥ים הַרְבֵּ֛ה יִחְיֶ֥ה הָאָדָ֖ם בְּכֻלָּ֣ם יִשְׂמָ֑ח. *Yiqtol* (irrealis) 3ms Qal √חיה and *yiqtol* (irrealis) or Jussive √שמח. Either the כי connects with the preceding verse as some sort of explanation for the motivation behind the statements there (although the connection is obscure) or, more likely in our opinion, it serves in its asseverative or emphatic function, "indeed!" (see JM §165a,e; cf. GKC §149d; WO §40.2.2b). The

אם introduces a conditional protasis, which exhibits the focus-fronting of the temporal adjunct NP שנים הרבה. The apodosis begins with the focus-fronted בכלם, which refers back to the previous fronted NP שנים הרבה. The verb is homonymously irrealis *yiqtol* or jussive. In either case, a deontic necessity or directive sense is fitting: "should be glad" or "let him rejoice." The alternative realis interpretation does not make as good of sense in the overall directive context of vv. 8-10 (see Krüger, 195).

וְיִזְכֹּר אֶת־יְמֵי הַחֹשֶׁךְ כִּי־הַרְבֵּה יִהְיוּ. *Yiqtol* (irrealis) or Jussive 3ms *Qal* √זכר and 3mp *Qal* √היה. In the Qal form of strong verbs the *yiqtol* used as an irrealis verb and the jussive are homonymous. In either case the form continues with the deontic/directive sense of the preceding verb to which it is conjoined. The NP את ימי החשך is the verbal complement, which is followed by a second, appositional, clausal complement כי הרבה יהיו, which indicates precisely what about the days of darkness should be remembered. Since the appositive complement is clausal, the כי serves as a nominalizer, allowing the clause to fill the role of a NP (see Fox 1999: 316 for a similar analysis).

כָּל־שֶׁבָּא הָבֶל. Participle ms Qal √בוא. A null copula clause with subject-copula-complement order. The subject, the quantifier כל, is modified by a restrictive ש relative clause that defines precisely what the כל quantifies. The participle בָא is homonymous with the *qatal* 3ms form, but the latter makes little sense in this context that focuses on the coming (future) days. Note that here and in v. 10, the more specific notion of ephemerality fits הבל in this context better than the notion of absurdity used elsewhere (see discussion at 1:2).

11:9 שְׂמַח בָּחוּר בְּיַלְדוּתֶיךָ וִיטִיבְךָ לִבְּךָ בִּימֵי
בְחוּרוֹתֶךָ וְהַלֵּךְ בְּדַרְכֵי לִבְּךָ וּבְמַרְאֵי עֵינֶיךָ וְדָע כִּי
עַל־כָּל־אֵלֶּה יְבִיאֲךָ הָאֱלֹהִים בַּמִּשְׁפָּט:

Be happy, young man, in your youth, and may your mind do you well in the days of your young manhood. Walk around on the paths of your mind and in the visions of your eyes. But know that God will bring you into judgment regarding all of these.

In the face of ignorance of life, Qoheleth urges here, as in the previous verse, that one should *choose* enjoyment over paralysis (see vv. 4-6). This advice is tempered, however, by Qoheleth's unswerving belief that everything falls within the purview of God's oversight, including the morality of one's actions in life.

שְׂמַח בָּחוּר בְּיַלְדוּתֶיךָ. Impv ms Qal √שמח. The NP בחור cannot be a complement of the monovalent שׂמח, and imperatives do not take NP subjects. The only syntactic role that בחור can play, then, is as a vocative (see Miller 2010 on vocative syntax). The PP בילדותיך is an adjunct localizing the activity or experience of being happy.

וִיטִיבְךָ לִבְּךָ בִּימֵי בְחוּרוֹתֶךָ. Jussive 3ms Hiph √יטב. The form יְטִיבְךָ is formally ambiguous between jussive and irrealis *yiqtol*; however, following an imperative, the jussive form is expected as continuing the directive sense. For morphophonological reasons (see Holmstedt 2000), the paradigm jussive form in the Hiphil, יַקְטֵל, becomes יַקְטִיל when a suffix (i.e., the plural וֹ-) or clitic pronoun (e.g., ךָ-) is attached, as here. The verb-subject order does not help determine if the verb is an irrealis *yiqtol* or a jussive since the modality of both forms would similarly trigger inversion to verb-subject. The PP בימי בחורותך is a temporal adjunct.

וְהַלֵּךְ בְּדַרְכֵי לִבְּךָ וּבְמַרְאֵי עֵינֶיךָ. Impv ms Piel √הלך. The motion verb הלך is bivalent in both the Qal and Piel and takes a locative complement. Thus, the complement of the verb is the compound PP בדרכי לבך ובמראי עיניך. Both PPs metaphorically describe the conduct in life as walking along a path in the direction one wishes (sees) to go.

וְדָע כִּי עַל־כָּל־אֵלֶּה יְבִיאֲךָ הָאֱלֹהִים בַּמִּשְׁפָּט. Impv ms Qal √ידע and *yiqtol* 3ms Hiph √בוא + 2ms clitic pronoun. The כי clause is the complement of the bivalent verb ידע. The כי by itself triggers inversion to verb-subject and here there is the addition of the fronted adjunct PP על כל אלה which would also have triggered inversion. The fronting of the PP is for focus, signaling that *it is for these reasons and none other* that God will bring the addressee into judgment. One should focus on what one knows and can choose in life and not be paralyzed by what one does not know or cannot choose.

11:10 וְהָסֵר כַּעַס מִלִּבֶּךָ וְהַעֲבֵר רָעָה מִבְּשָׂרֶךָ כִּי־
הַיַּלְדוּת וְהַשַּׁחֲרוּת הָבֶל:

Remove vexation from your mind and pass evil from your body because youth and black hair is a הבל.

This verse complements v. 9 by using the ephemerality of young age as a good reason to focus on the good things in life and avoid anything that detracts from them.

וְהָסֵר כַּעַס מִלִּבֶּךָ. Impv ms Hiph √סור. The Hiphil of סור is trivalent, taking both an NP complement ("what" is removed = the patient) and a PP complement specifying either the origin ("where" it came from) or the goal ("to where" it will be removed). Here the PP מלבך presents the origin.

וְהַעֲבֵר רָעָה מִבְּשָׂרֶךָ כִּי־הַיַּלְדוּת וְהַשַּׁחֲרוּת הָבֶל. Impv ms Hiph √עבר. Like הסר, the Hiphil of עבר is trivalent. Here רעה is the NP complement and the PP מבשרך is the second complement indicating the origin (and thus beneficiary of the removal process). The כי clause adds a motive for the verb העבר: one should remove from one's life anything that is an obstacle to enjoying life because one's youth is short enough as it is. On the article with nouns used in a generic way, see comment on העשק in 7:7. The notion of one's youthfulness becoming הבל seems to be a reference to how quickly it passes (its ephemerality) and becomes an object of nostalgic reminiscence.

וּזְכֹר אֶת־בּוֹרְאֶיךָ בִּימֵי בְּחוּרֹתֶיךָ עַד אֲשֶׁר לֹא־ 12:1
יָבֹאוּ יְמֵי הָרָעָה וְהִגִּיעוּ שָׁנִים אֲשֶׁר תֹּאמַר אֵין־לִי
בָהֶם חֵפֶץ:

And remember the one who created you in the days of your youth, while days of misfortune have not come and years have not arrived when you say, "I have no delight in them,"

In this verse Qoheleth moves further down the path toward old age and will transition to death in v. 2, which "serve to bring out the urgency of the advice" to enjoy life (Fox 1999: 316). The motivation for remembering the creation provided in v. 1b is the inevitability of old age, which changes one's ability to enjoy certain aspects of life. Note that vv. 1-7 constitute a single complex clause, with vv. 1b, 2, and 5 initiating three sections (עד אשר לא) that begin with temporally grounded motivations for remembering one's creator.

וּזְכֹר אֶת־בּוֹרְאֶיךָ בִּימֵי בְּחוּרֹתֶיךָ. Impv ms Qal √זכר. The את בוראיך is the NP complement of the bivalent verb זכר and the PP בימי בחורתיך is a temporal PP adjunct. The NP בוראיך appears to have the

form of a mp participle (here, a null-head relative rather than an agentive noun due to the presence of the 2ms clitic pronoun, which we take
to be the complement of the bivalent verb ברא; see discussion at 1:15).
The LXX and Vulgate take this word as a singular (or have בּוֹרְאָךְ in their
Vorlagen). No translation or commentary takes this as a polytheistic
statement and so the proposals for analyzing the word are many: (1) it is
a so-called plural of majesty (GKC §124; WO §7.4.3; see Schoors, 73);
(2) the confusion of III-א and III-ה roots (which occurs often in rabbinic
Hebrew), such that this form reflects ברא spelled as if from ברה (Gordis
1955: 330; Seow 1997: 351); (3) a scribal error for בּוֹרְךָ "your cistern"
or בְּאֵרֶךָ "your well," the former a metaphor for either the grave (Isa
14:19 // שְׁאוֹל) or one's wife (Prov 5:15) and the latter for a wife (Prov
5:15; Song 4:15) (see Crenshaw, 185; Longman, 264 n. 10, 267). The
issue for many is that mention of the creator is unexpected here (see Fox
1999: 322). It is possible that a wordplay is intended: a rabbinic tradition
traces this idea back to the root of a saying by R. ʿAkabyah b. Mahalalʾel
(m. Abot 3.1): to avoid sin, one should remember one's origin (באר),
one's end (בור), and one's creator (בורא) (Seow 1997: 351–52; similarly
Krüger, 197). On the use of the fp for the abstract (here, with בחורות
"youth"), see GKC §124; WO §7.4.3.

עַד אֲשֶׁר לֹא־יָבֹאוּ יְמֵי הָרָעָה. *Yiqtol* (irrealis) 3mp Qal √בוא. This
complex עַד PP is a (temporal) adjunct to the verb זכר. The preposition
עַד, like all Hebrew prepositions, requires an NP complement, which is
in this case fulfilled by the אשר nominalized clause. The sense of עַד can
be spatial "up to, as far as" a place (with a locative NP) or temporal "until,
during" an event (with a temporal NP, such as "evening," a nominalized
finite verbal clause, or an infinitival clause) (see WO §11.2.12). With
clausal complements, the clause may (as here) or may not be overtly
nominalized by אשר (HALOT, s.v. b). For this use of אשר and שׁ, see
Holmstedt 2016: 119–28. The meaning of עַד אשר לא is "while X has
not happened," which is functionally equivalent to "before X will happen," in which the (irrealis) *yiqtol* within the temporal protasis conveys a
future-in-the-past sense.

וְהִגִּיעוּ שָׁנִים אֲשֶׁר תֹּאמַר. *Qatal* (irrealis) 3cp Hiph √נגע and
yiqtol 2ms Qal √אמר. This clause continues within the domain of the
אשר following עַד. The conjoining of irrealis *qatal* to irrealis *yiqtol* is
conventional in BH, making it difficult to discern a semantic distinction between the two forms, though perhaps the irrealis *qatal* denotes
more properly a perfect sense here. Thus, it is the second conjunct of the

compound nominalized complement clause. In this conjunct the negative לֹא from the first half must be assumed to apply to this clause as well
(either by ellipsis of the negative or simply the initial לֹא taking wide
scope over both clauses). The subject NP שָׁנִים is modified by the relative
clause אֲשֶׁר תֹּאמַר, in which the head שָׁנִים could only be resumed by a
PP, "years that you say [about them] … ." In this case, the resumption is
null, though note that the relative head is linked to the anaphoric clitic
pronoun in the PP בהם within the embedded direct speech complement
of תאמר.

אֵין־לִי בָהֶם חֵפֶץ. A copular clause with אין as the negative copula,
the NP חפץ the subject, the PP לי the copular complement, and the PP
בהם an adjunct (locative or means) to the copula. The clause as a whole
is the direct speech complement of the verb of speaking תאמר within
the relative clause. The clitic pronoun in the PP בהם is 3mp, whereas its
antecedent שנים is fp (though with a masculine ending). Such masculine-
for-feminine gender agreement is not uncommon in the Hebrew Bible
(see JM §149b–c; Delsman; Schoors, 162–64, and Holmstedt 2009c)

12:2 עַד אֲשֶׁר לֹא־תֶחְשַׁךְ הַשֶּׁמֶשׁ וְהָאוֹר וְהַיָּרֵחַ וְהַכּוֹכָבִים וְשָׁבוּ הֶעָבִים אַחַר הַגָּשֶׁם׃

*while the sun and the light and the moon and the stars have not grown
dark and the clouds have not returned after the rain,*

This verse is a continuation of v. 1 and provides a second temporal
PP adjunct to the verb זכר. The main predicates are irrealis verbs through
v. 7, continuing as they do the temporal apodosis (see Cook 2013: 330,
338). Any semantic distinction between the irrealis *yiqtol* and *qatal* forms
is difficult to discern especially because of the uncertain imagery in the
passage. The imagery relates to the end of human life, which is implicitly
likened to the light(s) and the rain that are followed by darkness and
clouds, respectively (see Fox 1999: 333–49 for an extended discussion of
the imagery and vv. 1-7).

עַד אֲשֶׁר לֹא־תֶחְשַׁךְ הַשֶּׁמֶשׁ וְהָאוֹר וְהַיָּרֵחַ וְהַכּוֹכָבִים. *Yiqtol*
(irrealis) 3fs Qal √חשׁך. The first half of the compound אשר complement of עד is a negative verbal clause with a compound subject. The
verb-subject order reflects verb-raising, triggered by either the אשר or
the negative לֹא. The verb תחשׁך is 3fs, whereas the compound subject
would naturally be resolved as mp; such lack of gender and/or number

agreement is not particularly rare in the Hebrew Bible in general or the book of Ecclesiastes in particular (see comment on v. 1).

וְשָׁ֣בוּ הֶעָבִ֔ים אַחַ֖ר הַגָּֽשֶׁם. *Qatal* (irrealis) 3cp Qal √שוב. This clause constitutes the second half of the compound אשר complement. As in v. 1, the negative לא from the first conjunct must be assumed to apply to this conjunct as well.

12:3   בַּיּ֗וֹם שֶׁיָּזֻ֙עוּ֙ שֹׁמְרֵ֣י הַבַּ֔יִת וְהִֽתְעַוְּת֖וּ אַנְשֵׁ֣י הֶחָ֑יִל
       וּבָטְל֤וּ הַטֹּֽחֲנוֹת֙ כִּ֣י מִעֵ֔טוּ וְחָשְׁכ֥וּ הָרֹא֖וֹת
       בָּאֲרֻבּֽוֹת׃

on the day that the keepers of the house tremble and the men of character are stooped over and those who grind cease because they have become few and those looking through the windows have become dark,

Continuing the subsection of vv. 2-5, this verse is a complex PP temporal adjunct. As Fox argues (1999: 322–23), this PP must modify the events within v. 2 (the light going dark or the clouds returning or both) because the remembering (v. 1) must take place prior to the events described in vv. 2-5. In other words, the ב-PP brackets the event it qualifies by including it in the temporal situation it describes (vs. עד of vv. 1b and 2, which excludes the main event by specifying that the subordinate event is [or should be, in this case] situated after the main event). Thus, while vv. 1b and 2 can modify זכר since their information occurs after, the ביום of v. 3 does not modify זכר since it makes little practical sense to "remember your creator ... on the day of death (i.e., the funeral specified in v. 5)." Rather, one should remember *before* this dark day when old age moves toward its inevitable outcome, regardless of social status or wealth.

בַּיּ֗וֹם שֶׁיָּזֻ֙עוּ֙ שֹׁמְרֵ֣י הַבַּ֔יִת. *Yiqtol* (irrealis) 3mp Qal √זוע and Participle mp (bound) Qal √שמר. The verb זוע "to tremble" occurs only here and in Esth 5:9 in Hebrew within the Bible (and also twice in Aramaic: Dan 5:19; 6:27; it may also occur in the word מְזַעְזְעָיךְ of Hab 2:7, although this word is often derived from √זעה).

וְהִֽתְעַוְּת֖וּ אַנְשֵׁ֣י הֶחָ֑יִל. *Qatal* (irrealis) 3cp Hith √עות. The verb עות in the Hithpael means "to be bent, stooped." The men who are stooped are qualified by the noun חיל, "power, wealth, property, character." It is not clear if a particular nuance of חיל was intended by Qoheleth; what is clearer in the context of the verse is that this group should be understood as the other end of the spectrum established initially by שֹׁמְרֵי הַבַּיִת—both the servants (//טוֹחֲנוֹת in 3b) and the owners (//הָרֹאוֹת בָּאֲרֻבּוֹת in 3b) are moving toward their last days.

וּבָטְלוּ הַטֹּחֲנוֹת כִּי מִעֵטוּ. *Qatal* (irrealis) 3cp Qal √בטל and Participle fp Qal √טחן. The כי clause provides the reason that the grinding women have ceased their activity: they are dying off. The verb בטל, "to be inactive, cease working" (HALOT, s.v.) is a *hapax legomenon*. The meaning is determined by using both Semitic cognates (Akkadian, Ethiopic, and Arabic use the related root to mean "to cease" or "to be inactive"; HALOT, s.v.); the LXX has ἤργησαν, which is the 3pl aorist active indicative from ἀργέω "to lie idle, do nothing" (Liddell and Scott, s.v.).

וְחָשְׁכוּ הָרֹאוֹת בָּאֲרֻבּוֹת. *Qatal* (irrealis) 3cp Qal √חשׁך and Participle fp Qal √ראה. The participle is the copular complement of a null-head, ה-marked relative clause, which as a whole is the subject of the monovalent חשׁך. The PP בָּאֲרֻבּוֹת is the complement of bivalent ראה. The women who look through windows are the wealthy and privileged in society and parallel the אנשׁי החיל in the first half of the verse.

12:4   וְסֻגְּרוּ דְלָתַיִם בַּשּׁוּק בִּשְׁפַל קוֹל הַטַּחֲנָה וְיָקוּם לְקוֹל הַצִּפּוֹר וְיִשַּׁחוּ כָּל־בְּנוֹת הַשִּׁיר:

and the double doors in the street bazaar are shut when the sound of the mill has become low, and one rises at the sound of the bird, and all the daughters of the song are bent over,

This verse continues within the domain of the ביום שׁ in v. 3. It expands on the gloomy circumstances of the day of a sudden funeral (v. 5) that has interrupted the normal activity of the city.

וְסֻגְּרוּ דְלָתַיִם בַּשּׁוּק. *Qatal* (irrealis) 3cp Pual √סגר. The NP דלתים is the subject of the passive, monovalent סברו. The PP is a locative adjunct. The prepositional complement שׁוק is a rare noun in the Bible, occurring only here, v. 5, Prov 7:8, and Song 3:2.

בִּשְׁפַל קוֹל הַטַּחֲנָה. Inf Constr Qal √שׁפל. The verb שׁפל in the Qal is a stative verb, "to be low," and so has a *yiqtol* form with the /a/ theme vowel, e.g., וַיִּשְׁפַּל (Isa 2:9). Although the infinitive form with the /o/ vowel typically overrides the /a/ theme vowel, there are a few cases, as here, in which the /a/ theme vowel is preserved (JM §49c). This ב-PP/infinitive clause is an adjunct to the verb סגרו and provides further information regarding the temporal circumstances of the shutting of the double doors.

וְיָקוּם֙ לְק֣וֹל הַצִּפּ֔וֹר. *Yiqtol* (irrealis) 3ms Qal √קום. There is no overt subject for the verb יקום nor is one discernible from the the the preceding context, making it an impersonal construction. The ל-PP is an adjunct to the monovalent verb יקום and specifies the event that triggers the verbal action. On the use of ל as the temporal locative "at," see WO §11.2.10c, #6. While the individual words and the syntax of the clause are clear, what the resulting whole means is not clear. See Seow 1997: 357–58 for a survey of the proposals.

וְיִשַּׁ֖חוּ כָּל־בְּנ֥וֹת הַשִּֽׁיר. *Yiqtol* (irrealis) 3mp Qal √שחח. The verb is often analyzed as a Niphal "to keep low; make low sounds" (HALOT), with the normal assimilation of the initial נ to the שׁ of the root and *patah* (rather than the *qames* of the strong verb Niphal pattern) due to the gemination of ח, which is not marked by a *dagesh* but is implicit (JM §18b, 20a–b). By its form, it could also be analyzed as a Qal "to cower, crouch; bow down," with the gemination of the שׁ due to the use of the "Aramaising" pattern (JM §82h) and the *patah* theme vowel on the pattern of the stative verb (even though this verb is not stative semantically; see JM §82h, where this verb is listed as a possible Qal "to bend"). In the context, the Qal meaning is more felicitous since during a funeral the professional singers would not be silent or sing quietly but would be bent over in the traditional posture of lamentation (so also Fox 1999: 326; cf. Seow 1997: 359–60). On the gender mismatch between the mp verb ישחו and the fp כל בנות השיר, see comments on v. 1.

12:5   גַּ֣ם מִגָּבֹ֤הַּ יִרָ֙אוּ֙ וְחַתְחַתִּ֣ים בַּדֶּ֔רֶךְ וְיָנֵ֤אץ הַשָּׁקֵד֙
וְיִסְתַּבֵּ֣ל הֶֽחָגָ֔ב וְתָפֵ֖ר הָֽאֲבִיּוֹנָ֑ה כִּֽי־הֹלֵ֤ךְ הָֽאָדָם֙
אֶל־בֵּ֣ית עוֹלָמ֔וֹ וְסָבְב֥וּ בַשּׁ֖וּק הַסֹּפְדִֽים׃

—even of the High One they are afraid, and terrors are in the path, and the almond tree puts forth blossoms, and the grasshopper stuffs itself, and the caper is scattered when man goes to his eternal house and the lamenters mull around in the street bazaar,

Much in this verse is opaque. One can only speculate on the object of fear for the initial clause (we follow Fox's speculation; see below) and what Qoheleth intended by the reference to the trees and the חגב

("grasshopper"?) is equally enigmatic. Only the latter part of the clause is clear: whatever the former events or situations, the point seems to be that they are dark and occur during the funeral procession that represents the culmination of the ominous imagery in vv. 3-4.

גַּם מִגָּבֹהַּ יִרָאוּ. *Yiqtol* (irrealis) 3mp Qal √ירא. The גם marks focus on the fronted מִן-PP. Apparently, fearing מגבה is contrary to expectations, but why someone would fear something or someone "high" escapes us. Only Fox's suggestions makes much sense to us, that the adjective גבה might be a reference to God, perhaps like the epithets השמים [Rosh Hash 2.7] or המקום [Pes 10.5] in early rabbinic texts: "as [the songstresses] bow down, they dread the power lurking over their heads" (1999: 327). The lack of the article may seem to be an obstacle to taking גבה itself as an epithet (we would expect הַגָּבֹהַּ "the high one"), but an anarthrous adjective can be substantival and the resulting "a high place" could refer to God's abode (and by synecdoche, God himself).

וְחַתְחַתִּים בַּדֶּרֶךְ. A null copula clause with a ב-PP complement. The NP חַתְחַת is derived from √חתת and means "terrors." These may be figurative terrors associated with the ritual of a funerary procession, or if God is the source of real fear to the people who are mourning this death, then these terrors could be quite real.

וְיָנֵאץ הַשָּׁקֵד. *Yiqtol* (irrealis) 3ms Hiph √נצץ. The consonants of the verb suggest the root נאץ, which means "to spurn" in the Qal. This, of course, makes no sense with "almond tree" as the subject. The Masoretic vocalization (note the *qameṣ* under the prefix) suggests either a II-ו root or a II-III root. There is a rarely used root נוץ, which may mean "to flee," but this suffers a similar lack of contextual sense as נאץ. There are two lexical entries for נצץ, one of which appears to mean "to sparkle," while the other means "to blossom" in the Hiphil (see HALOT, s.v.; DCH, s.v.). It is only this last verb that makes any contextual sense, which is why it is the overwhelming choice of commentators (and is supported by the LXX's ἀνθήσῃ). How the consonantal text came to include the א is unclear.

וְיִסְתַּבֵּל הֶחָגָב. *Yiqtol* (irrealis) 3ms Hith √סבל. Note the metathesis of the dental ת of the Hithpael and the sibilant ס of the root—this is normal with roots that have a sibilant in first position; apparently it is a general Semitic phenomenon to avoid dental-sibilant sequences of consonants (JM §17b). The verb סבל in the Qal means "to bear a heavy load," and in the Hithpael is passive "to be burdened" or perhaps reflexive, "to burden oneself." With a grasshopper among the spring blossoms, the connotation could be "to stuff itself (with food)," which results in the grasshopper growing fat.

וְתָפֵר הָאֲבִיּוֹנָה. *Yiqtol* (irrealis) 3fs Hiph √פרר. The verb as pointed and vocalized in the MT is a Hiphil, which is the only *binyan* used for פרר, excepting three cases of the Hophal (Isa 8:10; Jer 33:2; Zech 11:11). The problem with the Hiphil here is that there is no overt complement for the bivalent verb; moreover, it is unclear what kind of null complement we might reconstruct, since what would a caper fruit break or frustrate? (Longman [266 n. 26] appears to confuse transitive "break" with unaccusative "break"; his analysis is untenable.) The LXX has διασκεδασθῇ, which is the aorist passive of διασκεδάζω "to disperse, scatter; thwart, jeopardize," the active form used to translate Hiphil פרר in numerous cases. Interestingly, the passive διασκεδασθῇ is used only here in the LXX, which lends some credence to revocalizing תָפֵר as a Hophal, תֻפַּר "(it) was broken" or "it was scattered." Some emend to תפרה from √פרה "to bear fruit" or תפרח from √פרח "it sprouts," conjecturing the haplography of the ה or ח due to the following ה on האבינה (see discussion in Gordis 1955: 336; Fox 1999: 238).

כִּי־הֹלֵךְ הָאָדָם אֶל־בֵּית עוֹלָמוֹ. Participle ms Qal √הלך. As we noted at 1:6, the expected order for clauses with participles is subject-participle, regardless of the presence of the initial כי. In most example of participle-subject order, a clear pragmatic reason, such as focus, motivates the fronting of the participle (see, e.g., Gen 3:5 כי ידע אלהים; Holmstedt 2002: 230–31). The fronting may serve to highlight the theme of death (= "going") that unites the disparate imagery of the passage. However, we can discern no clear reason for fronting of the participle here; the general opacity of the verse may be the cause.

וְסָבְבוּ בַשּׁוּק הַסֹּפְדִים. *Qatal* (irrealis) 3cp Qal √סבב and Participle mp Qal √ספד. The subject of the clause is the participle הספדים, which is used substantivally, "those who lament" ≈ "lamenters" (see comment at 1:15). This clause remains within the scope of the כי clause, which appears to have influenced the verb-subject order.

12:6 עַד אֲשֶׁר לֹא־יֵרָחֵק* חֶבֶל הַכֶּסֶף וְתָרֻץ גֻּלַּת הַזָּהָב
וְתִשָּׁבֶר כַּד עַל־הַמַּבּוּעַ וְנָרֹץ הַגַּלְגַּל אֶל־הַבּוֹר:

while the silver rope has not been torn apart, and the gold bowl has not been crushed, and a jar has not been broken over the spring, and the wheel to the well has not been crushed,

Verse 6 begins the third temporal situation that grounds the imperative זכר in v. 1. Though the images presented in vv. 6-7 are not wholly transparent, it seems clear that they continue the theme of death that was the culmination of the previous section. The message appears to be that death is inevitable and universal—no matter one's nature (whether one is a cord, a bow, a jar, or a wheel), everyone dies.

עַד אֲשֶׁר לֹא-יֵרָחֵק* חֶבֶל הַכֶּסֶף. *Yiqtol* (irrealis) 3ms Qal √רחק. The *Ketiv* has the consonants ירחק but the vowels of a Niphal. Since the Niphal does not exist in this root (and would make no sense, since it is a monovalent verb in the Qal), it is best understood as a Qal, thus יִרְחַק. However, "while he is not distant" makes no contextual sense either. The *Qere* presents the root רתק, which only occurs here and in the Pual in Nah 3:10, כָּל-גְּדוֹלֶיהָ רֻתְּקוּ בַזִּקִּים "all its important people shall be bound in fetters." Presumably the Niphal would be similarly passive, "to be bound," though that does little to clarify the sense of this clause. We have followed those who emend to Niphal ינתק "to be torn in two/apart" (see, e.g,. HALOT, s.v. רתק; Barton, 196; Fox 1999: 329–30; cf. Seow 1997: 365). On אשר עד, see v. 1. Note that that the negative לא must be assumed to apply to all the clauses in the verse, which are all within the domain of the אשר.

וְתָרֻץ גֻּלַּת הַזָּהָב. *Yiqtol* (irrealis) 3fs Qal √רצץ. The verb-subject word order has been triggered by the אשר that introduces the entire compound clause. What a gold bowl refers to is unclear. The form of the verb תרץ is problematic. Paradigmatically, it looks like a 3fs/2fs *yiqtol* from the II-ו root √רוץ. But the meaning of רוץ does not fit the context at all. Moreover, the use of the Niphal נָרֹץ from √רצץ later in the verse suggests a form of רצץ "to crush, oppress." The Qal is active and bivalent, but why would a bowl "(not) crush" something here? Rather than proposing a monovalent ("intransitive"), passive, or even impersonal active for the Qal (see DCH, s.v. רצץ; Seow 1997: 366; Longman, 266), the Niphal vocalization תֵּרֹץ is sometimes suggested (see, e.g., HALOT, s.v. רצץ; Fox 1999: 330; Krüger, 191), and we follow it here.

וְתִשָּׁבֶר כַּד עַל-הַמַּבּוֹעַ. *Yiqtol* (irrealis) 3fs Niph √שבר. The verb תשבר has been raised higher than the subject כד due to the initial אשר. The PP על המבוע is a locative adjunct of the passive, monovalent תשבר.

וְנָרֹץ הַגַּלְגַּל אֶל־הַבּוֹר. *Qatal* (irrealis) 3ms Niph √רצץ. As with the last two clauses, verb-subject order has been triggered by the אֲשֶׁר at the beginning of the compound clause. The PP אל הבור does not modify the verb (what would it mean that something was "crushed to the well"?), but is an NP-internal modifier of הגלגל, i.e., the to-the-well wheel. For NP-internal PPs, see also 1:1; 2:7, 13, 26; 3:1; 5:11; 7:6; 9:17.

12:7 וְיָשֹׁב הֶעָפָר עַל־הָאָרֶץ כְּשֶׁהָיָה וְהָרוּחַ תָּשׁוּב אֶל־
הָאֱלֹהִים אֲשֶׁר נְתָנָהּ:

and the dirt shall return to the land like it was, and the breath returns to God who gave it.

Verse 7 brings the unit begun in 11:7 to a close by reinforcing the ultimate reason to seize the day: God made us mortal and at some point we all return to the dirt with which he made us and the רוח, either wind or spirit, returns to God. Both the עפר and the רוח are clear allusions to the mythologies of Genesis 1–2—the עפר from Gen 2:7 and the רוח from Gen 1:2 (and perhaps linking to the "breath" in 2:7).

וְיָשֹׁב הֶעָפָר עַל־הָאָרֶץ כְּשֶׁהָיָה. Jussive 3ms Qal √שוב and *qatal* 3ms Qal √היה. The verb-subject word order reflects the use of the irrealis verb (here the jussive), which triggers verb-subject order. The jussive form is unexpected given the string of irrealis *qatal* and *yiqtol* forms and the clear *yiqtol* of the same root in the following clause. It may be that this is a defectively spelled *yiqtol* that was subsequently vocalized as a jussive, which would demand some directive meaning, such as "May the dust return to the earth." The שׁ nominalizes the following clause, which in this case has but one overt constituent, היה, so that it may function as the NP complement required by the preposition כ.

וְהָרוּחַ תָּשׁוּב אֶל־הָאֱלֹהִים אֲשֶׁר נְתָנָהּ. *Yiqtol* (irrealis) 3fs Qal √שוב and *qatal* 3ms Qal √נתן + clitic pronoun 3fs as its complement. The subject-verb order suggests that the verb תשוב, which is not the explicitly irrealis form like ישב in the preceding clause, is realis. However, the clause continues the lengthy and complex temporal protasis, strongly suggesting that the form is irrealis and the subject is fronted for contrastive focus with העפר "dirt" of the previous verse.

12:8   הֲבֵל הֲבָלִים אָמַר הַקּוֹהֶלֶת הַכֹּל הָבֶל:

"A total הבל*," said the Qoheleth, "everything is a* הבל*."*

Just as Qoheleth begins the report of his investigation of human life, so he concludes it. This verse serves as the conclusion to the final unit (11:7–12:7), advocating a carpe diem attitude, and the book as a whole. Note that the metanarrator breaks into Qoheleth's first-person narrative here. This narrative shift signals the transition to the end of the book. The near repetition in 12:8 of the book's motto from 1:2 provides the envelope structure that signals that the character Qoheleth's first-person narration of his experiment is complete. This verse is a single clause with the direct speech surrounding the quotative frame (see comment on 1:2).

הַקּוֹהֶלֶת. On the form of this noun and its meaning, see 1:1. This is the only occurrence in the book (excepting 7:27 as it is often emended) that includes the article, "the Qoheleth."

12:9-14 The Epilogue (or: the Narrator's Conclusion)

The primary interpretive issue for the final six verses of the book is whether they constitute an intentional unit and how this unit (or units) relates to the body of the book. The inclusio signaled by הכל הבל in 12:8, the shift to the book's narrator as the sole voice in v. 9, and the general viewpoint of the discussion—that the narrator is looking back at Qoheleth's argument and offering an assessment—all point to vv. 9-14 as an epilogue or perhaps a conclusion for the book (vs. Qoheleth's conclusion in v. 8).

More complicated is the unity of the section: were vv. 9-11 a first ending and vv. 12-14 a later addition? Additionally, there is little consensus on the relationship of the narrator's voice (and views) to the voice and views of Qoheleth. Our view is that vv. 9-14 are an originally intentional unit and that the narrator is the author, who differs from Qoheleth only in that he (the author-narrator) created Qoheleth as the literary fiction to present the experiment (which was a real experiment for Qoheleth but a thought experiment for the author).

For summaries of the complexities and the arguments, see, among many, Seow 1997: 391–96; Fox 1999: 144–45, 363–75; Shields: 47–109.

12:9   וְיֹתֵר שֶׁהָיָה קֹהֶלֶת חָכָם עוֹד לִמַּד־דַּעַת אֶת־הָעָם
וְאִזֵּן וְחִקֵּר תִּקֵּן מְשָׁלִים הַרְבֵּה:

And that Qoheleth was wise was an advantage; more (than this), he con-
tinually taught the people knowledge and would test and seek (and) arrange
many proverbs.

The first point the narrator makes about Qoheleth is that he was
not a cloistered intellectual detached from community and so from "real
life." In addition to this experiment, he lived the life of a typical sage.
Thus, his "day job" endows this current project with gravitas.

וְיֹתֵר שֶׁהָיָה קֹהֶלֶת חָכָם. *Qatal* 3ms Qal √היה. On יתר, see discussion at 2:15. The collocation of יתר and שׁ is unique in ancient Hebrew
(the closest parallel is יותר מש "beyond the fact that" in Mishnaic
Hebrew, though the מן is a critical part of that idiom). In all other places,
יתר is either the noun "advantage" or the noun used adverbially "excessively, too much." All attempts to turn יתר שׁ here into a conjunction
(e.g., "furthermore") have no grammatical support even if they result in
a sensible textual transition (see Shields: 55–57 for a survey of proposals).
We suggest that שׁ nominalizes the following clause so that it functions as
the subject of a null copula clause for which יתר is the copular complement. Besides being grammatical, this also seems to have some Masoretic
support, since prosodically the שׁ is not associated with יתר (note the
disjunctive טעם on יתר). Within the nominalized clause the adjective
חכם (which is the copular complement of the copula היה) carries restrictive semantics: "that Qoheleth was wise is … ." Though the grammar in
this analysis is clear and well attested, the resulting meaning within the
discourse remains somewhat obscure: precisely how does "that Qoheleth
was wise was an advantage (for him?)" relate to the following clause? We
have interpreted the relationship as an additive one (see next comment,
on עוד), as our best guess.

עוֹד לִמַּד־דַּעַת אֶת־הָעָם. *Qatal* (irrealis) 3ms Piel √למד. While
עוד is typically a verbal adjunct, here it appears to reflect the rare conjunctive use (DCH, s.v. 2b), which may be supported by the disjunctive
טעם, "moreover." The notion seems to be that though Qoheleth was so
wise, he did not keep his wisdom for himself but passed it on through
teaching others. The verb למד in the Piel can be bivalent but is most
often trivalent as here, with both what was taught, דעת, and to whom
it was taught, העם (see also Deut 4:5, 14; 5:31; 11:19; 31:19, 22; Judg

3:2; 2 Sam 1:18; 22:35; Isa 40:14; Jer 2:33; 9:13, 19; Pss 25:4, 9; 34:12; 51:15; 94:10; 119:12, 26, 64, 66, 68, 108, 124, 135, 171; 132:12; Dan 1:4). The עוֹד adverb here and the verb-subject word order in v. 10, suggest that the series of *qatal* forms are all irrealis habitual, describing what Qoheleth was wont to do.

וְאָזֵן וְחִקֵּר תִּקֵּן מְשָׁלִים הַרְבֵּה. *Qatal* (irrealis) 3ms Piel √אזן, √חקר, and √תקן. Each of the three verbs is bivalent, though there is only one available overt complement, the NP משלים הרבה. There are two syntactic analyses that make sense: either the three verbs are considered a compound and share the single complement (also sometimes called "right node raising" or "shared constituent coordination"; see Crystal, 418), or the first two verbs have a null complement that is gapped back from the final position in the clause (see Miller 2007: 168, esp. n. 11). Since Miller argues that backward ellipsis/gapping does not occurs in prose, we adopt the first analysis (i.e., right node raising).

12:10 בִּקֵּשׁ קֹהֶלֶת לִמְצֹא דִּבְרֵי־חֵפֶץ וְכָתוּב יֹשֶׁר דִּבְרֵי אֱמֶת:

Qohelet would seek to find words of delight and what was written correctly, words of truth.

בִּקֵּשׁ קֹהֶלֶת לִמְצֹא דִּבְרֵי־חֵפֶץ. *Qatal* (irrealis) 3ms Piel √בקש and Inf Constr Qal √מצא. The bivalent Piel בקש takes either an NP complement (see, e.g., נערה in 1 Kgs 1:2) or, as here, a ל-PP/infinitive clause. Within the infinitive clause, the subject is null and the complement of the bivalent מצא is the compound NP consisting of דברי־חפץ and the null-subject of the participial relative clause. On the verb-subject word order as suggesting an irrealis habitual sense, see on עוד למד above.

וְכָתוּב יֹשֶׁר דִּבְרֵי אֱמֶת. Participle (passive) ms Qal √כתב. Seow takes כתוב as a mispointed infinitive, i.e., כְּתוֹב. This is unnecessary, though, since the text as pointed makes good grammatical sense, as a null-head, unmarked relative clause, with the passive participle as the complement of the null copula, "(the thing that was) written … ." The NP ישר is an adjunct indicating the manner of the writing activity (and so, by extension, the resulting product). The NP דברי אמת is in apposition to the null-subject of the כתוב relative clause and clarifies the content.

12:11 דִּבְרֵי חֲכָמִים כַּדָּרְבֹנוֹת וּכְמַשְׂמְרוֹת נְטוּעִים בַּעֲלֵי
אֲסֻפּוֹת נִתְּנוּ מֵרֹעֶה אֶחָד:

The words of the wise are like goads, and like nails sunk in are well-grouped sayings, (which) are given by one shepherd.

This verse appears to present a proverb that contextualizes the activity of sages like Qoheleth (so also Murphy, 125; Longman, 238; Shields: 69). Their words, like Qoheleth's long and just finished narrative, poke and prod, often painfully, but always in the direction deemed wisest by the shepherd.

דִּבְרֵי חֲכָמִים כַּדָּרְבֹנוֹת. A null copula clause with an NP subject דברי חכמים and a PP complement כדרבנות. The meaning of דרבן is "goad."

וּכְמַשְׂמְרוֹת נְטוּעִים בַּעֲלֵי אֲסֻפּוֹת. A null copula clause, Participle (passive) mp Qal √נטע and fp Qal √אסף. The subject is the NP בעלי אספות. The NP בעלי is bound to the participle (passive) fp Qal √אסף. The meaning of בעלי אספות, "masters of gatherings," is unclear: does this phrase refer to men in charge of *assemblies* or people or men in charge of *gathering sayings*? Fox argues that it refers to "well-grouped sayings" due to the nature of בעל to refer to species, thus, "assembled (sayings) belonging to the same type" (1999: 353–54). The copular complement is the כ-PP כמשמרות נטועים and the NP משמרות (referring to nail or nail-like objects; the referent here is likely nails sunk in to stick and so another way of describing a goad) is bound to the participle נטוע. On the gender mismatch between fp משמרות and mp נטועים, see comment on 12:1. The word order of the first two cola is precisely opposite. Whereas the first colon presents the expected subject–null copula–complement order, the second colon has complement–null copula–subject. Rather than suggesting any topic or focus-fronting explanation for the כ-PP complement in the second colon (we can think of no good explanation), the context of the poetic tricolon suggests to us that the order reflects a forced chiastic structure (similarly, Shields, 73).

נִתְּנוּ מֵרֹעֶה אֶחָד. *Qatal* 3cp Niph √נתן. The מִן-PP provides the agent of the passive verb. This last colon is an unmarked relative clause, though whether it modifies the closer בעלי אספות or the fronted כמשמרות נטועים is unclear. Logic suggests that shepherds are not the only (and may not even be the primary) source of wisdom and so the relative head is more naturally goads, which the shepherd applies as needed. But the addition of אֶחָד (see below) hints that the narrator may be hijacking this proverb and suggesting that "one shepherd" (not just any old shepherd, but one particular shepherd) is more attentive to goading. And so the syntax and interpretation are equally ambiguous, perhaps intentionally so.

רֹעֶה אֶחָד. The numeral אחד is an adjunct of the NP רעה, "one shepherd." Many commentators argue that אחד may function as an indefinite article and so this generically refers to "a shepherd," or "any shepherd" (see, e.g., Seow 1997: 388; Longman, 279; Fox 1999: 355). But the generic reading would have been more easily captured by omitting the numeral אחד, which prompts us to ask why it is there (and explains why every serious commentary pauses to discuss the function of אחד here; see Shields, 76–84 for an excellent summary of proposals). We suggest that the author has taken a known proverb and modified it by adding the אחד in the final colon precisely as a not-so-subtle allusion to his identification of the "goading shepherd" with his book's protagonist (and also perhaps by virtue of the author-character relationship, himself). Thus, the רעה אחד refers to Qoheleth.

12:12 וְיֹתֵר מֵהֵמָּה בְּנִי הִזָּהֵר עֲשׂוֹת סְפָרִים הַרְבֵּה אֵין
קֵץ וְלַהַג הַרְבֵּה יְגִעַת בָּשָׂר׃

And more than they, my son, be warned. For the making of many writings no end exists, and to meditate much is a work of flesh.

וְיֹתֵר מֵהֵמָּה בְּנִי הִזָּהֵר. On יתר, see discussion at 2:15; in this verse the collocation יתר מ is often understood, on the basis of the Mishnaic meaning of יותר מ ("more than they" or "beyond them") or even the conjunctive "furthermore" (Gordis 1955: 344; Murphy, 125; Seow 1997: 388; Longman, 276; Fox 1999: 354). We prefer, however, to interpret it in keeping with its use elsewhere in the book as "too much of these," understanding it as a warning against spending too much time in speculative wisdom in contrast to Qoheleth's advice to enjoy life.

עֲשׂוֹת סְפָרִים הַרְבֵּה אֵין קֵץ. Inf Constr Qal √עשׂה. The structure of this אין negative copula clause is similar to the two copula clauses in vv. 3:4b and 5ab, where the infinitives also lacked the expected ל (see comment at 3:4). In this clause the עשׂות phrase is the complement (like the ל + infinitives in 3:2-8) to the negative copula אין and קץ as the subject, "(with regard to) the making of many books no end exists."

וְלַהַג הַרְבֵּה יְגִעַת בָּשָׂר. A null copula clause. The ostensible noun להג and its adjunct הרבה are the subject, and the bound phrase יגעת בשׂר is the copular complement. The noun להג is a *hapax legomenon*. It may be cognate to Arabic *lahija* "to be devoted, dedicated" and Syriac *lahgā* "glow, vapor" (HALOT, s.v.); however, some argue that it is better understood as a ל preposition plus some form of the root הגה "to mutter, groan" > "meditate" (HALOT, s.v.; see Ps 1), an otherwise unattested noun הג (perhaps "with regard to much meditation"), or an anomalously apocopated infinitive construct ("to meditate much"; the expected form is לַהֲגוֹת). The LXX's μελέτη supports the derivation from הגה, since it translates הֶגֶה, הָגוּת, or הִגָּיוֹן in Pss 19:15; 49:4; Job 37:2; Lam 3:62; and the verb μελετάω translates הגה in Josh 1:8; Isa 16:7; 27:8; 33:18; 38:14; 59:3, 13; Pss 1:2; 2:1; 37:30; 38:13; 63:7; 71:24; 77:13; 90:9; Job 27:4; Prov 8:7; 15:28; 24:2. Moreover, as Whitley notes, להג is not simply a *hapax* in the Bible, it does not exist in postbiblical Hebrew either (104). If the connection to הגה is correct, the syntax is simple enough if it is a shortened infinitive, since the ל-PP/infinitive clause would be the subject of the null copula clause. However, if הג is a noun, then the ל-PP would be a fronted topic and the subject itself would be null, "with regard to meditation, (it) is flesh-wearying"; this type of structure in Hebrew typically requires an overt resumptive (e.g., הוא) referring back to הג in the fronted phrase. This latter syntactic option is less likely due to the complication and unusual lack of resumption. The noun יגעת is the bound form of the feminine singular יְגִיעָה, which is another *hapax legomenon* in the verse. What is unique about יגיעה, though, is the gender form, not the basic lexeme, since the masculine יגיע "toil, labor; product" occurs elsewhere (Gen 31:42; Deut 28:33; Isa 45:14; 55:2; Jer 3:24; 20:5; Ezek 23:29; Hos 12:9; Hag 1:11; Pss 78:46; 109:11; 128:2; Job 3:17; 10:3; 39:11, 16; Neh 5:13). The challenge is determining the meaning of יגיעה bound to בשׂר—most suggest some variant of "wearies the flesh" (see, e.g., Murphy, 123). But it is unlikely that the noun יגיעה refers to a resultative activity, "making X be weary"; rather, it is better to take יגיעה as a synonym for its masculine counterpart, יגיע "toil, product." The collocation of יגיעה and בשׂר, in the context of Qoheleth's contrast between the לב and the בשׂר (see 2:3; 11:10), refers to study that is not guided by the לב. The contrast between the לב and the בשׂר is analogous to the Apostle Paul's contrast between the flesh and the spirit (see, e.g., Rom 7:18).

12:13 סֹ֣וף דָּבָ֔ר הַכֹּ֖ל נִשְׁמָ֑ע אֶת־הָאֱלֹהִ֤ים יְרָא֙ וְאֶת־
מִצְוֺתָ֣יו שְׁמ֔וֹר כִּי־זֶ֖ה כָּל־הָאָדָֽם׃

The end of the matter is (that) everything has been heard. Fear God and keep his commands, for this is the whole (portion) of man.

Over and against speculative wisdom as found in Qoheleth's experiment, the epilogue author advocates keeping the directive to fear God from traditional wisdom (e.g., Prov 1:7).

סֹ֣וף דָּבָ֔ר הַכֹּ֖ל נִשְׁמָ֑ע. A null copula clause, in which סוף דבר is the subject and the complement is הכל נשמע, itself clausal. Although נשמע could be a participial relative—even without the "matching" article (see Holmstedt 2013c, 2016: 69–77)—such an analysis makes little contextual sense. Rather, הכל is the subject of a null copula clause with the participle as the complement, "everything has been heard." And this whole clause is the complement (unmarked by שׁ, אשר, or כי) of the higher null copula.

אֶת־הָאֱלֹהִ֤ים יְרָא֙. Impv ms Qal √ירא. The complement את האלהים is fronted for focus—"fear God (and nothing else)."

וְאֶת־מִצְוֺתָ֣יו שְׁמ֔וֹר. Impv ms Qal √שמר. As in the last clause, the complement את מצותיו is focus-fronted, though the focus lies primarily on the 3ms clitic pronoun referring back to האלהים "fear his (and no one else's) instructions."

כִּי־זֶ֖ה כָּל־הָאָדָֽם. A null copula clause, with the deictic זה (pointing back to the two previous imperative clauses) as the subject and the quantifier phrase כל האדם as the complement. The phrase כל האדם is opaque unless we read it elliptically for כל חלק האדם "whole portion/lot of humankind"—i.e., the only thing humans can effectively do since it is their assignment in life (see 3:22; 5:17; 9:9). On כל האדם, see also discussion at 3:13 and 5:18.

12:14 כִּ֤י אֶת־כָּל־מַעֲשֶׂ֔ה הָאֱלֹהִ֖ים יָבִ֣א בְמִשְׁפָּ֑ט עַ֖ל כָּל־
נֶעְלָ֑ם אִם־ט֖וֹב וְאִם־רָֽע׃

For every deed God will bring into judgment, concerning every hidden thing, whether (it is) good or whether (it is) bad.

כִּ֤י אֶת־כָּל־מַעֲשֶׂ֔ה הָאֱלֹהִ֖ים יָבִ֣א בְמִשְׁפָּ֑ט עַ֖ל כָּל־נֶעְלָ֑ם. *Yiqtol* 3ms Hiph √בוא and Participle ms Niph √עלם. After both an initial subordinator as well as a fronted NP, we expect to see verb-subject order. So, unless the subject-verb order reflects a shift in Hebrew syntactic patterns in this late book, the position of הָאֱלֹהִים before the verb יָבִא must reflect a second focus-fronted NP—"because every deed (not just *one*, or even *many*, but *every!*) God (and no one else) will bring into judgment." The PP בְּמִשְׁפָּט is the locative complement of the trivalent Hiphil of בוא. The עַל-PP, which includes the participle נֶעְלָם—itself actually inside a null-head, unmarked relative, "[thing] [that] is hidden" > "hidden [thing]" (see comment at 1:15)—is an adjunct.

אִם־טוֹב וְאִם־רָע. Two null copula, null-subject clauses with the solitary adjectives טוֹב and רַע as the copular complements.

WORKS CITED

Andersen, Francis I. 1974. *The Sentence in Biblical Hebrew*. The Hague, The Netherlands: Mouton.

Ashby, William J. 1988. "The Syntax, Pragmatics, and Sociolinguistics of Left- and Right-Dislocations in French." *Lingua* 75: 203–29.

Bailey, Charles-James N. 1973. *Variation and Linguistic Theory*. Arlington, Va.: Center for Applied Linguistics.

Baranowski, Krzysztof. 2011. "The Article in the Book of Qoheleth." Pages 31–51 in Ἐν πάσῃ γραμματικῇ καὶ σοφίᾳ: *Saggi di linguistica ebraica in onore di Alviero Niccacci, ofm, Studium Biblicum Franciscanum Analecta*, edited by G. Geiger. Jerusalem: Franciscan Printing Press.

Bartholomew, Craig. 2009. *Ecclesiastes*. Baker Commentary on the Old Testament: Wisdom and Psalms. Grand Rapids: Baker.

Barton, George A. 1908. *A Critical and Exegetical Commentary on the Book of Ecclesiastes*. ICC 17. Edinburgh: T&T Clark.

Bauer, H., and P. Leander. 1922. *Historische Grammatik der hebräischen Sprache des Alten Testamentes*. Halle: Max Niemeyer.

Bekins, Peter J. 2013. "Non-Prototypical Uses of the Definite Article in Biblical Hebrew." *Journal of Semitic Studies* 58 (2): 225–40.

Beldman, David J. H. 2013. "Framed! Structure in Ecclesiastes." Pages 137–61 in *The Words of the Wise Are Like Goads: Engaging Qohelet in the 21st Century*, edited by Mark J. Boda, Tremper Longman III, and Cristian G. Rata. Winona Lake, Ind.: Eisenbrauns.

Bhat, D. N. S. 2004. *Pronouns*. Oxford: Oxford University Press.

Brown, Francis, S. R. Driver, and C. A. Briggs. 1979. *The New Brown-Driver-Briggs Hebrew-English Lexicon*. Peabody, Mass.: Hendrickson.

Buth, Randall. 1999. "Word Order in the Verbless Clause: A Generative-Functional Approach." Pages 79–108 in *The Verbless Clause in Biblical Hebrew: Linguistic Approaches*, edited by C. L. Miller. Winona Lake, Ind.: Eisenbrauns.

Bybee, Joan L., and Östen Dahl. 1989. "The Creation of Tense and Aspect Systems in the Languages of the World." *Studies in Language* 13: 51–103.

Carnie, Andrew. 2006. *Syntax: A Generative Introduction.* 2nd ed. Introducing Linguistics 4. Malden, Mass.: Blackwell.

———. 2010. *Constituent Structure.* 2nd ed. Oxford Surveys in Syntax and Morphology Oxford: Oxford University Press.

Christianson, E. S. 1998. *A Time to Tell: Narrative Strategies in Ecclesiastes.* JSOTSup 280. Sheffield: Sheffield Academic.

Clines, David J. A., ed. 1993–2011. *The Dictionary of Classical Hebrew.* 8 vols. Sheffield: Sheffield Academic.

Comprehensive Aramaic Lexicon. http://cal.huc.edu.

Cook, John A. 2005. "Genericity, Tense, and Verbal Patterns in the Sentence Literature of Proverbs." Pages 117–33 in *Seeking Out the Wisdom of the Ancients: Essays Offered to Honor Michael V. Fox on the Occasion of His Sixty-Fifth Birthday*, edited by R. L. Troxel, K. G. Friebel and D. R. Magary. Winona Lake, Ind.: Eisenbrauns.

———. 2008. "The Hebrew Participle and Stative in Typological Perspective." *Journal of Northwest Semitic Languages* 34 (1): 1–19.

———. 2012a. "Detecting Development in Biblical Hebrew Using Diachronic Typology." Pages 83–95 in *Diachrony in Biblical Hebrew*, edited by Cynthia L. Miller-Naudé and Ziony Zevit.

———. 2012b. *Time and the Biblical Hebrew Verb: The Expression of Tense, Aspect, and Modality in Biblical Hebrew.* Linguistic Studies in Ancient West Semitic 7. Winona Lake, Ind.: Eisenbrauns.

———. 2013. "The Verb in Qohelet." Pages 309–42 in *The Words of the Wise Are Like Goads: Engaging Qohelet in the 21st Century*, edited by Mark J. Boda, Tremper Longman III, and Cristian G. Rata. Winona Lake, Ind.: Eisenbrauns.

———. 2016. "Verbal Valency: The Intersection of Syntax and Semantics." In *Contemporary Examinations of Classical Languages (Hebrew, Aramaic, Syriac, and Greek): Valency, Lexicography, Grammar, and Manuscripts*, edited by Timothy Martin Lewis, Alison G. Salvesen, and Beryl Turner. Perspectives in Linguistics and Ancient Languages 5. Piscataway, N.J.: Gorgias.

Cook, John A., and Robert D. Holmstedt. 2013. *Beginning Biblical Hebrew: A Grammar and Illustrated Reader.* Grand Rapids: Baker.

Creason, Stuart. 1991. "Discourse Constraints on Null Complements in Biblical Hebrew." *University of Chicago Working Papers in Linguistics* 7: 18–47.

Crenshaw, James L. 1987. *Ecclesiastes*. Old Testament Library. Philadelphia: Westminster.

Crystal 2008. *A Dictionary of Linguistics and Phonetics*. 6th ed. Oxford: Blackwell.

Dahood, Mitchell Joseph. 1952a. "Canaanite-Phoenician Influence in Qoheleth." *Biblica* 33: 191–221.

———. 1952b. "Canaanite-Phoenician Influence in Qoheleth." *Biblica* 33: 30–52.

Dalman, Gustaf. 1960. *Grammatik des jüdisch-palästinischen Aramäisch*. Darmstadt: Wissenschaftliche Buchgesellschaft.

Davila, James R. 1990. "Qoheleth and Northern Hebrew." Pages 69–87 in *Sopher Mahir: Northwest Semitic Studies Presented to Stanislav Segert (Maarav 5–6)*, edited by E. M. Cook. Winona Lake, Ind.: Eisenbrauns.

———. 1994. "Dialectology in Biblical Hebrew: A North Israelite Dialect? Synchronic and Diachronic Considerations." Paper presented at the Annual Meeting of the Society of Biblical Literature. Chicago.

Delitzsch, Franz. 1875. *Biblischer Commentar über Das Alte Testament: Hoheslied und Koheleth*. Leipzig: Dörffling & Franke.

Delsman, W. C. 1991. "Die Inkongruenz im Buch Qoheleth." Pages 27–37 in *Studies in Hebrew and Aramaic Syntax: Presented to Professor J. Hoftijzer on the Occasion of His Sixty-Fifth Birthday*, edited by K. Jongeling, H. L. Murre-van den Berg, and L. Van Rompey. Leiden: Brill.

Diessel, Holger. 1999. *Demonstratives: Form, Function, and Grammaticalization*. Typological Studies in Language 42. Amsterdam: John Benjamins.

Doron, Edit. 1986. "The Pronominal 'Copula' as Agreement Clitic." Pages 313–65 in *The Syntax of Pronominal Clitics*, edited by Hagit Borer. New York: Academic.

Dresher, Bezalel Elan. 1994. "The Prosodic Basis of the Tiberian Hebrew System of Accents." *Language: Journal of the Linguistic Society of America* 70 (1): 1–52.

———. 2012. "Methodological Issues in the Dating of Linguistic Forms: Considerations from the Perspective of Contemporary Linguistic Theory." Pages 19–38 in *Diachrony in Biblical Hebrew*, edited by Cynthia L. Miller-Naudé and Ziony Zevit. Winona Lake, Ind.: Eisenbrauns.

Driver, Samuel R. 1892 [1998]. *A Treatise on the Use of the Tenses in Hebrew and Some Other Syntactical Questions*. 3rd ed. Oxford: Clarendon. [Reprint, with introductory essay by W. R. Garr. Grand Rapids: Eerdmans.]

————. 1913. *Introduction to the Literature of the Old Testament*. Revised ed. New York: Charles Scribner's Sons.

Fassberg, Steven E. 1999. "The Lengthened Imperative קָטְלָה in Biblical Hebrew." *Hebrew Studies* 40: 7–13.

Ferguson, Charles A. 1959. "Diglossia." *Word* 15: 325–40.

Forbes. 2014. "On Dating Biblical Hebrew Texts: Constraints and Options." Paper presented at the 2014 ISLP Symposium in St. Petersburg, Russia.

————. 2016. "Crystallization of BH Texts and Diachronic Inversion." Paper presented at the 2016 ISLP session in Stellenbosch, South Africa.

Fox, Michael V. 1989. *Qoheleth and His Contradictions*. JSOTSup 71. Decatur, Ga.: Almond Press.

————. 1999. *A Time to Tear Down & A Time to Build Up: A Rereading of Ecclesiastes*. Grand Rapids: Eerdmans.

————. 2004. *Ecclesiastes* קהלת. The JPS Bible Commentary. Philadelphia: The Jewish Publication Society.

Fox, Michael V., and Bezalel Porten. 1978. "Unsought Discoveries: Qoheleth 7:23–8:1a." *Hebrew Studies* 19: 26–38.

Fredericks, Daniel C. 1988. *Qoheleth's Language: Re-evaluating Its Nature and Date*. Ancient Near Eastern Texts and Studies 3. Lewiston, N.Y.: Edwin Mellen.

Golsman, Y. A. P. 2004. "Qoheleth." Pages 64–112 in *Biblia Hebraica Quinta: Fascicle 18: General Introduction and Megilloth*, edited by A. Schenker. Stuttgart: Deutsche Bibelgesellschaft.

Gordis, Robert. 1949. "The Translation-Theory of Qoheleth Re-examined." *Jewish Quarterly Review* 40: 103–16.

————. 1955. *Koheleth—The Man and His World*. 2nd augmented ed. Texts and Studies of the Jewish Theological Seminary of America 19. New York: Jewish Theological Seminary of America.

————. 1968. *Koheleth—The Man and His World: A Study of Ecclesiastes*. 3rd augmented ed. New York: Schocken Books.

Gordon, Cyrus H. 1955. "North Israelite Influence on Postexilic Hebrew." *Israel Exploration Journal* 5: 85–88.

Gross, Walter. 1987. *Die Pendenskonstruktion im Biblischen Hebräisch: Studien zum althebräischen Satz I*. Arbeiten zu Text und Sprache im Alten Testament 27. St. Ottilien: EOS.

Harris, Alice C., and Lyle Campbell. 1995. *Historical Syntax in Cross-Linguistic Perspective*. Cambridge Studies in Linguistics. Cambridge: Cambridge University Press.

Heijmans, Shai. 2013. "Greek Loanwords." Pages 148–51 in *Encyclopedia of Hebrew Language and Linguistics*. Vol. 2: *G–O*, edited by Geoffrey Khan. Leiden: Brill.

Hoftijzer, Jacob, and Karel Jongeling. 1995. *Dictionary of the North-West Semitic Inscriptions*. 2 vols. Handbook of Oriental Studies: The Near and Middle East 21. Leiden: Brill.

Holmstedt, Robert D. 2000. "The Phonology of Classical Hebrew: A Linguistic Study of Long Vowels and Syllable Structure." *Zeitschrift für Althebraistik* 13 (2): 145–56.

———. 2001. "Headlessness and Extraposition: Another Look at the Syntax of אשר." *Journal of Northwest Semitic Languages* 27 (1): 1–16.

———. 2002. "The Relative Clause in Biblical Hebrew: A Linguistic Analysis." Ph.D. diss., University of Wisconsin.

———. 2005. "Word Order in the Book of Proverbs." Pages 135–54 in *Seeking Out the Wisdom of the Ancients: Essays Offered to Honor Michael V. Fox on the Occasion of His Sixty-Fifth Birthday*, edited by R. L. Troxel, D. R. Magary, and K. G. Friebel. Winona Lake, Ind.: Eisenbrauns.

———. 2006. "Issues in the Linguistic Analysis of a Dead Language, with Particular Reference to Ancient Hebrew." *Journal of Hebrew Scriptures* 6 (11): 1–21.

———. 2007. "The Etymologies of Hebrew *ăšer* and *šeC-*." *Journal of Near Eastern Studies* 66 (3): 177–91.

———. 2008a. "The Restrictive Syntax of Genesis i 1." *Vetus Testamentum* 58: 56–67.

———. 2008b. "The Relative Clause in Canaanite Epigraphic Texts." *Journal of Northwest Semitic Languages* 34 (2): 1–34.

———. 2009a. "Word Order and Information Structure in Ruth and Jonah: A Generative-Typological Analysis." *Journal of Semitic Studies* 54 (1): 111–39.

————. 2009b. "אֲנִי וְלִבִּי: The Syntactic Encoding of the Collaborative Nature of Qohelet's Experiment." *The Journal of Hebrew Scriptures* 9 (29): 1–26.

————. 2009c. "So-Called 'First-Conjunct Agreement' in Biblical Hebrew." Pages 105–29 in *Afroasiatic Studies in Memory of Robert Hetzron: Proceedings of the 35th Annual Meeting of the North American Conference on Afroasiatic Linguistics,* edited by C. Häberl. NACAL 35. Newcastle on Tyne: Cambridge Scholars.

————. 2010. *Ruth: A Handbook on the Hebrew Text.* Waco, Tex.: Baylor University Press.

————. 2011. "The Typological Classifications of the Hebrew of Genesis: Subject-Verb or Verb-Subject?" *The Journal of Hebrew Scriptures* 11 (14): 1–39.

————. 2012. "Historical Linguistics and Biblical Hebrew." Pages 97–124 in *Diachrony in Biblical Hebrew,* edited by Cynthia L. Miller-Naudé, and Ziony Zevit. Winona Lake, Ind.: Eisenbrauns.

————. 2013a. "The Grammar of שׁ and אשׁר in Qohelet." Pages 283–307 in *The Words of the Wise Are Like Goads: Engaging Qohelet in the 21st Century,* edited by Mark J. Boda, Tremper Longman, III, and Cristian G. Rata. Winona Lake, Ind.: Eisenbrauns.

————. 2013b. "Pro-drop." Pages 265–67 in *Encyclopedia of Hebrew Language and Linguistics.* Vol. 3: *P–Z,* edited by Geoffrey Khan. Leiden: Brill.

————. 2013c. "Relative Clause: Biblical Hebrew." Pages 350–57 in *Encyclopedia of Hebrew Language and Linguistics.* Vol. 3: *P–Z,* edited by Geoffrey Khan. Leiden: Brill.

————. 2013d. "Hypotaxis." Pages 220–22 in *Encyclopedia of Hebrew Language and Linguistics.* Vol. 2: *G–O,* edited by Geoffrey Khan. Leiden: Brill.

————. 2013e. "Investigating the Possible Verb-Subject to Subject-Verb Shift in Ancient Hebrew: Methodological First Steps." *Kleine Untersuchungen zur Sprache des Alten Testaments und seiner Umwelt* 15: 3–31.

————. 2013f. "The Syntax and Pragmatics of Subject Pronouns in Phoenician." Pages 84–110 in *Linguistic Studies in Phoenician Grammar: In Memory of J. Brian Peckham,* edited by Robert D. Holmstedt, and Aaron Schade. Winona Lake, Ind.: Eisenbrauns.

————. 2014. "Critical at the Margins: Edge Constituents in Biblical Hebrew." *Kleine Untersuchungen zur Sprache des Alten Testaments und seiner Umwelt* 17: 109–56.

————. 2016. *The Relative Clause in Biblical Hebrew*. Linguistic Studies in Ancient West Semitic 10. Winona Lake, Ind.: Eisenbrauns.

————. Forthcoming. *Biblical Hebrew Syntax: A Linguistic Sketch*. Grand Rapids: Baker Academic.

Holmstedt, Robert D., and Andrew R. Jones. 2014. "The Pronoun in Tripartite Verbless Clauses in Biblical Hebrew: Resumption for Left-Dislocation or Pronominal Copula?" *Journal of Semitic Studies* 59 (1): 53–89.

————. Forthcoming. "Apposition in Biblical Hebrew: Structure and Function." *Kleine Untersuchungen zur Sprache des Alten Testaments und seiner Umwelt*.

Holmstedt, Robert D., and John Screnock. 2016. "Writing a Descriptive Grammar of the Syntax and Semantics of the War Scroll (1QM): The Noun Phrase as Proof of Concept." Pages 67–106 in *The War Scroll, War and Peace in the Dead Sea Scrolls and Related Literature: A Tribute to Martin G. Abegg*, edited by K. S. Baek, K. Davis, and Peter W. Flint. Leiden: Brill.

Holmstedt, Robert D., and Alexander T. Kirk. 2016. "Subversive Boundary Drawing in Jonah: The Variation of אשר and שׁ as Literary Code-Switching." *Vetus Testamentum* 66: 542–55.

Hopper, Paul J., and Elizabeth Closs Traugott. 2003. *Grammaticalization*. 2nd ed. Cambridge Textbooks in Linguistics. Cambridge: Cambridge University Press.

Hurvitz, Avi. 1990. "Qoheleth's Language: Re-Evaluation of Its Nature and Date." *Hebrew Studies* 31: 144–54.

————. 2006. "The Recent Debate on Late Biblical Hebrew: Solid Data, Experts' Opinions, and Inconclusive Arguments." *Hebrew Studies* 47: 191–210.

————. 2007. "The Language of Qoheleth in Its Historical Setting within Biblical Hebrew." Pages 23–34 in *The Language of Qohelet in Its Context: Essay in Honour of Prof. A. Schoors on the Occasion of His Seventieth Birthday*, edited by A. Berlejung and P. Van Hecke. Leuven: Peeters.

————. 2012. "The 'Linguistic Dating of Biblical Texts': Comments on Methodological Guidelines and Philological Procedures." Pages

267–79 in *Diachrony in Biblical Hebrew*, edited by Cynthia L. Miller-Naudé and Ziony Zevit. Winona Lake, Ind.: Eisenbrauns.

Isaksson, Bo. 1987. *Studies in the Language of Qoheleth, with Special Emphasis on the Verbal System*. Studia Semitica Upsaliensia 10. Stockholm: Almqvist & Wiksell.

Jacobson, P. 2006. "Constituent Structure." Pages 58–71 in *Encyclopedia of Language and Linguistics*. Vol. 3, edited by Keith Brown. Boston: Elsevier Science.

Janse, Mark. 2014. "Greek Loanwords in Hebrew and Aramaic." Pages 122–23 in *Encyclopedia of Ancient Greek Language and Linguistics*. Vol. 2: *G–O*, edited by Georgios K. Giannakis. Leiden: Brill.

Jastrow, Marcus. 1996 [1903]. *A Dictionary of the Targumim, the Talmud Babli and Yerushalmi, and the Midrashic Literature*. New York: Judaic Press.

Jones, Andrew R. 2010. "The Relative Clause in Ancient Hebrew Texts: A Quantitative and Comparative Analysis." Unpublished ms.

Joosten, Jan. 2007. "The Syntax of Volitive Verbal Forms in the Book of Qoheleth in Historical Perspective." Pages 47–61 in *The Language of Qohelet in Its Context: Essay in Honour of Prof. A. Schoors on the Occasion of his Seventieth Birthday*, edited by A. Berlejun and P. Van Hecke. Leuven: Peeters.

Joüon, Paul. 1923. *Grammaire de L'Hebreu Biblique*. Corrected 1965 ed. Rome: Pontifical Biblical Institute.

Joüon, Paul, and Takamitsu Muraoka. 2006. *A Grammar of Biblical Hebrew*. Rev. ed. Subsidia Biblica 27. Rome: Pontifical Biblical Institute.

Kautzsch, Emil. 1910. *Gesenius' Hebrew Grammar*. Translated by A. E. Cowley. 2nd Engl. ed. Oxford: Clarendon.

Kaye, Alan S. 2002. "Comment." *International Journal of the Sociology of Language* 157: 117–25.

Koehler, Ludwig, Walter Baumgartner, and Johann Jakob Stamm, eds. 1994–2000. *The Hebrew and Aramaic Lexicon of the Old Testament*. Translated and edited under the supervision of M. E. J. Richardson. Leiden: Brill.

König, Eduard. 1897. *Historisch-Kritisches Lehrgebäude der hebräischen Sprache*. 3 vols. Leipzig: Hinrichs.

Kroch, Anthony. 1989. "Reflexes of Grammar in Patterns of Language Change." *Language Variation and Change* 1: 199–244.

———. 2001. "Syntactic Change." Pages 699–729 in *The Handbook of Contemporary Syntactic Theory*, edited by Mark Baltin and Chris Collins. Malden, Mass.: Blackwell.

Krüger, Thomas. 2004. *Qoheleth.* Translated by O. C. Dean Jr. Hermeneia. Minneapolis: Fortress.

Kummerow, David. 2013. "Object Predication in Tiberian Hebrew— A Typological Approach to the Nonverbal Copula." *Kleine Untersuchungen zur Sprache des Alten Testaments und seiner Umwelt* 16: 1–135.

Kutscher, Eduard Yechezkel. 1982. *A History of the Hebrew Language.* Jerusalem: Magnes.

Lauha, Aarre. 1978. *Kohelet.* Biblischer Kommentar Altes Testament 19. Neukirchen-Vluyn: Neukirchener Verlag.

Lichtheim, Miriam. 1980. *Ancient Egyptian Literature.* Vol. 3: *The Late Period.* Berkeley: University of California Press.

Liddell, Henry George, and Robert Scott. 1889. *An Intermediate Greek-English Lexicon.* Oxford: Clarendon.

Linafelt, Tod, and F. W. Dobbs-Allsopp. 2010. "Poetic Line Structure in Qoheleth 3:1." *Vetus Testamentum* 60: 249–59.

Lohfink, Norbert. 2003. *Qoheleth.* A Continental Commentary. Minneapolis: Fortress.

Longman, Tremper. 1998. *The Book of Ecclesiastes.* New International Commentary on the Old Testament. Grand Rapids: Eerdmans.

Mallinson, Graham, and Barry J. Blake. 1981. *Language Typology: Cross-linguistic Studies in Syntax.* North-Holland Linguistic Series. Amsterdam: North-Holland Publishing.

Mankowski, Paul V. 2000. *Akkadian Loanwords in Biblical Hebrew.* Harvard Semitic Studies 47. Winona Lake, Ind.: Eisenbrauns.

Marshall, Phillip. 2013. "Relative and Complement Clauses: Discerning the Difference." Unpublished ms.

Meade, John D. and Peter J. Gentry. 2012. "Evaluating Evaluations: the Commentary of *BHQ* and the Problem of הוֹלֵלוֹת in Ecclesiastes 1:17." Pages 197–212 in *Sophia-Paideia: Sapienza e Educazione (Sir 1,27). Miscellanea di studi offerti in onore del prof. Don Mario Cimosa*, edited by G. Bonney and R. Vincent. Nuova Biblioteca di Scienze Religiose 34. Roma: Libreria Ateneo Salesiano.

Meek, Russell L. 2016. "Twentieth and Twenty-first-century Readings of *Hebel* (הֶבֶל) in Ecclesiastes." *Currents in Biblical Research* 14 (3): 279–97.

Miller, Cynthia L. 1996. *The Representation of Speech in Biblical Hebrew Narrative*. Harvard Semitic Monographs 55. Atlanta: Scholars Press.

———. 2005. "Ellipsis Involving Negation in Biblical Poetry." Pages 37–52 in *Seeking Out the Wisdom of the Ancients: Essays Offered to Honor Michael V. Fox on the Occasion of His Sixty-Fifth Birthday*, edited by Ronald L. Troxel, Kevin G. Friebel, and Dennis R. Magary. Winona Lake, Ind.: Eisenbrauns.

———. 2007. "Constraints on Ellipsis in Biblical Hebrew." Pages 165–80 in *Studies in Comparative Semitic and Afroasiatic Linguistics Presented to Gene B. Gragg*, edited by C. L. Miller. Chicago: Oriental Institute of the University of Chicago.

———. 2010. "Vocative Syntax in Biblical Hebrew Prose and Poetry: A Preliminary Analysis." *Journal of Semitic Studies* 55 (2): 347–64.

Miller, Douglas B. 2002. *Symbol and Rhetoric in Ecclesiastes: The Place of Hebel in Qoheleth's Work*. Academia Biblica 2. Atlanta: Society of Biblical Literature.

Murphy, Roland. 1992. *Ecclesiastes*. Word Biblical Commentary 23A. Dallas: Word Books.

Naudé, Jacobus A. 1990. A Syntactic Analysis of Dislocations in Biblical Hebrew. *Journal of Northwest Semitic Languages* 16: 115–30.

———. 1991. "Qumran Hebrew as a Null Subject Language." *South African Journal of Linguistics* 9 (4): 119–25.

———. 1993. "On Subject Pronoun and Subject Noun Asymmetry: A Preliminary Survey of Northwest Semitic." *South African Journal of Linguistics* 11 (1): 17–28.

———. 1999. "Syntactic Aspects of Co-ordinate Subjects with Independent Personal Pronouns." *Journal of Northwest Semitic Language* 25 (2): 75–99.

———. 2003. "The Transitions of Biblical Hebrew in the Perspective of Language Change and Diffusion." Pages 189–214 in *Biblical Hebrew: Studies in Chronology and Typology*, edited by Ian Young. London: T&T Clark.

Nevalainen, Terttu, and Helena Raumolin-Brunberg. 2003. *Historical Sociolinguistics*. London: Pearson.

Pahk, Y. S. 1998. "The Significance of אשר in Qoh 7, 26: 'More Bitter than Death is the Woman, if She is a Snare.'" Pages 373–83 in *Qohelet in the Context of Wisdom*, edited by A. Schoors. Leuven: Peeters.

Pérez Fernández, Miquel. 1997. *An Introductory Grammar of Rabbinic Hebrew*. Translated by John Elwolde. Leiden: Brill.

Pintzuk, Susan. 2003. "Variationist Approaches to Syntactic Change." Pages 509–28 in *The Handbook of Historical Linguistics*, edited by Brian D. Joseph and Richard D. Janda. London: Blackwell.

Porten, Bazalel, and Ada Yardeni. 1986. *Textbook of Aramaic Documents from Ancient Egypt*. 4 vols. The Hebrew University Department of the History of the Jewish People, Texts and Studies for Students 1. Winona Lake, Ind.: Eisenbrauns.

Provan, Ian. 2001. *Ecclesiastes/Song of Songs*. New International Version Application Commentary. Grand Rapids,: Zondervan.

Pustet, Regina. 2003. *Copulas: Universals in the Categorization of the Lexicon*. Oxford Studies in Typology and Linguistic Theory. Oxford: Oxford University Press.

Qimron, Elisha. 1986. *The Hebrew of the Dead Sea Scrolls*. Harvard Semitic Studies 29. Atlanta: Scholars Press.

Rad, Gerhard von. 1972. *Wisdom in Israel*. Translated by J. D. Martin. Nashville: Abingdon.

Rendsburg, G. A. 1990. *Diglossia in Ancient Hebrew*. New Haven, Conn.: American Oriental Society.

———. 1996. "Linguistic Variation and The 'Foreign' Factor in the Hebrew Bible." *Israel Oriental Studies* 15: 177–90.

———. 2006. "Israelian Hebrew in the Song of Songs." Pages 315–23 in *Biblical Hebrew in Its Northwest Semitic Setting: Typological and Historical Perspectives*, edited by Steven E. Fassberg and Avi Hurvitz. Jerusalem: Magnes.

Revell, E. J. 1993. "Concord with Compound Subjects and Related Uses of Pronouns." *Vetus Testamentum* 43 (1): 69–87.

———. 1995. "The Two Forms of First Person Singular Pronoun in Biblical Hebrew: Redundancy or Expressive Contrast?" *Journal of Semitic Studies* 40 (2): 199–217.

Rezetko, Robert, and Ian Young. 2014. *Historical Linguistics & Biblical Hebrew: Steps Toward an Integrated Approach*. Ancient Near Eastern Monographs 9. Atlanta: Society of Biblical Literature.

Rezetko, Robert, and Martin Naaijer. 2016a. Review of Avi Hurvitz, in collaboration with Gottlieb, Leeor, Hornkohl, Aaron, and Mastéy, Emmanuel, *A Concise Lexicon of Late Biblical Hebrew: Linguistic Innovations in the Writings of the Second Temple Period* (VTSup 160; Leiden: Brill, 2014). *Journal of Hebrew Scriptures* 16: 1–23.

————. 2016b. "An Alternative Approach to the Lexicon of Late Biblical Hebrew." *Journal of Hebrew Scriptures* 16 (1): 1–39.

Rothstein, Susan. 1995. "Small Clauses and Copular Constructions." Pages 27–48 in *Small Clauses,* edited by Anna Cardinaletti and Maria Teresa Guasti. San Diego: Academic.

Rousseau, F. 1981. "Structure de Qohelet 1:4-11 et Plan du Livre." *Vetus Testamentum* 31: 200–17.

Sáenz-Badillos, Angel. 1993. *A History of the Hebrew Language.* Translated by John Elwolde. Cambridge: Cambridge University Press.

Salyer, G. D. 2001. *Vain Rhetoric: Private Insight and Public Debate in Ecclesiastes.* JSOTSup 327. Sheffield: Sheffield Academic.

Schoors, Anton. 1992. *The Preacher Sought to Find Pleasing Words: A Study of the Language of Qoheleth.* Part I: *Grammar.* Orientalia Lovaniensia Analecta 41. Leuven: Peeters.

Scott, R. B. Y. 1965. *Proverbs, Ecclesiastes.* Anchor Bible 18. Garden City, N.Y.: Doubleday.

Screnock, John, and Robert D. Holmstedt. 2015. *Esther: A Handbook on the Hebrew Text.* Baylor Handbook on the Hebrew Bible. Waco, Tex.: Baylor University Press.

Segal, M. H. 1927. *A Grammar of Mishnaic Hebrew.* Oxford: Oxford University Press.

Seow, Choon-Leong. 1996. "Linguistic Evidence and the Dating of Qohelet." *Journal of Biblical Literature* 115 (4): 643–66.

————. 1997. *Ecclesiastes.* Anchor Bible 18C. Garden City, N.Y.: Doubleday.

Shields, Martin A. 2006. *The End of Wisdom: A Reappraisal of the Historical and Canonical Function of Ecclesiastes.* Winona Lake, Ind.: Eisenbrauns.

Shlesinger, Yitzhak. 1999. "תפוצת כינויי הזיקה 'ש-' ו'אשר' בספר קהלת." Pages 91–109 in מחקרים בלשון העברית העתיקה והחדשה מוגשים למנחם צבי קדרי, edited by Shimon Sharvit. Ramat-Gan: Bar-Ilan University Press.

Shulman, Ahouva. 1996. "The Use of Modal Verb Forms in Biblical Hebrew Prose." Ph.D. diss., University of Toronto.

Shupak, N. 1997. "The Eloquent Peasant, The Complaint of Khakheperré-Sonb, and The Prophecies of Neferti." Pages 93–110 in *The Context of Scripture.* Vol. 1: *Canonical Compositions from the Biblical World,* edited by W. W. Hallo and K. W. Younger. Leiden: Brill.

Siewierska, Anna. 1988. *Word Order Rules*. Croom Helm Linguistics Series. London: Croom Helm.

Smith, Carlotta S. 2008. "Time with and without Tense." Pages 227–50 in *Time and Modality*, edited by Jacqueline Guéron and Jacqueline Lecarme. Studies in Natural Language and Linguistic Theory. Dordrecht: Springer.

Subtelny, Maria E. 2004. "The Tale of the Four Sages Who Entered the *Pardes*: A Talmudic Enigma from a Persian Perspective." *Jewish Studies Quarterly* 11: 3–58.

Thomason, Sarah Grey. 2003. "Contact as a Source of Language Change." Pages 687–712 in *The Handbook of Historical Linguistics*, edited by Brian D. Joseph and Richard D. Janda. London: Blackwell.

van der Merwe, Christo H. J. 2009. "Another Look at the Biblical Hebrew Focus Particle גַּם." *Journal of Semitic Studies* 54 (2): 313–32.

van der Merwe, Christo H. J., Jacobus A. Naudé, and Jan H. Kroeze. 1999. *A Biblical Hebrew Reference Grammar*. Biblical Languages: Hebrew 3. Sheffield: Sheffield Academic.

Waltke, Bruce K., and Michael O'Connor. 1990. *An Introduction to Biblical Hebrew Syntax*. Winona Lake, Ind.: Eisenbrauns.

Whitley, Charles Francis. 1979. *Koheleth: His Language and Thought*. New York: de Gruyter.

Whybray, R. N. 1978. "Qoheleth the Immoralist? (Qoh 7:16-17)." Pages 191–204 in *Israelite Wisdom: Theological and Literary Essays in Honor of Samuel Terrien*, edited by John G. Gammie et al. Missoula, Mont.: Scholars Press.

Wise, Michael O. 1990. "A Calque from Aramaic in Qoheleth 6:12; 7:12; and 8:13." *Journal of Biblical Literature* 109 (2): 249–57.

Wolfram, Walt, and Natalie Schilling-Estes. 2003. "Dialectology and Linguistic Diffusion." Pages 713–35 in *The Handbook of Historical Linguistics*, edited by Brian D. Joseph and Richard D. Janda. London: Blackwell.

Wright, A. G. 1968. "The Riddle of the Sphinx: The Structure of the Book of Qoheleth." *Catholic Biblical Quarterly* 30: 313–34.

Young, Ian. 1993. *Diversity in Pre-Exilic Hebrew*. Tübingen: Mohr.

Young, Ian, Robert Rezetko, and Martin Ehrensvärd. 2008. *Linguistic Dating of Biblical Texts*. 2 vols. London: Equinox.

Ziv, Yael. 1994. "Left and Right Dislocation: Discourse Functions and Anaphora." *Journal of Pragmatics* 22: 629–46.

GLOSSARY

Like all technical fields, linguistics thrives on specialized terminology. Unfortunately, the terminology often results in some opacity, if not confusion, for biblical and textual studies students and scholars who have not been trained in linguistics. And yet, it is often not desirable to avoid all technical terminology: doing so would not only result in unwieldy verbosity but remove studies like this from their explicit grounding in a linguistic theory and/or specific linguistic studies. To facilitate the nonlinguist's reading of this volume, we provide here a short list of linguistic terms used throughout the introduction and verse-by-verse comments. For convenience and to point the reader to perhaps the single most useful linguistics volume for the nonlinguist, we have based as many definitions as possible on David Crystal's *A Dictionary of Linguistics and Phonetics* (6th ed. Oxford: Blackwell, 2008). The number in brackets after an entry is the page number where the definitions can be found in Crystal 2008.

Adjectival (*see* adjective)
Adjective [11]. "A term used in the grammatical classification of words to refer to the main set of items which specify the attributes of nouns."
Adjunct [12]. "[An] optional or secondary element in a construction: an adjunct may be removed without the structural identity of the rest of the construction being affected."
Adverb(ial) [14]. "A term used in the grammatical classification of words to refer to a heterogeneous group of items whose most frequent function is to specify the mode of action of the verb. ... Syntactically, one can relate adverbs to such questions as *how*, *where*, *when* and *why*, and classify them accordingly, as adverbs of 'manner,' 'place,' 'time,' etc."

Adversative [15]. "In grammar and semantics, a form or construction which expresses an antithetical circumstance. Adversative meaning can be expressed in several grammatical ways (as "adversatives"), such as through a conjunction (*but*), adverbial (*however, nevertheless, yet, in spite of that, on the other hand*), or preposition (*despite, except, apart from, notwithstanding*)."

Agreement [18]. "A traditional term used in grammatical theory and description to refer to a formal relationship between elements, whereby a form of one word requires a corresponding form of another (i.e., the forms agree)."

Anacoluthon [24]. "A traditional rhetorical term, sometimes encountered in linguistic studies of conversational speech. It refers to a syntactic break in the expected grammatical sequence within a sentence, as when a sentence begins with one construction and remains unfinished, e.g., *The man came and—are you listening?* 'Anacolutha' have come to be especially noticed in linguistic studies as an area of performance features which a grammar of a language would aim to exclude." See also GKC §167b.

Anaphora (also anaphoric pronoun, long-distance anaphora) [25]. The process or result of a linguistic item (e.g., pronoun) deriving its interpretation from some previously expressed unit or meaning (the antecedent). Anaphoric reference is one way of marking the identity between what is being expressed and what has already been expressed. In such a sentence as "He did that there," each word is anaphoric and is thus anaphorically related to a corresponding referent in the preceding context. Anaphora operates *within* clause boundaries and clause boundaries, although the greater the distance between the anaphor and its antecedent, the greater potential there is for other constituents that also agree with the anaphor to intervene and create difficulty for interpretation.

Apocopation [30]. "A term used in comparative philology, and sometimes in modern phonology, to refer to the deletion of the final element in a word; often contrasts with aphaeresis and syncope."

Apposition(al) [31]. "A traditional term retained in some models of grammatical description for a sequence of units which are constituents at the same grammatical level, and which have an identity or similarity of reference."

> **Appositive.** The second (or third, fourth, etc.) item in an appositional structure.

Appositive Head. The first item in an appositional structure.

Appositive of Attribution. An appositive that describes the head. ("X, being Y").

Appositive of Equivalence. An appositive that is equated with the head ("X, that is/namely Y").

Appositive of Inclusion. ("X, for example/especially Y").

Nonrestrictive Appositive. An appositive that does not define or limit the head.

Restrictive Appositive. An appositive that defines or limits the head.

Aspect (*see* Tense-Aspect-Mood)

Asseverative כי. The use of כי to reinforce an affirmation (see JM §164b, although we take it to be a stronger reinforcement than described there). Translatable by English as "certainly, indeed."

Assimilation [39]. "A general term in phonetics which refers to the influence exercised by one sound segment upon the articulation of another, so that the sounds become more alike, or identical."

Bound (construction). A morpheme is bound if it "cannot occur on its own as a separate word" (Crystal 2008, 59). The so-called construct state of nouns involves a variant form of the noun that is bound to the following noun (bound construction).

Bivalent (*see* valency).

Casus Pendens (*see* dislocation).

Clause [78]. "[A] unit of grammatical organization smaller than the sentence but larger than phrases, words, or morphemes."

> **Comparative clause**. A clause in which two entities are compared (e.g., Prov 22:1, מִכֶּסֶף וּמִזָּהָב חֵן טוֹב "Favor is better than silver and than gold").

> **Conditional clause** [99]. "[A clause] whose semantic role is the expression of hypotheses or conditions."

> **Nominalized clause**. A subordinate clause, typically introduced by כי or אשר, which functions syntactically in the main clause as an NP would. Nominalized clauses can thus function as the subject of the main clause or as a complement of the verb.

Null copula clause (*see* copula).

Purpose clause. A clause expressing the reason for which an action was taken.

Reduced (*see* small clause).

Relative clause. A subordinate clause that modifies a noun phrase.

Head. The relative head, or pivot, is the word modified by the relative clause.

Nonrestrictive Relative. A relative clause that does not define or limit the modified noun phrase.

Restrictive Relative. A relative clause that defines or limits the modified noun phrase.

Unmarked Relative. A relative clause that is not introduced by a relative pronoun.

Result clause [415]. "[A] clause ... whose meaning expresses the notion of consequence or effect."

Small clause [440]. "[A] clause that contains neither a finite verb nor an infinitival *to*."

Subordinate clause. A clause (of any kind) that is subordinated within a larger clause (*see* subordination).

Temporal clause. A subordinate clause indicating when the events of the main clause occur.

Clitic [80]. "A term used in grammar to refer to a form which resembles a word, but which cannot stand on its own as a normal utterance, being phonologically dependent upon a neighboring word (its host) in a construction."

Complement [92]. "A term used in the analysis of grammatical function, to refer to a major constituent of sentence or clause structure, traditionally associated with 'completing' the action specified by the verb. In its broadest sense, complement therefore is a very general notion, subsuming all obligatory features of the predicate other than the verb, e.g. objects (e.g., *She kicked the ball*) and adverbials (e.g., *She was in the garden*)." This notion of *obligatory completion* extends to PPs and NPs as well, so that these phrases also can require complements (e.g., *to the bank*).

Concessive [98]. "In grammar, referring to a word or construction which expresses the meaning of 'concession'. The point expressed in the main clause continues to be valid despite the point being made in the subordinate clause (the concessive clause). In English, the most widely used markers of concession are *although* and *though*."

Conjunction [101]. "[An] item or a process whose primary function is to connect words or other constructions."

Constituent [104]. "A linguistic unit which is a functional component of a larger construction."

Construct (*see* bound construction).

Copula (verbal, nonverbal, null) [116]. A "linking verb, i.e., a verb which has little independent meaning, and whose main function is to relate other elements of clause structure, especially subject and complement." In Hebrew, the verbal copula is היה. The verbal copula is omitted more often than not in favor of a null copula (i.e., a phonologically unexpressed copula) that defaults to the tense-aspect of the discourse context. Null copula clauses are variously referred to as "nominal clauses" or "verbless clauses." A nonverbal copula is an overt constituent (i.e., not a null item, but an overt item such as a pronoun) that is used to link the two components of a copular clause. See Pustet; also see Doron; Rothstein; Kummerow; and Holmstedt and Jones 2014 for further discussion of the copula in Hebrew.

Covert (*see* null).

Deixis/deictic [133]. The process of (and as an adjective, the words used in) referring directly to the personal, temporal or locational characteristics of the situation within which an utterance takes place, whose meaning is thus relative to that situation; e.g., the first- and second-person pronouns אַתֶּם, אַתְּ, אַתָּה, אֲנַחְנוּ, אֲנִי, and אַתֵּן are deictic, as are the demonstrative זֹאת, זֶה, and אֵלֶּה, and also nonpronominal words such as הִנֵּה and עַתָּה. Within a discourse, deixis is relativized and thus concerns the backwards or forwards reference in discourse (anaphora and cataphora respectively), e.g., English "that," "the following," "the former." See Diessel for a typological discussion of demonstratives and deixis.

Demonstrative [135]. A class of items whose function is to point to an entity in the situation or elsewhere in a sentence. The Hebrew items זֹאת, זֶה, and אֵלֶּה (and when used to modify nouns, הֵם, הִיא, הוּא, and הֵן) have their reference fixed by gestures, speaker knowledge, or other means. Depending on their grammatical role, they are often called "demonstrative determiners" (בַּיּוֹם הַהוּא "On that day") or "demonstrative pronouns" (מַה זֹּאת עָשִׂיתָ "What is this you have done?"). Demonstratives fall within the general class of deictic expressions, and are sometimes contrasted with "pure indexicals." See Diessel 1999 for a typological discussion of demonstratives.

Dislocation (Left and Right) [273, s.v. left dislocation; 418, s.v. right dislocation]. A type of sentence in which one of the constituents appears in initial (left) or final (right) position and its canonical position is filled by a pronoun or a full lexical noun phrase with the same reference, e.g. "John, I like him/the old chap" or "I know that woman/her, Julie." See Gross; Naudé 1990, Holmstedt 2014.

Exceptional Case Marking (ECM). A term used in generative linguistic theory for a class of verbs, such as "believe" and "consider," which may take a clausal complement and assign accusative (object) case to the subject of the embedded clause (e.g., "John considers him a genius"). Though not studied for BH, an example is identified with the verb מצא "find" in Eccl 7:26.

Exclamative [177]. "Traditionally, an exclamation refers to any emotional utterance, usually lacking the grammatical structure of a full sentence, and marked by strong intonation, e.g., *Gosh! Good grief!*" The most common exclamative in Hebrew is the deictic הִנֵּה, though the exclamative use of כִּי also occurs (this is sometimes referred to as the "asseverative" כִּי).

Extraposition (extraposed) [182]. "A term used in grammatical analysis to refer to the process or result of moving (or extraposing) an element from its normal position to a position at or near the end of the sentence."

Focus (fronting) [192–93]. "A term used by some linguists in a two-part analysis of sentences which distinguishes between the information assumed by speakers, and that which is at the centre (or 'focus') of their communicative interest; 'focus' in this sense is opposed to presupposition. (The contrast between given and new information makes an analogous distinction.) For example, in the sentence *It was Mary who came to tea*, Mary is the focus (as the intonation contour helps to signal). Taking such factors into account is an important aspect of intersentence relationships: it would not be possible to have the above sentence as the answer to the question *What did Mary do?*, but only to *Who came to tea?*" In Hebrew, constituents are typically fronted (*see* fronting) to indicate focus; see Holmstedt 2014.

Fronting [201]. "[Any] transformation which transposes a constituent from the middle or end of a string to initial position. For example, the rule of '*Wh*-fronting' places a *Wh*-phrase (e.g. *where, which books*) in initial position, transposing it from the underlying noninitial position (cf. *John walked there → John walked where → where did John walk*)." See Holmstedt 2014.

Gapping [166]. Gapping occurs when "[an unambiguously specifiable] part of the structure has been omitted, which is recoverable from a scrutiny of the context." See Miller 2005, 2007.

Genitive. A term properly used to describe a particular *case*, borrowed in the study of Hebrew (particularly in WO's description) to describe various way in which a noun can be modified along the lines of English "of."

Gnomic. A term used to describe a clause, or a verb within a clause, that communicates a general truth or maxim.

Grammaticalization [218, s.v. grammar]. The process whereby a word with semantic content is used to express grammatical functions. An example of grammaticalization (grammaticization) is the use of the English motion verb go, as in "She is going to London," "which has become a marker of tense in "It's going to rain." A case of grammaticalization in Hebrew concerns the word אֲשֶׁר, which seems have been a noun "step, place" in prebiblical Hebrew (based on Semitic evidence) but has grammaticalized into a function introducing nominal (relative, complement) clauses. See Holmstedt 2007, 2016: 89–101 for discussions of אשׁר and grammaticalization.

Heavy Noun Phrase Shift (**HNPS**). A cross-linguistically common phenomenon wherein "heavy" or complex constituents are moved to the right of "lighter" or less complex constituents (see Holmstedt 2014, where it is discussed with "extraposition").

Interrogative [251]. "A term used in the grammatical classification of sentence types, and usually seen in contrast to declarative. It refers to verb forms or sentence/clause types typically used in the expression of questions, e.g. the inverted order of *is he coming?*, or the use of an interrogative word (or simply 'interrogative'), often subclassified as interrogative adjectives (e.g. *which*), adverbs (e.g. *why*) and pronouns (e.g. *who*)."

Inversion [254]. "A term used in grammatical analysis to refer to the process or result of syntactic change in which a specific sequence of constituents is seen as the reverse of another."

Linguistic Typology [499, s.v. typological linguistics]. A branch of linguistics that studies the structural similarities between languages, regardless of their history, as part of an attempt to establish a satisfactory classification, or typology, of languages. Typological comparison is thus distinguished from the historical comparison of languages—the province of comparative philology and historical linguistics—an its groupings may not coincide with those set up by the historical method. For example, in respect of the paucity of inflectional endings, English is closer to Chinese than it is to Latin.

Mood (*see* Tense-Aspect-Mood).

Monovalent (*see* valency).

Nominal Clause (*see* copula).

Noun Phrase (NP) [367, 333]. "A single element of structure [consisting] minimally of the noun"; NPs may consist of a single noun (e.g., דָּבָר "thing") or may contain additional constituents that modify the noun (e.g., הַדָּבָר הַקָּשֶׁה אֲשֶׁר אֶעֱשֶׂה מָחָר "the difficult thing that I am going to do tomorrow").

Null copula (*see* copula).

Null (covert) [335]. "An application in generative grammar of the mathematical use of this term, with the general meaning of empty or zero, as in 'null-subject' (a phonologically empty constituent, PRO) or 'null element'"; in other words, a constituent that exists but is not phonologically overt (verbalized).

Null (covert) complement. A phrase used to refer to a constituent that must exist, given the argument structure of a verb or noun phrase, but is not phonologically overt. Null complements may or may not be reconstructable from context.

Null (covert) subject. A phrase used to refer to a subject that must exist, given the argument structure of a verb, but is not phonologically overt. Null-subjects may or may not be reconstructable from context.

Null (covert) verb. A verb that is not phonologically overt (*see* gapping).

Overt (*see* null).

Partitive. A preposition used to "[refer] to part of the noun (or noun equivalent) after the preposition" (WO §11.2.11e) (e.g., אֶחָד מִן־ הַסָּרִיסִים "one of the eunuchs").

Pivot (*see* clause; head; relative clause).

Predicate. [381]. "[A] major constituent of sentence structure ... containing all obligatory constituents other than the subject," within a "two-part analysis" of clauses (*see* subject).

Prepositional Phrase (PP) [383]. "[The] set of items which typically precede noun phrases (often single nouns or pronouns), to form a single constituent of structure." "[Prepositions] can combine with not only an NP but also a PP (e.g. *since before breakfast*) [or] a clause (e.g. *since they finished their breakfast*)."

Pronoun [391–92]. A term referring to the closed set of items which can be used to substitute syntactically for a noun phrase. Pronouns are often divided into classes, such as personal, demonstrative, interrogative, reflexive, indefinite, and relative. Additionally, anaphor and deixis differences indicate that first and second-person pronouns must be distinguished from third-person pronouns. Such a divide is clear in Hebrew, where the third-person subject pronouns הוּא, הִיא, הֵם, and הֵן are also used as distal demonstratives and, as argued above, nonverbal copulas. See Bhat 2004 on pronouns in general and Holmstedt 2013f for a discussion of pronouns in Phoenician that is directly applicable to BH.

Proper Noun (PN) [392]. "The name of an individual person, place, etc."

Relative Clause (*see* clause).

Resumptive (resumption) [415]. "[An] element or structure which repeats or in some way recapitulates the meaning of a prior element." In Hebrew, resumption occurs especially in relative clauses, where pronouns are the typical resumptive element, for example, הָאָרֶץ אֲשֶׁר עָבַרְנוּ בָהּ (Num 13:32, "the land that they explored *it*").

Small Clause (*see* clause).

Subject [461]. "[A] major constituent of sentence or clause structure, traditionally associated with the 'doer' of an action, as in *The cat bit the dog*. [Many] approaches make a twofold distinction in sentence analysis between subject and predicate" (*see* predicate).

Subordination [462]. "A term used in grammatical analysis to refer to the process or result of linking linguistic units so that they have different syntactic status, one being dependent upon the other, and usually a constituent of the other."

Substantive [463]. A term referring to "items which function as nouns, though lacking some of the formal characteristics of that class (cf. the 'substantival function' of adjectives, in the poor, the rich, etc.)."

Tense (*see* Tense-Aspect-Mood).

Tense-Aspect-Mood (TAM). A bundle of features present in verbs.

> **Aspect** [38]. "A category used in the grammatical description of verbs (along with tense and mood), referring primarily to the way the grammar marks the duration or type of temporal activity denoted by the verb."

> **Mood** [312]. "Mood (modality, or mode) refers to a set of syntactic and semantic contrasts signaled by alternative paradigms of

the verb, e.g. indicative (the unmarked form), subjunctive, imperative. Semantically, a wide range of meanings is involved, especially attitudes on the part of the speaker toward the factual content of the utterance, e.g. uncertainty, definiteness, vagueness, possibility."

Tense [479]. "A category used in the grammatical description of verbs (along with aspect and mood), referring primarily to the way the grammar marks the time at which the action denoted by the verb took place."

Topic (fronting) [48]. "The entity (person, thing, etc.) about which something is said, whereas the further statement made about this entity is the comment." In Hebrew, constituents are fronted (*see* fronting) to indicate topic.

Trivalent (*see* valency)

Valency [507]. "The number and type of bonds which syntactic elements may form with each other"; in particular in this book, the number of arguments necessary to complete a verb phrase.

Avalent. The valency of a verb requiring no arguments [subject and complements].

Monovalent. The valency of a verb requiring one argument.

Bivalent. The valency of a verb requiring two arguments.

Trivalent. The valency of a verb requiring three arguments.

Verb Phrase (VP). The phrase of which the verb is the head, that is, the predicate of a verbal clauses (*see* predicate).

Verbless Clause (*see* copula)

APPENDIX: TRANSLATION

¹·¹*These are the words of Qoheleth, the son of David, king in Jerusalem.* ²*"A total* הבל*!" said Qoheleth, "A total* הבל*! Everything is a* הבל.

¹·³*What profit belongs to a man in exchange for all his toil that he does under the sun?* ⁴*A generation goes and a generation comes; that is, the world always remains the same.* ⁵*The sun rises and the sun sets: for its place, it longs—it rises back there.* ⁶*Going to the south, turning around to the north—round, round goes the wind, and upon its rounds the wind returns.* ⁷*All the rivers are going to the sea, yet the sea—it is not full! To the place that the rivers go—there they go continually.* ⁸*All the words are wearying: man is not able to speak, the eye is not satisfied by seeing, and the ear is not filled from hearing.* ⁹*Whatever has been—it is what will be. Whatever has happened—it is what will happen. There is nothing new under the sun.* ¹⁰*A thing exists about which one might say, "See this—it is new!" It has already existed for the ages that were before us.* ¹¹*No remembrance belongs to the former (generations); additionally, no remembrance will belong to the latter (generations) that will exist, among (those who) will be at the latter (time).* ¹²*I am Qoheleth. I have been king over Israel in Jerusalem.* ¹³*I set my* לב *to seek and to investigate with wisdom concerning all that has happened under the heavens. It is a severe task (that) God has given to men to be occupied with.* ¹⁴*I have seen all the events that have happened under the sun, and look—the whole thing is a* הבל *and chasing wind.* ¹⁵*What is bent is not able to become straight, and what is lacking is not able to be counted.* ¹⁶*I spoke, I, with my* לב*, "I—look!—have made myself great and have added (to myself) wisdom over all who were before me over Jerusalem." And my* לב *(also) has seen much wisdom and knowledge.* ¹⁷*I set my* לב *to know wisdom; and knowing blindness and folly—I came to know that even this was chasing wind.* ¹⁸*Because in an abundance of wisdom exists an abundance of vexation and he who will add knowledge will add pain.*

^{2:1}*I said, I with my* לב: *Come, I will make you experienced in joy; look upon (what is) good. See—even this is a* הבל*!* ²*Regarding "laughing," I said "Senseless!" Regarding happiness—what does it accomplish?* ³*I set out, along with my* לב, *to drag my flesh along with wine (though my* לב *was leading by wisdom), and to grasp foolishness, until I might see which is good for humans, which they might do under the heavens (for) the number of the days of their life.* ⁴*I made my deeds great; I built houses for myself; I planted vineyards for myself.* ⁵*I made gardens, that is, royal gardens, for myself and I planted a tree of every fruit in them.* ⁶*I made water pools for myself to water from them a growing tree forest.* ⁷*I acquired male and female servants, and home-born slaves belonged to me, also much livestock—cattle and sheep—belonged to me, more than all who were before me in Jerusalem.* ⁸*I gathered for myself both silver and gold and royal and provincial property; I appointed for myself male and female singers and the delights of humans, many concubines.* ⁹*I became greater and added more (things) than anyone who was before me in Jerusalem; even my wisdom stood by me.* ¹⁰*All (the things) that my eyes desired I did not withhold from them; I did not withhold my* לב *from any joy, because my* לב *was happy from all my toil—and this was my share from all my toil.* ¹¹*But (when) I faced, I, all my works that my hands had done and the toil that I had worked to do, See!—the whole (thing) was a* הבל *and chasing wind; there is no profit under the sun.* ¹²*I turned, I, to see wisdom and inanity and foolishness, that what the man who comes after the king (does)—(it) is (a thing) that they have already done!* ¹³*I saw, I, that the profit of wisdom is more than (the profit of) foolishness, like the profit of light is more than (the profit of) darkness.* ¹⁴*As for the wise man—his eyes are in his head. But the fool in darkness is walking. Yet I have come to know, even I, that one fate befalls them all.* ¹⁵*I said, I with my* לב, *"Like the fool's fate am even I; it will befall me! Why have I become wise, I, then, so much?" I spoke with my* לב *that this too was a* הבל. ¹⁶*Because remembrance is never for the wise alongside the fool; because already (in) the coming days, all is forgotten. How the wise dies with the fool!* ¹⁷*I came to hate life, because the event that has happened under the sun was terrible to me, because everything is a* הבל *and chasing wind.* ¹⁸*I came to hate, I, all my toil, which I did under the sun, which I must leave it to the man who comes after me.* ¹⁹*Who knows whether he will be a wise man or a fool, and will rule over my toil that I did and concerning which I became wise under the sun. This too is a* הבל*!* ²⁰*I turned around, I, to put my* לב *in a state of despair about all the toil that I did under the sun,* ²¹*because there is a man whose gain is by wisdom and by knowledge and by skill, but to a man who has not done it he must give it, his portion (this too is a* הבל *and a great tragedy!);* ²²*because what endures for man in*

exchange for all his toil and striving of his heart, which he has done under the sun? ^{23}*Indeed, all his days are pains and grief is his business; even at night his mind has not "lain down to sleep." This too—it is a* הבל*!* ^{24}*A better thing does not exist for man (than) that he eat and drink and show himself good in his toil. Even this I saw, I, that it is from the hand of God.* ^{25}*Because who can eat? Who can suffer, apart from him/me?* ^{26}*Because to a man who is good before him he has given wisdom, knowledge, and joy; but to the offender he has given the business of gathering and collecting in order to give (everything) to the one who is good before God. Even this is a* הבל *and chasing wind.*

$^{3:1}$*For everything exists a season and a time, for every delight/matter under the sun:*

^{2}*A time exists for birthing and a time exists for dying,*
a time exists for planting and time exists for uprooting something that is planted.

^{3}*A time exists for killing and a time exists for healing,*
a time exists for breaking down and a time exists for building.

^{4}*A time exists for crying and a time exists for laughing,*
a time of wailing exists and a time of gaiety exists.

^{5}*A time exists for casting stones and a time exists for collecting stones,*
a time exists for embracing and a time exists for being distant from embracing.

^{6}*A time exists for seeking and a time exists for losing,*
a time exists for keeping and time exists for throwing out.

^{7}*A time exists for rending and time exists for sewing together,*
a time exists for being silent and a time exists for speaking.

^{8}*A time exists for loving and a time exists for hating,*
a time exists for war and a time exists for peace.

^{9}*What is the profit of the worker in exchange for (the labor) that he does?* ^{10}*I have seen the occupation that God has given to men to be occupied with.* ^{11}*He has made everything fitting in its time; yet he has put "eternity" in their mind without man's ability to find out the work that God has done from beginning to end.* ^{12}*I have come to know that there is no good (thing) among them [humanity], except to take joy and to do pleasure in one's life,* ^{13}*and also the whole (portion) of man is that he eats and drinks and experiences goodness in all his acquisition(s)—it is the gift of God.* ^{14}*I have come to know that all that God does, it will be forever. There is no adding upon it and there is no diminishing from it—God has done (it), that they should be afraid of him.* ^{15}*Whatever is—it was already, and what is to be already has been, and God will seek what is pursued.* ^{16}*And again I saw under the sun the place of justice—there was wickedness!—and the place of righteousness—there was wickedness!* [17]*I said, I with my* לב, *"The righteous and the wicked God will judge," because there is a time for every matter and over every deed there.* [18]*I said, I with my* לב, *concerning humans, "God should test them and should see that they are cattle, they to themselves,"* [19]*because the fate of man and the fate of the cattle—one fate belongs to them!; like the death of the one—thus is the death of the other, and one spirit belongs to all, and the advantage of man over cattle is nothing. Indeed, everything is a* הבל! [20]*Everything goes to one place; everything came from the dirt and everything returns to the dirt.* [21]*Who knows (if) the spirit of mankind—it is what goes up above, while the spirit of the cattle—it is what goes down to the earth?* [22]*And I saw that a better thing does not exist than that man takes joy in his works, because it is his portion, because who can lead him to consider whatever will be after him?*

[4:1]*Then I turned, I, and I saw all the oppressions that happen under the sun. And look, the tears of the oppressed—they have no comforter; from the hand of their oppressors (comes) power, and they have no comforter,* [2]*(while) I praise the dead, who have already died, more than the living, who are yet living.* [3]*And better than the both of them is (the person) who has not yet existed, who has not seen the evil event that has happened under the sun.* [4]*I saw, I, all the acquisition(s) and all the success of work—that it is (out of) the jealousy of a man because of his neighbor. This too is a* הבל *and chasing the wind.* [5]*The fool folds his hands and eats his flesh.* [6]*The fullness of a palm (with) quietness is better than the fullness of a two handfuls (with) acquisition(s) and chasing wind.* [7]*And I returned, I, and saw a* הבל *under the sun.* [8]*There is one but no second (indeed no son or brother belongs to him), yet there is no end to all of his toil, nor will his eyes (Kt) be sated (by) riches. "(So) for whom am I toiling and depriving myself of goodness?" This too is a* הבל *and it is an unfortunate task.* [9]*Two are better than one, who have a good wage in exchange for their toil.* [10]*Because if they should fall, one can raise his companion, but woe to him, the one that falls and there is no second (person) to raise him up.* [11]*Also, if two lie down, they will keep warm, but for one—how can he get/keep warm?* [12]*And if someone should overpower him—the one, the two can stand against him [i.e., the aggressor]. And a three-ply thread will not quickly be torn.* [13]*A poor but wise youth is better than an old but foolish king who still does not know to be careful,* [14]*because from the prison he [= old king] had come out to be king, even though a poor one [= youth] was born in his [= old king's] reign.* [15]*I saw all the living who were walking under the sun (being) with the second youth, who will stand in his [= old king] place.* [16]*There is no end to all the people, that is, to all who he [= youth] was before them, yet those after will not be happy with him [= youth]. Indeed, this too is a* הבל *and chasing wind.* [17]*Watch your feet (Kt) when you go to the house of God: to listen is more acceptable than fools giving a sacrifice, because they do not know how to do bad.*

⁵:¹ *Don't be hasty with regard to your mouth and don't let your mind hurry to bring out a word before God, because God is in the heavens and you are upon the earth. Therefore let your words be few.* ²*Because "the dream comes in abundance of activity and a voice of a fool (comes) in abundance of words." ³When you make a vow to God, do not delay in fulfilling it, because there is no delight in fools. (The thing) that you vow fulfill.* ⁴*That you do not vow is better than that you do and do not fulfill (it).* ⁵*Do not let your mouth cause your flesh to sin, and do not say before the messenger, "Indeed, it is an error!" Why should God become angry at the sound of you and (so) destroy the work of your hands?* ⁶*Because in the abundance of vacuous visions and many words—indeed fear God.* ⁷*If oppression of the poor and robbery of righteous judgment you see in the province, don't be amazed at the matter, because one high above (another) high one is watching, and ones higher than them (are also watching).* ⁸*And the profit of land—he (Qr) is over everything, a king of an arable country.* ⁹*He who loves money will not be sated by money, and whoever loves abundance (will) not (be sated) by the product. This too is a* הבל. ¹⁰*When good things increase, those who consume it increase; and what benefit belongs to its owner except what his eyes see (Kt)?* ¹¹*The sleep of the worker is sweet whether he eats little or much, but the satisfaction of the rich—it does not allow him to sleep.* ¹²*There is a sickly misfortune (that) I have seen under the sun: wealth is kept by its owner, to his misfortune.* ¹³*When that wealth perished in an unfortunate business and he had begotten a son, there was nothing in his [i.e., the son's] hand.* ¹⁴*Like he came out from the womb of his mother, naked he will again go, like he came. Nothing will he be able to take in exchange for his toil that he may bring into his [= his son's] hand.* ¹⁵*And this also is a sickly misfortune: like he came—so he will go. What is profit for him who toils for wind?* ¹⁶*Also, all his days he shall eat in darkness, that is, (with) great anger, his sickness, and wrath!* ¹⁷*Look, (the thing) that I saw, I, is good—that to eat and to drink and to see goodness in all his toil that he does under the sun, (for) the number of the days of his life (Qr) that God has given him, because it is his lot, is good.* ¹⁸*Also, the whole (portion) of man is that God has given him wealth and possessions and has given him the power to eat from it and to bear his portion and to be happy in his toil. This—it is a gift of God,* ¹⁹*because he will not much call to mind the days of his life, because God keeps (him) busy with the joy of his mind.*

⁶:¹ *A misfortune that I have seen under the sun exists, and it is severe upon the human.* ²*A man to whom God has given riches and possessions and*

wealth—he does not lack for his appetite anything that he craves, but God does not authorize him to eat from it, because a "foreign" man will eat it. This is a הבל *and it is a severe sickness.* ³*If a man begets a hundred and lives many years and complains* that the days of his years would occur but his appetite would not be sated by goodness and he would not have a (proper) burial, I say, "The stillborn is better than him!,"* ⁴*because in a breath he would have come and into the darkness he would go and in the darkness his name would be covered.* ⁵*Not even the sun has he seen or known—more rest belongs to this one [the stillborn] than the other one [the aged, unsatisfied man]!* ⁶*And if he lived a thousand years, twice, he would not have seen goodness. Doesn't everything go to one place?* ⁷*All of man's labor is for his mouth, and yet his appetite is never filled.* ⁸*Indeed, what profit belongs to the wise more than the fool? What belongs to the poor (who) knows how to walk before the living?* ⁹*A vision of the eyes is better than a walk of the appetite. This too is a* הבל *and chasing wind.* ¹⁰*Whatever has been—its name has already been called. That he is man is known, but he is not able to contend with the one who is mightier (Kt) than he.* ¹¹*Indeed, many words are increasing* הבל*. What advantage belongs to man?* ¹²*Because who knows what is good for man in life, that is, the number of the days of his life of* הבל *(and he spends them like a shadow)? Because who can tell man what will be after him under the sun?*

⁷:¹*A name is better than fine oil, and the day of death better than the day of one's birth.* ²*To walk into the house of mourning is better than to walk into the house of feasting, because it is the end of every man and the living should pay attention.* ³*Anger is better than laughing because in gloominess the mind will be good.* ⁴*The mind of the wise (ones) is in the house of mourning, while the mind of the fools is in the house of feasting.* ⁵*To listen to the rebuke of a wise man is better than a man who listens to the song of fools,* ⁶*because, like the sound of thorns under the cooking-pot—so is the laughter of fools (this too is a* הבל*),* ⁷*because oppression makes a wise man a fool, and a gift destroys the mind.* ⁸*The end of a matter is better than its beginning; patience is better than arrogance.* ⁹*Don't be hasty with your spirit to become angry, because anger settles in the lap of fools.* ¹⁰*Don't say, "What has happened?," that is, that the former days have been better than these, because you do not ask about this out of wisdom.* ¹¹*Wisdom is good with an inheritance and (it is) an advantage for those who see the sun.* ¹²*Although "(Living) in the shadow of wisdom is (living) in the shadow of money," the advantage of knowledge is (that) wisdom keeps its owner alive.* ¹³*See the work of God, that who is able to straighten (the thing) that he has twisted?* ¹⁴*On the day of goodness, be in good, and on the day of adversity, consider that, indeed, God made this one*

(day of goodness) like (he has made) that one (day of adversity), for the purpose that man does not find anything after him. ¹⁵*I have seen all sorts in my* הבל *days. A righteous person perishes in his righteousness and a wicked person prolongs (his days) in his evilness.* ¹⁶*Don't be a very "righteous" man nor consider yourself excessively wise. Why should you be shocked?* ¹⁷*Don't be very wicked nor be a fool. Why should you die in (what is) not your time?* ¹⁸*That you grab ahold of this is good, but also do not rest your hand from that, because a God-fearer fulfills all of them. (*¹⁹*Wisdom gives strength to the wise more than ten rulers who were in the city.)* ²⁰*Because, man—a righteous one does not exist in the land, who does good and does not sin.* ²¹*Also, don't pay attention to any of the words that they speak; (in order) that you don't hear your servant cursing you.* ²²*Because, also, many times your mind has known that even you (Qr) have cursed others.* ²³*All this I have tested with wisdom. I said, "I shall become wise," but it is too distant for me.* ²⁴*Distant is whatever has happened, and most deep. Who can find it?* ²⁵*I turned around, I and my* לב, *to understand and to investigate and seek wisdom and accounting and to understand irrational wickedness, stupidity, and foolishness.* ²⁶*I find more bitter than death "the woman," who is snares, and her mind is nets, her hands are fetters. (The one) pleasing before God will escape from her, but the offensive one will be captured by her.* ²⁷*See, this I found—said Qoheleth—, one to one to find a conclusion.* ²⁸*(The one) whom my soul sought continually I did not find. One man out of a thousand I found but "a woman" among all these I did not find.* ²⁹*Only, see—this I found, that God made man (to be) straightforward but they seek many schemes.*

^{8:1}*Who is like the wise, and who knows a matter's interpretation? A man's wisdom will illumine his face, and the "strength" of his face will be (thus) changed.* ²*As for me, a king's command obey, that is, according to the manner of an oath (to) God.* ³*Don't panic because of him—leave! Don't stand (around) during a bad word, because everything that he desires he does.* ⁴*Because a king's word is power, and who dares to say to him, "What are you doing?"* ⁵*He who keeps a commandment will not know a bad word, and a wise mind knows a time and a judgment,* ⁶*that for every matter there is a time and a judgment; that the man's evil is severely upon him;* ⁷*that he does not know whatever will be; that when it will be who can tell him?* ⁸*No man is a ruler over the wind in order to contain the wind, and control over the day of death does not exist, nor does release in war exist, and wickedness cannot save its owner.* ⁹*I have seen all of this (while) setting my* לב *to every deed that happens under the sun, a time when the man rules over (another) man—to his misfortune.* ¹⁰*And then I saw wicked people buried, and they used to come*

and go from a place of a holy one. But they would be forgotten in the city, who have acted justly. This too is a הבל, [11]that a decision is not made quickly (regarding) the deed of evil, therefore the mind of humans is full within them to do evil; [12]that a sinner does evil a hundred (times) and prolongs himself. Yet I also know that wellness belongs to those who fear God—whom they should be afraid of! [13]And wellness will not belong to the wicked person and he will not lengthen days, as a shadow—(he) who does not have fear before God! [14]There is a הבל that has happened on the earth, that there are righteous people who (a thing) befalls them just like the deed of the wicked, and there are wicked people who (a thing) befalls them like the deed of the righteous. I say that this too is a הבל! [15]I praised, I, happiness, (namely), that there is no good thing for man under the sun but to eat and drink and be happy! It will accompany him in his labor (during) the days of his life which God has given him under the sun. [16]At (the time) that I set my לב to understand wisdom and to consider the business that has happened on the earth, indeed even during day and night he sees no sleep in his eyes, [17]I saw the whole work of God, that man is not able to "find out" the deed that has happened under the sun, because man toils to seek but does not find. Even if the wise man intended to understand, he could not "find (it) out."

[9:1]Indeed, all of this I set to my לב, that is, in order to examine all of this: that the righteous and the wise and their works are in the hand of God; whether love or hate, no man knows everything before them. [2]Everything is like (that) which belongs to everyone. One fate belongs to the righteous and the wicked, to the good <and the bad>, to the clean and the unclean, to he who sacrifices and he who does not sacrifice; (so too) the good person is like the sinner (and) he who makes an oath is like (the one) who is afraid of an oath. [3]This is a tragedy in all that has happened under the sun, that there is one fate for everything and also the mind of humans is full of evil and lack of reason is in their mind during their lives and he who is after each (is joined) to the dead. [4]Indeed, whoever is joined (Qr) to all the living has confidence, because, even as a dog, life is better than a lion that is dead, [5]because the living know that they will die, but the dead—they do not know anything, and they have no more reward, because memory of them has been forgotten. [6]Their love, hate, and jealousy have already perished, and a portion no longer belongs to them forever in all that happens under the sun. [7]Go, happily eat your food and gladly drink your wine, because God has already accepted your deeds. [8]At every time let your clothes be white and do not let oil be lacking on your head. [9]Enjoy life with the woman whom you love all the days of your הבל life, whom he has given to you under the sun all your הבל days, because *it is your lot in life and in exchange for your labor that you did under the sun.* ¹⁰*All that your hand finds to do with your strength, do, because no deed or accounting or knowledge and wisdom exists in Sheol, where you are going.* ¹¹*I again considered under the sun that the race is not to the swift nor the battle to the mighty, nor even food to the wise, riches to the discerning, or favor to the skillful, because time and change happen to them all,* ¹²*because, indeed, man does not know his time. Like fish that are caught in a bad net and like birds that are snagged in a trap—like them humans are ensnared at a time of misfortune, when it falls upon them suddenly.* ¹³*Also this I saw (about) wisdom under the sun. And it was impressive to me.* ¹⁴*A small city (people are in it, a few)—a great king came to it and surrounded it and built against it great towers,* ¹⁵*but he found a poor wise man in it and he saved—he!—the city by his wisdom. But no one remembered that poor man!* ¹⁶*So I said, I, wisdom is better than might: the wisdom of the poor is despised, and his words—they are not heeded.* ¹⁷*The words of the wise in calm are heeded more than the shout of a ruler among fools.* ¹⁸*Better is wisdom than instruments of war; one offender destroys much goodness.*

^{10:1}*Dead flies stink, (it) putrefies a perfumer's oil. More weighty than wisdom, than honor is a little foolishness.* ²*The mind of a wise man (goes) to his right, but the mind of a fool (goes) to his left.* ³*And also, on the road, when a fool (Qr) is walking, his mind is lacking, so that he says to everyone (that) he is a fool!* ⁴*If the spirit of the ruler rises against you, don't leave your place, because healing/calmness sets aside great offenses.* ⁵*There is a tragedy that I saw under the sun, like a mistake that proceeds from the ruler.* ⁶*The fool/folly is set in many high places and the rich dwell in humility.* ⁷*I saw servants on horses and princes walking like servants on the ground.* ⁸*(He who) digs a pit will fall into it, and (he who) breaks down/through a wall—him a snake will bite.* ⁹*He who uproots [= quarries] rocks may be hurt by them, he who splits wood may be endangered by them.* ¹⁰*If one has blunted the iron and he has not sharpened (its) edges, then he must exert (his) power; that is, an advantage to working skillfully (Qr) is wisdom.* ¹¹*If the snake bites without a charm, then there is no advantage to the charmer.* ¹²*The words of the mouth of the wise (are) gracious, but the lips of the fool will swallow him.* ¹³*The beginning of the words of his mouth are foolishness, and the end of his mouth is evil inanity.* ¹⁴*But the fool will multiply words! Man cannot know what will happen, and what will happen after him—who can tell him?* ¹⁵*The toil of the fools will weary him, he who does not (even) know (how) to get to town!* ¹⁶*Woe belongs to you, O Land, whose king is a servant and your princes feast in the morning.* ¹⁷*Fortunate are you, O Land whose king is a*

noble and whose princes eat at the (proper) time—with manliness and not with drinking! [18]Through laziness the (roof) beams will become sagged and through slackness of hands the house will leak. [19]For laughter they make food and wine will gladden life; and money answers everything. [20]Also, in your thinking do not insult a king, or in the rooms of your bed do not insult a rich man, because the birds of the skies carry the sound and the winged creature (Kt) reports a word.

[11:1]Cast your bread upon the surface of the water, because in a number of days you will find it. [2]Give one portion to seven or even to eight, because you cannot know what will be calamitous on the earth. [3]If the clouds are filled with rain, they will empty (it) out on the earth, and if a tree falls in the south or in the north, the place that the tree falls—there it remains. [4]He who observes wind will not sow and he who watches clouds will not harvest. [5]Just as you do not know what the path of the wind is, (which is) like bones in the belly of the pregnant woman, so you cannot know the work of God, who does everything. [6]In the morning, sow your seed and in the evening don't let your hand rest, because you do not know which will prosper, whether this or that, or if both of them are equally good. [7]The light is sweet and for the eyes to see the sun is good. [8]Indeed—if a man lives many years, in all of them he should be happy, and he should remember the days of darkness, that they will be many. All that is coming is ephemeral. [9]Be happy, young man, in your youth and may your mind do you well in the days of your young manhood. Walk around on the paths of your mind and in the visions of your eyes. But know that God will bring you into judgment regarding all of these. [10]Remove vexation from your mind and pass evil from your body, because youth and black hair is a הבל.

[12:1]And remember the one who created you in the days of your youth, while days of misfortune have not come and years have not arrived when you say, "I have no delight in them," [2]while the sun and the light and the moon and the stars have not grown dark and the clouds have not returned after the rain, [3]on the day that the keepers of the house tremble and the men of character are stooped over and those who grind cease because they have become few and those looking through the windows have become dark, [4]and the double-doors in the street-bazaar are shut when the sound of the mill has become low, and one rises at the sound of the bird, and all the daughters of the song are bent over, [5]—even of the High One they are afraid and terrors are in the path and the almond tree puts forth blossoms and the grasshopper stuffs itself and the caper is scattered, when man goes to his eternal house and the lamenters mull around in the street-bazaar, [6]while the silver rope has not been torn *apart (Kt*) and the gold bowl has not been crushed and a jar has not been broken over the spring and the wheel to the well has not been crushed,* ⁷*and the dirt shall return to the land like it was and the breath returns to God who gave it.* ⁸*"A total* הבל*," said the Qoheleth, "Everything is a* הבל*."*

^{12:9}*And that Qoheleth was wise was an advantage; more (than this), he continually taught the people knowledge and would test and seek (and) arrange many proverbs.* ¹⁰*Qohelet would seek to find words of delight and what was written correctly, words of truth.* ¹¹*The words of the wise are like goads and like nails sunk in are well-grouped sayings, (which) are given by one shepherd.* ¹²*And more than they, my son, be warned. For the making of many writings no end exists, and to meditate much is a work of flesh.* ¹³*The end of the matter is (that) everything has been heard. Fear God and keep his commands, for this is the whole (portion) of man.* ¹⁴*For every deed God will bring into judgment, concerning every hidden thing, whether (it is) good or whether (it is) bad.*

INDEX OF LINGUISTIC ISSUES